STUDY GUIDE
FOR OREGON

PROPERTY MANAGEMENT

JOHN JEDDELOH

FOURTH EDITION

Published in the United States of America by
Real Estate Publishers, Inc.
8316 N. Lombard #329
Portland, Oregon 97203-3727

WWW.REALESTATEPUBLISHERS.COM
E-mail: INFO@REALESTATEPUBLISHERS.COM

Library of Congress Catalog Card Number 99-66090
ISBN 1-878572-20-2

First printing, January, 2003
Second printing, December, 2003

Cover Design: Architectural elevation of house © 2002 Bruinier & Associates, Inc., Portland, Oregon, 800-379-3828, reproduced with permission. Bruinier & Associates sells stock building plans and plan books for residential, commercial, duplexes, rowhouses and multifamily. Plans are available in traditional format or on CD-ROM. They also do custom architectural design. You can see their work at HTTP://WWW.BRUINIER.COM, or e-mail PLANS@BRUINIER.COM.

Contents

Introduction

The *Study Guide For Oregon Property Management* offers a thorough introduction to the study of property management in Oregon and is especially structured to prepare students to take the Oregon real estate license examinations. The text is part of the Study Guide series – other texts in the series include *Study Guide For Oregon Real Estate Law*, *Study Guide For Oregon Real Estate Finance*, *Study Guide For Oregon Real Estate Practices*, *Study Guide For Oregon Real Estate Contracts* and *Study Guide For Oregon Real Estate Agency*. Used in conjunction with the other texts in the series, this text will give the reader an excellent foundation in real estate. It is an invaluable tool for anyone interested in property management, real estate investments, mortgage lending, title work, escrow and real estate development.

This book is divided into five sections covering all aspects of the practical side of Oregon real estate, with special consideration to those topics which are covered on Oregon real estate licensing examinations. Following the first five sections is a section containing forms commonly used in Oregon property management. And finally, this fourth edition includes a new section containing pertinent legal cases on landlord-tenant issues.

Because many people using this book will be preparing for the examinations, we have taken great care to ensure that all examination subjects are covered thoroughly, and in proportion to their importance on the real estate examinations. In addition, we have included sample examination questions, many of which have been used on past state exams.

The author, John Jeddeloh, began his real estate career in 1971 and since then has worked in brokerage, property management, appraisal and investing. There is nothing in the field of real estate that he has not done.

The sample questions and text material are from the author's personal knowledge of the real estate licensing examinations in Oregon and from his many years of teaching prelicense courses in both public and private schools in Oregon. The author has 20 years of classroom experience teaching prelicense real estate full-time. There is no one as familiar with the Oregon real estate licensing examinations as he is. Before entering the real estate field, Mr. Jeddeloh worked for a large commercial bank in Oregon and also taught public secondary schools. Mr. Jeddeloh has an undergraduate degree in Education and did his graduate work in Business Administration, Law and Finance. Students who have taken his live instruction classes are always impressed by his ability to explain complex subjects clearly and understandably.

The author's combination of knowledge and experience have resulted in this book being the most comprehensive text available for the study of real estate property management in Oregon.

Getting a Real Estate License

Real estate brokerage is a relatively young profession compared to other professional fields such as medicine and law. Real estate agents were almost totally unregulated until 1908 when the National Association of Real Estate Boards was formed (currently the National Association of Realtors®). In fact, the chief purpose for which the National Association of Real Estate Boards was formed was to create a Code of Ethics and to encourage government licensing of real estate agents.

Even then, membership and adherence to the Code of Ethics was voluntary. Oregon led the nation by creating the first effective real estate licensing law in 1919. Today, this law is known as the Oregon Real Estate License Act, and is augmented by numerous Administrative rules promulgated by the Oregon Real Estate Agency. The Real Estate License Law requires that you hold one of several different kinds of real estate licenses in order to engage in what the law refers to as "professional real estate activity." Which kind of license you obtain depends on what kind of real estate activity you plan to do, and whether you plan to work independently or hire other agents. Most of these real estate licenses require completion of a separate license examination.

Most persons new to the real estate profession must get a ***brokers license*** as their first license. A brokers license entitles you to engage in all kinds of professional real estate activity except appraisal. (Appraisal is considered a separate field and appraisers are licensed by the Oregon Appraiser Certification and Licensure Board.) A real estate broker can work independently (after three years experience), or cooperatively with other brokers. If you wish to run a real estate company and have other brokers working for the company, then you need a ***principal brokers license***. With some exceptions, you cannot get a principal brokers license in Oregon without meeting additional educational requirements and having three years of experience as a broker. The most notable exceptions to these rules are for out of state licensees or for persons who have held a license in another state and now reside in Oregon. Partial or full waiver of the time requirement is also possible if you can demonstrate substantial experience related to real estate, although a full waiver is granted only in exceptional circumstances. Since each individual's situation will be unique, if you feel you might qualify for a waiver, and wish to apply directly for a principal brokers license, you should contact the Oregon Real Estate Agency to determine the exact requirements. Their address is: Oregon Real Estate Agency, 1177 Center Street N.E., Salem, Oregon 97310, Telephone (503) 378-4170.

Assuming, however, that you are new to the profession and do not have significant previous real estate experience, you will need to start with the regular brokers license if you wish to engage in real estate sales. If you wish to conduct property management activity, and your professional real estate activity will be limited to property management, then you may wish to consider the special property managers license (see *Property managers license* on the next page).

There are four requirements to obtain a brokers license. You must

- Be 18 years of age,
- Be of good character,
- Demonstrate competence in Oregon Real Estate Law, Real Estate Finance, Real Estate Practices, Property Management, Real Estate Agency, Real Estate Contracts, and Real Estate Brokerage, and you must
- Take and pass the national and state (Oregon) real estate brokers exams.

Since most persons have no problem with the first two requirements, let us confine our discussion to the last two.

You must demonstrate competence in the seven subject areas by taking and passing a course in each subject area in a school where the course(s) have been approved by the Oregon Real Estate Agency.

The real estate examinations consist of the Oregon exam (also called the state exam) and the national exam. These exams are always given at the same time, which is every month on the third or fourth Saturday (except La Grande test center, which is only three times a year, and Bend, which is six times a year). You must pass both exams with a score of 75% or better. If you pass one exam, but fail the other, you need to retake only the exam you failed, provided that you finally pass it within 12 months of passing the first exam.

Both exams are made up of totally objective multiple choice questions. The Oregon exam consists of 50 questions and the national exam has 150 questions. Most states now split their examinations into a state portion and a national portion (also sometimes called "multi-state" or "uniform" exam). As a result, if you ever move to another state you will usually only have to take the state portion in the new state, since most states now recognize Oregon's national exam as meeting the same requirements as their national, multi-state or uniform exam.

In order for a course to be approved by the Oregon Real Estate Agency it must meet certain requirements. In particular, a course in Oregon Property Management must cover the material presented in this text. Another requirement is that you must actually spend the time taking the course, either in a tape presentation with an instructor present, in a live classroom setting, or by approved distance education (e.g., by the internet or through correspondence).

Property managers license: In early 1988 it became possible to obtain a special license as a property manager. The requirements for the property managers license are the same as for the brokers license, except that the examinations and courses are different. To obtain a property managers license you need to demonstrate competence only in Oregon Property Management. In addition you must take a general examination on property management consisting of 150 questions. You should bear in mind that a property manager licensee is limited strictly to property management; you cannot be involved in any real estate activity that involves a sale. For example, you could lease a property to a tenant, but you could not do a lease-option because if the option is exercised it would result in a sale. Note also that brokers and principal brokers can also do property management, so if you want to be involved in both sales and property management, then the brokers license is the one to get.

Applying for the Examinations: The deadline for applying for any real estate exam is generally the fifth day of the month in which you wish to take the exam. In other words, if you want to take an exam scheduled for the third Saturday in December, you must apply no later than December 5. Note that your application must be postmarked by December 5, not received in Salem by December 5.

However, you should mail your application as soon as possible. Many test centers have limited space (especially the Portland center). If the test center you have chosen is filled when your application is received, then you will be assigned the next closest center where space is available.

The fee for the examination is $75 for the brokers national and state (or either exam separately), and the property managers exam is also $75. In addition, you must submit a fingerprint card the first time you apply to take an examination. The fingerprint card must be completed by an official qualified to take fingerprints. The Real Estate Agency charges $40 for processing the fingerprint card. The fingerprint card will be submitted to the FBI for criminal activity check. You can take the examination(s) at any time, but no license will be issued until the check is completed. This can take several months, so the fingerprint card should be submitted immediately once you have made the decision to obtain the license. You can submit the fingerprint card with the fee for processing it alone and send in the exam application later. The fingerprint card must be obtained from the Real Estate Agency; generic fingerprint cards from other agencies are not acceptable.

You may obtain an exam application, fingerprint card and *Examination Information* booklet from the Oregon Real Estate Agency (see address and phone on the previous page). These materials are also available free of charge at the most real estate schools.

Study Hints

Successful students know that if you master the terminology of a given subject area, you will have mastered that subject. This is particularly true of real estate because you will encounter an overwhelming number of new terms to learn. Don't let a new word get by you without learning its meaning and how it is used. About half the exam items are really just vocabulary questions – testing your knowledge of real estate terminology. So if you know the language of real estate thoroughly, you will have the subject well in hand at exam time. To assist you in mastering real estate vocabulary, you will find a *Key terms* section at the end of the reading in each section. Each of the key terms listed is italicized where it first appears in the preceding text, so you can easily check on its meaning and usage.

Always be sure you understand a topic thoroughly before going on to the next topic. Since you will forget material as you progress through the course, you should start a program of systematic review of the material previously studied. A wise man once said "if you want to increase your vocabulary, use a new word three times a day for three days and it will be yours forever." This works because people learn best by a sequence of learning, forgetting, relearning, forgetting, relearning, and so on. Each time you learn-forget-relearn you double the time before you will forget the material.

Another good study trick is to look for common elements and ways to tie information together. If you try to memorize facts in isolation, it is very difficult to remember them for long enough to pass an exam. But if you get an overall picture, the individual facts are easier to remember. After all, individual facts make more sense when you have a framework to place them in.

Do not be alarmed if you find your retention is poor at first. It is not uncommon for students to retain only 20-30% of the information after just one reading. But if you do not give up, you will find that successive readings (plus attendance at the lectures for which this text was designed) will increase your memory remarkably.

Exam Techniques

At the end of each section in this text you will find various sample exam questions which are similar to the type of questions you will find on the real estate exams given by the Real Estate Agency. You should be sure you practice with these questions, as they are the most important part of the text if you are planning on taking licensing exams.

There are three basic question types. Probably the most prevalent type is the *completion* or *fill-in* type of question (see examples below). Almost as common is the *double true-false* format, and occasionally you will encounter a *Roman numeral* type of question. But regardless of the type of question, all test questions are comprised of two parts. The first part is called the ***stem***, and it is the part that actually "asks the question." The stem is followed by three ***distracters*** or ***foils***, which are the three wrong answer choices, and, of course, the correct answer.

For example, in the following question, the stem is in regular print, and the distracters or foils are underlined. The correct answer is in italics:

In real estate, a preliminary sales contract is called

(A) <u>a listing agreement</u>.

(B) <u>a lease-option</u>.

(C) *an earnest money agreement.*

(D) <u>an offering</u>.

Many students make silly mistakes answering questions because they were never taught the simple ground rules for answering questions. The rules are really very easy:

1. Read the stem and the first answer (answer A) as an entire sentence. Then decide whether the statement is true or false. Using your pencil, make a notation of your decision next to the answer.

2. Read the stem again, this time followed by the second answer (answer B). Again, decide whether the statement is true or false and mark your decision next to the answer. Repeat the process for the last two answers (C and D). It is important to remember to read the stem over again each time.

3. When you have finished, the correct answer will be obvious – whichever answer is the "odd man out" is the correct answer. In other words, if you marked three answers false and one answer true, then the one marked true must be the correct answer. Similarly, with some types of negative questions, you may mark three answers true and one answer false. Then the one marked false is the correct answer.

When you finish the above question, it should look like this:

In real estate, a preliminary sales contract is called

f (A) a listing agreement.

f (B) a lease-option.

t (C) an earnest money agreement.

f (D) an offering.

Be sure to mark your decision for each answer. Do not attempt to trust your memory. By the time you finish reading the fourth answer, you could easily have forgotten what you decided about the first answer. This technique is not only useful for avoiding silly mistakes, but also when you are not sure of the answer and must make a partial guess.

These questions are really the same type of question. The only difference is that in the fill-in question an actual blank appears in the question, while the completion question contains an assumed blank at the end of the stem. For example –

The _______ is the interest held by the vendor during the term of a land sales contract.

(A) equitable title (C) naked title

(B) marketable title (D) insurable title

or

The interest held by the vendor during the term of a land sales contract is the

(A) equitable title. (C) naked title.

(B) marketable title. (D) insurable title.

After you answered the above questions, your answer section should have looked like this

f (A) equitable title. *t* (C) naked title.

f (B) marketable title. *f* (D) insurable title.

The fill-in or completion format is especially useful for testing knowledge of vocabulary items. Since testing your familiarity with real estate terminology is a fundamental part of the real estate exams, you will find many fill-in and completion questions.

Double true-false questions

The second most commonly encountered exam question type is the double true-false question. These questions come in one of two formats, e.g.

According to the Real Estate License Law, the
I. Real Estate Commissioner is the seventh member of the Real Estate Board.
II. decisions of the Real Estate Commissioner cannot be appealed.
(A) I only (C) Both I and II
(B) II only (D) Neither I nor II

or sometimes the format is like this –

According to the Real Estate License Law,
(A) the Real Estate Commissioner is the seventh member of the Real Estate Board.
(B) the decisions of the Real Estate Commissioner cannot be appealed.
(C) both A and B are true.
(D) neither A nor B is true.

In answering the double true-false question, follow exactly the same rules as for the fill-in or completion question. That is, first read the stem and the first answer (Roman numeral I in the first example, and (A) in the second format). Decide whether the statement is true or false, and mark your decision next to the answer. Then read the stem again, followed by the second answer, and decide whether this statement is true or false. Again mark your decision next to the answer. When you have marked both answers, the correct choice is obvious.

Double true-false questions are popular with test makers because they are easy to write. They are hard on students, however, because if you have to guess at one of the answers, you have only a 50-50 chance.

After you have answered the above question, it should look like this:

According to the Real Estate License Law, the
t I. Real Estate Commissioner is the seventh member of the Real Estate Board.
f II. decisions of the Real Estate Commissioner cannot be appealed.
(A) I only (C) Both I and II above
(B) II only (D) Neither I nor II above

or

According to the Real Estate License Law,
t (A) the Real Estate Commissioner is the seventh member of the Real Estate Board.
f (B) the decisions of the Real Estate Commissioner cannot be appealed.
(C) Both A and B above are true.
(D) Neither A nor B above is true.

Roman numeral questions

A third type of question which occasionally occurs on the real estate exams is the Roman numeral question. This question is similar to the double true-false question above, but instead of having two answers (I and II), it has three or more answers. As a result, the choices (A, B, C and D) may have a variety of choice combinations. For example –

Which of the following would be an encumbrance on a real estate title?
I. A land sales contract
II. An easement
III. A trust deed
IV. A mortgage
(A) I, III and IV only (C) IV only
(B) III and IV only (D) All of the above

Answer the Roman numeral question the same way as you answered the preceding question formats. That is, read the stem followed by each answer in turn and decide whether it is true or false, mark your decision, and continue until you have marked each answer. Always re-read the stem for each answer. When you have marked all the answers, you can easily select the correct answer. After you have completed the above question, the Roman numeral section should look like this –

t I. A land sales contract
t II. An easement
t III. A trust deed
t IV. A mortgage

Notice that regardless of the question format, you always mark your true-false decisions next to each answer and always re-read the stem with each answer. The importance of this technique cannot be overstressed. It is very common for students to let the first answer color their thinking about the second answer. *You cannot do this.* Each answer is distinct and separate from each other and must be considered in isolation. Making your true-false markings as you decide about each answer is the only way to ensure that you will do this properly.

Question sets

On rare occasions, you may encounter on the real estate exams a set of two or more questions which are related to each other. In other words, data from a question is referred to and used in one or more following questions. However, you will never find a set of questions where you must get the answer correct to the first one before you can get the answer correct for the following question(s). In other words, the questions may use common data, but they must be kept separate to the extent that missing a previous question will not cause you to miss a subsequent question.

Frequently, when this technique is employed, there will be a chart or graph to which a number of questions will be directed. These questions are unpopular with test makers because it becomes hard to store the questions individually and they become inflexible when trying to make up a new exam.

One situation on the real estate exams, however, does consistently make use of the question set technique. When testing your knowledge of listing agreements and earnest money receipts, the Real Estate Agency usually includes a "narrative" – that is, a story about how a transaction is to take place. The narrative is followed by a sample listing agreement or earnest money receipt. The listing agreement or earnest money receipt will contain blanks, several of which are numbered. One or more questions then follow, and each question asks what should be placed in one of the numbered blanks. Note that all the questions use the same common data (the narrative), but each question is separate and distinct from the others. That is, you can miss any one question but still have an equal opportunity to get all the others correct.

Ranking the answers

Many times, when answering a test item, you might find that you are unsure of the right answer. Since there is no penalty on the real estate exams for guessing, by all means you should answer the question. But some students have problems deciding which answer to choose. If this happens to you, it may be helpful to use a *ranking technique*, a modification of the true-false marking system discussed above. For example, suppose we had the same completion question we used previously,

> The interest held by the vendor during the term of a land sales contract is the
>
> (A) equitable title. (C) naked title.
> (B) marketable title. (D) insurable title.

Except that this time, suppose you are not sure of the answer. Suppose that you read the stem and answer (A) and decide that it is definitely false, so you mark it false. Then you read the stem again with answer (B), and you decide that the answer is probably true. So you mark (B) as true. When you read the stem again followed by answer (C), you decide that this is a true statement also, so you mark (C) as true. Finally, you read the stem the fourth time followed by answer (D), and this time you also decide the statement is true. When you mark answer (D) as true, you are faced with a dilemma – which is the correct answer among (B), (C) and (D)? Only one answer can be true, but you answered three with true –

> The interest held by the vendor during the term of a land sales contract is the
>
> *f* (A) equitable title. *t* (C) naked title.
> *t* (B) marketable title. *t* (D) insurable title.

The answer is to rank the ones of which you are unsure. It is usually easiest to do this in pairs. For example, ask yourself the question, "Do I like (B) better than (C)?" If you answer yourself that you like (C) better than (B), then eliminate (B) by marking it false. Next, decide between the two remaining choices, (C) and (D). Ask yourself which of these two you think is more likely to be true. If you decide (C) is more likely to be true than (D), then eliminate (D) by marking it false. By this process of elimination you have arrived at the decision that (C) is the correct answer. This method works because it is human nature to get confused when we have too many choices to make, but it is always easy to decide between just two items at a time.

Elimination technique

Sometimes you might encounter a problem where you have no idea whether any of the answers is right or not. In this situation, you might still be able to save the day. Many times you can get at the correct answer to a question by eliminating the answers you know are not correct. If you can eliminate three answers as definitely wrong, then you know the fourth answer has to be the correct one.

Use your subconscious mind

Another trick used by successful test takers is to exert a reluctance to change their answers. Good students know that the subconscious mind is a powerful force. They know that they may not be able consciously to remember the answer, but if they ever read the information in the past it is still stored somewhere in their unconscious mind. Therefore, a good rule of thumb when guessing is to stick by your first answer. Of course, when checking over your test at the end you may discover that you completely misunderstood the question, in which case you are certainly justified in changing your answer.

Work the answers backwards

There is another clever technique which is very useful for certain difficult math questions. While the math questions on the real estate exams are a lot easier than many people fear, still there may occasionally be a math problem that is especially difficult. For example, look at the following problem –

> A seller told an agent that she wanted to net $160,000 from the sale of her lot, which she felt had a market value of about $180,000. She told the agent that the agent could have everything over the $160,000 as commission. However, the agent did not wish to take a listing on this basis, and decided to list it at a set price which would include the amount the seller wished to net plus a commission of 6%. At what price should the agent list?
>
> (A) $160,000 (C) $170,213
>
> (B) $169,600 (D) $180,000

Now, the way to calculate this correctly is to divide the $160,000 the seller wishes to net by 94%. This is because $160,000 is 94% of what the agent needs to list the property for. However, if you cannot remember how to do the problem, you can still get the right answer another way.

Obviously, one of the four answers above is correct. So you can figure out which is the correct answer just by calculating which one works. Take your calculator, subtract 6% of each answer from that answer in turn, until you find the answer that will leave you with $160,000. As you can see, this technique can make stubborn math problems a breeze.

Learn to smell the answers

Good test takers are usually people who have taken a lot of standardized tests and therefore have come to understand these principles. They have also developed a second sense – they almost seem to be able to "smell" wrong answers put in deliberately to mislead them. The best way for you to develop this second sense is to practice, practice, practice. Go over each and every sample test question without fail.

One thing you can do which will help you develop this second sense is to watch out for key words in a question. Pay particular attention to negative words such as not, least, except, and so forth. Also pay close attention to words such as never, and always. In the real world, things are seldom absolute, so answers containing the words "never" and "always" tend to be untrue.

Pay attention also to the grammatical flow of the question. If there seems to be an abrupt change when you leave the stem and start reading the answer, this can be a clue that the answer is not true. On the other hand, answers which are long, wordy or full of qualifications tend to be true statements. Of course, all of this advice can really only be useful in those cases where you are reduced to guessing anyway. If you know the material, you won't need to worry about second-guessing the test makers.

Choosing the best answer

Many students complain that the test questions seem to have more than one correct answer. They report that one answer may be better than another, but it confuses them when two or more answers are both technically correct. In reality, students who find more than one correct answer are students who really do not understand the material thoroughly. In fact, very few questions have two correct answers and force you to choose the better of the two. The fact is that students who have learned some of the material, but not all of it, find they are able to discriminate down to the last two choices, both of which sound correct to them. But if they knew the material better, they would realize that only one of these last two is really correct.

Incomplete answers

Don't let an incomplete statement fool you. For example, suppose you read the stem of a question and the first answer and it reads "For a valid escrow to exist, there must be: (A) an escrow agent and escrow instructions." You immediately conclude that this is a false statement, because there are several other requirements to create a valid escrow in addition to "an escrow agent and escrow instructions." Wrong! If you read the statement all by itself, it is a true statement, because an escrow agent and escrow instructions are required for a valid escrow. The fact that there are other requirements is irrelevant to the truth of this statement.

Don't "what if" the question

One of the most common mistakes students make is to add material or facts to a question that is not stated. People tend to jump to conclusions and make unwarranted assumptions. This can lead to errors. Consider the following question –

> An office manager has assigned all the leads during one afternoon to Hans Schmidt, a broker licensed with the company. Consuelo Moreno, another of the brokers is also in the office at the same time. In the middle of the afternoon, Mr. and Mrs. Gomez come in to inquire about buying a property. If the broker assigns the buyers to Moreno,
> (A) this is steering.
> (B) the broker has violated the Fair Housing Act.
> (C) both A and B above are correct.
> (D) neither A nor B above is correct.

The correct answer is (C), because assigning clients to brokers on the basis of race, religion, national origin, sex, mental or physical handicap or familial status (having children), is a called *steering* and is a violation of the Fair Housing Act. But many students read this question and add the assumption that the buyers do not speak English. Then they add the assumption that the buyers do speak Spanish, that Schmidt does not speak Spanish, and that Moreno does speak Spanish! Notice that the stem and the answers do not address the language issue at all, so you must assume that everyone speaks English.

Do the easy questions first

You can maximize your probability of success if you do not let the difficult questions slow you down. If you are taking the national and Oregon exams, you will have almost two whole minutes per question. Since most questions won't take more than about 30 seconds, this will be plenty of time. But if you spend 15 minutes on one tough question, and as a result lack time to finish all of the easy questions, you will be the loser.

To avoid this, the best technique is to answer all the easy questions first. Leave the more difficult questions for a second pass later. After you have finished the easy ones, you will find that you have lots of time left to go back and do the harder ones. Furthermore, you will be more relaxed, more mentally conditioned to the test, and you may have found some material which jogged your memory about one of the harder questions you skipped earlier. Some students still skip some of the especially difficult questions on their second pass and save them for a third pass later. If you follow this approach, you can be sure that, if you run out of time, the questions you didn't have time to finish were the questions you had the least chance of getting right anyway.

Double-check your work

When you finally finish the exam, make a final double-check of your work. Don't forget to check your answer sheet – remember that you get no credit for the right answer unless it is clearly marked with pencil in the proper place on the answer sheet. If you skip a question, be especially careful to place your answers in the right space on the answer sheet. Also be sure that your name and other information is correct. When students talk over the exam afterwards with other students, they usually realize that they made at least one, stupid, silly mistake. In fact, the average error rate is about one silly mistake per 50 exam questions, even when you are trying your best to be careful. If you have time remaining, check your work over carefully; this is no time to get sloppy.

Get ahead of the game

As the day for the exam draws near, you will quite naturally feel nervous and apprehensive. This is really a senseless time for you to feel this way! If you studied well, then you are as prepared to take the exams as any of the other people you will meet at the test center. If you haven't done your work by now, well, it's probably too late anyway. So whether you are prepared or not, it makes no sense to worry. The best course of action for the last couple of days before the exams is to continue to review and study, but *relax*! Of course, it also helps to get plenty of rest, watch your diet, and don't let the rest of the world get in your way, but the most important factor is to stay relaxed.

Make your final preparations for the exam several days in advance. Since you may have to drive some distance, be sure to set the alarm clock early enough. Also tend to other mundane matters such as getting together your pencils, admission ticket, identification, calculator (don't forget fresh batteries), and even fill up the car with gas. Get your family to help you for the last couple of days by taking the rest of your usual chores off your back to allow you time to review in peace and quiet. If you can do all this, you can sit down to take the exam feeling confident that you are as prepared as it is possible to be and that ***nothing is going to stand in the way of your success!***

LEASEHOLD ESTATES

MANY DIFFERENT KINDS OF INTERESTS CAN EXIST IN REAL ESTATE AT THE same time. For example, an owner may have leased the property to a tenant, so both the owner and the tenant have interests in the same property simultaneously. Or perhaps the owner has mortgaged the property to a bank. Then the bank clearly has an interest in the property also. The word ***interest*** is a broad term that encompasses any kind of right in the real property.

There are many kinds of interests that can exist in the same property simultaneously. In addition to leasing or mortgaging your property, you can give your neighbor an easement across it, you can give a buyer an option to buy it, and you can even list it for sale with a real estate broker, among many other possibilities.

Most of these interests are more properly discussed in a general real estate law text, but one particular kind of interest that we will explore in detail in this section is an ***estate***. An estate is a possessory interest in real estate. In other words, if you have a right of possession, your interest is properly referred to as an estate. A possessory interest could arise through ownership of the property, or by being a renter or lessee.

Estates are further classified as ***present estates*** and ***future estates***, that is, the right to current possession, or the right to possession at some time in the future. For example, if you own a property, but lease it to a tenant, the tenant has the present estate, and you have the future estate – the right to possession after the lease is over. There are many ways to create a future estate, as we shall see later.

Modern Oregon real estate law is based on English common and statutory legal principles. Early England was a class society with serfs at the bottom of the social scale and various levels of lords rising up to the king or queen at the top. In the beginning,

NOTES

serfs were not permitted to own real estate – only the lords were allowed that privilege. Later, a third class arose, called "freemen." A freeman was not a lord, but did have the right to own real property. With the signing of the Magna Charta in 1215, all Englishmen who were not lords became freemen – the serf class was abolished. From that point on, any Englishman could own real property. For the most part, women were accorded the same rights in real property as men.

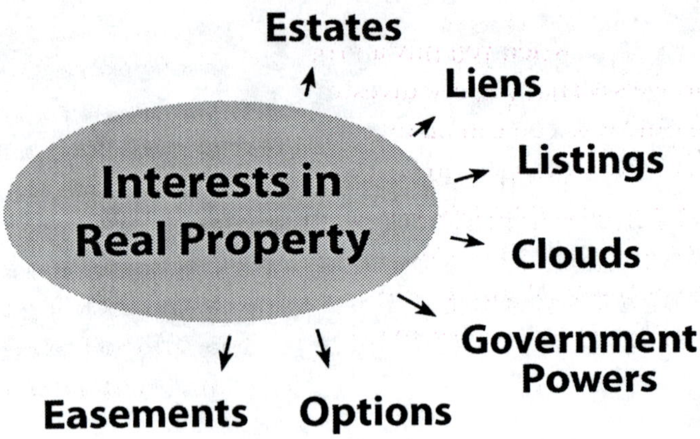

There can be an unlimited number of interests in a given piece of real estate, most of which can exist at the same time. For example, you can own the property (an estate), but have a mortgage to the bank (a lien), lease it to a tenant, grant your neighbor an easement across it, give your brother an option to buy it, and list it with a real estate broker.

There are so many possible interests that we categorize them. There are many different kinds of estates, for example, so many that we will devote this entire section of the book to them. The diagram shows only some of the major groups of interests.

What does all this have to do with modern real estate? Today we still use the terms and concepts developed during this early period of history. One important concept is ***ownership***. In early England ownership was a right which could only be held by a freeman or better, so ownership interests today are still called ***freeholds*** or ***freehold estates***. Possessory interests which are not ownerships are called ***less than freehold estates***, or sometimes ***leaseholds***.

Estates of inheritance

As we have seen, estates in real property are divided into freeholds and less than freeholds (leaseholds). Let us begin our discussion of these interests with the freehold estates. Freeholds are further classed as ***estates of inheritance*** (usually called ***fees***) and ***estates not of inheritance*** (more commonly referred to as ***life estates***).

A fee estate (or estate in fee) is said to be an estate of inheritance because the owner can leave it to his or her heirs. A life estate, on the other hand, is said to be an estate not of inheritance because the estate terminates upon the death of the owner. That is, if you have a life estate, you own the property, but only for your lifetime. Your ownership ends upon your death. And if your ownership ends upon your death, then there is nothing for you to leave to your heirs. Of course, ownership must continue to be vested in someone even after your death. Who the property would go to after your death (the future possessory estate) is determined by rules which we will discuss later.

Fees are further divided into ***fees tail*** and ***fees simple***. A fee tail (also sometimes called an ***estate in fee tail*** or an ***entailed estate***) is an estate which is granted to the holder and to a certain class of the holder's heirs, normally the children or other family members. The idea is to keep the property in the family. Therefore, if a holder of a fee tail were to attempt to deed the property outside of the class of heirs, the deed would be void. Fees tail are not recognized in Oregon. If you wish to keep property within the family, then the modern approach is to set up a family trust. The advantage of a trust is that the trust is a separate legal entity which can also own stocks, bonds and other personal property as well.

The word "simple" in the expression "fee simple" really just means "not tail." In other words, if you have a fee simple, you can leave the estate to whomever you wish and you can also sell or give away the property during your lifetime. Because the fee tail

NOTES

is not recognized in Oregon, the only kind of fee that still exists is the fee simple. As a result, many knowledgeable persons leave the word "simple" out. In Oregon today, a "fee title" is a "fee simple title."

Fees simple are further divided into those fees which are ***absolute*** and those which are ***defeasible*** (also called ***qualified fees*** or fees which are ***subject to divestiture***). The words "absolute" and "defeasible" refer to how the owner's title is vested. The vesting of title means delivery of the ownership rights and is normally accomplished by a deed. The opposite of vesting is ***divestiture*** (or ***divestment***). In other words, when you buy a property you are vested in title, and when you no longer own it, we say that you are divested.

If your title is vested absolutely, this means that the only way you can be divested is your voluntary act (you deed or will it to someone else), or involuntarily through an operation of law (condemnation, foreclosure, etc.). But if your title is defeasible, then the person you acquired title from has created a ***condition*** and if you violate the condition, you can be divested. Therefore, a defeasible title can be divested voluntarily or involuntarily the same as a title which is vested absolutely and, in addition can be divested if the owner violates the condition. Fortunately, defeasible fees are very rare, so real estate agents are unlikely to run into them in a normal real estate practice.

Of course, if a title is defeasible, then there is a question as to who will gain ownership if the present owner violates the condition and is divested. Normally, the title will revert to the person who set up the condition in the first place. For example, suppose someone deeds property to you and adds to the deed a clause which says that the conveyance is "only so long as the premises shall be used for residential purposes, and if they should cease to be used for residential purposes, then the estate herein granted shall automatically revert to the grantor or the grantor's heirs." Now, if you violate the condition, the title will automatically go back (revert) to the person you got it from. The right to take the title back is called a ***right of reverter, estate in reversion, reversionary interest (estate)*** or just simply a ***reverter***.

In some cases, the grantor does not wish to get the property back, but rather wishes it to go to a third party. But if the property goes to a third party we can't call the future estate a right of reverter, since the word "revert" implies that it returns to the grantor. Instead, if the property is to go to a third party we say that the third party has an ***executory interest***.

As a practical matter, Oregon law recognizes three types of defeasible fees. A ***fee simple determinable*** or ***determinable fee simple***, which is also sometimes called a ***fee simple upon special limitation***, is created by using words such as "for so long as," "while," "during" and the like, together with a statement of the grantor's automatic right of reverter. For example, the language "only so long as the premises shall be used for residential purposes, and if they should cease to be used for residential purposes, then the estate herein granted shall *automatically* revert to the grantor or the grantor's heirs" is an example of a determinable fee. Note that the fee reverts to the grantor automatically upon the violation of the condition.

A ***fee simple on a condition subsequent*** is similar, except that the right of reverter is actually is a ***right of entry***, sometimes also called a ***power of termination*** or ***possibility of reverter***. The grantor has the right to get the property back, but the right is not automatic. Upon violation of the condition, the grantor must re-enter the premises and take action to recover the estate. Language used to create this interest typically includes phrases such as "on condition that," "provided" and the like. The same residential-only restriction as in the fee simple determinable above could be recast as a fee simple on a condition subsequent by changing it to read "on condition that the premises are used for residential purposes, and if they should not be used for residential purposes, then the grantor or the grantor's heirs may re-enter and terminate the estate herein created."

NOTES

When it is desired to have the property go to a third party in the event the condition is breached, then the grantor can create a ***fee simple subject to an executory interest***. This estate is frequently used when the grantor wishes to make the conveyance force someone to act in a certain way, e.g., "I hereby convey this property to Suzie, provided that she marry within the next ten years, and if she should fail to do so, then the fee shall vest absolutely in her brother, Joe." In this case Joe has an executory interest and Suzie has a fee simple subject to her brother's executory interest.

By special statute in Oregon, a determinable fee or a fee simple subject to a condition subsequent become absolutely vested if the condition is not violated within 30 years, even if the grantor places a longer time limit on it. This statute does not apply to estates which are subject to an executory interest, however.

From the preceding discussion, you can see that a fee simple title which is vested absolutely is the highest ownership interest in real property that is possible. You will commonly hear people refer to this interest as a "fee simple absolute" as a short way of describing it. In fact, since the word "simple" is unnecessary in Oregon, you could really shorten this to just "fee absolute." And since defeasible fees are rare, if you say just "fee" or "fee title," everyone normally assumes that you mean a fee simple title absolutely vested.

Estates not of inheritance

A fee title is called an estate of inheritance because the owner can leave it to his or her heirs. A life estate, on the other hand, is said to be an estate not of inheritance because the estate terminates upon the death of the owner. Nevertheless, always remember that life estates are ownership interests in real property (freeholds). The difference is that the duration of a fee title is potentially perpetual, where life estates have a duration measured by someone's life. The life which measures the ownership period is called the ***governing life***. This can be the life of the donor, of the recipient, or it can be the life of an unrelated third party. It can even be for the life of the survivor of a stipulated group of persons.

The governing life is normally simply the life of the holder of the life estate – called the ***life tenant***. In fact, unless there is some language stating otherwise, the legal presumption is that the governing life is that of the life tenant. If the life estate is for another person's life, then it is called a life estate ***pur autre vie***. The term pur autre vie is Old French which, literally translated, means "for another life." A life estate pur autre vie can be created directly by the grantor – e.g., "I hereby convey this property to you for the life of your brother." But the life tenant can sell the life estate, and if the life tenant were to do so, a life estate pur autre vie would also be created.

For example, suppose you convey a life estate to your sister. Since you specify no other governing life, we presume the governing life is the life of the life tenant, in this case, your sister. Now suppose your sister deeds the property to your brother. An ordinary Oregon deed, without any special language, is presumed to convey all of the grantor's right, title and interest in the property. Therefore, your brother has now received exactly the interest your sister had, no more and no less. Since your sister held an ownership interest for her life, that is exactly what your brother now holds – an ownership interest for your sister's life. In other words, your brother now has a life estate pur autre vie.

Your brother in the preceding example may also be motivated to see that your sister lives a long and healthy life since, upon her death, fee title reverts to you. Life estates always terminate upon the death of the governing life and thereafter fee title must vest in someone. The presumption is (unless there is language to the contrary), that the life estate reverts to the grantor. Note then, that the life estate is normally followed by a right

NOTES

of reverter (also called an estate in reversion or reversionary interest). Of course, these are the same familiar terms we used previously to describe the right of the grantor to get the property back when the estate was a defeasible fee.

When the life estate is to go to a third party rather than back to the grantor, then the future interest is called a ***remainder***. Notice here that the concept of the remainder and the concept of the executory interest we discussed above are the same. Nevertheless, when the future estate follows a life estate it is called a remainder and when it follows a fee estate it is called an executory interest.

Life estates are sometimes created when an owner in fee title conveys a remainder to someone but retains a life estate in the property. Parents frequently convey a remainder in their property to their children, reserving a life estate. This reduces the dollar value of their estate and thereby lowers future estate taxes. At the same time that they are lowering future estate taxes, the parents can take advantage of the gift exclusions which allow them to give substantial sums to any individual without any tax liability. A tax benefit also accrues when you donate property to a qualified charitable or religious organization. Older people frequently donate property to such organizations, but reserve a life estate in the property. The donation gives them a tax break while they are alive and can still enjoy the tax savings.

You can also create a life estate that is defeasible. For example, suppose you want to grant a life estate to someone, but you also want to receive monthly income from the life tenant, and you want the life estate to terminate if the rent is not paid. Then you might grant a life estate "for so long as the sum of X dollars is paid monthly, and if not so paid, then the estate herein created shall automatically terminate and revert and revest in the grantor." This would create a determinable life estate. Note that you now have two rights of reverter – you have the right to get the property back when the life tenant dies, and you also have the right to get the property back if the life tenant violates the condition by not paying the monthly rent.

Since a life estate is an ownership interest, the life tenant is free to use the property in any way, including selling it. The only restriction is that the life tenant cannot do anything which would be injurious to the interests of the holder of the future estate. And, of course, the life tenant has no power or authority to bind the holder of the future estate to any agreements with others.

Even though the rights of the life tenant are subsidiary to the rights of the holder of the future estate, the life tenant can mortgage or lease the life estate or create other interests within it. But what would happen if a life tenant mortgaged the property on a 30-year mortgage, and then died before the mortgage was paid off? In this case, the lender's mortgage would be extinguished. The holder of the future interest would become vested in fee simple absolute and unencumbered by the mortgage. The logic is that the lender took a mortgage on a life estate, so the lender should have known that the life estate could terminate at any time. If the mortgage is an interest which depends on the life estate, then it is extinguished if the life estate is extinguished. The same results would occur if the life tenant were to lease the life estate. If the life tenant dies, the lessee may be forced to move even if the lease is not yet over. Lenders and lessees in these situations commonly protect themselves by obtaining the signature of the holder of the future interest on the mortgage or lease. Then the future interest is also mortgaged or leased so, if the property reverts, the mortgage or lease remains intact.

Anyone who holds a future interest in real estate has a right to expect that the holder of the present interest will maintain the premises in reasonable condition and not allow ***waste***. Waste occurs when a holder of a present possessory estate acts (or fails to act) in such a fashion as to cause a lowering of the value of the interest of those who have

NOTES

a future estate in the property. So, while a life tenant can do anything with the property, this right does not extend to waste.

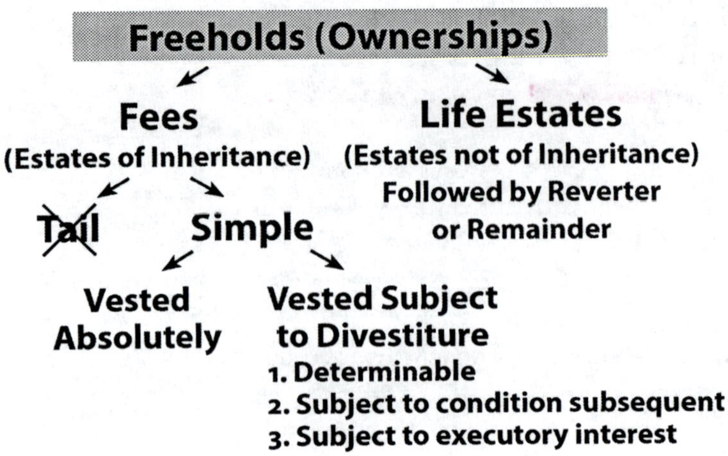

Estates are categorized as freeholds and less than freeholds. Here we see a diagram showing how the freeholds are further categorized as fees and life estates. Fees were originally either tail or simple, but the fee tail is not recognized in Oregon, leaving us with only the fee simple. Ordinarily a fee simple is vested absolutely, but if the grantor wishes it can be vested with a condition. Violating the condition makes the grantee lose the title, so if there is a condition we say the vesting is subject to divestiture, or defeasible. There are three ways to vest the title subject to divestiture.

The bundle of rights

All freeholders (owners) are said to be vested with ***seizin*** (also frequently spelled "seisin" or "seizen") to the property they own. A legal expression commonly used is to say that the owner is "seized of the estate."

Seizin makes the person vested with it responsible for the property. Chief among these responsibilities is the duty to pay the taxes. The owner's responsibilities also include liability for certain damages that might be caused by the land. For example, if the handrail is loose and, as a result, the local letter carrier falls and is injured, the owner is liable. Even if the letter carrier was delivering mail to a renter in the property, the owner is still liable. The owner also has the responsibility to obey the law and to abate any nuisances caused by the land.

On a more pleasant note, the party vested with seizin also has rights. These rights are referred to as the ***bundle of rights***. The bundle of rights is like a bundle of sticks, each of which represents one of the rights of ownership. These sticks include the right to do anything the owner wishes with the property. The owner may use and enjoy it, rent or lease it, mortgage it, sell it, or give it away. Every conceivable thing that could be done with the property is another stick in the bundle of rights. The bundle of rights even includes the right of the owner to do nothing at all.

The owner may exercise any of these rights with the entire property or just part of it. And the owner may simultaneously exercise one or more rights on part of the land while exercising other rights on another part of the land. The owner may exercise some or all the rights for a period of time and then change the use in the future. All or part of the rights may be granted to another for a period of time, for life, or forever. Or the owner may divide the rights and grant them to different individuals, again, for a period of time, for life or forever. The possibilities are endless.

When we refer to an owner granting one of these rights we say that the owner has given one of the "sticks from the bundle of rights." The concept that an owner can give or keep any stick is a concept that is used throughout the study of real estate. For example, when an owner gives a real estate broker a listing, the owner has given the broker one of the sticks from the bundle of rights – the right to sell the property. Always remember that any single stick or combination of sticks can be granted to anyone for any period of time the owner desires.

Exercise a

An ________ is an interest in real property in which the holder has a right of ________. Ownership estates in real property are called ________ and non-ownership estates are called ________ ________ ________ estates, or ________.

Freehold estates are categorized as ________ estates (estates of inheritance) and as ________ ________ (estates not of inheritance).

The fee ________ is not recognized in Oregon, leaving us with nothing but a fee ________. In Oregon an estate can be vested ________ or the vesting can be ________ to ________. There are three kinds of these fees, which are:

1. ________
2. ________
3. ________

These must be followed by a right of ________ or by an ________ ________.

The highest interest in real estate is the ________ ________ ________.

The length of a life estate is measured by the ________ life. If this life is other than the life of the ________ ________, then we say the life estate is a life estate ________ ________ ________.

Life estates are always followed by a future interest which will be either a right of ________ or a ________.

All freeholders, including life tenants, are said to be vested with ________ to the property, which gives them responsibilities and a ________ of ________, except that a life tenant is not allowed to commit ________ on the property.

Leasehold estates

Leaseholds are created by a ***lease*** or ***rental agreement***. The act of leasing or renting the property is legally referred to as a ***demise***. When the leasehold terminates, the owner retakes possession of the property. The right of the owner to retake possession is called a right of reverter (or estate in reversion, reversionary interest or estate, etc.) – the same term we encountered for the future interest after a defeasible fee or a life estate.

A leasehold estate is frequently referred to as a ***tenancy***. This term describes the act of possessing the property by the ***tenant***. A tenant is the party in possession. Legally, we use the word tenant to describe even an owner when the owner is in possession. Note that an "estate" is the possessory interest or right, and the "tenancy" is the act of possessing. While these concepts are slightly different, from a practical standpoint, when describing different interests in property, most people use the terms interchangeably.

NOTES

In the rest of this section we will discuss the various leasehold tenancies and the rights and duties of landlords and tenants generally. However, there is a special statute in Oregon called the "Oregon Residential Landlord and Tenant Law" which governs the relationships between landlords and tenants in residential tenancies. It is so detailed that we will devote a separate section to it.

Creating a less than freehold estate

To create a less than freehold estate generally requires only the signature of the owner. The tenant signifies acceptance of the terms by taking possession and paying rent. The common practice today, however, is to have the tenant sign the lease or rental agreement as well. If the tenant did not sign the lease, the tenant always has the potential claim that certain provisions of the lease were unknown, and therefore should not be binding.

If the agreement provides that any part of the tenancy is to last longer than a year in the future the agreement must be in writing in Oregon. This is required by a law called the ***Statute of Frauds***. Of course, even though the law does not require a short lease to be in writing, it is always a good idea to take any important contract in writing.

Responsibilities of the parties

A common question is the issue of maintenance. The original English common-law rule provided that the landlord had no responsibility for maintenance of the premises. Today, modern courts give the landlord the responsibility to provide at least some maintenance, particularly of items which involve health or safety hazards. The Oregon Residential Landlord and Tenant Law places extensive maintenance requirements on the landlord. However, in a non-residential setting, the landlord is usually only obligated to maintain the premises if there is an agreement to that effect, although the landlord may be liable for defects unknown to the tenant and for maintenance of common areas under the control of the landlord.

By the same token, the tenant is only obligated to maintain the premises as necessary to prevent waste. The tenant is not obligated to make extensive additions or improvements. Again, the Oregon Residential Landlord and Tenant Law, which only applies to residential rentals, relieves the tenant of most of the burden to maintain the premises and places it on the shoulders of the landlord.

What would happen if someone were injured on the premises during the tenancy? The general rule is that the landlord is liable unless the injury was caused by something under the tenant's control or by some improvement made by the tenant. For example, if you rent a property to a tenant and there is a loose step which causes a visitor to be injured, you are normally liable. If the rental agreement contains language which requires the tenant to perform all maintenance, then the tenant and you would most likely both be liable. On the other hand, if the stair was in good condition at the start of the tenancy, but the tenant damages it beyond ordinary wear and tear, then any resulting injury could conceivably be just the responsibility of the tenant. The issue of responsibility for injuries to each other and to third parties is an area of law where it is difficult to escape liability. The best course for both landlord and tenant is to assume that they will always be liable and plan accordingly.

The law recognizes an implied ***covenant of quiet enjoyment*** on which the tenant may rely. The covenant of quiet enjoyment means that the landlord is obligated to defend the landlord's title against any claims which would interfere with the tenant's right to uninterrupted possession of the premises. If the landlord cannot meet this requirement, then the tenant is relieved of the responsibility to pay rent. For example, suppose you

Notes

have leased space from the owner of a shopping center in which you operate a business. An owner whose property is adjacent to the shopping center claims an easement through the shopping center and, in fact, right through your space. If the owner of the shopping center is not successful in warding off the claim, and as a result you are forced to leave your space, then your lease is terminated and you have no further obligations to the lessor.

Types of less than freehold estates

Conceptually, there are two categories of less than freeholds. There is a ***tenancy at sufferance*** (without the owner's permission), and there is a ***tenancy at will*** (with permission). There are also two special types of tenancies at will, called a ***tenancy for years*** (for a fixed term, i.e., a lease) and a ***tenancy from period to period*** (periodic tenancy, which has a period that continuously renews until one party gives notice to the other, i.e., a month-to-month rental). It is also possible to be in possession with permission, but without either a fixed term or a period – as though the owner gave the tenant permission, but neglected to stipulate the specific terms.

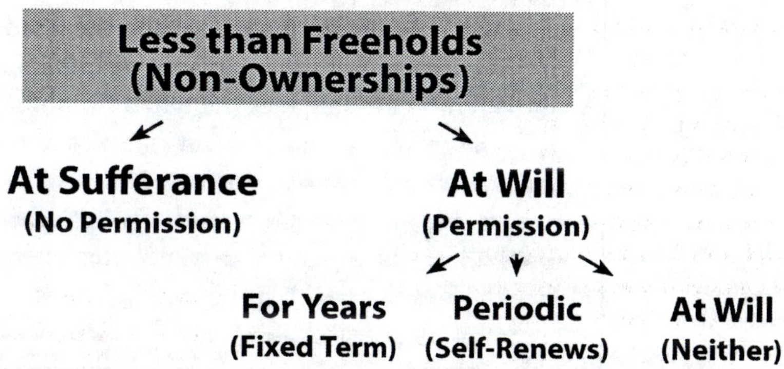

There are two kinds of less than freeholds. If the tenant is in possession without the permission of the owner it is at sufferance. If the tenant has permission it is at will. Tenancy at will can be for a fixed term, i.e., a lease, in which case it is a tenancy for years. Or a tenancy at will can have a period which continuously renews until one party gives notice. This would be called a periodic tenancy. If there is no fixed term and no period, then we call it a tenancy at will. Technically, a tenancy for years and a periodic tenancy are also "at will," but when the phrase is used alone it implies that there is no fixed term or period.

Although the tenancy for years and tenancy from period to period are actually types of tenancies at will, we don't generally say "tenancy at will for years," or "tenancy at will from period to period." We just say "tenancy for years" or "tenancy from period to period." At the same time, we reserve the phrase "tenancy at will" to mean permission, but with neither a fixed term nor a period. Most people just operate as though there were four separate types and define them individually.

Tenancy at will

The tenancy which gives the most rights to the tenant is the ***tenancy for years.*** Do not be confused by the word "years" – a tenancy for years is a tenancy for any fixed term, whether the term is a day, a month, a year, or longer. The tenancy for years is what most people think of when they think of a ***lease***. As everyone knows, a lease has a definite term with a beginning and an ending date. How often the rent is paid, or even whether there is rent, is irrelevant; it is the fixed term which makes the agreement a lease.

Leases also occasionally call for a fixed dollar amount during the term (a ***straight lease***). As a result, lay people commonly presume that there is some legal requirement that this be so. The truth is that leases usually contain cost-of-living clauses or tie the rent to some index or provide that the rent will be a percentage of the tenant's gross sales, among other possibilities. It is unusual to find a lease with a fixed amount of rent.

NOTES

Although most less than freeholds require the parties to give proper notice to each other in order to terminate the agreement, this is not the case with a tenancy for years. No notice is required to terminate a tenancy for years because it has a definite expiration date and the parties obviously knew when it would be over at the time they entered into the lease. Of course, if either party wishes to terminate the lease sooner, then notice may be required. Note that a party wishing to terminate a lease before its expiration has to have a valid reason, such as a breach by the other party.

When the tenant holds a tenancy for years, the owner's title is encumbered by the leasehold. Therefore, if the owner subsequently sells the property, the buyer will take title subject to the lease. Of course, it is possible to place a special termination clause in a lease which allows the lessor to cancel the lease upon a sale. It is also common to find leases where the tenant also has a right to cancel the lease upon the happening of some event such as the death or incapacity of the lessee, for example.

Unless a lease contains language prohibiting it, a lessee may ***assign*** his or her interest to another. An ***assignment*** occurs when you transfer rights under a contract to another. In the case of a lease, this means that you would transfer all of your rights for the entire premises and for the entire remaining term to a new tenant. Many times a lease will contain a clause requiring the lessor's approval for an assignment. The lessor, in this case, cannot unreasonably withhold consent without the risk of becoming liable to the tenant for damages the tenant might suffer as a result.

What if you transfer your rights to just a portion of the premises, or for only a part of the remaining term of the lease? Then this is called a ***sublease*** and, as with the assignment, the lessee may sublease unless the lease specifically prohibits it. Make note that a prohibition on assignment does not create a prohibition on subleasing, and vice-versa. And as with the assignment, if the lease requires the lessor's approval for a sublease, the approval cannot be unreasonably withheld. When a sublease has been created there will be two leases in existence. The lessee of the original lease will have become the lessor to the new tenant. In this situation we say the original lessee holds a ***sandwich lease***.

When the tenant assigns or subleases to another, this does not normally relieve the tenant from the obligation to pay the rent. If the new tenant fails to pay, the landlord has the right to look to the original tenant for payment. However, it is possible for the lessor to accept the new tenant and release the original tenant from liability, This is called a ***novation***. A novation occurs when an original contract is extinguished and replaced with a new contract.

When a lessee abandons the premises the lessor is nevertheless entitled to demand that the rent continue uninterrupted. The common-law rule is that the lessor can hold the tenant to the tenant's promise to pay the rent, regardless of whether the tenant has possession, because moving out was the tenant's own choice. However, in Oregon a landlord has a duty to ***mitigate***. To mitigate means to lessen a loss. Therefore, if the tenant moves out, the lessor must make a good faith attempt to locate a new tenant. When an acceptable tenant is found, the lessor must offset the obligations of the old tenant with whatever the new tenant pays. Of course, the old tenant remains liable for the period when the premises were vacant, and for the expenses the lessor incurred in obtaining the new tenant.

Another factor which may hinder the landlord's right to collect rent from the tenant is the possibility of a ***surrender***. A surrender occurs any time a holder of a present possessory interest relinquishes the premises and allows the holder of the future estate to take over immediately. A surrender of a lease would occur when the lessee moves out and gives possession of the premises back to the lessor prior to the termination of the lease. Of course the lessor need not accept the surrender. However, if the lessor does accept the surrender, the lessee is relieved of any further obligation under the lease.

NOTES

Tenancy from period to period

A more common tenancy (particularly in residential property) is the ***tenancy from period to period***, or ***periodic tenancy.*** This type of tenancy is characterized by a rental period, rather than a fixed term as in the tenancy for years. The period may be any period desired by the parties, such as month-to-month, week-to-week and the like. Agricultural properties are frequently rented on a year-to-year basis. Sometimes we refer to this type of tenancy by the period involved. For example, a ***month-to-month tenancy*** is a type of periodic tenancy where the period is monthly, and so on. Usually the parties in a periodic tenancy are referred to as ***landlord*** and ***tenant*** rather than as lessor and lessee, although the distinction is not carefully observed today.

A tenancy from period to period continues for an indefinite period, but can be terminated by either party upon giving proper notice to the other. At common law, the amount of the notice required is the amount of the period, so for a month-to-month tenancy, the notice required would be one month. However, there are several special statutes in Oregon which modify the common law rule. Nonresidential tenancies require a 60-day notice if from year to year and a 30-day notice if month-to-month. The Oregon Residential Landlord and Tenant Law provides for 31 days notice if the tenancy is month-to-month and ten days notice for week-to-week tenancies. Note that the ten day requirement for week-to-week tenancies applies only in residential rentals. Residential tenancies are also subject to shorter notice periods for certain breaches such as nonpayment of rent, damaging the premises, unpermitted pets, and the like.

Since proper notice is required to terminate a periodic tenancy, it is also required if there is to be a substantial modification of the tenancy. This would include matters such as rent increases.

Tenancies from period to period are encumbrances on the owner's title, the same as tenancies for years, so if the owner sells the property, the buyer must respect the rights of the tenant. Of course, the new owner can terminate a periodic tenancy with a relatively short notice, so the matter is not as significant as where a long term lease is involved.

Also as with leases, a periodic tenancy can be assigned or subleased, assuming there is no provision in the rental agreement which prohibits assignment or subleasing. Again, if the landlord declines to allow an assignment or sublease, the matter is not significant because the tenant can just give notice and terminate the tenancy.

Tenancy at will

A ***tenancy at will*** is created when an owner gives someone permission to occupy the premises. Remember that a tenancy for years and a periodic tenancy are both tenancies at will, since the owner has given permission. However, it is still a tenancy at will even if there is no fixed term or period. Notice that permission to occupy the premises can be given without stipulating how long the permission is good for, and without even charging rent.

Tenancies at will can be terminated by the owner only by giving proper notice, which is generally held to be 30 days. After all, the owner did give permission for the tenant's occupancy, so it is only fair that the owner give reasonable notice to vacate the premises.

A tenancy at will (unless for years or periodic) cannot be assigned or subleased. Tenancies at will which are not for years or periodic are not considered encumbrances on the owner's title, so a sale of the property extinguishes the tenant's rights and converts the tenancy into a tenancy at sufferance (see below).

NOTES

Tenancy at sufferance and trespass

When a right of possession is terminated, but the tenant does not leave, this is called a ***tenancy at sufferance***. Actually, this does not constitute a true interest in the property since the tenant has no legal grounds upon which to base a right of possession. Therefore, the owner can terminate a tenancy at sufferance without notice.

In order to create a tenancy at sufferance, the tenant must have originally entered into possession lawfully through some prior right which is now ended. For example, if you own the house you live in, sell the house to another, but then not leave after your sales contract requires you to deliver possession to the buyer, you are a tenant at sufferance. The term ***holdover tenant*** is sometimes applied to a tenant at sufferance.

When a tenant never had a legal right, but instead just takes possession of the property, it is called a ***trespass***. A trespasser, the same as a tenant at sufferance, has no legal right to possession, so the owner can terminate the tenancy without notice. A tenancy at sufferance and a trespass are both civil wrongs, so the owner can sue the tenant at sufferance or trespasser for possession or damages. But, unlike a tenancy at sufferance, a trespass is also a criminal act.

An owner faced with a tenant at sufferance or trespasser should be careful. What if the tenant at sufferance or trespasser offers money to the owner? Accepting money from a tenant at sufferance or trespasser may be held to constitute granting permission. Permission means the tenancy is at will (or better), so the owner must now give the tenant proper notice to terminate the tenancy.

Eviction

An ***eviction*** occurs when an owner forces a tenant to leave the premises. This can be an ***actual eviction*** (filing a suit) or a ***constructive eviction*** (forcing the tenant out). Actual evictions occur when the owner files a suit called a ***forcible entry and detainer***, (frequently abbreviated "F.E.D."). Sometimes you encounter the term with a extra word, such as ***forcible entry and wrongful detainer*** or ***forcible entry and unlawful detainer***. In this expression, the term "forcible" does not necessarily mean that the tenant is using force to enter or hold (detain) the premises, but only that the possession is without permission.

Assuming that the owner files a suit for forcible entry and detainer and wins the suit, the judge will grant the owner an ***order of restitution***. This means that the tenant is required to restore possession to the owner. If the tenant still refuses to comply, then the owner can ask the court to order the sheriff to remove the tenant and the tenant's possessions, by force if necessary.

When the owner takes matters into his or her own hands and forces the tenant out, this is called a ***constructive eviction***. For example, if the owner cuts off essential services or locks the tenant out, these actions would constitute constructive eviction. Constructive eviction of a residential tenant causes the landlord to be liable to the tenant for actual and punitive damages, plus the tenant's attorney's fees, so the use of constructive eviction is generally limited to non-residential tenancies.

Where the rental agreement or lease requires the owner to maintain the premises, and the owner fails to do so to the point where the premises become unusable or uninhabitable, this also constitutes constructive eviction. A claim that the owner has constructively evicted the tenant by failure to maintain the premises is a common complaint by a residential tenant.

Another remedy is a ***landlord's lien*** on certain chattels owned by the tenant and brought upon the premises. By statute, the lien attaches to the chattels 20 days after the

NOTES

rent becomes due and remains unpaid. Thereafter the landlord may retain the chattels to enforce collection of rent. If necessary, the landlord may have the chattels sold to satisfy the tenant's obligations. Whenever a party holds the personal property of another in order to force the payment of money, it is called ***distraint***. In this case, enforcement of the landlord's lien is really ***distraint for rent***. Distraint for rent is permitted only if the tenancy is non-residential, and would subject the owner to action by the tenant for actual and punitive damages if it is a residential tenancy.

Lease-options

In an ***option to buy*** the owner grants a buyer the right to buy the property at a certain price and terms for a period of time. For an option to be enforceable, the buyer must give something of value to the seller as consideration. Note that an option does not have to be an option to buy; it can be an option to sell, option to lease, or option to do anything else the parties desire. For example, suppose a buyer gives you a written document stating that the buyer will buy your property for $500,000 any time you are ready to sell it provided that you agree to sell it within the next 90 days and provided that you give the buyer $10. Upon receipt of the offer, you tender the $10 to the buyer. You now hold an option to sell.

Options to buy are frequently coupled with a lease. This is commonly called a ***lease-option***. In a lease-option, the optionee (holder of the option right) also has possession of the property through a lease. Always remember that a lease-option is really two separate documents – a lease and an option to buy. Either the lease or the option can stand on its own. This can create a problem if the tenant breaches the lease. Since the option is a separate agreement, the tenant could still exercise the option. To avoid this, most lease-option agreements provide that a breach of the lease extinguishes the option.

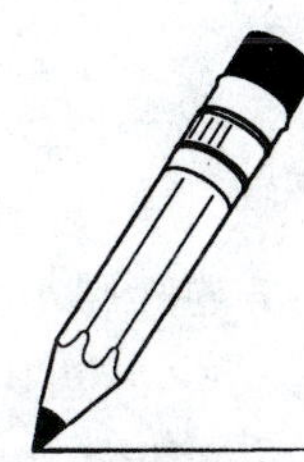

Exercise b

Less than freehold estates are created by a __lease__ *or, if for an indefinite time or on a periodic basis, by a* __rental__ __agreement__. *The creation of a less than freehold estate is called a* __demise__. *The party in possession of the is called a* __tenant__ *and the act of possessing is referred to as the* __tenancy__. *If a tenancy is for more than a year, its creation must be in* __writing__. *This is required by the Oregon* __statute__ *of* __frauds__.
Normally, the __tenant__ *is the party who must maintain the premises, although under the Oregon* __Residential__ __landlord__ *and* __tenant__ *Act, the responsibility to maintain lies with the* __landlord__. *The landlord also owes the tenant an implied* __Covenant__ *of* __quiet__ __enjoyment__.
When a tenancy is for a fixed term, it is called a tenancy __for__ __years__ *and it constitutes an* __encumberance__ *on the owner's title. Normally, the lessee can* __assign__ *his or her interest or can* __sub-lease__ *the premises, in which case a* __sandwich__ *lease is created. If the lessor accepts a new tenant, this is called a* __novation__. *In Oregon, if a tenant moves out of the*

premises, the lessor must attempt to ______________. If the lessor accepts a ______________ of the premises, the tenant's obligations under the lease are canceled.

When the tenancy continuously self-renews, it is called a ______________ tenancy. This type of tenancy can be terminated upon proper ______________ from one party to the other. If the tenancy is month-to-month, the required ______________ is ______ days. For year-to-year tenancies, a ______ -day ______________ is required.

When there is permission, but neither a fixed term nor a period, a tenancy ______ ______________ is created. This is not an ______________ on the owner's title and cannot be ______________ or ______________. A ______ - day notice is required to terminate it.

A tenancy ______ ______________ is created when a tenant lawfully in possession fails to leave at the termination of the tenancy. Such a tenant is also called a ______________ tenant. If the party in possession did not enter the premises legally, this constitutes a ______________ which is also a ______________ act, in addition to a civil wrong.

To force a tenant to move out, the owner can ______________ the tenant. This can be ______________, as where the owner files a suit, called a ______________ ______________ and ______________. By filing the suit, the owner is asking the court for an ______________ of ______________. If the owner attempts to force the tenant out, it is called ______________ eviction. In a non-residential tenancy, the owner is entitled to a ______________ lien against certain chattels belonging to the tenant. If the owner retains the chattels, it is called ______________ ______________ ______________.

A ______________ - ______________ gives the tenant possession of the property and an option to buy it.

KEY TERMS

The key to understanding any new field is the vocabulary used in that field. To maximize your comprehension of the material presented in this chapter, be sure you know the meaning and significance of the following terms. Remember that the majority of test questions primarily test knowledge of vocabulary.

Absolute
Actual eviction
Assign
Assignment
Bundle of rights
Condition
Constructive eviction
Covenant of quiet enjoyment
Defeasible
Demise
Determinable fee
Distraint for rent
Divestiture (Divestment)
Eminent domain
Entailed estate
Escalation clause
Escheat
Estate
Estate in fee tail
Estate in reversion
Estate not of inheritance
Estate of inheritance
Eviction
Executory interest
Fee
Fee simple
Fee simple determinable
Fee simple on a condition subsequent

Fee simple subject to an executory interest
Fee simple upon special limitation
Fee tail
Forcible entry and (unlawful) detainer
Freehold
Freehold estate
Future estate
Governing life
Holdover tenant
Interest
Landlord
Landlord's lien
Lease
Leasehold
Lease option
Less than freehold estate
Life estate
Life tenant
Mitigate
Month-to-month tenancy
Novation
Option to buy
Order of restitution
Ownership
Periodic tenancy
Possibility of reverter
Power of termination
Present estate
Pur autre vie
Qualified fee
Remainder
Rental agreement
Reversionary interest
Reverter
Right of entry
Right of reverter
Sandwich lease
Seizin
Statute of Frauds
Straight lease
Subject to divestiture
Sublease
Surrender
Tenancy
Tenancy from period to period
Tenancy for years
Tenancy at will
Tenancy at sufferance
Tenure
Trespass
Vesting
Waste

ANSWERS

To chapter exercises. If you couldn't figure out what to put in the blanks, find the answer here!

Exercise a

An ESTATE *is an interest in real property in which the holder has a right of* POSSESSION *Ownership estates in real property are called* FREEHOLDS *and non-ownership estates are called* LESS THAN FREEHOLD *estates, or* LEASEHOLDS *.*

Freehold estates are categorized as FEE *estates (estates of inheritance) and as* LIFE ESTATES *(estates not of inheritance).*

The fee TAIL *is not recognized in Oregon, leaving us with nothing but a fee* SIMPLE *. In Oregon an estate can be vested* ABSOLUTELY *or the vesting can be* SUBJECT *to* DIVESTITURE *. There are three kinds of these fees, which are:*

1. FEE SIMPLE DETERMINABLE (FEE SIMPLE ON SPECIAL LIMITATION)
2. FEE SIMPLE ON CONDITION SUBSEQUENT
3. FEE SIMPLE SUBJECT TO AN EXECUTORY INTEREST

These must be followed by a right of REVERTER *or by an* EXECUTORY INTEREST *.*

The highest interest in real estate is the FEE SIMPLE ABSOLUTE.
The length of a life estate is measured by the GOVERNING life. If this life is other than the life of the LIFE TENANT, then we say the life estate is a life estate PUR AUTRE VIE.
Life estates are always followed by a future interest which will be either a right of REVERTER or a REMAINDER.
All freeholders, including life tenants, are said to be vested with SEIZIN to the property, which gives them responsibilities and a BUNDLE of RIGHTS, except that a life tenant is not allowed to commit WASTE on the property.

Exercise b

Less than freehold estates are created by a LEASE or, if for an indefinite time or on a periodic basis, by a RENTAL AGREEMENT. The creation of a less than freehold estate is called a DEMISE. The party in possession of the is called a TENANT and the act of possessing is referred to as the TENANCY. If a tenancy is for more than a year, its creation must be in WRITING. This is required by the Oregon STATUTE of FRAUDS.
Normally, the TENANT is the party who must maintain the premises, although under the Oregon RESIDENTIAL LANDLORD and TENANT Act, the responsibility to maintain lies with the LANDLORD. The landlord also owes the tenant an implied COVENANT of QUIET ENJOYMENT.
When a tenancy is for a fixed term, it is called a tenancy FOR YEARS and it constitutes an ENCUMBRANCE on the owner's title. Normally, the lessee can ASSIGN his or her interest or can SUBLEASE the premises, in which case a SANDWICH lease is created. If the lessor accepts a new tenant, this is called a NOVATION. In Oregon, if a tenant moves out of the premises, the lessor must attempt to MITIGATE. If the lessor accepts a SURRENDER of the premises, the tenant's obligations under the lease are canceled.
When the tenancy continuously self-renews, it is called a PERIODIC tenancy. This type of tenancy can be terminated upon proper NOTICE from one party to the other. If the tenancy is month-to-month, the required NOTICE is 31 days. For year-to-year tenancies, a 60 -day NOTICE is required.
When there is permission, but neither a fixed term nor a period, a tenancy AT WILL is created. This is not an ENCUMBRANCE on the owner's title and cannot be ASSIGNED or SUBLEASED. A 30 - day notice is required to terminate it.
A tenancy AT SUFFERANCE is created when a tenant lawfully in possession fails to leave at the termination of the tenancy. Such a tenant is also called a HOLDOVER tenant. If the party in possession did not enter the premises legally, this constitutes a TRESPASS which is also a CRIMINAL act, in addition to a civil wrong.
To force a tenant to move out, the owner can EVICT the tenant. This can be ACTUAL, as where the owner files a suit, called a FORCIBLE ENTRY and DETAINER.
By filing the suit, the owner is asking the court for an ORDER of RESTITUTION. If the owner attempts to force the tenant out, it is called CONSTRUCTIVE eviction. In a non-residential tenancy, the owner is entitled to a LANDLORD'S lien against certain chattels belonging to the tenant. If the owner retains the chattels, it is called DISTRAINT FOR RENT.
A LEASE - OPTION gives the tenant possession of the property and an option to buy it.

PRACTICE QUESTIONS

The following practice questions are representative of the questions you will find on the final examination and on the licensing examinations given by the Oregon Real Estate Agency.

1. Which of the following would be closest in meaning to the word "estate"?
   (A) Possessory interest
   (B) Inheritable
   (C) Deed
   (D) Right of use

2. The term "estate" refers to
   (A) the owner's bundle of rights in the property.
   (B) the extent of the owner's interest in the property.
   (C) both A and B.
   (D) neither A nor B.

3. The right to possession, including use and enjoyment, as well as the right to dispose of property, most accurately describes
   (A) an estate.
   (B) ownership.
   (C) real estate.
   (D) a less than freehold.

4. An estate in real property
   (A) may exist simultaneously with another person who holds another estate in the same property.
   (B) involves a present or future right of possession.
   (C) may be of definite, indefinite, or unlimited duration.
   (D) All of the above are correct.

5. Estates in real property are classified mainly as to
   (A) the warranties the owner has.
   (B) the number of rights the owner has.
   (C) the length of their duration.
   (D) how many encumbrances there are.

6. At common law, which of the following would be an ownership interest in real property?
   I. A deeded two-week timeshare vacation home
   II. A residential condominium unit where the owners lease the land beneath them.
   (A) I only
   (B) II only
   (C) Both I and II
   (D) Neither I nor II

7. A fee estate is an estate which is
   (A) freely inheritable by the owner's family members.
   (B) of unlimited duration.
   (C) both A and B.
   (D) neither A nor B.

8. In real estate the word "fee" means
   (A) a less than freehold estate.
   (B) an estate of inheritance.
   (C) an estate used in the feudal period but which no longer is used.
   (D) a leasehold estate.

9. A fee simple absolute is an estate which is
   (A) free of encumbrances.
   (B) of indefinite duration.
   (C) both A and B.
   (D) neither A nor B.

10. A fee simple absolute estate can last
    I. for the life of the owner.
    II. after the life of the owner.
    (A) I only
    (B) II only
    (C) Both I and II
    (D) Neither I nor II

11. Which of the following would not be a characteristic of a fee simple absolute estate?
    (A) It must be free of encumbrances.
    (B) It must be freely transferable.
    (C) It must be inheritable.
    (D) It must be of indefinite duration.

12. The largest estate you can have in real property is called a
    (A) fee simple defeasible.
    (B) fee simple absolute.
    (C) freehold estate.
    (D) life estate.

13. When we say that an owner has a qualified fee, we mean that the owner has
(A) a property subject to one or more easements.
(B) the right of possession for a fixed term only.
(C) an ownership interest which is subject to a restriction on the use of the property.
(D) tenure by authority of the recorder of deeds.

14. Regarding a life estate, which of the following is not a correct statement?
(A) A life estate is a freehold.
(B) The life tenant is entitled to all the rents and profits from the property.
(C) The life tenant may dispose of the life estate by deed.
(D) There may be only one estate existing in a life estate at one time.

15. Which of the following would be an absolutely vested ownership interest which lasts for the duration of someone's life?
(A) A leasehold estate
(B) A remainder
(C) A life estate
(D) An executory interest

16. From the standpoint of the life tenant, a life estate is a
(A) leasehold for life. (C) remainder.
(B) reverter. (D) freehold.

17. A widow lady was willed her deceased husband's home for the rest of her natural life. She would have
(A) a life estate. (C) a possessory interest.
(B) a freehold estate. (D) all of the above.

18. Nevah Saydie was deeded some real estate for the rest of her life. Which of the following statements is not true in this case?
(A) She has a freehold estate.
(B) She has a fee simple estate.
(C) Her estate endures only for the length of her life.
(D) She may encumber the estate, but only for a period of time not exceeding her lifetime.

19. A life tenant may not
(A) lease the property.
(B) allow waste on the property.
(C) mortgage or otherwise allow a lien against the property.
(D) retain the profits from the property.

20. During the term of a life estate the life tenant
(A) is responsible for paying the taxes on the property.
(B) must accept legal liability for the property as an owner.
(C) must not allow the property to deteriorate.
(D) must do all of the above.

21. Assuming there are no deed restrictions to the contrary, a life tenant may do all of the following with the life estate except
(A) sell it. (C) mortgage it.
(B) rent it. (D) will it.

22. Max DeFraude leased some property to Candide L'Innocence on a five-year lease. Two years thereafter, DeFraude died, at which time his heirs discovered that he held a life estate in the property. DeFraude's heirs ask L'Innocence to vacate the property. If she contests their right to ask her to leave, a court would most likely find that the lease
(A) was valid for the remainder of its term.
(B) was invalid from the start, since a life estate cannot be leased.
(C) expired upon DeFraude's death.
(D) would be valid until L'Innocence's death.

23. In real estate law, the term "reversion" means
(A) that the property must pass to the grantee's heirs.
(B) that the property returns to the grantor.
(C) that the property is conveyed to another.
(D) the same as escheat.

24. When we say an owner has a bundle of rights, we mean that the owner has
(A) the right to use and enjoy the property.
(B) the responsibility to pay the taxes on the property.
(C) both A and B.
(D) neither A nor B.

25. An owner's bundle of rights includes the right to
    I. lease the property to another.
    II. demise the real estate.
    III. escheat the property to the state.
    (A) I only
    (B) I and II only
    (C) I, II and III
    (D) II only

26. Ownership of real estate includes
    (A) the right to use the land.
    (B) the right to possess the land.
    (C) both A and B.
    (D) neither A nor B.

27. A homeowners' association in a subdivision adopted a restriction in which "for sale" signs were prohibited. The restriction is unenforceable because it interferes with the
    I. right of the government to create such ordinances.
    II. owner's right to sell the property.
    (A) I only
    (B) II only
    (C) Both I and II
    (D) Neither I nor II

28. The bundle of rights for a fee simple estate compared to a life estate would be
    (A) greater in quantity.
    (B) fewer in quantity.
    (C) about the same.
    (D) exactly the same.

29. Which of the following would not be an estate in real property?
    (A) A remainder
    (B) A leasehold
    (C) A greater than freehold estate
    (D) All of the above are estates in real property.

30. An owner can change the estate from a fee simple title to a less than freehold by
    I. selling the mineral rights.
    II. a sale leaseback.
    (A) I only
    (B) II only
    (C) Both I and II
    (D) Neither I nor II

31. A holder of a fee simple estate will be left with a leasehold estate after
    (A) leasing the land on a long term lease for agricultural purposes.
    (B) assigning a right of way to a railroad company.
    (C) either A or B.
    (D) neither A nor B.

32. Freehold estates include
    (A) leases.
    (B) life estates.
    (C) both A and B.
    (D) neither A nor B.

33. An instrument which transfers possession of real estate, but does not transfer ownership, could be
    (A) a deed.
    (B) a lease.
    (C) a mortgage.
    (D) any of the above.

34. Mabel Barres owns a parcel of real property. She can change her fee simple title to less than a freehold estate by
    I. selling the mineral rights.
    II. a sale-leaseback arrangement.
    (A) I only
    (B) II only
    (C) Both I and II
    (D) Neither I nor II

35. Less than freehold estates are estates which are owned by
    (A) lessees.
    (B) life tenants.
    (C) both A and B.
    (D) neither A nor B.

36. A "demise" is a transfer of rights in real property which can be accomplished with
    (A) a will.
    (B) a lease.
    (C) either A or B.
    (D) neither A nor B.

37. A lease is an instrument used to transfer
    (A) possession of real property to another for a period of time.
    (B) ownership of trade fixtures.
    (C) both A and B.
    (D) neither A nor B.

38. The owner of real property who leases it to another is called
    (A) vendor.
    (B) lessee.
    (C) optionee.
    (D) lessor.

39. The interest that a tenant holds by virtue of a lease is called
    (A) a leasehold estate.
    (B) a less than freehold estate.
    (C) both A and B.
    (D) neither A nor B.

40. A lease for less than one year
(A) is enforceable even if oral.
(B) must be in writing.
(C) may be oral, but must be reduced to writing within 30 days.
(D) is completely unenforceable.

41. In order to create a valid month-to-month rental agreement, which of the following is not essential?
(A) In writing
(B) Offer and acceptance
(C) Consideration
(D) All of the above are unnecessary.

42. A lease of less than a year in duration should be in writing in order to
(A) make it binding.
(B) make it legal.
(C) avoid misunderstandings.
(D) benefit the tenant.

43. To be valid and enforceable, a lease must
I. state the consideration.
II. be delivered.
III. be acknowledged.
(A) I only
(B) I and II only
(C) II only
(D) II and III only

44. When describing the premises to be rented in an apartment lease, the contract should include the
(A) legal description of the property.
(B) street address of the building.
(C) dimensions of the space.
(D) tax lot number of the property.

45. All of the following are examples of leaseholds except
(A) an estate at sufferance.
(B) a life estate.
(C) an estate for years.
(D) a tenancy from year-to-year.

46. Which of the following is not a type of leasehold estate?
(A) Tenancy by the entirety
(B) Estate from period to period
(C) Tenancy at will
(D) Tenancy at sufferance

47. Which of the following would be a less than freehold estate?
(A) Property held by an owner which is subject to an easement
(B) Property which is held under a lease
(C) Real estate less the subsurface rights
(D) All of the above are examples of less than freeholds.

48. In real estate law the term "tenancy" refers to
(A) the holding of a possessory interest in real estate.
(B) a position where an owner refuses to grant possession.
(C) the right of the owner to regain possession after a lease.
(D) an estate of inheritance.

49. The lessor of a leasehold estate may be
(A) a fee simple owner.
(B) a life tenant.
(C) a lessee.
(D) any of the above.

50. Regarding landlord-tenant relationships, which of the following is true?
(A) The holder of an estate at will is said to have a less than freehold interest in real estate.
(B) The holder of the fee title to land which is rented to another is said to have a freehold interest.
(C) When a less than freehold interest is created, the fee title is encumbered.
(D) All of the above are correct statements.

51. During a valid tenancy a landlord has a
(A) tenancy for years.
(B) right of reverter.
(C) tenancy at will.
(D) tenancy at sufferance.

52. The term "reversion" best describes the interest of the
(A) county in an action for escheat.
(B) state in an action for escheat.
(C) lessor under a leasehold.
(D) beneficiary under a trust deed.

53. Examples of less than freehold estates include
I. a fee simple estate.
II. a 99-year lease.
III. a mortgage.
(A) I only
(B) I and II only
(C) II only
(D) II and III only

54. A leasehold would be
    I. a chattel real.
    II. an estate in remainder.
    III. personalty.
    (A) I only
    (B) I, II and III
    (C) I and III only
    (D) II and III only

55. A landlord and tenant reached a verbal agreement on a five-year lease. The lease was drawn up, signed by the landlord and delivered to the tenant. Upon receipt of the lease, the tenant moved into the premises, but did not ever sign the lease. If the tenant does not pay the rent stipulated in the lease, the landlord can
    (A) successfully sue to collect the rent.
    (B) collect nothing, as the tenant did not sign the lease.
    (C) collect nothing, as the tenant had a tenancy at will which does not require consideration.
    (D) collect nothing, provided the tenant moves out immediately after being made aware of the landlord's demand for payment.

56. The terms and conditions of a written lease can be changed only by
    (A) the surrender and acceptance of the old lease and the creation of a new one.
    (B) a written codicil to the original lease.
    (C) a modification agreement signed by the lessor only.
    (D) a modification agreement signed by the lessee only.

57. A tenant's lease provided that the lessor guaranteed the right to use the property without interference. This is called a covenant
    (A) of quiet enjoyment.
    (B) of seizin.
    (C) of title.
    (D) against nuisances.

58. In every lease the lessor gives the lessee an implied covenant of
    (A) further assurance.
    (B) seizin.
    (C) compliance.
    (D) quiet enjoyment.

59. In a lease the covenant of quiet enjoyment is
    (A) a covenant where the owner promises to refrain from interfering with the tenant's business in leased commercial space.
    (B) assurance to the tenant that the landlord's title is not defective and therefore the tenant will not be dispossessed by persons asserting a paramount title.
    (C) assurance to the tenant that premises are fit for the use for which they were intended.
    (D) assurance to the landlord that the tenant will conduct business on the premises in a manner to ensure the enjoyment of the premises by other tenants.

60. When a residential property has been rented to a tenant in Oregon, the tenant automatically has the landlord's assurance
    (A) of quiet enjoyment.
    (B) that the property will meet minimum standards of habitability.
    (C) of both A and B.
    (D) of neither A nor B.

61. A tenant in a commercial building informed the landlord that there had developed a crack in the ceiling. The lease provided that any repairs were the responsibility of the tenant. However, to maintain good tenant relations, the landlord agreed to fix the crack. After the landlord repaired the crack, plaster fell, injuring the tenant, as a direct result of the landlord's faulty repair. If the tenant wishes to recover damages from the landlord, the tenant will be able to recover
    (A) nothing, as the landlord was not obligated to repair the ceiling in the first place.
    (B) the cost of re-repairing the ceiling, but nothing for the damages.
    (C) for damages, but not the cost of re-repairing the ceiling.
    (D) for damages as well as the cost of re-repairing the ceiling.

62. If the tenant should allow harm to come to the premises, either willfully or by negligence, this is called
    (A) waste.
    (B) functional obsolescence.
    (C) unlawful trespass.
    (D) violating a covenant.

63. Unless prohibited by the terms of the agreement, a lessee may
    I. mortgage the leasehold interest.
    II. install trade fixtures and remove them upon vacating the premises.
    (A) I only
    (B) II only
    (C) Both I and II
    (D) Neither I nor II

64. An estate for years
    (A) is of indefinite duration.
    (B) automatically renews itself on termination.
    (C) requires either party to have just cause to terminate prior to expiration.
    (D) All of the above are correct.

65. A tenant signed an agreement with an owner for the use and possession of the owner's property for a period of 30 days. The tenant has
    (A) an estate for years.
    (B) a month-to-month tenancy.
    (C) a periodic tenancy.
    (D) an estate at sufferance.

66. A less than freehold estate which has a definite expiration date is called
    (A) a tenancy for years.
    (B) an estate from period to period.
    (C) a tenancy at will.
    (D) a fee simple determinable.

67. A tenant rented a property on a monthly basis from April 1 through August 31. The tenancy was
    (A) a tenancy from period to period.
    (B) for years.
    (C) a tenancy for years.
    (D) from year to year.

68. A lease of real estate is generally considered to be
    (A) an encumbrance on the title to the property.
    (B) an estate for years.
    (C) both A and B.
    (D) neither A nor B.

69. Which of the following is true regarding an estate for years?
    (A) It automatically terminates on the stated expiration date.
    (B) It must be for at least one year.
    (C) It terminates on the death of either principal.
    (D) All of the above are true statements.

70. Which of the following interests automatically renews itself?
    (A) Tenancy for years
    (B) Periodic tenancy
    (C) Tenancy at will
    (D) Tenancy at sufferance

71. An estate in land which runs from year to year is called
    (A) a freehold estate.
    (B) an estate at will.
    (C) an estate for years.
    (D) a periodic tenancy.

72. A tenant whose commercial lease was about to expire entered into negotiations with the lessor for an extension of the lease. They agreed to continue the tenancy on a year-to-year basis with either party to have the option to terminate on 60 days notice. This agreement created a tenancy
    (A) at will.
    (B) for life.
    (C) for years.
    (D) from period to period.

73. A tenant held a lease for one year which expired. After the expiration of the lease the tenant remained in possession and the lessor began to accept rent on a monthly basis. The tenant now has
    (A) an estate in remainder.
    (B) a tenancy for years.
    (C) a tenancy from period to period.
    (D) a tenancy at sufferance.

74. A farmer rented a property on a yearly basis where the law provided that either party could terminate the arrangement with 60 days notice. This was most likely
    (A) a tenancy for years.
    (B) a tenancy from period to period.
    (C) a tenancy at will.
    (D) a life estate.

75. An estate at will is
    (A) an inheritance of property through an estate.
    (B) a tenancy of uncertain duration.
    (C) both A and B.
    (D) neither A nor B.

76. Under an estate at will,
    I. 30 days notice is required to terminate the tenancy.
    II. the tenancy is created with the permission of the owner.
    (A) I only
    (B) II only
    (C) Both I and II
    (D) Neither I nor II

77. In Oregon, how much notice is required to terminate a tenancy at will?
(A) No notice is required.
(B) A 24-hour notice is required.
(C) A 30-day notice is required.
(D) The amount of notice required depends on the length of time the tenant has been in possession.

78. An estate which can be terminated by either party at any time would be
(A) an estate for years.
(B) a tenancy at sufferance.
(C) a tenancy at will.
(D) a tenancy from period to period.

79. As a general rule in landlord-tenant relationships, the landlord can terminate which of the following tenancies on the shortest notice?
(A) Tenancy at will
(B) Tenancy at sufferance
(C) Tenancy from month to month
(D) Tenancy from period to period

80. A tenant possessed a property for five years without the permission of the owner. This means that the tenant's interest was a
(A) tenancy at sufferance.
(B) tenancy for years.
(C) periodic tenancy.
(D) tenancy at will.

81. A person who originally had a lease but stayed on the premises after the termination of the lease is
(A) a tenant at sufferance.
(B) a holdover tenant.
(C) both a tenant at sufferance and a holdover tenant.
(D) neither a tenant at sufferance nor a holdover tenant.

82. Under Oregon law, how much notice is required to terminate a tenancy at sufferance?
(A) No notice is required.
(B) A 24-hour notice is required.
(C) A 30-day notice is required.
(D) The amount of notice required depends on the length of time the tenant has been in possession.

83. The type of tenancy which gives the lessee the fewest rights is the
(A) tenancy at sufferance.
(B) tenancy at will.
(C) tenancy from period to period.
(D) tenancy for years.

84. Which of the following are synonymous in real estate?
I. Estate for years — Periodic estate
II. Estate at will — Tenancy at sufferance
(A) I only (C) Both I and II
(B) II only (D) Neither I nor II

85. In an agreement for the possession of real estate, the
I. owner need give no notice to terminate the tenancy if the tenant is without permission.
II. term "rent" indicates that the estate is from period to period.
(A) I only (C) Both I and II
(B) II only (D) Neither I nor II

86. A notice is required to terminate
I. an estate from period to period.
II. an estate for years.
III. a tenancy at will.
(A) I only (C) I, II and III
(B) I and II only (D) I and III only

87. Which of the following would be an estate for an indefinite period?
(A) Tenancy for years
(B) Encumbrance
(C) Freehold estate
(D) Easement appurtenant to the land

88. Leaseholds which are of indefinite duration include
(A) tenancies for years. (C) both A and B.
(B) tenancies at will. (D) neither A nor B.

89. A lessee had five years remaining on a lease. The lessee wished to enter into an agreement where another person would take over all the remaining rights the lessee had in the property. This would be known as
(A) an assignment of lease.
(B) a gross lease.
(C) a sublease.
(D) a net lease.

90. Typically, a sublease constitutes
(A) the same as an assignment of the lessee's interest.
(B) a transfer of the entire leasehold interest of the lessee.
(C) a transfer of a portion of the leasehold interest of the lessee.
(D) both A and B.

91. A lessee decided to sublet the entire estate to a third party. The new lessee will become a
(A) landlord.
(B) grantor.
(C) trustee.
(D) tenant.

92. When all or part of a tenant's rights in a property are subleased to another,
(A) primary responsibility for the rent payments shifts to the new tenant.
(B) the original tenant remains fully liable to the lessor for the rent payments.
(C) both A and B are correct.
(D) neither A nor B is correct.

93. When a tenant under a lease subleases the property,
(A) the new tenant becomes directly obligated to the lessor for the rent payments.
(B) the original lease is canceled and a new lease is created between the lessor and the new tenant.
(C) both A and B are correct.
(D) neither A nor B is correct.

94. A tenant assigned the lease to another. The tenant
(A) transferred the right of possession for the entire remaining term of the lease.
(B) retained secondary liability for payment of the rent of the new tenant does not pay.
(C) accomplished the same thing as a sublease.
(D) did both A and B.

95. A tenant under a lease also held an option to buy. If the tenant assigned the lease to a new tenant, the option to buy
(A) could be voided by the owner.
(B) would become illegal under the provisions of the Statute of Frauds.
(C) would render the option unenforceable.
(D) would constitute a transfer of the option to the new lessee.

96. A tenant leased a building for two years. After six months the tenant moved out and stopped paying rent. The landlord can demand payment of
(A) rent to the end of the month only.
(B) rent until the expiration of the statutory notice period.
(C) rent for the entire remaining term of the lease.
(D) nothing.

97. A tenant under a lease stayed in possession of the property after the termination of the lease. The tenant's possession was not in good faith. The landlord had already leased the property to a new tenant, but the new tenant was unable to take possession because the original tenant did not vacate the premises. The landlord is entitled to sue the original tenant for damages and recover
(A) up to two month's rent as punitive damages.
(B) rent for the actual period the tenant stayed in wrongful possession.
(C) the greater of A or B above.
(D) the lesser of A or B above.

98. Hendrickson leased office space from Vulture Enterprises, Inc. on a five-year lease. After three years of the lease, Hendrickson abandoned the premises and ceased making rent payments. Vulture Enterprises, Inc.
I. could sue for the entire unpaid balance of the lease.
II. must make a reasonable effort to re-rent the premises and, if successful, must lower the damages they claim by the amount received from the new tenant.
(A) I only
(B) II only
(C) Both I and II
(D) Neither I nor II

99. An owner of a retail building did not receive the periodic rent when it was due, so the landlord called the water bureau and had the water turned off in order to force the tenant out. You would say that
I. this constituted constructive eviction.
II. the landlord had a legal right to do this.
(A) I only
(B) II only
(C) Both I and II
(D) Neither I nor II

100. When the tenant under a lease holds over after the termination of the lease, the
   I. landlord may physically remove the tenant and the tenant's personal property.
   II. tenant is considered at law to be merely a trespasser.
   (A) I only (B) II only (C) Both I and II (D) Neither I nor II

101. A court-enforced order removing a lessee is called
   (A) constructive eviction.
   (B) eviction.
   (C) surrender.
   (D) both A and C.

102. A forcible entry and wrongful detainer action would normally be used by a
   I. lessor. II. lessee.
   (A) I only (B) II only (C) Both I and II (D) Neither I nor II

103. Alpha leased property to Beta. Upon the termination of the lease Beta refused to sign a new lease. In this case Alpha can
   (A) sue Beta for breach of the lease and bad faith.
   (B) bring a court action for specific performance.
   (C) oust Beta from the property.
   (D) obtain a judgment against Beta for the rent under new terms.

104. An apartment was leased to a couple and their children. Shortly after the lease began the parents of the wife moved in. The landlord can
   (A) do nothing.
   (B) increase the rent.
   (C) evict the parents only.
   (D) evict the parents, their children and the wife's parents.

105. A lessor was required by the terms of a lease to maintain the premises, but did not do so. When the premises become so deteriorated that the tenant can no longer safely use them, this is known as
   (A) eviction by dispossession.
   (B) actual eviction.
   (C) constructive eviction.
   (D) a forcible entry and detainer.

106. A lessee had possession of real property under a five-year lease. During the lease, the lessor died. As a result of the death of the lessor,
   (A) the heirs could evict the tenant as soon as they gain title.
   (B) the lease continued for the remainder of its term.
   (C) as soon as the heirs gain title they must reaffirm the lease or they will lose their right to collect rent from the tenant.
   (D) as soon as the heirs gain title they can evict the tenant after at least 30 days notice.

107. A tenant held possession of premises under a lease which had several years left before expiration. If the owner wished to sell the building,
   (A) the owner must give the tenant a first option to match the buyer's offer and buy the building.
   (B) the lease would become a sublease.
   (C) a sale would have no effect on the rights of the tenant.
   (D) the tenant would have to move out as soon as the buyer takes title and gives at least 30-days notice unless the tenant could renegotiate a new lease with the new owner.

108. A lease would be terminated by
   (A) exercise of eminent domain by the government.
   (B) a successful eviction by the lessor.
   (C) either A or B above.
   (D) neither A nor B.

109. A lessor and lessee got together and agreed to terminate a lease. This would be called a
   (A) rescission.
   (B) surrender and acceptance.
   (C) revocation.
   (D) cancellation.

110. A lease may be terminated by
   I. mutual consent.
   II. breach of the terms and conditions of the lease.
   (A) I only (B) II only (C) Both I and II (D) Neither I nor II

111. A lessee may terminate an ordinary lease
(A) if the lessor interferes with the lessee's quiet enjoyment of the property.
(B) if the lessor sells the property.
(C) upon the death of the lessor.
(D) if the lessor becomes delinquent in paying an underlying mortgage.

112. Which of the following would terminate a lease?
I. Death of the landlord or tenant
II. Sale of the property
(A) I only
(B) II only
(C) Both I and II
(D) Neither I nor II

113. When leased real estate is sold and the lease is silent regarding a sale of the property, the lease
(A) must be renewed at expiration.
(B) expires upon the sale.
(C) becomes a sublease.
(D) is binding on the new owner.

114. Franklin was the owner of a building that has been leased to Tomlin on a 20-year lease. Franklin died at the end of the eleventh year of the lease. Which of the following is true regarding this situation?
I. Franklin's heirs and devisees will become the new lessors.
II. A new lease must be negotiated with Franklin's heirs and devisees.
(A) I only
(B) II only
(C) Both I and II
(D) Neither I nor II

115. A tenant has a two-year lease and has one year remaining. If the landlord sells the building, the
(A) sale would not cancel the tenant's current lease.
(B) new landlord will have to decide whether or not to extend the lease for its remaining term.
(C) tenant's lease is automatically cancelled.
(D) lease will be terminated by 60 days notice from the new owner to the tenant.

116. A lease can always be terminated by
I. selling the building.
II. death of the tenant.
III. abandonment of the leased premises by the tenant.
IV. expiration of the term of the lease.
(A) I, II, III and IV
(B) II and IV only
(C) III and IV only
(D) IV only

117. Which of the following would not be grounds for a landlord to terminate a lease and sue to evict the tenant?
(A) Sale of the property
(B) Unlawful use of the property
(C) Noncompliance of health codes
(D) Violation of building rules

118. An owner leased a house to a tenant for one year but did not put the lease in writing. A few months thereafter, the owner sold the house. In this situation, the
(A) tenant must move out any time the buyer demands it.
(B) tenant must move out if the buyer gives at least 30 days notice.
(C) tenant's lease is binding on the buyer.
(D) sale of the property was illegal.

119. A landowner leased land to a tenant, who in turn leased it to a sublessee who will use the property for a sandwich shop. Who holds the sandwich lease?
(A) The landowner.
(B) The lessee
(C) The sublessee.
(D) The assignee.

ANSWERS

To practice questions. If you chose the wrong letter, here's the right one! The explanations are designed to clarify your understanding.

1. **A** There are many possible interests in real estate which can exist at the same time. An estate is defined as a right to possession of the property. However, not all estates are inheritable (tenancy at will, for example). A right of use is the definition for an easement, not an estate. A deed is a piece of paper, not a possessory interest.
2. **C** An estate is defined as a right to possession of the property. Since a right to possession may be for different time periods, for life or forever, therefore there are numerous different types of estates. The greater the holder's right of possession, the greater the number of sticks in the bundle of rights.
3. **B** An estate is defined as a right of possession. A less than freehold may be a right of possession, but does not include the right to dispose of the property. Ownership may not necessarily include a present right of possession as, for example, when an owner leases the property to a tenant.
4. **D** An owner can lease or rent the property to a tenant, so the owner holds a right of reverter (future estate), while the tenant has the present possessory interest, thereby creating two estates in the property at the same time. An estate can be for a definite time period (for years), for life (life estate), or forever (fee title).
5. **C** Whether or not an estate is subject to encumbrances has to do with the quality of the title, but it has nothing to do with the quantity of the title. Warranties refer to the promises that a seller would make in the deed as to the quality of the title (i.e., free and clear, encumbered, and so forth). An estate can be for a definite time period (for years), for life (life estate), or forever (fee title), so the length of the duration is the normal way estates are classified.
6. **A** Because the timeshare is deeded means that the owners have a freehold (ownership) interest. The fact that the interest is only for a recurring two-week period is irrelevant. Unless there is some restriction, the owners have the right of possession for those two weeks forever. However, a leasehold interest, is considered personal property, not real estate so, because the owners of the leasehold condominium own a leasehold, they do not have an ownership interest in real property.
7. **C** A fee estate is defined as a "freehold estate of inheritance." In this respect it is contrasted with the other kind of freehold, a life estate. Therefore, a fee estate is inheritable. The fact that others may also inherit does not render untrue the statement "a fee estate is an estate which is freely inheritable by the owner's family members." Since fee estates are inheritable, they can potentially last forever and are therefore of unlimited duration.
8. **B** A fee estate is defined as a "freehold estate of inheritance." A less than freehold estate is a synonym for a leasehold estate, and is a possessory interest, but without ownership.
9. **B** A fee is defined as a "freehold estate of inheritance." The quality of the title (encumbered or not) has nothing to do with the quantity of the estate (fee, life estate, less than freehold, etc.). The term "absolute" in the phrase "fee simple absolute" does not mean "free and clear." It means that the estate is not subject to divestiture. In other words, a fee title which is mortgaged is still probably a fee simple absolutely vested.
10. **C** A fee is a "freehold estate of inheritance." The fact that a fee simple absolute can last longer than the life of the owner does not make it an untrue statement to say that a fee simple absolute can last for the life of the owner.
11. **A** The quality of the title (encumbered or not) has nothing to do with the quantity of the estate (fee, life estate, less than freehold, etc.). A fee simple absolute is freely transferable, since the ability to transfer a thing to another is a fundamental right of ownership. A fee estate is defined as a "freehold estate of inheritance."
12. **B** A fee simple defeasible, a fee simple absolute and a life estate are all freehold estates, therefore, all are ownership interests. A life estate is ownership only for life, a defeasible title is one which can revert or vest an executory interest in another because it was created with a condition. Only the fee simple absolute is unconditional (absolute) and potentially of

unlimited duration, therefore it is the highest interest possible.

13. **C** A defeasible title is one which can revert or vest an executory interest in another because it was created with a condition. "Qualified" is a synonym for "defeasible."

14. **D** A freehold is an ownership interest. Since life estates are freeholds, the life tenant has a bundle of rights which includes the right to do anything at all with the property. This includes transferring the life estate to another, renting it, leasing it, mortgaging it, etc. Therefore, the life tenant can create multiple estates within the life estate.

15. **C** Ownerships are called freeholds, which can be either fee titles (perpetual) or life estates (for a lifetime). Either can be vested absolutely, or vested subject to divestiture (defeasible). If defeasible, it may be followed by a future estate, which is a reverter, remainder or executory interest. A leasehold estate is a right of possession, but without ownership.

16. **D** A life estate is a freehold, not a leasehold estate. When there is a life estate, someone else will hold a right of reverter (estate in reversion) or a remainder (estate in remainder).

17. **D** Ownerships are called freeholds, which can be either fee titles (perpetual) or life estates (for a lifetime). Estates are defined as having a right of possession.

18. **B** Ownerships are called freeholds, which can be either fee titles (perpetual) or life estates (for a lifetime). Life estates and fee estates are both freeholds, but a life estate lasts only for someone's lifetime, where a fee estate is potentially of unlimited duration. The owner of a life estate has the same rights as the owner of a fee title, including the right to encumber it. However, the life estate is extinguished upon the death of the governing life, therefore all interests (including encumbrances) which depend on its existence would be extinguished also.

19. **B** A fundamental principle of law is that whenever there is a future interest, the holder of the present estate is not allowed to permit waste of the property. Therefore, the life tenant must maintain the premises, ordinary wear and tear excepted. However, the life tenant is free to encumber or grant any other interest in the life estate.

20. **D** Since the life estate is a freehold, the life tenant is vested with seizin. This means that the life tenant not only has the bundle of rights, but also has the responsibilities of ownership, including accepting legal liability for the property and the responsibility to pay the taxes. Whenever there is a future interest, the holder of the present estate is not allowed to permit waste of the property.

21. **D** An owner of a life estate is free to do anything with the life estate, including selling or encumbering it. However, a life estate terminates upon the death of the life tenant, so the life tenant can only sell what he or she has – ownership until the end of the governing life. Similarly, any encumbrances such as a rental or lease agreement or a mortgage would be extinguished at the end of the life estate. Since a will does not take effect until the death of the testator, at the point it takes effect, the life estate no longer exists. Therefore, the life tenant cannot will the life estate, because it would not exist after the death of the life tenant.

22. **C** Although the life tenant is free to do with the life estate whatever the life tenant desires, the life tenant can nevertheless not create a greater estate than the life estate. In other words, if the life tenant wishes to lease the life estate, then the lessee takes a leasehold on the life estate, since the life tenant had no authority to lease the future interest as well. Therefore, upon the termination of the life estate, the leasehold is also extinguished.

23. **B** A reversion occurs whenever a person conveys rights to another, but gets the rights back later. Rights of reversion typically occur when there is a defeasible fee, when there is a life estate, or when there is a lease.

24. **A** All freeholders (owners) are said to be vested with seizin to the property. Being vested with seizin creates in the owner the bundle of rights and also makes the owner responsible for the property. However, the responsibilities are not part of the bundle of rights.

25. **B** A demise is another term for a rental or lease. The government has the right to take the property when the owner dies without a will and no natural heirs capable of inheriting. This is called the government's right of escheat. It is not part of the rights of the owner.

26. **C** A right of possession is an estate and a right of use is an easement. Both are part of the bundle of rights. Do not become confused by the fact that an owner can grant an easement (right of use) to another. The fact that the owner no longer holds a particular stick in the bundle of rights does not mean

that the right no longer exists – it merely means that the right is vested in another.

27. **D** In this case neither the association, nor government agencies, nor private parties can restrict the right of the owner to place a "for sale" sign on the property. The right to sell the property can be vested in another, as where there is a deed covenant. To refuse to allow a "for sale" sign would, however, violate constitutional guarantees by infringing on the right to freedom of speech. Even then, it would only be a constitutional issue if a government agency attempted to make the rule. The government cannot restrict freedom of speech, but private parties generally can.

28. **A** A fee simple estate is an estate whose duration is potentially perpetual, whereas the life estate only lasts for the life of the life tenant. Therefore the fee simple absolute is the greater estate and has a greater number of sticks in the bundle of rights.

29. **C** The definition of an estate is any possessory interest, whether through ownership or otherwise. Therefore, remainders (right to possession in the future) and leaseholds (right to present possession without ownership) are estates. However, there is no such thing as a "greater than freehold estate."

30. **B** Selling the mineral rights does not change the fee estate into a less than freehold. A sale-leaseback transaction occurs when the owner sells the property, and then leases it back from the buyer. Therefore the sale leaseback would result in the owner no longer holding a fee estate but holding a less than freehold in its place.

31. **D** Assigning a right of way (creating an easement) or leasing the property will encumber a fee estate, but will not destroy it.

32. **B** An estate is a possessory interest, so all the choices are estates. Estates are classified as freeholds (ownerships) and less than freeholds (possession without ownership. Freeholds are further classified as fees and life estates. Less than freeholds include estates for years, periodic estates, estates at will and estates at sufferance.

33. **B** A mortgage does not transfer either ownership or possession; it merely creates a lien (encumbers) the real estate to make it collateral for a debt. Deeds and leases both transfer a right of possession, but deeds also convey ownership.

34. **B** An estate is any interest in property which gives the holder a right of possession. There are two kinds of estates, freehold (ownership) and less than freehold (non-ownership). Conveying mineral or oil rights does not cause a loss of the right of possession. If an owner leases his or her land to someone else, the owner still has a freehold (ownership). The only thing that would cause the ownership to become a leasehold would be to sell the property and lease it back from the buyer.

35. **A** "Life tenant" is the term used to describe an owner of a life estate, which is a freehold. The term "lessee" is used to describe a tenant who holds a less than freehold estate.

36. **C** The term "demise" refers to the creation of a less than freehold estate. Less than freehold estates are commonly created by lease or rental agreement. A will can also grant ownership in one person, but subject to a right of possession for a time to be vested in another person.

37. **A** Trade fixtures are personal property. A bill of sale is used to transfer personal property, the same as a deed is used to convey real property.

38. **D** The party granting an interest is always the "-or" word, and the party receiving the interest is the "-ee" word. Therefore, the lessor leases to the lessee. A vendor is a seller. An optionee is a person who receives an option.

39. **C** The terms are identical in meaning. However, some people use the word leasehold in certain contexts as a synonym for "tenancy for years." Nevertheless, technically, the two terms mean the same thing.

40. **A** The Statute of Frauds in Oregon requires all contracts which involve real property to be in writing lest they be void. The Statute of Frauds even includes an authorization to deal in the real property of another (such as a property management or listing agreement), and further provides that an authorization to deal in the real property of another is void if it fails to state the agent's compensation with reasonable certainty. However, an exception to the Statute of Frauds is a lease for less than a year.

41. **A** To be valid and enforceable all contracts must have a legal object and agreement of the parties (meeting of the minds). The agreement normally comes about by the process of offer and acceptance. In contracts other than contracts for personal services a contract must also be supported by consideration. The Statute of Frauds requires all contracts involving real property to be in writing lest they be void. An exception to the Statute of Frauds is a contract to create a leasehold for a year or less or of indefinite duration.

42. **C** The Oregon Statute of Frauds requires all contracts involving real property to be in writing lest they be void. A lease for a year or less is an exception.

43. **A** Most contracts require consideration to be valid and enforceable. Delivery refers to the intent of a grantor of a deed to convey the title to the buyer. Acknowledgment normally occurs when a notary public witnesses a signature. Acknowledgment is not normally required for a contract to be valid and enforceable.

44. **B** To be valid and enforceable, contracts must meet certain requirements. If the contract involves real property it must describe or reference the property with certainty. Normally this is done by a legal description. In the creation of less than freehold estates, the street address is acceptable in Oregon courts. Oregon statutes specifically provide that a tax lot number is not a valid description of property.

45. **B** Less than freehold estates (leaseholds) are either at sufferance (without permission) or at will (with permission). If the estate is at will, it could be for years (a fixed term), periodic, or without stipulating either a fixed term or a period.

46. **A** Leaseholds are either at will (with the owner's permission) or at sufferance (without permission). A tenant at sufferance has no rights in the property. If at will, it could be for years (for a fixed term, i.e., a lease), from period to period (i.e., month to month) or just "at will," that is, with permission but without a fixed term or period. A tenancy by the entirety is an ownership by husband and wife.

47. **B** A lease is a type of less than freehold estate. Less than freehold interests, easements, subsurface rights vested in another, and many other interests are encumbrances on the fee title. The less than freehold is the only encumbrance that is a possessory interest.

48. **A** The right of the owner to recover possession after the termination of a less than freehold estate is called a right of reverter (estate in reversion). An estate of inheritance is a fee. "Tenancy" means the act of possessing, or being in possession of, real property. It is applied equally to the owner as to a renter. In other words, whoever is in possession is the tenant, and the tenant's act of possessing is called the tenancy.

49. **D** Clearly, the owner can lease the property to another. A life tenant holds a life estate, which is an ownership interest. The holder of the life estate (life tenant) can lease the premises to another for a term not exceeding the end of the life estate. Also, a lessee can sublease to another, and so would become a lessor as well as a lessee.

50. **D** Less than freeholds include tenancy for years, periodic tenancy, tenancy at will, and tenancy at sufferance. Whenever a freeholder creates a subsidiary interest it has the effect of encumbering the freehold. The fact that an encumbrance is created, however, does not diminish the quantity of the estate C it is still a fee simple absolutely vested. It merely affects the quality of the estate.

51. **B** There are four kinds of less than freehold estates – estate for years, periodic estate, estate at will, and estate at sufferance. The right of the owner to recover possession after the termination of a less than freehold estate is called a right of reverter (estate in reversion).

52. **C** Any time someone has a future right to the property, such as a landlord's right to retake possession after a lease, it is called a "reverter," or sometimes an "estate in reversion."

53. **C** Only the 99-year lease is a less than freehold estate. A fee simple is a freehold, not a less than freehold. A mortgage is not a possessory interest (estate), and therefore is neither a freehold nor a less than freehold.

54. **C** A "chattel real" is an interest in real property which is classified as personal property. A right of possession under a less than freehold is so considered. "Personalty" is a term which is a synonym for "chattels," so a leasehold interest is also personalty. An estate in remainder is the right to the fee title upon the death of a life tenant, and is therefore real property.

55. **A** Leases (as well as deeds) need not be signed by the grantee, only by the grantor (lessor or landlord). In other words, the lessee's acceptance of the terms of the lease is evidenced by the fact that the lessor gave the lessee a copy of the lease, whereupon the lessee moved in. The act of taking possession constitutes agreement to the terms.

56. **A** A surrender of a lease occurs when the lessor agrees to release the tenant from further liability under the lease. While the lessor is under no legal obligation to accept the surrender, if the lessor does accept the surrender, the original lease is deemed to be extinguished. If a lessor and a lessee agree mutually to a modification of an existing lease, this is deeded to be the same as surrender and acceptance, followed by the creation of a new lease. Another term for this is "novation."

57. **A** Even if the lease says nothing, there is an implied covenant of quiet enjoyment in a lease. The covenant of quiet enjoyment means that the lessor will defend his or her title to the property to the extent necessary to protect and guarantee the tenant's right to uninterrupted possession.
58. **D** The covenant of quiet enjoyment is an implied provision in a lease or a deed that the tenant's or buyer's possession of the property will not be interrupted by someone asserting a paramount title.
59. **B** The covenant of quiet enjoyment is the lessor's promise that lessee's possession of the premises will not be interrupted by someone with a superior title. For example, if the property is mortgaged and the lender forecloses, the foreclosure may extinguish the lease. If it does, the lessor would be in violation of the covenant of quiet enjoyment.
60. **C** The covenant of quiet enjoyment means that the lessor will defend his or her title to the property to the extent necessary to protect and guarantee the tenant's right to uninterrupted possession, and is implied in all leases. Habitability standards are required by the Oregon Residential Landlord and Tenant Law, but this law applies only to residential properties. Rentals and leases of non-residential property need contain no promise of habitability.
61. **C** Since this is a commercial lease, the lessor had no obligation to repair. However, you must always accept legal liability for your wrongful acts, even if done gratuitously. Therefore, since the lessor did repair the ceiling, the lessor is now liable for damages caused by the fact that it was not repaired properly.
62. **A** Any act or failure to act which causes a loss of value or utility is called waste. A fundamental principle of real property law is that whenever there is a future possessory interest, such as the landlord's right of reverter, the holder of the present possessory estate may not allow waste. This is not violating a covenant contained in the lease because the fact that the tenant may not permit waste need not be stated as a covenant; it is common law.
63. **C** A mortgage is a device which makes property collateral for a debt. Anything you own can be mortgaged, including a leasehold interest in real property. Of course, if the lender holds a mortgage on a leasehold, a foreclosure cannot gain the lender any greater title than the leasehold. Trade fixtures are defined as items installed by a tenant in rented or leased premises, and the tenant is generally permitted to remove them, provided the tenant repairs any damage caused by their removal and restores the premises. Therefore, trade fixtures, unlike ordinary fixtures, are considered personal property.
64. **C** Less than freehold estates include tenancy (estate) for years, tenancy (estate) from period to period, tenancy (estate) at will, and tenancy (estate) at sufferance. Of these, the tenancy for years is the only one where the time span is fixed. It is fixed in the original agreement, therefore neither party need give notice to the other to terminate. Nor can either party terminate before the end of the fixed term, unless the party wishing to terminate can claim that the other has breached the agreement.
65. **A** Do not let the word "period" confuse you. The fact that the possession was for exactly 30 days means it is a tenancy for years, not periodic. Periodic tenancies have no fixed ending date; they renew over and over for each successive period until one of the parties gives notice to the other.
66. **A** There are three ways to give a tenant permission to occupy the premises – tenancy for years (for a fixed term), periodic tenancy (of indefinite term, self-renews until one party gives notice to the other), and tenancy at will (neither a fixed term nor a period).
67. **B** Do not let the phrase "on a monthly basis" confuse you. Since there is a definite expiration to the arrangement, the tenancy is for years, not periodic.
68. **C** Although some people use the word "lease" as a synonym for "leasehold" and "less than freehold," in common usage it is considered another term for a tenancy for years.
69. **A** A tenancy for years could be for any term the parties desire and is not limited to one year, or to a time span in multiples of a year. The death of either the lessor or the lessee does not terminate a tenancy for years. The heirs of the lessor must take title subject to the lease, and the heirs of a lessee must continue to pay the lease and continue to hold the right of occupancy.
70. **B** Tenancy or estate from period to period (periodic tenancy or estate) differs from the tenancy for years in that it self-renews each period until one of the parties gives notice to the other. It is, therefore, a tenancy of indefinite duration. Both tenancy from period to period and tenancy for years are (technically) special types of tenancies at will, but most people use the term to mean the owner has granted permission, but without a fixed term (tenancy for years) or a period (periodic tenancy). A tenant at sufferance has no permission, and therefore no legal rights.

71. **D** Do not confuse a "tenancy for years" (lease) with a "tenancy from year to year." A tenancy from year to year is a special type of periodic tenancy where the period happens to be a year.

72. **D** If the lessor and lessee had successfully negotiated an extension of the lease, it would have been a tenancy for years, since an extension of the lease implies a new fixed ending date. Instead they agreed to a periodic tenancy (tenancy from period to period). Do not confuse a "tenancy for years" (lease) with a "tenancy from year to year." A tenancy from year to year is a special type of periodic tenancy where the period happens to be a year.

73. **C** In this case, the landlord accepted rent from the tenant, thus giving the tenant a legal right (permission of the owner) to remain in possession. Therefore, this is a tenancy at will or better; most likely from period to period.

74. **B** By statute in Oregon, a tenancy from year to year can be terminated by either party upon giving 60 days notice to the other. It is the only periodic tenancy which calls for a 60-day notice.

75. **B** An estate at will is a less than freehold estate which has nothing to do with inheritance.

76. **C** Since the owner has given the tenant permission to occupy the premises, the law requires the owner to give the tenant reasonable notice to quit. But since there is no period involved, the notice has been fixed at a flat 30 days.

77. **C** Since the owner has given the tenant permission to occupy the premises, the law requires the owner to give the tenant reasonable notice to quit. But since there is no period involved, the notice has been fixed at a flat 30 days.

78. **B** Since a tenant at sufferance has no permission, the owner need give no legal notice to terminate the tenancy. An estate for years (lease) also requires no notice, as the parties knew when it would be over when they entered into the agreement. However, a lease cannot be terminated at any time; it requires a cause.

79. **B** A tenancy at sufferance is one which is without legal right, therefore the landlord need give no notice at all.

80. **A** There are four types of less than freehold estates: Estate for years (a fixed term), periodic estate (of indefinite duration, until one party gives notice to the other), estate at will (permission of the owner but without a period or a fixed term, and estate at sufferance. Of these, the estate at sufferance is the only one without the owner's permission.

81. **C** One who holds over wrongfully has no permission, so "holdover tenant" is a synonym for a tenant at sufferance.

82. **A** Since a tenant at sufferance has no permission, the owner need give no legal notice to terminate the tenancy.

83. **A** There are four types of less than freehold estates: tenancy for years (a fixed term), periodic tenancy (of indefinite duration, until one party gives notice to the other), tenancy at will (permission of the owner but without a period or a fixed term, and tenancy at sufferance. Of these, the tenancy at sufferance is the only one without the owner's permission.

84. **D** An estate for years is a right of possession for a fixed term, i.e., a lease. A periodic estate is a right of possession that self-renews from period to period until one party gives notice to the other. An estate at will is permission to occupy the property, but without a fixed term or a specified period. An estate (tenancy) at sufferance is possession without permission, as a holdover tenant.

85. **A** "Rent" is the term used for the consideration paid by the tenant, regardless of the type of tenancy involved.

86. **D** All tenancies require notice to terminate if the tenancy involved the permission of the owner. However, notice was given to a tenant for years (i.e., a tenant under a lease) at the moment of entering into the tenancy, since the estate for years has a definite expiration date. Therefore, as a technicality, notice is not required to terminate a tenancy for years. A tenant at sufferance does not have the permission of the owner, so no notice is required.

87. **C** An encumbrance is not normally an estate, since an estate must be a possessory interest. An easement is a right of use, not a right of possession, so it is not an estate. A tenancy for years is an estate for a fixed term, not an indefinite period. Freeholds are always estates for an indefinite (although not necessarily perpetual) time.

88. **B** A tenancy for years is a lease, and therefore has a fixed ending date. A tenancy at will, is merely permission to occupy without stating a period or fixed term. A tenancy at will continues until the owner gives the tenant notice.

89. **A** When all the possessory rights are transferred to the new party, it is an assignment. If the lessee gives a portion of the rights, such as a portion of the space or a portion of the remaining term, then it is a sublease.

90. **C** An assignment places a new party (the assignee) in the shoes of one of the original parties to a contract (the assignor). In the case of a lease, this means that the new tenant takes the place of the original tenant. The new tenant has the same contractual rights, because the lease is still the original lease. A sublease, however is a new lease, where the original lessee remains a lessee of the owner, and becomes the lessor to the new tenant. In a sublease there will be two leases on the same premises. An assignment transfers all the rights to the new tenant, so if the new tenant is to have only a portion of the premises, or only a portion of the remaining term, or is to pay more or less rent, then the sublease is the appropriate instrument.

91. **D** The term "tenant" refers to the party in possession of the real estate. The original lessee was a tenant, so by granting a right of possession to a third party, the third party gains right of possession, and thereby becomes a tenant.

92. **C** Normally, when a tenant subleases or assigns to a third party, the original tenant is not relieved of the responsibility to pay. Nevertheless, assuming the lessor agreed to the assignment or sublease, the lessor will expect payment to come first from the third party and will only look to the original tenant for payment in the event the new tenant fails to pay.

93. **D** When the transfer is a sublease rather than an assignment, the new tenant is responsible only to the original tenant, since the original tenant has become the landlord (lessor) to the new tenant. The original lease is canceled only if there is a surrender and acceptance, but there cannot be a surrender and acceptance because cancellation of the old lease would extinguish the original tenant's right of possession. If the original tenant's right of possession is extinguished, then the original tenant cannot sublease to the new tenant, since there would be no interest to grant.

94. **D** An assignment is a transfer of all rights in a contract to a new party. A sublease is a new lease instrument that grants only a portion of the leasehold interest to the new tenant. The original tenant is not relieved of liability to the landlord in either case.

95. **D** Normally, a lease and option (lease option) is written as one contract where the option is dependent upon the tenant not being in default of the lease. Assuming this to be the case, then an assignment of the lease contract is also an assignment of the option, since the option is part of the same contract.

96. **C** Normally a lease is a grant of a possessory interest by the lessor and a promise to pay by the lessee. The right of possession could be extinguished by various factors, including eviction. The promise to pay is independent of the right of possession, so if the tenant moves out, the tenant is still responsible for the rent until the end of the tenancy.

97. **B** The lessor is entitled to be made whole, but no more. In this case the lessor must forego rent from the new tenant during the period of time the new tenant did not have possession, so the lessee must pay the lessor for that period of time. There may be a possibility of additional actual damages as a consequence of the tenant's failure to leave – i.e., damages to compensate for the lessor's liability to the new tenant.

98. **C** The lessor is entitled to be made whole, but no more. In Oregon, a lessor must make a good faith attempt to mitigate the loss in the event a tenant abandons the premises. Anything the lessor can get from a new tenant must be used to offset the liability of the old tenant.

99. **C** To file a suit for eviction (F.E.D. or forcible entry and detainer) is called an actual eviction. When a landlord forces a tenant out some other way, it is called constructive eviction. Even a mere failure to maintain the premises to the point where they become uninhabitable, constitutes constructive eviction, if the landlord was the party responsible for maintenance. Constructive eviction makes a landlord legally liable to a tenant for damages if the tenancy is residential. However, there are no restrictions on constructive eviction for commercial property.

100. **D** The distinction between a tenant at sufferance and a trespasser is twofold. First, a tenant at sufferance is a party who entered the premises originally under some legal right of possession, but has remained in possession after the legal right ended. Second, a tenancy at sufferance and a trespass are both civil wrongs – that is, a landlord can summarily evict either one. A trespass, however, is also a criminal act. As for physically removing the tenant, the law might allow this if it were other than a residential lease and there were extenuating circumstances. Normally, however, the landlord must bring an eviction proceeding and, if the tenant still refuses to leave, ask the court to order the sheriff to move the tenant out.

101. **B** Actual eviction is when the landlord files suit (forcible entry and detainer) to regain possession. If the landlord forces the tenant out by action, or failure to act when required, this is called construc-

tive eviction. Surrender is when the tenant leaves the property and the landlord agrees to take it back, thus terminating the tenant's remaining obligations under the lease.

102. **A** Since a forcible entry and (wrongful) detainer action (F.E.D.) is an eviction proceeding, it would be the lessor would be the plaintiff and the tenant would be the defendant.

103. **C** If the tenant's lease has expired and the tenant does not agree to a new lease, then the tenant is a tenant at sufferance. A landlord can evict a tenant at sufferance without notice. A suit for breach of the lease cannot be successful because there is no new lease. Specific performance is a remedy with a plaintiff asks the court to order the other party to perform a contract as originally agreed.

104. **D** If the lease was to the couple and their children, then others are not permitted to occupy the premises. When the couple allowed the wife's parents to move in they breached the lease. This breach allows the landlord the right to evict the tenants. The parents have no legal right to be there, so they are tenants at sufferance. The landlord can evict tenants at sufferance without notice.

105. **C** "Forcible entry and detainer" (F.E.D.) is the older term for a suit to evict. Filing an F.E.D. is an actual eviction. Forcing the tenant out by diminishing services or locking the tenant out is constructive eviction. Failing to maintain the premises under a tenancy where the landlord has a duty to maintain can become constructive eviction if the failure to maintain renders the premises unusable.

106. **B** The death of either party has no effect on a normal lease. The heirs of the lessee may retain possession, provided they continue to perform the lease. Similarly, the heirs of the lessor will automatically take title to the property subject to the lease.

107. **C** A sale of the building has no more effect than its conveyance through a will. The lease is an encumbrance which a new owner must take the title subject to.

108. **C** When the government exercises the right of eminent domain (condemnation), normally the government takes the entire property in fee title. Therefore the rights of the lessee would also be taken. Eviction (forcible entry and detainer) also extinguishes the leasehold estate.

109. **B** The result is the same as cancellation or rescission, but it is normally called a surrender and acceptance. The lessee surrenders possession to the lessor, who accepts it. Acceptance of a surrender is deemed to extinguish not only the lease, but also the tenant's obligation to pay.

110. **C** Mutual cancellation or rescission are always options in any contract. Breach of a contract by one party excuses the other from the requirement to perform it further.

111. **A** When there is an underlying mortgage, then the mortgage normally already existed as an encumbrance on the title at the time the lessee accepted the lease. Therefore, the tenant took the lease subject to the rights of the lender. If the lender should foreclose, the foreclosure will extinguish the lease. However, until the lease is actually extinguished by a foreclosure, the tenant's lease is intact and the obligation to pay continues. A covenant of quiet enjoyment is the lessor's promise that nothing will interfere with the title so as to abridge the tenant's right of possession. Allowing the lender to foreclose would be a breach of the covenant of quiet enjoyment. A tenancy for years and a periodic tenancy are not terminated by the death of either party.

112. **D** Death of a party to a contract does not terminate ordinary contracts, including leases. The estate of the deceased party must continue to perform the lease. A sale of the property also does not terminate a lease because the lease is an encumbrance on the owner's title. The buyer must take title subject to the lease.

113. **D** Unless there is a specific provision in a lease allowing termination upon a sale, the buyer must always take title subject to the lease.

114. **A** A devisee is the person who receives real property in a will. Death terminates only contracts for services.

115. **A** A lease is an encumbrance on the title. Encumbrances are defined as matters which burden the title and survive a sale. Therefore the buyer must take title subject to the lease.

116. **D** A lease is considered an encumbrance on the owner's title, so the buyer takes title subject to it. Death of either party to a contract does not terminate the contract, unless it is a contract for services. If the tenant abandons the premises the lease is not terminated unless the landlord takes it as a surrender.

117. **A** A lease is an encumbrance on the owner's title, so if the property is sold the buyer takes title subject to the lease.

118. **C** The fact that the lease was not in writing is irrelevant in this case. A lease for less than a year

need not be in writing to be enforceable. There may be an issue of notice, however, assuming the tenant was in possession of the premises, then the buyer took the title subject to the lease.

119. **B** When we refer to the holder of a lease, we mean the party who has the right of possession. In this case, the (original) lessee is holding the lease in the middle, which is the sandwich lease.

OREGON RESIDENTIAL LANDLORD-TENANT ACT

FOR AS LONG AS THERE HAVE BEEN LANDLORDS AND TENANTS THEIR RELATIONSHIPS have been the subject of legal disputes. Until recently, the legal relationship between a landlord and tenant has been in many ways out of step with the realities of modern life. In the late 1960s the federal government funded a project sponsored by the American Bar Association to create a Model Residential Landlord-Tenant Code, which was finally published in 1969. Subsequently, the National Conference of Commissioners on Uniform State Laws drafted the Uniform Residential Landlord and Tenant Act (URLTA) in 1972. This was adopted by the American Bar Association at its mid-year convention in August, 1972 with a recommendation that it be enacted in all states. In 1973 the Oregon Legislature became one of the first states to enact legislation based on the URLTA when it passed the original Oregon Residential Landlord and Tenant Act.

Today many states have adopted residential landlord-tenant laws based on the URLTA, but the laws in each state vary slightly from the original, including the Oregon Residential Landlord-Tenant Act. Still, the common elements of state residential landlord-tenant laws today makes it easier for tenants moving from one state to the next to understand the law.

In 1974 the American Bar Association adopted amendments to the original URLTA, most of which were incorporated as amendments to the Oregon Residential Landlord-Tenant Act. Since its passage in 1973, the Oregon Residential Landlord-Tenant Act has seen many other amendments, as well as court interpretations.

As could be inferred from its name, the Oregon Residential Landlord and Tenant Act applies only to residential property. Even so, the act excludes certain rental arrangements, such as –

Notes

- Institutional residential facilities, such as schools and colleges, medical care facilities, religious institutions, and the like
- Rental of a property by a purchaser prior to the closing of a sale, such as when the buyer moves in before closing, or by a seller after a sale, provided in both cases the term does not exceed 90 days
- Occupancy of premises operated by a fraternal or social organization, by a member of the organization
- Rental of premises in a hotel or motel on a transient basis, but not if the rental is periodic such as weekly or monthly
- Premises occupied by a resident manager of a landlord or owner, because the arrangement is for employment more than a rental arrangement
- Occupancy by an owner of a condominium or cooperative built on leased land
- Occupancy by a squatter, defined as one in possession illegally but not as a hold-over tenant
- Vacation occupancy
- Agricultural property, when it is rented as a business, but rental of a farmhouse separately is within the scope of the Act

It should be noted that the Act includes extensive provisions governing tenancies in mobile home parks and tenancies in floating homes. These provisions are included in the last portion of the Act (ORS 90.505 to 90.875), which apply only to rental of a space for a mobile or floating home. The first portion of the Act (ORS 90.100 to 90.475) applies to all residential tenancies, including mobile home and floating home space rentals. The first section also applies to mobile and floating homes where the landlord owns the mobile or floating home (in which case the last section does *not* apply). Except where specifically mentioned, in this section we will refer only to the first part of the Oregon Residential Landlord and Tenant Act.

Rental agreements

The Oregon Residential Landlord and Tenant Act does not stipulate the content of rental agreements, except that certain provisions are prohibited. These include –

- Waiver of the tenant's rights under the Residential Landlord and Tenant Act
- Agreement that the landlord has a judgment against the tenant without having to file suit
- Waiver of landlord's liability (called an ***exculpation clause***)

A landlord who includes any of these provisions and attempts to enforce it on the tenant may be liable to the tenant for actual damages and up to three months rent as punitive damages, as well as attorney's fees.

Although the landlord need not do so in the rental agreement itself, the landlord must disclose certain items in writing to the tenant. These include the name and address of the person authorized to manage the premises, and the name and address of an owner, or agent of the owner on whom the tenant can serve legal notices and demands. In addition, for properties containing one to four units, the landlord must disclose to the tenant at the beginning of the rental agreement if the property is subject to foreclosure, including a property tax foreclosure.

The landlord must also disclose to the tenant if a portion of any of the tenant's utility bills will be used to benefit the landlord or others in the complex. For example, if outside lighting which illuminates the whole parking lot is wired into one of the units, then the tenant in that unit is being charged for utility services which benefit other tenants, and that fact must be disclosed to the tenant in writing at the start of the tenancy.

Unless the rental agreement stipulates otherwise, certain matters are presumed. These include –

NOTES

- Rent is payable at the premises and on the first day of the period
- The tenancy is presumed to be month-to-month unless the parties have specifically created a tenancy for a fixed term or for week to week
- If the amount of the rent is not stipulated, the tenant is obligated to pay fair market rent

Of course, the above are merely presumptions. If the parties wish, they can stipulate other arrangements. However, the only periodic rentals that are permitted are week to week and month to month. Quarterly, semi-annual, year-to-year or other periodic tenancies are not permitted.

A landlord is required to give a tenant a copy of a written rental agreement. In addition, the landlord must keep a copy of the rental agreement on the premises, if there is a resident manager. If there is no resident manager, then a copy must be kept at the address of the person who is designated in the rental agreement as the manager. The landlord must permit the tenant to inspect the rental agreement during reasonable hours. The tenant is entitled to a copy of the rental agreement upon request, although the landlord may charge the tenant for the expense of copying.

Deposits and fees

Prior to the Oregon Residential Landlord and Tenant Act, tenants were frequently frustrated in their attempts to recover deposits, even though they left the premises in good condition. To remedy this situation, the Act stipulates that a ***security deposit*** is refundable – that is, it is subject to being refunded. This does not mean that a landlord cannot retain a security deposit if the tenant breaches the agreement. But it does mean that the tenant is entitled to receive a refund of the deposit or an accounting of why the landlord is not refunding the deposit, or a partial refund and partial accounting. The landlord must give the refund or accounting to the tenant within 31 days after the end of the tenancy or the landlord is liable to the tenant for twice the amount of the deposit as damages.

Security deposits can be used only to repair damages to the premises made by the tenant or failure to pay rent. The statute specifically prohibits forfeiture of the deposit when its purpose was to ensure that a tenant would rent the premises for a specified term.

If a property rented to a tenant is sold, and the previous owner was holding a tenant's security deposit, the new owner automatically becomes liable to the tenant for refund of the deposit. For this reason, it is customary for a buyer to ask the seller to turn all deposits over to the buyer at closing.

The statute also address a ***last month's rent deposit***. A last month's rent deposit is also defined as refundable, and is subject to the same rules as for security deposits. If the landlord takes a last month's rent deposit it can be used only to pay the last month's rent. It cannot be used for damages or other breaches by the tenant. A last month's rent deposit is subject to the same rules as any other deposit.

Only a deposit or last month's rent deposit are refundable. If the landlord wishes to retain the funds, they can be labeled a non-refundable fee or charge. The statute allows fees to be charged only once, although exceptions are made for recurring items, such as late rent fees, dishonored check fees, and so on.

The statute allows a "nonrefundable" deposit "for the purpose of securing the execution of a rental agreement" (ORS 90.297). A deposit to secure the execution of a rental agreement means a deposit to hold the premises for a tenant while the tenant makes up his or her mind whether or not to rent it. If the tenant does rent the premises, the land-

NOTES

lord is required to credit the tenant with the full amount of the deposit. If the tenant does not rent the premises, then the landlord may retain the deposit.

In the past it was common for landlords to increase their profits by charging a credit report fee in excess of their actual costs. The statute defines this as an ***applicant screening charge***, and the landlord is prohibited from charging more than the average cost of obtaining information on the applicant, including the landlord's labor costs. Because the amount could be disputed by tenants, most landlords use an outside service which simply bills the landlord at a flat rate. Even if the landlord does the screening, the amount cannot exceed what is customary in the area. The landlord must give a receipt for the amount to the applicant.

The landlord is prohibited from requiring an applicant screening charge unless the landlord adopts written screening criteria, discloses to the applicant the amount of the charge, and the process by which the landlord will conduct the screening (i.e., what the landlord will check), and tells the applicant of his or her right to contest any incorrect information. The landlord must also give the applicant an estimate of the approximate number of rental units of the type sought by the applicant that are, or within a reasonable future time will be, available to rent from that landlord. The estimate must include the approximate number of applications previously accepted and remaining under consideration for those units. The landlord is prohibited from accepting an applicant screening charge if the landlord has no vacancies available or will not in the foreseeable future.

The landlord must also comply with the provisions of the federal Fair Credit Reporting Act.

To make Oregon landlord-tenant law parallel to federal consumer credit reporting laws, the landlord must advise the prospective tenant what the screening entails and of their right to dispute any information contained in it. If the applicant is turned down, the landlord must disclose the name and address of the agency which supplied the screening information.

Exercise 4a

The Oregon Residential Landlord and Tenant Act would apply to which of the following?

- ❑ *Residency in an elder care facility*
- ❑ *A week-to-week rental of a single room in a hotel*
- ❑ *An apartment occupied by a resident manager*
- ❑ *A leasehold condominium rented to a tenant on a month-to-month basis*
- ❑ *Seller renting the house back from the buyer for 120 days after closing the sale*
- ❑ *Rental of a small single-tenant retail building*

A landlord must disclose to a tenant in writing if a portion of the tenant's ____________ bills will benefit others in the complex. For one to four unit buildings, disclosure must also be made if the property is the subject of ____________ action. A rental agreement must contain the name and address of the ____________ or other person on whom the tenant can service notices and demands. The tenant is entitled to a ____________ of the rental agreement at the time of entering into it.

If the landlord collects advance funds from the tenant and labels the funds a ___deposit___ *then the funds are subject to being* ___refunded___ *. If a charge is nonrefundable, it should be called a* ___fee___ *. If a landlord takes a deposit for last month's rent, it is* ___refundable___ *. Refundable items must be returned to the tenant, or an* ___accounting___ *within* ___31___ *days after the termination of the tenancy.*

Habitability standards

Prior to the Residential Landlord and Tenant Act, there were occasions when tenants were unable to make their landlords provide safe, clean and decent housing. While the majority of landlords were reasonably conscientious about the condition of their property, the Act now provides mandatory minimum standards. These include –

- Water- and weatherproofing of all exterior surfaces, including windows and doors
- Plumbing facilities, including a water supply capable of producing hot and cold water, furnished to appropriate fixtures and connected to an adequate sewage disposal system
- Adequate heating facilities
- Electrical wiring and lighting maintained in good working order
- Premises which are clean, sanitary and free of debris, filth, rubbish, garbage, rodents and vermin at the start of the tenancy
- Appropriate garbage receptacles, maintained in good condition, including garbage removal, and separate containers for recyclables in communities with a recycling program
- Floors, walls, ceilings, stairways and railings maintained in good repair
- Ventilating, air conditioning, elevators and other appliances maintained in good repair if supplied or required to be supplied by the landlord
- Safety from fire hazards, including a working smoke detector at the start of the tenancy
- Working locks and keys for all doors and latches for windows, except where local law prohibits latches on windows

Most of the above standards include the provision that the premises and fixtures were in compliance with applicable building codes at the time they were installed. However, the Residential Landlord and Tenant Act does not specifically state that the landlord's failure to comply with a building or housing code is an automatic violation of the habitability standards.

If the premises do not meet the habitability standards, the landlord and the tenant may enter into an agreement that the tenant is to make repairs. To do so the agreement must be in writing, and the landlord cannot use the agreement to evade responsibility or to lessen the landlord's duties to other tenants. The tenant must receive adequate consideration for the work.

Tenant obligations

A frequent complaint of landlords is that tenants abuse the premises. To remedy this problem, the Residential Landlord and Tenant Act creates specific obligations of the tenant. The tenant must –

- Use the premises in a reasonable manner, as a dwelling unit only, and considering the use for which they were intended
- Keep the premises as clean and sanitary and free of debris, filth, rubbish and garbage as their condition permits

NOTES

- Dispose of all waste from the premises in a clean and safe manner, including complying with state law regarding the disposal of needles and other infectious waste
- Keep all plumbing fixtures as clean as their condition permits
- Use the facilities in a reasonable manner, including electrical, plumbing, sanitary, heating, ventilating, air conditioning equipment and other facilities and appliances, including elevators
- Not remove or tamper with a properly working smoke detector, including removal of batteries, and test and replace batteries as needed at least once every six months
- Not deliberately or negligently destroy, damage or remove any part of the premises, or allow anyone else to do so
- Behave and require other persons on the premises with the consent of the tenant to behave in a manner that will not disturb the peaceful enjoyment of the premises by neighbors.

Rules

Many times a landlord will find it necessary to adopt occupancy rules. Such rules become enforceable immediately unless they constitute a substantial modification of the tenant's rental agreement, in which case the rules take effect only if the tenant agrees in writing. A rule must –

- Promote the safety, convenience or welfare of the tenants, preserve the landlord's property, or make a fair distribution of services and facilities
- Be reasonably related to the purpose for which it is adopted
- Be applied equally and fairly to all tenants
- Be clear and explicit
- Not be used in order to evade the landlord's responsibilities

Rules can go into effect upon giving notice of them to the tenants. However, if the rule is adopted after the tenancy has begun, and the rule would work a substantial modification of the tenant's rights, the rule does not go into effect as to that tenant until the tenant consents to it in writing.

Alternate energy devices

When a tenant desires to install an alternate energy device, the tenant must first secure the landlord's written permission. The statute does not specifically provide that the landlord is under any obligation to grant such permission. The Act does specify that the landlord may require the tenant to secure waivers of liability and waivers of the right to a construction lien from installers. The landlord may also require that the tenant post a bond to ensure that the tenant will restore the premises at the end of the tenancy.

If the landlord does grant the tenant permission to install an alternate energy device, the device remains the property of the tenant, unless the parties specifically agree otherwise in writing.

Access

A landlord is entitled to enter the premises to inspect, make repairs or alterations, supply services, or show the premises to prospective purchasers, lenders, tenants or contractors. Normally, the landlord must give the tenant 24 hours notice prior to entering the premises. However, there are exceptions, including –

- Emergencies
- Under order of a court
- Access to the exterior for purpose of giving notices to the tenant

NOTES

- If the landlord has reason to believe the premises have been abandoned
- To allow workers and others to make repairs requested by the tenant during reasonable hours
- To show the unit to potential buyers, provided there is an agreement where the tenant receives consideration for the permission

If the landlord enters the premises because of an emergency the landlord must notify the tenant within 24 hours after the entry. The notice must include the date and time of the entry, names of the parties who entered, and the nature of the emergency.

The landlord cannot abuse the right of access or harass the tenant. If the landlord fails to give proper notice, or harasses the tenant, the tenant may obtain an injunction to prevent a further occurrence and may obtain a judgment against the landlord for damages in the amount of one month rent. If the tenant refuses to grant access, the landlord can file suit to compel the tenant to allow access and obtain judgment for the expenses incurred.

Even when the landlord gives notice, the tenant has the right to deny access, which the landlord must honor at the time. The landlord may then proceed with a suit to compel the tenant to grant access, or simply give the tenant notice to terminate the tenancy.

Attorney's fees

In most cases, the prevailing parties to a suit are only entitled to recover attorney's fees from the other party if there is a written agreement calling for attorney's fees. The Oregon Residential Landlord and Tenant Act, however, provides by statute that either party may recover attorney's fees from the other, whether there is a written agreement or not.

Abandonment

If desired, the Oregon Residential Landlord and Tenant Act permits a rental agreement to require a tenant to notify the landlord of an absence in excess of seven days. If the rental agreement contains such a provision, then the landlord may enter the premises without notice after the tenant has been absent for seven days.

If the tenant has abandoned the premises, then the landlord must make a reasonable effort to re-rent the premises for a fair rental value. If the previous tenant (who abandoned the premises) had paid rent in advance, upon re-renting the premises the landlord must refund rent for any overlapping period. The concept is that the landlord may not collect rent for the same space for the same period of time from two different tenants.

Tenant's personal property

The Landlord and Tenant Act contains extensive provisions which balance the landlord's right to recover possession and dispose of abandoned property as quickly as possible, with the tenant's right to be sure that property which is not really abandoned is not lost without proper notice.

Oregon Revised Statutes 90.425 provides three circumstances under which a landlord may remove and/or dispose of a tenant's personal property. The first occurs when a tenancy terminates by expiration, surrender or abandonment and the landlord "reasonably believes" that the tenant has no intention of asserting a claim to the property. The second occurs when the landlord has been awarded restitution of the premises in an eviction proceeding and, without formal eviction by the sheriff, the tenant has been absent for seven days. The third possibility is for the landlord to take possession of property after the sheriff has formally evicted a tenant.

In any of the above cases, the landlord may remove the property from the premises to safe storage. The storage may be the landlord's own premises, or may be a

NOTES

commercial storage facility. In all cases, the landlord must give written notice to the tenant before the landlord can dispose of the property. The notice must be personally delivered or sent by first class mail (not certified or registered mail), with possibly multiple copies – one to the premises, and one to the tenant's last known address or post office box. The notice must state that the landlord considers the property abandoned and give the tenant five days to respond (eight days if mailed, or 45 days if the personal property is a manufactured or floating home). The notice must advise the tenant that if the tenant does not respond the landlord will dispose of the property.

If the tenant responds, the landlord must give the tenant 15 days (30 days for recreational vehicles) to remove the property following receipt of the tenant's response. If the tenant appears and wishes to reclaim the property, the landlord is entitled to recover reasonable expenses for removal and storage before returning the property to the tenant.

Assuming the tenant does not claim the property and the property is worth selling, the landlord must proceed with a public sale of the property. If the property is of so little value that the amount which could be received by selling it is probably less than the cost of the sale and the costs already incurred, then the landlord may dispose of the property. The statute provides that "dispose of the property" means that the landlord may destroy the property or give it to anyone not related to the landlord, or to a charitable organization, but the landlord may not keep the property.

If the landlord proceeds with a sale, the landlord may retain from the proceeds only specified amounts. These include the costs of the removal, storage and notice and any unpaid rent. The landlord must tender the surplus to the tenant. If the landlord cannot locate the tenant, then the landlord must send the surplus to the county treasurer.

If a landlord seizes and retains a tenant's personal property in violation of the law, the tenant may recover damages from the landlord up to twice the amount of the tenant's actual damages. In addition, the landlord loses the right to collect for damages to the premises not caused by gross negligence and the tenant is relieved of the responsibility to pay any unpaid rent.

The statutes also prohibit a landlord from creating or enforcing a lien on the tenant's personal property. As to rentals covered by the Act, ***distraint for rent*** is abolished. Distraint for rent is the landlord's right to seize the tenant's personal property to satisfy the tenant's unpaid obligations to the landlord.

Retaliatory conduct

The Oregon Residential Landlord and Tenant Act allows the tenant to exercise any of an extensive list of rights without fear of retaliation by the landlord and it is illegal for the landlord to take action against the tenant for exercising any of these rights. These rights include –

- Filing or threatening to file a complaint with any governmental agency of violation(s) of building, housing or health codes, discrimination laws or regarding the delivery of mail
- Complaining to the landlord of the landlord's failure to make required disclosures in a rental agreement, landlord's violation of habitability standards, landlord's abuse of access, landlord's constructive eviction, or landlord's breach of the rental agreement
- Defending a suit for eviction (if successful and within the preceding six months)
- Forming a tenants' union
- Complaining that the landlord has failed to give at least 30 days notice of rent increases
- Testifying against the landlord

It is considered ***retaliatory conduct*** if the landlord, in response to any of the foregoing, increases the rent, decreases services, serves notice to terminate the tenancy, or evicts or threatens to evict a tenant. For retaliatory conduct, the tenant may recover up to two months rent as damages or twice the actual damages suffered by the tenant, whichever is greater. Retaliatory conduct is also a valid counterclaim against a landlord's suit for eviction.

Nevertheless, a tenant loses all right to claim retaliatory conduct if the tenant is in default in paying the rent, or if the tenant caused the problem of which the tenant is complaining. Also, the landlord does not engage in retaliatory conduct by evicting a tenant when the property is in such condition that repairs to bring it into compliance with the code would be so extensive as to deprive the tenant of the use of the premises.

Exercise 4b

The Residential Landlord and Tenant Act requires the landlord to maintain the premises in at least habitable *condition. This requires that the landlord supply and maintain which of the following items?*

- ☐ *Storm doors and windows*
- ☑ *An air conditioner which the landlord has supplied*
- ☑ *A water heater*
- ☐ *A heating outlet or fixture in each separate room in the structure*

If a landlord adopts rules which promote the safety of the tenants and which are applied fairly and equally to all tenants, the rules go into effect immediately / upon notice.

Many times the landlord desires access to the premises. Give the amount of notice the landlord must give the tenant before entering the premises in each of the following cases:

0 *The landlord has a written agreement to lower the rent by $10 per month in order to show the premises to prospective buyers*

0 *The landlord wishes to cross the grounds and post a notice for the tenant on the front door.*

0 *The landlord notified the tenant 30 days earlier that workers would be entering without notice in order to make repairs to the plumbing equipment*

0 *There is water pouring out of the bathroom window*

A rental agreement may require a tenant to notify the landlord of any expected absence by the tenant in excess of 7 *days. If it does, and the tenant is absent for this time, the landlord may presume that the premises have been* abandoned.

If there is abandoned personal property, the landlord must give the tenant 5 *days notice to claim it, or* 8 *days notice if mailed. If the tenant claims it, the landlord may recover the costs of [Choose the one(s) which are correct]* ☑ *Removal* ☑ *Storage* ☑ *Mailing the Notice* ☑ *Unpaid Rent. If the landlord sells personal property belonging to a tenant, the proceeds of the sale must be turned over to the* tenant*, but if the* *tenant cannot be located, then the landlord must turn the funds over to the county. In a residential tenancy, distraint for rent is not permitted.*

Which of the following would be considered retaliatory conduct?

- [ ] *Raising the rent to pay for bringing the property up to habitability standards*
- [x] *Evicting a tenant who forms a tenants' union and organizes a rent strike*
- [x] *Taking away a parking right because the tenant asked the city to inspect the property*

Tenant's remedies

If the landlord fails to live up to the requirements of the rental agreement or the Residential Landlord and Tenant Act the tenant has various remedies. The statute creates different remedies if the landlord's breach is a failure to supply ***essential services*** as opposed to other less serious matters. Essential services are defined as including (but not limited to) heat, water and electricity.

For failure to supply essential services, the tenant may give notice to the landlord of the breach and the tenant's intent to terminate the rental agreement in 30 days if the landlord does not remedy the breach within seven days. If the landlord remedies the breach within the seven days, the tenancy is not terminated. If lack of the essential service poses an imminent or serious threat to the health or safety of the tenant, the tenant may terminate the rental agreement in 48 hours unless the landlord remedies the breach within that time.

For essential services, if the tenant gives written notice to the landlord and the landlord refuses or neglects to supply the essential services, then the tenant may immediately procure the required essential services and deduct the cost from the rent. Or the tenant may recover damages from the landlord in the amount of the diminished rental value of the premises. Or, as yet another alternative, the tenant may secure substitute housing at the landlord's expense and need not pay rent to the landlord during the time of the landlord's non-compliance. In other words, during the time when the landlord neglects or refuses to supply essential services, the tenant may obtain free rent in comparable substitute housing.

The tenant may also have cooking appliances and refrigerators repaired if supplied by the landlord, after giving reasonable written notice to the landlord. The tenant may deduct the cost of the repair (up to $500) from the rent.

If the landlord's breach is other than a failure to supply essential services, then the procedure is the same, but the landlord has 30 days to remedy the breach. However, if the landlord breaches the agreement in substantially the same way within six months, then the tenant only need give 14 days notice.

Regardless of whether the landlord breaches the rental agreement or fails to provide habitable premises, the tenant may obtain an injunction against the landlord's continued violation. Or the tenant may choose to sue the landlord for damages caused by the landlord's noncompliance.

NOTES

Tenant counterclaims

If the landlord attempts to evict the tenant for nonpayment of rent, or sues the tenant for unpaid rent, the tenant may counterclaim for any damages the tenant feels is owed by the landlord. If the tenant's counterclaim is successful, the court must offset the claims of the landlord by the amount of the tenant's counterclaim. To prevail in a counterclaim, the tenant need not prove that the landlord had actual notice, or should have been aware of the facts on which the tenant's counterclaim is based.

For example, suppose the landlord files an eviction (forcible entry and detainer, see below), claiming that a month's rent in the amount of $1,000 is past due. However, the tenant counterclaims that the property did not meet habitability standards and the landlord failed to maintain the premises, causing the rental value to be diminished by $300 per month for the past four months – so the tenant's total counterclaim is for $1,200. If the court agrees that the tenant's counterclaim is just, then the landlord actually owes the difference ($200) to the tenant, and the landlord's suit to evict will be dismissed.

However, where a landlord has sued to evict a tenant and the tenant's counterclaims are less than the amount of rent owing, the tenant must pay the remainder of the rent to the court to retain possession.

Landlord's remedies

When a landlord files a suit to evict a tenant, this is called an ***actual eviction***. The legal expression is an action for ***forcible entry and (wrongful) detainer***, usually abbreviated "F.E.D.." When a landlord attempts to force a tenant out by refusing or deliberately neglecting to supply essential services, this is called a ***constructive eviction***.

While constructive eviction is not barred in other types of tenancies, the Oregon Residential Landlord and Tenant Act does not permit its use for residential tenancies. A landlord who attempts constructive eviction is subject to damages for the tenant's actual loss or twice the amount of the monthly rent, whichever is greater.

Notices

When a landlord gives a tenant proper notice and the tenant remains unlawfully in possession, the landlord may file an eviction proceeding. Similarly, the tenant can move out and terminate the tenancy upon proper notice to the landlord. If the tenancy is month to month, either party may give the other 31 days notice at any time without needing a reason. Similarly, ten days notice is required if the tenancy is week to week. If the tenancy is for years (lease), then neither party can give the other notice unless the other party has breached the lease.

For month-to-month tenancies, the landlord can give the tenant 30 days notice if the tenant has significantly breached the rental agreement or has failed to comply with the requirements of the Residential Landlord and Tenant Act relating to health and safety. If the tenant remedies the breach within 14 days, the tenancy is reinstated. But if the same breach occurs within six months, the landlord need give the tenant only ten days notice, and the tenant has no right to reinstate the tenancy by remedying the breach. Note that a landlord would ordinarily only use this provision of the statute if the tenancy is a lease, since the landlord can give notice without needing a reason if the tenancy is periodic.

If the tenancy is week to week, the 30-day notice above is reduced to seven days and the tenant must remedy the breach within four days to avoid termination of the tenancy. If the same breach occurs within six months, the landlord can give a four-day notice and the tenant cannot reinstate the tenancy by remedying the breach.

NOTES

For an unpermitted pet, the landlord may give the tenant ten days notice. The tenant may reinstate the tenancy by removing the pet within the ten days. A pet is defined as a dog, cat, or other pet "capable of causing damage to persons or property." If the tenant has an unpermitted pet again within six months, the landlord can give the tenant ten days notice and the tenant cannot terminate the notice by removing the pet.

If the tenant fails to pay the rent when due, the landlord can give the tenant 72 hours notice after a seven-day grace period. If the tenancy is month-to-month, the landlord has the option to give the tenant 144 hours notice after a four-day grace period. If the tenant pays the rent in full within the 72 hours (or 144 hours), the tenancy is reinstated. However, the landlord is not obligated to accept partial rent.

In most cases, when a statute gives a time period or deadline, the due date or beginning date does not count. For example, if your mortgage payment is due on the first, but you have a 15-day grace period, then you may make the payment without penalty through the sixteenth of the month. However, for purposes of the 72-hour or 144-hour notices, the statute provides the notice begins at 11:59 PM the day the notice is given and runs 72 or 144 hours thereafter. For example, suppose the rent is due on the first and the tenant fails to pay it. The landlord can give a 72-hour notice any time on the eighth day. The notice starts to run at one minute before midnight of the 8th of the month. The tenant can avoid terminating the tenancy by paying the rent in full at any time until one minute before midnight of the 11th of the month. The 72 or 144 hours runs without regard to Saturdays, Sundays or holidays.

Late charges may not be imposed before the fourth day after the due date. A late charge may not exceed the greater of

(A) A reasonable flat amount which is customary in the market

(B) Five percent of the periodic rent, or

(C) A daily charge, starting on the fifth day, not exceeding one thirtieth of either (A) or (B) above.

Most professional landlords charge the five percent, since the alternatives invite argument. Failing to pay a late charge is not the same as failing to pay rent. In other words, if the landlord has given the tenant 72 or 144 hours notice, the landlord must accept the rent as sufficient to terminate the notice. If there is also a late charge due and unpaid, the landlord can give the tenant a subsequent 30 day notice for breach of the rental agreement.

The landlord may give 24 hours notice if –

- The tenant, someone in the tenant's control, or the tenant's pet inflicts, or threatens to inflict personal injury on the landlord, on other tenants, on any other person on the premises with the permission of the owner, or on any neighbor living in the vicinity.
- The tenant, or someone in the tenant's control intentionally inflicts substantial damage to the premises
- The tenant has vacated the premises, the rental agreement or lease does not permit subleasing or assignment, yet someone other than the tenant remains in possession
- The tenant or someone in the tenant's control commits an act which is outrageous in the extreme. An act which is "outrageous in the extreme" is defined as "more extreme or serious than an act that warrants a 30-day termination ... [for cause]." Oregon Revised Statutes 90.400 provides that acts which are outrageous in the extreme include, but are not necessarily limited to, drug activity, prostitution, intimidation, or burglary.

NOTES

Service of notices

In general, notices from either party to the other may be served personally or by first class mail addressed to the other's last known address. There are, however, different types of service which are required under certain circumstances. Certified mail is not only not required, but specifically does not constitute proper notice unless simultaneously accompanied by the mailing of another copy of the notice by regular first class mail. When notice is served by mail, three additional days must be allowed unless the notice is also posted on the premises.

Waiver

As a rule, a landlord is deemed to have waived the right to terminate a tenancy because of a breach by the tenant if the landlord accepts rent from the tenant while knowing of the tenant's breach. The landlord also waives the right to enforce any other provision of the rental agreement if the landlord accepts performance by the tenant which varies from the provisions of the agreement.

However, the landlord and tenant may agree after the breach that the landlord's acceptance of rent or other performance by the tenant does not constitute a waiver.

The most important issue is whether acceptance of rent by the landlord would be a waiver of a notice to terminate the rental agreement. In general, acceptance of rent for a period beyond the time stated in the notice would be evidence that the landlord is willing to continue the tenancy, so the notice would thereby be extinguished. But acceptance of rent for the rest of the time up to the time stated in the notice does not invalidate the notice.

A special rule applies for a 72- or 144-hour notice for non-payment of rent. While acceptance of partial rent would normally be considered poor management practice, acceptance of partial rent before giving a 72- or 144-hour notice does not extinguish the right of the landlord to give a 72- or 144-hour notice if the tenant fails to pay the balance as required. If the landlord agrees to accept the balance of the rent on a certain date in the future and the tenant fails to do so, the landlord can give the tenant another 72- or 144-hour notice without having to give the tenant an additional grace period.

Manufactured and floating homes

The last portion of the Oregon Residential Landlord and Tenant Act contains special provisions which apply only to manufactured dwelling and mobile home parks, and floating home moorage facilities. (Although the term ***mobile home*** is still commonly used, the statutory term is ***manufactured dwelling*** or ***manufactured housing***.) These provisions include –

- Rent increases require 90 days notice, and the landlord must be available for meetings with tenants either individually or as a group.
- A landlord cannot charge extra for a pet, either as a special fee or as increased rent, for a tenant who is renting space for a home owned by the tenant.
- The landlord must provide rules and cannot adopt rule changes without notice to the tenants, and the rules go into effect in 60 days unless 51% of the tenants object within 30 days.
- Rental contracts must be in writing and contain various special provisions.
- Tenants cannot be required to give more than 30 days notice.
- Landlords cannot dictate whom the tenant may choose as supplier of fuel, furnishings, goods, services or accessories and cannot require the tenant to pur-

NOTES

chase a home from a particular dealer, nor can dealers require, as a condition of a sale, that the buyer set up the home in any particular facility.

- Bylaws, rental agreements and occupancy rules may not contain provisions which limit the tenants reasonable right to assemble peaceably or canvas on the common areas of the facility, nor can the landlord prevent tenants from speaking or inviting speakers to speak on political issues.
- Landlords must give reasonable cause to terminate a tenancy, and must give at least 30 days notice (20 days notice for the same offense within six months); except for nonpayment of rent, harming or threatening to harm persons on the premises, or outrageous conduct, in which case the usual 24-hour notice applies.
- If a facility is to be closed, the landlord must give the tenant 365 days notice. The landlord need give only 180 days notice if the landlord finds an alternative space and pays the tenant's actual moving expenses up to $3,500. The tenant may waive these notices if the landlord and tenant reach an agreement otherwise.
- If there is a tenants' association, the association may request notice prior to the sale of the park, in which case the landlord must immediately give notice to the tenants upon listing the park.
- If an owner of a manufactured dwelling or floating home wishes to sell the dwelling, the landlord may not require the owner to remove the dwelling from the park for the purpose of selling it, pay the landlord a commission, or deny the owner the right to place a reasonable "for sale" sign on the dwelling.

Exercise 4c

If a landlord fails to provide an essential service, the tenant can give the landlord a notice of the tenant's intent to terminate the agreement in ____ days if the landlord does not provide the essential service within ____ days. If the matter does not involve an essential service, then the tenant can give the landlord notice of intent to terminate the rental in ____ days if the landlord fails to remedy the breach within ____ days. When a property does not meet habitability standards, the tenant can ____ for loss of rental value, which can be used as a defense in a suit for ____ ____ and ____. When a landlord attempts to force a tenant out, this is called ____ eviction and would subject the landlord to damages.

To terminate tenancies without stating a cause, ____ days notice is required for month-to-month tenancies and ____ days notice is required for week-to-week tenancies. For an unpermitted pet, the landlord can give the tenant ____ days notice. For failure to pay rent, the landlord can give the tenant ____-____ notice after a ____-____ grace period, or for month-to-month tenancies, a ____-____ notice after a ____-____ grace period. For conduct which is outrageous in the extreme the landlord can give the tenant ____ ____ notice. Notice can be by personal service or by ____ ____ mail.

The Oregon Residential Landlord and Tenant Act applies to (Choose which)

- ☐ *Manufactured housing*
- ☐ *Floating homes*

REFERENCES

The following is required reading to ensure your success on the exams. Many of the practice questions at the end of this chapter, as well as state exam questions, are drawn from the following reading.

Oregon Revised Statutes Chapter 90 (ORS 90.100 to 90.875), the Oregon Residential Landlord-Tenant Act

Note: The text in this chapter is a general introduction to the Residential Landlord-Tenant Act. Anyone engaging in property management must study the actual statutes in detail. In addition, many exam questions are taken directly from the statutes.

KEY TERMS

The key to understanding any new field is the vocabulary used in that field. To maximize your comprehension of the material presented in this chapter, be sure you know the meaning and significance of the following terms. Remember that the majority of test questions primarily test knowledge of vocabulary.

Abandonment
Actual eviction
Alternate energy device
Constructive eviction
Counterclaim
Deposit
Distraint for rent
Essential services
Exculpation clause
Fee
Forcible entry and detainer
Habitability standards
Last month's rent deposit
Manufactured dwelling
Mobile home
Retaliatory conduct
Squatter
Security deposit
Waiver

ANSWERS

To chapter exercises. If you couldn't figure out what to put in the blanks, find the answer here!

Exercise 4a

The Oregon Residential Landlord and Tenant Act would apply to which of the following?

- ❏ *Residency in an elder care facility*
- ■ *A week-to-week rental of a single room in a hotel*
- ❏ *An apartment occupied by a resident manager*
- ■ *A leasehold condominium rented to a tenant on a month-to-month basis*
- ■ *Seller renting the house back from the buyer for 120 days after closing the sale*
- ❏ *Rental of a small single-tenant retail building*

A landlord must disclose to a tenant in writing if a portion of the tenant's ___UTILITY___ *bills will benefit others in the complex. For one to four unit buildings, disclosure must also be made if the property is the subject of* ___FORECLOSURE___ *action. A rental agreement must contain the name and address of the* ___OWNER___ *or other person on whom the tenant can service notices and demands. The tenant is entitled to a* ___COPY___ *of the rental agreement at the time of entering into it.*

If the landlord collects advance funds from the tenant and labels the funds a ___DEPOSIT___ *then the funds are subject to being* ___REFUNDED___. *If a charge is nonrefundable, it should be called a* ___FEE___. *If a landlord takes a deposit for last month's rent, it is* ___REFUNDABLE___. *Refundable items must be returned to the tenant, or an* ___ACCOUNTING___ *within* ___30___ *days after the termination of the tenancy.*

Exercise 4b

The Residential Landlord and Tenant Act requires the landlord to maintain the premises in at least ___HABITABLE___ *condition. This requires that the landlord supply and maintain which of the following items?*

- ❑ *Storm doors and windows*
- ■ *An air conditioner which the landlord has supplied*
- ■ *A water heater*
- ❑ *A heating outlet or fixture in each separate room in the structure*

If a landlord adopts rules which promote the safety of the tenants and which are applied fairly and equally to all tenants, the rules go into effect ___IMMEDIATELY___.

Many times the landlord desires access to the premises. Give the amount of notice the landlord must give the tenant before entering the premises in each of the following cases:

__-0-__ *The landlord has a written agreement to lower the rent by $10 per month in order to show the premises to prospective buyers*

__-0-__ *The landlord wishes to cross the grounds and post a notice for the tenant on the front door.*

__-0-__ *The landlord notified the tenant 30 days earlier that workers would be entering without notice in order to make repairs to the plumbing equipment*

__-0-__ *There is water pouring out of the bathroom window*

A rental agreement may require a tenant to notify the landlord of any expected absence by the tenant in excess of __7__ *days. If it does, and the tenant is absent for this time, the landlord may presume that the premises have been* ___ABANDONED___.

If there is abandoned personal property, the landlord must give the tenant __5__ *days notice to claim it, or* __8__ *days notice if mailed. If the tenant claims it, the landlord may recover the costs of [Choose the one(s) which are correct]* ■ *Removal* ■ *Storage* ■ *Mailing the Notice* ■ *Unpaid Rent. If the landlord sells personal property belonging to a tenant, the proceeds of the sale must be turned over to the* ___TENANT___, *but if the* ___TENANT___ *cannot be located, then the landlord must turn the funds over to the county. In a residential tenancy,* ___DISTRAINT___ *for* ___RENT___ *is not permitted.*

Which of the following would be considered retaliatory conduct?

- ❑ *Raising the rent to pay for bringing the property up to habitability standards*
- ■ *Evicting a tenant who forms a tenants' union and organizes a rent strike*
- ■ *Taking away a parking right because the tenant asked the city to inspect the property*

Exercise 4c

If a landlord fails to provide an essential service, the tenant can give the landlord a notice of the tenant's intent to terminate the agreement in __30__ *days if the landlord does not provide the essential service within* __7__ *days. If the matter does not involve an essential service, then the tenant can give the landlord notice of intent to terminate the rental in* __30__ *days if the landlord fails to remedy the breach within* __14__ *days. When a property does not meet habitability standards, the tenant can* ___COUNTERCLAIM___ *for loss of rental value, which can be used as a defense in a suit for* ___FORCIBLE___ ___ENTRY___ *and* ___DETAINER___.

When a landlord attempts to force a tenant out, this is called ___CONSTRUCTIVE___ *eviction and would subject the landlord to damages.*

To terminate tenancies without stating a cause, __31__ *days notice is required for month-to-month tenancies and* __10__ *days notice is required for week-to-week tenancies. For an unpermitted pet, the landlord can give the ten-*

ant ___10___ days notice. For failure to pay rent, the landlord can give the tenant __72__ __HOURS__ notice after a _7_ - __DAY__ grace period, or for month-to-month tenancies, a _144_ - __HOUR__ notice after a __4__ - _DAY_ grace period . For conduct which is outrageous in the extreme the landlord can give the tenant _24_ __HOURS__ notice. Notice can be by personal service or by ___FIRST___ ___CLASS___ mail.

The Oregon Residential Landlord and Tenant Act applies to (Choose which)

- *Manufactured housing*
- *Floating homes*

PRACTICE QUESTIONS

The following practice questions are representative of the questions you will find on the final examination and on the licensing examinations given by the Oregon Real Estate Agency.

1. The Oregon Residential Landlord and Tenant Act relates to
   (A) a tenancy by the entirety.
   (B) a commercial lease.
   (C) a tenancy for life.
   (D) rental of a residential condominium.

2. The Oregon Residential Landlord and Tenant Act does not apply to a rental of
   (A) a room in a college dormitory.
   (B) an off-campus apartment for married students, rented from a college.
   (C) a motel room which is rented by the month.
   (D) a house which the owner has sold but is to occupy for up to six months after closing the sale.

3. An owner of which of the following must comply with the Oregon Residential Landlord and Tenant Act when renting the property?
   (A) A space in a manufactured housing facility
   (B) A manufactured dwelling in a manufactured dwelling facility
   (C) A manufactured dwelling on land where the landlord owns both the land and the dwelling
   (D) All of the above are within the scope of the Oregon Residential Landlord and Tenant Act.

4. The Oregon Residential Landlord and Tenant Act applies to all of the following except
   (A) a roomer occupying a dwelling unit in which the kitchen and bathroom are shared.
   (B) the owner of a manufactured dwelling who rents space in a park.
   (C) the occupant of premises that are used primarily for agricultural purposes.
   (D) the occupant of an apartment owned by a public housing authority.

5. Which of the following are under the jurisdiction of the Residential Landlord and Tenant Act?
   (A) Tenants renting farm property and using it primarily for agricultural purposes
   (B) Students renting off-campus housing owned by the school
   (C) Apartments occupied by residential managers employed by the owner of the building
   (D) Holders of proprietary leases in cooperative housing units

6. The Oregon Residential Landlord and Tenant Law applies to all of the following except
   (A) a roomer in a dwelling unit where the kitchen and bathroom are shared.
   (B) a tenant in an apartment owned by a public housing authority.
   (C) the owner of a mobile home who rents space in a mobile home park.
   (D) holders of proprietary leases in a cooperative.

7. The Oregon Residential Landlord and Tenant Act applies to which of the following?
   I. Mobile home spaces
   II. Rooms in college dormitories
   III. Moorage spaces for floating homes
   (A) I only
   (B) I and II only
   (C) I and III only
   (D) II and III only

8. The definition of "dwelling units" under the Landlord and Tenant Law includes all of the following except
   (A) The rental space for a mobile home.
   (B) Houseboats rented by a family for residential use.
   (C) A part of a structure used by a family as a sleeping place only.
   (D) A hotel room rented by a family for seven days.

9. Which of the following statements concerning rental agreements in Oregon is false?
   (A) The name and address of the person authorized to manage the premises must be disclosed.
   (B) The tenant must be notified of a service he pays that directly benefits other tenants as well.
   (C) A rental agreement may include provisions prohibited by Oregon statute as long as the tenant agrees to their inclusion.
   (D) A copy of the rental agreement must be given to the tenant.

10. According to the Oregon Residential Landlord and Tenant Act, a tenant must be given notice when a rental agreement is signed of
    I. utilities the tenant must pay and which benefit other tenants.
    II. foreclosure suits filed against the property, but only if there are more than four units.
    III. the name and address of the owner or person authorized to manage the property.
    (A) I only (C) I and III only
    (B) I, II and III (D) II and III only

11. Under the Oregon Landlord and Tenant Act, a tenant who rents a unit in a duplex must be notified, at the time the rental agreement is executed, of which of the following?
    I. Any pending suit against the landlord to foreclose a mortgage pertaining to the property
    II. The name and address of any person authorized to manage the property
    (A) I only (C) Both I and II
    (B) II only (D) Neither I nor II

12. Which of the following statements about rental agreements entered into in Oregon is true?
    I. An agreement may state that a tenant waives his or her rights to the conditionally refundable security deposit.
    II. If an agreement is for a term less than one month, the rent is payable at the beginning of the term.
    (A) I only (C) Both I and II
    (B) II only (D) Neither I nor II

13. Under the Oregon Landlord and Tenant Act a tenant may recover damages if the landlord
    I. tries to enforce provisions in the rental agreement which the landlord knew were prohibited by state law.
    II. knowingly failed to provide normal essential services.
    III. failed to disclose to the tenant that the tenant would be required to pay for electricity which benefited other tenants.
    (A) I only (C) II and III only
    (B) II only (D) I, II and III

14. A tenant installed a solar water heater in residential premises with the landlord's permission. In this case, the
    I. water heater automatically becomes the property of the landlord.
    II. tenant is relieved of any responsibility for damage caused by the installation.
    (A) I only (C) Both I and II
    (B) II only (D) Neither I nor II

15. A "security deposit" would include monies paid by a tenant for
    (A) a non-refundable cleaning fee.
    (B) a refundable deposit.
    (C) payment of rent.
    (D) a non-refundable credit check fee.

16. "Security deposits" include monies paid by a tenant for a
    I. refundable deposit. II. credit check charge.
    (A) I only (C) Both I and II
    (B) II only (D) Neither I nor II

17. According to the Oregon Residential Landlord and Tenant Act, the security deposit
    (A) may be kept by the landlord on termination of the lease and is considered income earned.
    (B) is a predetermined sum charged the tenant providing the tenant protection against unreasonable charges for cleaning or damages at the end of the lease.
    (C) must be returned to the tenant within 31 days, or the landlord must provide the tenant with a written accounting for the portion of the deposit not returned.
    (D) is not regulated by the law, but is determined by the provisions of the rental agreement.

18. Under the Oregon Residential Landlord and Tenant Act, security deposits
    I. may be claimed by the landlord to repair damages caused by the tenant.
    II. are forfeited to the landlord if the tenant fails to maintain a tenancy for a specified amount of time.
    (A) I only (C) Both I and II
    (B) II only (D) Neither I nor II

19. A landlord can use a tenant's conditionally refundable deposit
    I. whenever there is a broken window in the premises.
    II. to repair damage from ordinary wear and tear caused by the tenant.
    (A) I only (C) Both I and II
    (B) II only (D) Neither I nor II

20. Upon termination of a tenancy, a tenant's conditionally refundable deposit may be expended by the property manager to repair a
    I. door jamb broken by the tenant.
    II. carpet torn by a guest of the tenant.
    (A) I only (C) Both I and II
    (B) II only (D) Neither I nor II

21. A landlord may claim all or part of a tenant's conditionally refundable deposit for the cost of
    (A) repairing a window broken by a tenant.
    (B) a tenant failing to rent an apartment for at least six months.
    (C) creating a reserve fund to replace items damaged by normal wear and tear.
    (D) the property manager's phone calls to the tenant.

22. Which of the following statements is correct concerning a tenant's security deposit?
    (A) A security deposit must be forfeited to the landlord if the tenant fails to maintain the tenancy for a specified period.
    (B) A security deposit could be used by the landlord to repair damages caused by the tenant, not including wear and tear.
    (C) When a property is sold, the landlord must refund tenants' deposits before the sale is closed in escrow.
    (D) All of the above are correct.

23. A property manager, in order to claim a part of a conditionally refundable deposit, must give an accounting to the tenant within
    (A) seven days after termination of tenancy.
    (B) 14 days after termination of tenancy.
    (C) 31 days after termination of tenancy.
    (D) 45 days after termination of tenancy.

24. Regarding the Oregon Residential Landlord and Tenant Act, which of the following is correct?
    (A) A refundable deposit must always be given back to the tenant within 30 days after the termination of the tenancy.
    (B) A cleaning fee must always be given back to the tenant in full within 30 days after the termination of the tenancy.
    (C) A cleaning fee need never be refunded.
    (D) A security fee must be refunded in full, unless the unit is damaged.

25. A landlord rented a single-family home to a tenant, and took a $450 security deposit, stipulating that the deposit could be used to cure any and all defaults. The tenant accepted the terms and moved in. A few days later the tenant moved out without giving the landlord any notice. The rent is $800 per month. The tenant caused no harm to the premises. When the tenant asks for the deposit back, the
    (A) landlord must refund it in full.
    (B) landlord can retain all of it.
    (C) tenant is entitled to an accounting of why it was not refunded.
    (D) landlord can retain all of it but must give the tenant an accounting.

26. A tenant of a rented home in Oregon has the right to
    I. a habitable, livable unit.
    II. quiet enjoyment of the rented home.
    (A) I only (C) Both I and II
    (B) II only (D) Neither I nor II

27. A landlord rented a house to a tenant and accepted a $500 deposit from the tenant, plus $1,600 for the first and last months' rent. The tenant later gave the landlord proper notice and moved out, leaving the premises clean and undamaged. Forty-five days later the tenant sued the landlord for the deposit because the landlord had not refunded it. Under these circumstances, the landlord must pay
    (A) $500.
    (B) $500, plus the tenant's costs and attorney's fees.
    (C) $1,000, plus the tenant's court costs and attorney's fees.
    (D) nothing.

28. Unless otherwise agreed, all rents are payable
    (A) in advance.
    (B) at the end of the month.
    (C) by the tenth of the month.
    (D) by the fifteenth of the month.

29. Which of the following would be prohibited by the Oregon Residential Landlord and Tenant Act?
    (A) A provision in a rental agreement which requires a late charge if the rent is two days late.
    (B) A landlord's refusal to return a cleaning deposit when the landlord had to spend more than the amount of the deposit to have the premises cleaned after the tenant moved out.
    (C) A tenant's attempt to recover a deposit from a current owner, even though the deposit had originally been given to a previous owner.
    (D) An owner designating the premises manager as the person to receive service of legal papers.

30. The term "essential services," under the Oregon Residential Landlord and Tenant Act, is defined so as to include, among other things,
    (A) curtains.
    (B) water and electricity.
    (C) television antenna.
    (D) all of the above.

31. The absence of which of the following would render a property unhabitable under the definition in the Oregon Landlord and Tenant Act?
    I. Hot and cold running water
    II. Connection to a sewage disposal system
    III. Adequate heating facility
    (A) I only (C) II and III only
    (B) II only (D) I, II and III

32. It is a responsibility of landlords, according to the Oregon Landlord and Tenant Act, to provide
    I. storm doors and storm windows.
    II. trash and garbage receptacles.
    (A) I only (C) Both I and II
    (B) II only (D) Neither I nor II

33. Under the Oregon Landlord and Tenant Act, landlords are responsible to provide
    I. adequate trash and garbage receptacles.
    II. weather- and waterproof roofs and exteriors.
    (A) I only (C) Both I and II
    (B) II only (D) Neither I nor II

34. The Oregon Residential Landlord and Tenant Law requires the landlord to provide tenants which of the following services?
    I. Garbage receptacles
    II. Electrical lighting
    III. Locks and keys to entrance doors
    (A) II only (C) II and III only
    (B) I and II only (D) I, II and III

35. Under the Oregon Residential Landlord and Tenant Act, which of the following would a landlord be required to do?
    I. Maintain the air conditioning equipment
    II. Maintain the grounds free from rubbish during the tenancy
    (A) I only (C) Both I and II
    (B) II only (D) Neither I nor II

36. The term "essential services" as defined under the Oregon Residential Landlord and Tenant Act would include which of the following?
    (A) Adequate heating facilities
    (B) Garbage containers
    (C) Maintenance of an air conditioner which was on the premises at the start of the tenancy
    (D) All of the above.

37. The term "essential services" under the Residential Landlord and Tenant Act is defined to include
    (A) heat, water and electricity.
    (B) garbage disposal unit at the landlord's expense.
    (C) window screens, curtains and drapes.
    (D) all of the above.

38. If a tenant has an essential service repaired and deducts the cost from the rent, the tenant may also
(A) terminate the tenancy with ten days notice to the landlord.
(B) terminate the tenancy with 14 days notice to the landlord.
(C) recover damages from the landlord.
(D) do none of the above.

39. Under the Oregon Landlord and Tenant Act a tenant may do which of the following if the landlord fails to provide an essential service and the tenant has properly notified the landlord of the problem?
I. Find substitute housing during the period of the landlord's noncompliance and not pay rent for the period of the noncompliance
II. Recover the actual and reasonable cost or fair and reasonable value of the substitute housing
(A) I only
(B) II only
(C) Either I or II
(D) Neither I nor II

40. Under Oregon law, the tenant may terminate the rental agreement if the landlord does not repair a burned out water heater within
(A) 48 hours.
(B) seven days.
(C) two weeks.
(D) 20 days.

41. In most cases, a residential tenant in Oregon may obtain damages from a landlord who fails to provide an essential service if the
I. tenant notified the landlord of the problem.
II. condition was caused by negligence on the part of the tenant.
(A) I only
(B) II only
(C) Both I and II
(D) Neither I nor II

42. A tenant notified the landlord of a problem with the wiring. The landlord did nothing, so on the 11th day the tenant called an electrician. The tenant in this case
(A) will have to pay the electrician.
(B) was within the law in hiring the electrician.
(C) has no recourse against the landlord, because the tenant did not wait the statutory 30 days.
(D) both B and C are correct.

43. A tenant in a residential rental notified the landlord in writing of a problem, but the landlord did nothing. Which of the following would the tenant be allowed to pay for and deduct from the rent?
(A) Repainting the exterior of the building
(B) A bill for $500 for repairing the furnace
(C) Unpaid water bill when the water has not yet been shut off
(D) None of the above

44. A tenant notified the landlord in writing that a wiring problem had developed and the tenant was without electricity. Ten days passed without the landlord correcting the problem. The tenant called an electrician to do the work. The tenant
(A) should have waited another ten days before having the work done.
(B) was legally correct in having the electrician do the work.
(C) has no recourse against the landlord.
(D) must take the landlord to court to settle this problem.

45. A landlord rented an apartment, which was at the top of a flight of stairs. The rental agreement required the tenant to do all necessary repairs in return for lower than market rent. One day the tenant notified the landlord of a defect in the stairs. The landlord attempted to repair the stairs, but did an inadequate job. Subsequently, the tenant fell on the stairs and was injured. Who is liable in this case?
I. The tenant
II. The landlord
(A) I only
(B) II only
(C) Both I and II
(D) Neither I nor II

46. A landlord rented a house to a tenant who likes children. The neighbor children took to playing on the roof, causing the roof to leak. Under these circumstances it would be
(A) the responsibility of the landlord to have the roof repaired.
(B) the responsibility of the tenant to have the roof repaired.
(C) the responsibility of the landlord to have the roof repaired, but the landlord has just cause to terminate the rental agreement.
(D) a shared responsibility to have the roof repaired.

47. A landlord had a house rented to a tenant and the water heater went out. The rental agreement stipulated that all maintenance was to be performed by the tenant in return for a lower than market rent. In this case, the
   (A) tenant must repair the water heater or pay to have it repaired.
   (B) landlord must repair the water heater or pay to have it repaired.
   (C) tenant must repair the water heater, but the landlord must pay for any parts required.
   (D) landlord has the final responsibility to see that the water heater is repaired, and cannot charge the tenant for the cost.

48. An apartment owner knew the premises had defects, so the owner wrote the rental agreements so the tenants could take no action if the units are not habitable. If a tenant wishes, the tenant may
   (A) do nothing regarding the landlord's violation of habitability standards.
   (B) give the landlord proper notice of the needed repairs and, if the landlord refuses to repair, sue the landlord to force the landlord to supply habitable units.
   (C) request that the landlord comply with the habitability standards of the Oregon Residential Landlord and Tenant Act and, if the landlord refuses, cause the repairs to be made and deduct the cost from the rent.
   (D) do either B or C.

49. A residential tenant in Oregon may recover damages if the landlord
   I. rents property after the city has served notice that the premises violate the housing code.
   II. refuses to rent to a blind person because of a guide dog and the landlord has a "no pets" policy.
   III. refuses to provide locks for entrance doors.
   (A) I and II only (C) II only
   (B) I, II and III (D) II and III only

50. A tenant in an apartment building invited some friends over. The friends insisted on playing loud music to the point where other tenants complained to the manager. The landlord can
   (A) do nothing, as the disturbance was not caused by the tenant.
   (B) give the tenant a 30-day notice, whether on a lease or month-to-month rental agreement.
   (C) give the tenant a 24-hour notice, whether on a lease or month-to-month rental agreement.
   (D) give the tenant a 10-day notice, whether on a lease or month-to-month rental agreement.

51. A tenant may lawfully
   (A) leave a car up on blocks as long as it is within its assigned parking space.
   (B) perform minor car repairs if the premises include an enclosed garage.
   (C) wash the tenant's car on the premises.
   (D) do any of the above.

52. A landlord may terminate a lease and sue to evict the tenant for all of the following reasons except
   (A) unlawful use of the premises.
   (B) failure of the tenant to agree to waive his or her rights under the Oregon Landlord and Tenant Act.
   (C) non-compliance of building rules.
   (D) abuse of the premises.

53. Under the Oregon Landlord and Tenant Act, a rental agreement may require a tenant to
   I. notify the owner when the tenant will be absent from the premises for more than seven days.
   II. agree to limit the landlord's liability that may arise from the landlord's negligence.
   (A) I only (C) Both I and II
   (B) II only (D) Neither I nor II

54. Which of the following is true under the Oregon Residential Landlord and Tenant Act?
   I. A tenant may be required to notify the landlord of an absence from the premises in excess of seven days.
   II. A tenant must notify the landlord in writing of the tenant's intention to terminate a periodic tenancy.
   (A) I only (C) Both I and II
   (B) II only (D) Neither I nor II

55. If a landlord wishes to adopt rules for a residential property, they are enforceable only if
  I. they apply equally to all tenants in a fair manner.
  II. the tenant has notice of the rules at the time the rules are adopted or in the rental agreement.

(A) I only
(B) II only
(C) Both I and II
(D) Neither I nor II

56. An owner of an apartment building became tired of complaints from the tenants about the behavior of other tenants around the swimming pool, so the landlord adopted a reasonable list of "pool rules" and posted them by the pool. Which of the following is true in this case?
(A) The rules cannot be enforced on a tenant until the tenant agrees to them in writing.
(B) The rules go into effect immediately.
(C) The rules must be enforced equally and fairly among all tenants.
(D) Both B and C are correct.

57. According to the Oregon Landlord and Tenant Act a landlord may adopt rules concerning a tenant's use and occupancy of the premises. The landlord's rules are enforceable only if, among other things,
  I. the rules apply to all tenants in the premises in a fair manner.
  II. the tenant has notice of the rules at the time the rental agreement is signed or when the rules are adopted.

(A) I only
(B) II only
(C) Both I and II
(D) Neither I nor II

58. Which of the following regarding the Oregon Residential Landlord and Tenant Act is false?
(A) A tenant must use the premises in such a manner as to ensure the safety and quiet enjoyment of the other tenants.
(B) A tenant may be required to notify the landlord if the tenant will be away from the property for more than seven consecutive days.
(C) A tenant of an apartment may refuse the landlord access to the property unless the tenant has been given 24 hours notice or unless there is an emergency.
(D) A tenant of a mobile home may refuse to comply with any rules adopted by the landlord after the tenant enters into the rental agreement.

59. Under the Oregon Residential Landlord and Tenant Act, a landlord may enter the premises
(A) without notice if under court order.
(B) by giving the tenant 24 hours notice.
(C) without notice if there is an emergency.
(D) in any of the above cases.

60. Unless otherwise agreed, the landlord is required by the Oregon Landlord and Tenant Act to give a tenant 24 hours notice to
  I. show the property to a prospective purchaser.
  II. enter the property to make non-emergency repairs.

(A) I only
(B) II only
(C) Both I and II
(D) Neither I nor II

61. According to the provisions of the Oregon Residential Landlord and Tenant Act it is true that
  I. a tenant of an apartment may refuse the landlord access to the property unless the tenant has been given 24 hours notice or unless there is an emergency.
  II. a tenant must use the premises in such a manner as to ensure the safety and quiet enjoyment of the other tenants.

(A) I only
(B) II only
(C) Both I and II
(D) Neither I nor II

62. A tenant, under the Oregon Landlord and Tenant Act, may be entitled to damages if a landlord does which of the following?
  I. The landlord makes an unlawful entry of the tenant's home.
  II. The landlord of a single family house failed to disclose a pending suit to foreclose a mortgage on the property at the time the tenant signed the rental agreement.
  III. The landlord failed to disclose to the tenant that a portion of the tenant's electricity bill would be for services used for the benefit of other tenants.

(A) I only
(B) III only
(C) II and III only
(D) I, II and III

63. Under the Oregon Residential Landlord and Tenant Act, a tenant can recover damages if the landlord
   I. tries to enforce illegal provisions in the rental agreement.
   II. knowingly fails to provide essential services.
   III. fails to disclose to the tenant that the tenant would be required to pay for electricity for the benefit of other tenants.
   (A) I only (C) II only
   (B) I, II and III (D) II and III only

64. The Oregon Landlord and Tenant Act provides that a landlord may be entitled to damages if a tenant does which of the following?
   I. The tenant remains in possession after the expiration of the rental agreement without the landlord's permission
   II. The tenant refuses to allow the landlord lawful access to the property
   (A) I only (C) Both I and II
   (B) II only (D) Neither I nor II

65. A landlord raised the rents for certain tenants who are troublemakers. Which of the following could a tenant lawfully do without fear of reprisal?
   (A) File a complaint about discrimination.
   (B) Form a tenants' union.
   (C) Complain to the bureau of buildings about the condition of the premises.
   (D) Any of the above.

66. A landlord may terminate a tenancy if a residential tenant complains to city officials about a
   I. health hazard the landlord failed to correct.
   II. building code violation which the tenant caused.
   (A) I only (C) Both I and II
   (B) II only (D) Neither I nor II

67. A tenant of a rented home in Oregon has a right to
   (A) orally give the landlord legal notice of needed repairs.
   (B) complain without reprisal.
   (C) join tenant associations.
   (D) do both B and C above.

68. In Oregon, retaliatory conduct by the landlord is illegal against a tenant who
   (A) joins a tenant union.
   (B) complains to a government agency about sanitary conditions of the dwelling.
   (C) complains to the landlord about the habitability of the dwelling.
   (D) does any of the above.

69. An Oregon landlord may terminate the tenancy because the tenant did which of the following?
   I. Refused to remove a pet which violates the rental agreement
   II. Complained to the city about a health hazard the landlord refused to correct
   III. Complained to the city about a building code violation which was caused by the lack of the tenant's care
   (A) I and II only (C) II only
   (B) I and III only (D) III only

70. In Oregon, retaliatory conduct by the landlord is illegal against a tenant who
   (A) joins a tenants' union.
   (B) complains to a government agency about unsanitary conditions of a dwelling.
   (C) complains to the landlord about the habitability of a dwelling.
   (D) does any of the above.

71. Under Oregon Residential Landlord and Tenant Law, a tenant is entitled to
   (A) terminate a month-to-month rental agreement after 30 days written notice.
   (B) have a written accounting for the use of the security deposit and a return of any deposit balance within 31 days after moving.
   (C) electrical lighting.
   (D) all of the above.

72. Which of the following must a residential tenant do in Oregon?
   I. Notify the landlord of an absence over seven days but only if the agreement requires it.
   II. Notify the landlord of an intention to terminate the tenancy.
   (A) I only (C) Both I and II
   (B) II only (D) Neither I nor II

73. A landlord who had rented a house on a month-to-month rental agreement discovered that the tenant had moved and left a few pieces of furniture, which the landlord deemed had a market value of $250. The landlord found the tenant's new address and gave the tenant eight days notice that the landlord deemed the furniture to be abandoned. If the tenant does not respond to the notice within eight days the landlord may immediately
   I. sell the personal property at public auction.
   II. destroy the property if the landlord determines it to be of no value.
   (A) I only
   (B) II only
   (C) Both I and II
   (D) Neither I nor II

74. A landlord may, according to the Oregon Landlord and Tenant Act, do which of the following with personal property abandoned by a tenant who has terminated the tenancy?
   I. Destroy the property if the value of the property is so low that the cost of storage and the conduct of a sale would exceed the amount realized from the sale
   II. Sell the tenant's personal property and apply the proceeds towards cost of storage and unpaid rent
   (A) I only
   (B) II only
   (C) Both I and II
   (D) Neither I nor II

75. A landlord seized a tenant's personal property in an effort to collect rent past due on an apartment the tenant had leased. The landlord claimed the right to take possession of the property under a concept of law known as "distraint." In Oregon, distraint for rent
   (A) is prohibited under the Landlord and Tenant Act.
   (B) is permitted if the rental agreement specifically includes this landlord right.
   (C) is permitted only for residential property.
   (D) is prohibited under the Landlord and Tenant Act if the rent owed the landlord is less than $500.

76. An owner rented a house with a separate garage. The tenant failed to pay the rent, so the owner locked the garage and refused to allow the tenant to use it until the tenant paid. In this case, the
   (A) landlord could be liable for two months' rent as punitive damages.
   (B) tenant can successfully sue to recover possession of the premises and force the landlord to unlock the garage.
   (C) tenant can legally terminate the rental agreement.
   (D) tenant can do any of the above.

77. A landlord owned a condominium which was rented to a tenant. After three months the tenant failed to pay the rent, so the landlord shut off the water to the unit. In this case, the tenant
   (A) could hold the landlord liable for two months rent as damages.
   (B) can sue to recover possession and force the landlord to turn the water back on.
   (C) can legally terminate the rental agreement.
   (D) can do any of the above.

78. The Oregon Landlord and Tenant Act permits notices for increases in rent and notices to terminate tenancies to be delivered by
   I. first class mail.
   II. personal delivery.
   (A) I only
   (B) II only
   (C) Either I or II unless the rental agreement provides otherwise
   (D) Neither I nor II

79. A forcible entry and wrongful detainer could be used by a landlord to terminate a tenancy for which of the following?
   I. Non-payment of rent on a month-to-month tenancy
   II. Tenant who holds over after expiration of lease and does not pay rent
   III. Tenant who keeps a pet in violation of the rental agreement
   (A) I only
   (B) I, II and III
   (C) II only
   (D) III only

80. According to the Oregon Residential Landlord and Tenant Act, a landlord may
    I. increase rents at any time with 30 days written notice if the tenancy is month to month.
    II. claim the conditionally refundable security deposit when a tenant fails to maintain tenancy for a specified term.
    (A) I only
    (B) II only
    (C) Both I and II
    (D) Neither I nor II

81. A landlord may evict a tenant for all of the following except
    (A) unlawful use of the premises.
    (B) refusing to agree to waive the tenant's rights under the Residential Landlord and Tenant Law.
    (C) failure to comply with building rules.
    (D) abuse of the premises.

82. A notice is required to terminate most residential tenancies. In Oregon, to terminate a
    (A) month-to-month tenancy without cause, a 31-day notice is required.
    (B) week-to-week tenancy without cause, a seven-day notice is required.
    (C) year-to-year tenancy without cause, a six-month notice is required.
    (D) monthly lease without cause, a 31-day notice is required.

83. When a tenant has not paid the rent and the due date was more than twelve days ago, how much notice must the landlord give the tenant in order to terminate the tenancy?
    (A) After the tenth day no notice is required.
    (B) A minimum 72-hour notice is required.
    (C) A 30-day notice is required.
    (D) The required notice depends on the length of the period.

84. A landlord may give a tenant 24 hours notice to terminate a month-to-month rental agreement
    (A) when the rent remains unpaid more than seven days past the due date.
    (B) when the tenant is threatening the other tenants.
    (C) when the tenant is disturbing the quiet enjoyment of other tenants.
    (D) in any of the above situations.

85. If a tenant is damaging the premises, the landlord may
    (A) seek to have the tenant's behavior enjoined by the court.
    (B) give the tenant 24-hours notice to terminate.
    (C) successfully sue the tenant for the cost of the repairs.
    (D) do any of the above.

86. Under Oregon law, in a month-to-month tenancy, the landlord automatically has the right to
    (A) terminate the tenant's occupancy after 31-day notice.
    (B) show the unit to a prospective renter without giving the current tenant prior notice.
    (C) quadruple damages from a tenant who refuses to move after proper notice has been given.
    (D) raise the rent of a tenant if the tenant forms a tenants' union.

87. The Oregon Residential Landlord and Tenant Act gives a landlord the right to
    (A) terminate the tenancy if the tenant refuses to remove a pet which is kept on the premises in violation of the rental agreement.
    (B) enter the premises with less than 24 hours' notice in an emergency.
    (C) require the tenant give the landlord notice if the tenant will be absent from the property for more than seven days.
    (D) do any of the above.

88. Under which of the following circumstances may a landlord not terminate a rental agreement and take possession of the property as provided for by Oregon law and with the landlord's 24 hours written notice to the tenant?
    (A) Ted vacated the premises, having subleased the property to Eric. Ted's rental agreement prohibited subleasing.
    (B) Michael failed to pay rent within seven days of the date the rent was due.
    (C) A pet owned by Susan, the tenant, seriously threatened personal injury upon Tom, another tenant.
    (D) A guest in the home of Dorothy, the tenant, seriously injured another tenant.

89. A landlord may terminate a tenancy with only ten days notice if the tenant has done which of the following more than once during a six-month period?
    I. Kept a dog or other pet capable of harming the property in violation of the rental agreement
    II. Failed to comply with provision of the rental agreement relating to health and safety.
    (A) I only
    (B) II only
    (C) Both I and II
    (D) Neither I nor II

90. A landlord is permitted to give the tenant on a month-to-month tenancy less than 30 days notice to terminate the tenancy if the tenant is in violation of which of the following?
    I. Keeping a pet on the premises, which is prohibited in the rental agreement
    II. Failing to pay rent within seven days of the date it is due
    (A) I only
    (B) II only
    (C) Both I and II
    (D) Neither I nor II

91. Ed, the landlord, served a 30-day notice to terminate the month-to-month tenancy of Patrick, the tenant, effective June 20. According to Oregon law, if Ed accepts payment for rent for the period of June 1, the day Patrick's rent is normally due, until June 20, Ed
    (A) must serve another 30 days termination notice to Patrick.
    (B) must serve a ten days termination notice to Patrick.
    (C) must, within 72 hours of accepting the rent, advise Patrick that the termination notice is still in force.
    (D) does not have to do any of the above.

92. A landlord gave a tenant a 31-day notice to terminate the tenancy on August 12. If the rent is due on August 1 and the landlord accepts rent on that date for the period ending August 12, the landlord
    (A) must serve an additional 31-day notice in order to terminate the tenancy.
    (B) must serve a ten-day notice to terminate.
    (C) must, within 72 hours, advise the tenant that the termination notice is still in effect.
    (D) need do none of the above.

93. A landlord served the tenant with a 31-day notice to terminate on June 20. If the rent is due on June 1 and the landlord accepts the normal rent on that date and keeps it, the landlord
    (A) must serve an additional 31-day notice in order to terminate the tenancy.
    (B) must serve a ten-day notice to terminate.
    (C) must, within 72 hours, advise the tenant that the termination notice is still in effect.
    (D) need do none of the above.

94. An owner wanted a month-to-month tenant to move out, so the owner delivered a 31-day notice on July 31. A few days later, the owner accepted rent to August 31. Which of the following is true?
    (A) The tenant must move immediately.
    (B) The landlord is required to give the tenant an additional 31-day notice if the reason for terminating the tenancy is so the landlord can move into the property.
    (C) The tenant is entitled to another 31-day notice because the rent payment canceled the notice.
    (D) The landlord can evict the tenant if the tenant does not move by August 31.

95. A landlord came by to find out why the tenant had not paid the rent, and discovered that the tenant had left. The landlord located the tenant and sued for the rent due for the month, since the tenant left without notice. Meanwhile the landlord re-rented the premises three days after the tenant left. In this case, the
    (A) landlord can collect from both the old and the new tenants.
    (B) court will deduct the rent collected for the remainder of the month from the new tenant from the amount owed by the old tenant.
    (C) landlord cannot collect anything from the old tenant.
    (D) landlord cannot legally collect anything from the new tenant.

96. Tom rented an apartment for $975 on a month-to-month tenancy with rent due on the first day of every month. The landlord sent Tom a 30-day notice to terminate the tenancy effective May 20. According to the Oregon Landlord and Tenant Act, what amount will Tom be required to pay on May 1 for rent?
(A) $471 (C) $648
(B) $629 (D) $975

97. An apartment is rented for $600 per month and the rent is due on the first of the month. The landlord sent the tenant a notice effective May 20. How much will the tenant owe on May 1?
(A) $213 (C) $400
(B) $387 (D) $600

98. A landlord of a residential property in Oregon may
(A) terminate the tenancy if the tenant keeps a pet in violation of the rental agreement.
(B) enter the premises with less than 24 hours notice in an emergency.
(C) require the tenant to give the landlord advance notice of an absence of more than seven days.
(D) do any of the above.

99. Under the Residential Landlord and Tenant Act a landlord may be entitled to damages if a tenant
I. remains in possession after the expiration of the rental agreement without permission.
II. refuses the allow the landlord lawful access to the premises.
(A) I only (C) Both I and II
(B) II only (D) Neither I nor II

100. Which of the following cases would not create the right to give the tenant 24 hours notice?
(A) Tenant vacated the premises after subleasing to a new tenant; lease prohibited subleasing
(B) Tenant failed to pay the rent within seven days of the date the rent was due
(C) Tenant's pet threatened personal injury to another tenant
(D) Tenant's guest seriously injured another tenant

101. The landlord of a mobile home space may do which of the following under the Oregon Residential Landlord and Tenant Act?
I. Require tenants to purchase fuel from a specific supplier
II. Charge a fee for the sale of the tenant's mobile home without a written contract naming the landlord as agent
III. specify the size and placement of a "for sale" sign on a mobile home owned by the tenant
(A) I, II and III (C) II and III only
(B) II only (D) III only

102. A tenant who rents a space in a mobile home park has the legal right to
(A) sell the mobile home without having to move it out of the park.
(B) place a "for sale" sign on the mobile home.
(C) have the buyer of the mobile home take over the rental even if the landlord objects.
(D) do both A and B.

87%

ANSWERS

To practice questions. If you chose the wrong letter, here's the right one! The explanations are designed to clarify your understanding.

1. **D** The scope of the Oregon Residential Landlord and Tenant Act is limited to less than freehold estates in residential property. A tenancy by the entirety is a co-ownership between husband and wife. A "tenancy for life" is another expression for "life estate, which is an ownership interest (freehold)."

2. **A** Exemptions to the Oregon Residential Landlord and Tenant Act include tenancies in institutions such as nursing homes, educational, religious, fraternal and social organizations; tenancy by a buyer prior to the closing of a purchase of the property; transient occupancy of hotel and motel facilities; occupancy by a squatter, vacation tenancy, tenancy of a resident manager; tenancy in a cooperative housing unit, and tenancy in property primarily used for agricultural purposes (ORS 90.110). However, the exemption for educational institutions specifically does not apply to off-campus housing. Also, rental of a house by a buyer prior to closing the sale or by a seller back from the buyer after the sale are exempt, but only if the period does not exceed 90 days. And hotel/motel tenancies are not exempt if they are week to week or month to month.

3. **D** The Oregon Residential Landlord and Tenant Act defines dwelling unit as including space rentals in floating home and manufactured housing facilities, even if the housing unit is owned by the tenant, i.e., rental of the space only. The term "dwelling unit" also includes the manufactured or floating home itself if it is owned by the landlord.

4. **C** Oregon Revised Statutes 90.110 excludes property used primarily for agricultural purposes. The fact that a bathroom and kitchen are shared is irrelevant. It is also immaterial if the dwelling unit is owned by a public agency.

5. **B** Oregon Revised Statutes 90.110 excludes property used primarily for agricultural purposes, apartments of resident managers (except for the eviction procedures), and cooperative housing units. It also excludes occupancy for educational purposes, but only if the property is located on the campus of the educational institution.

6. **D** Oregon Revised Statutes 90.110 excludes cooperative housing units. It does not matter if a kitchen and bath are shared, nor is it relevant if the property is owned by a government agency. There are extensive provisions in the statutes relating to mobile and floating homes, and the renting of space in facilities for such housing.

7. **C** The Oregon Residential Landlord and Tenant Act specifically exempts "Residence at an institution, public or private, if incidental to detention or the provision of medical, geriatric, educational, counseling, religious or similar service, but not including residence in off-campus nondormitory housing." (ORS 90.110). There are no exemptions for the rental of manufactured dwellings (mobile homes) or floating homes (houseboats). There are extensive provisions relating to the rental of a space in either a manufactured housing facility, or a floating home facility.

8. **D** The Residential Landlord and Tenant Act provides extensive sections on manufactured and mobile homes, in addition to houseboats and floating homes. It also includes either the rental of the structure, or of the space for a structure owned by the tenant. However, ORS 90.110 (4) excludes "transient occupancy in a hotel or motel" from the Residential Landlord and Tenant Act.

9. **C** Oregon Revised Statutes 90.305 provides "The landlord shall disclose to the tenant in writing at or before the commencement of the tenancy the name and address of: (a) The person authorized to manage the premises; and (b) An owner of the premises or a person authorized to act for and on behalf of the owner for the purpose of service of process and receiving and receipting for notices and demands." Oregon Revised Statutes 90.315 states "(2) The landlord shall disclose to the tenant in writing at or before the commencement of the tenancy any utility or service that the tenant pays directly to a utility or service provider that benefits, directly, the landlord or other tenants." Oregon Revised Statutes 90.245 states that a prohibited provision in a rental agreement is unenforceable. Oregon Revised Statutes 90.240 states "(2) The landlord shall provide the ten-

ant with a copy of any written rental agreement and all amendments and additions thereto."

10. **C** Oregon Revised Statutes 90.315 requires disclosure if any of the tenant's future utility bills will benefit others in the complex. Oregon Revised Statutes 90.310 requires disclosure to new tenants if the property is four units or less and under any kind of foreclosure action. Oregon Revised Statutes 90.305 requires the disclosure of the name and address of the person responsible for managing the property.

11. **C** Oregon Revised Statutes 90.305 requires the landlord to disclose the name and address of the person responsible for managing the premises. For properties of four units or less, Oregon Revised Statutes 90.310 requires the landlord to disclose to new tenants if the property is the subject of any kind of foreclosure action.

12. **B** Oregon Revised Statutes 90.245 states "a rental agreement may not provide that the tenant ... agrees to waive or forego rights or remedies under this chapter." Oregon Revised Statutes 90.240 states "... periodic rent is payable at the beginning of any term of one month or less and otherwise in equal monthly or weekly installments at the beginning of each month or week, depending on whether the tenancy is month-to-month or week-to-week."

13. **D** Oregon Revised Statutes 90.245 provides "... if a landlord deliberately uses a rental agreement containing provisions known by the landlord to be prohibited and attempts to enforce such provisions, the tenant may recover in addition to the actual damages of the tenant an amount up to three months periodic rent." Oregon Revised Statutes 90.365 gives the tenant the right to damages if the landlord fails to provide normal essential services within a reasonable time after the tenant gives the landlord notice. Oregon Revised Statutes 90.315 (2) states "The landlord shall disclose to the tenant in writing at or before the commencement of the tenancy any utility or service that the tenant pays directly to a utility or service provider that benefits, directly, the landlord or other tenants."

14. **D** Oregon Revised Statutes 90.265 provides that if a tenant installs an alternative energy device with the owner's permission, then the tenant remains the owner of the device, not the property owner, unless there is a written agreement to the contrary. The owner is not obligated to give permission, and may require that the tenant agree to take certain responsibilities as a condition of granting permission.

15. **B** Oregon Revised Statutes 90.100 (35) states "'Security deposit' means any refundable payment or deposit of money, however designated, the primary function of which is to secure the performance of a rental agreement or any part of a rental agreement, but does not mean a fee." An "applicant screening charge" is defined separately in the statute.

16. **A** Oregon Revised Statutes 90.100 (35) states "'security deposit' means any refundable payment or deposit of money, however designated, the primary function of which is to secure the performance of a rental agreement or any part of a rental agreement, but does not mean a fee." And section (3) defines "applicant screening charge" as "any payment of money required by a landlord of an applicant prior to entering into a rental agreement with that applicant for a residential dwelling unit, the purpose of which is to pay the cost of processing an application for a rental agreement for a residential dwelling unit."

17. **C** By definition, a "deposit" is refundable. The Oregon Residential Landlord and Tenant Act requires the landlord to refund the deposit, or an accounting (or partial refund and partial accounting) within 31 days after the termination of the tenancy (ORS 90.300).

18. **A** Oregon Revised Statutes 90.300 provides "a security deposit or prepaid rent shall not be required or forfeited to the landlord upon the failure of the tenant to maintain a tenancy for a minimum number of months in a month-to-month tenancy." Oregon Revised Statutes 90.300 also provides that a security deposit may be forfeit for failure to pay rent or "to repair damages to the premises caused by the tenant, not including ordinary wear and tear."

19. **D** Oregon Revised Statutes 90.300 provides "The landlord may claim from the security deposit only the amount reasonably necessary: (a) to remedy the tenant's defaults in the performance of the rental agreement including, but not limited to, unpaid rent; and (b) to repair damages to the premises caused by the tenant, not including ordinary wear and tear."

20. **C** Oregon Revised Statutes 90.300 provides "the landlord may claim from the security deposit only the amount reasonably necessary ... to remedy the tenant's defaults in the performance of the rental agreement including, but not limited to, unpaid rent; and ... to repair damages to the premises caused by the tenant, not including ordinary wear and tear."

21. **A** Oregon Revised Statutes 90.300 provides "the landlord may claim from the security deposit

only the amount reasonably necessary ... to remedy the tenant's defaults in the performance of the rental agreement including, but not limited to, unpaid rent; and ... to repair damages to the premises caused by the tenant, not including ordinary wear and tear. It further provides "a security deposit or prepaid rent shall not be required or forfeited to the landlord upon the failure of the tenant to maintain a tenancy for a minimum number of months in a month-to-month tenancy."

22. **B** Oregon Revised Statutes 90.300 provides "... a security deposit or prepaid rent shall not be required or forfeited to the landlord upon the failure of the tenant to maintain a tenancy for a minimum number of months in a month-to-month tenancy." It also provides "the holder of the landlord's interest in the premises at the time of termination of the tenancy is bound by this section," in other words, a buyer of the property inherits the original landlord's obligation to refund the security deposit. Although a buyer of the property would be well advised to ask the seller to turn over the security deposits at closing, there is no law requiring it.

23. **C** Oregon Revised Statutes 90.300 (10) provides "In order to claim all or part of any prepaid rent or security deposit, within 31 days after the termination of the tenancy and delivery of possession the landlord shall give to the tenant a written accounting that states specifically the basis or bases of the claim. The landlord shall give a separate accounting for security deposits and for prepaid rent."

24. **C** Only a "deposit" is defined by statute as refundable, so if the funds are described as a "nonrefundable fee" or "nonrefundable charge," the landlord may retain the funds without a reason and without giving the tenant an accounting.

25. **D** Oregon Revised Statutes 90.300 provides "The landlord may claim from the security deposit only the amount reasonably necessary: (a) to remedy the tenant's defaults in the performance of the rental agreement including, but not limited to, unpaid rent; and (b) to repair damages to the premises caused by the tenant, not including ordinary wear and tear." Because the tenant failed to give notice, the tenant is liable for another month's rent, for which the landlord can use the security deposit. The landlord must always give the tenant a refund of the deposit or an accounting within 31 days after the termination of the tenancy.

26. **C** Oregon Revised Statutes 90.320 specifies a long list of maintenance requirements. These are referred to as the "habitability standards." All rental agreements and leases in Oregon contain a presumed covenant of quiet enjoyment. The covenant of quiet enjoyment is the landlord's warranty that the tenant's occupancy of the premises will be uninterrupted by persons claiming a paramount or superior title.

27. **C** The landlord must refund the deposit or give the tenant an accounting (or partial refund and accounting for the rest) within 31 days after the termination of the tenancy. The penalty for the landlord's failure to refund or account for a deposit is twice the amount of the deposit, plus the tenant's attorney's fees (ORS 90.300).

28. **A** The common law in England, and therefore the common law in the United States, is that rent is always due at the end of the period. Since this does not work in modern practice, Oregon has a statute which provides that rent is always due in advance, unless there is an agreement to the contrary. There is a grace period for payment, but the rent is still due and payable at the beginning of the period.

29. **A** Late charges of all types are legal, although the Oregon Residential Landlord and Tenant Act does not permit the landlord to evict a tenant after a 72-hour or 144-hour notice if the default is merely failure to pay a late charge, although it does constitute grounds to terminate the tenancy with 30 days notice. Late charges also cannot be imposed for the first four days of delinquency (ORS 90.260). Oregon Revised Statutes 90.300 provides that a landlord may retain a security deposit (or portion thereof) for damages caused by the tenant, not including ordinary wear and tear, or for failure to pay rent, but not for failing to maintain the tenancy for a specific period of time (ORS 90.300). When a property is sold, the statute requires that the "holder of the landlord's interest at the time of the termination of the tenancy is bound by this section." It does not require the seller to turn the deposits over to the buyer, but the buyer usually demands it as a condition of the sale agreement. The statute requires the landlord to designate someone on whom the tenant can serve notices and demands. It does not specify any particular person, so the owner can designate anyone the owner desires. It is common practice to designate the premises manager.

30. **B** Heat, water and electricity are specifically stated to be essential services (ORS 90.100).

31. **D** Oregon Revised Statutes 90.320 (habitability standards) define a dwelling as uninhabitable if it lacks "a water supply approved under applicable law, which is ... capable of producing hot and cold

running water ... Connected to a sewage disposal system approved under applicable law" or "adequate heating facilities which conform to applicable law at the time of installation and maintained in good working order."

32. **B** The habitability standards of the Oregon Residential Landlord and Tenant Act require the landlord to provide adequate trash and garbage receptacles. A landlord must also maintain "Effective waterproofing and weather protection of roof and exterior walls, including windows and doors" (ORS 90.320). However, storm doors and windows are not required.

33. **C** The habitability standards of the Oregon Residential Landlord and Tenant Act require the landlord to provide adequate trash and garbage receptacles. A landlord must also maintain "Effective waterproofing and weather protection of roof and exterior walls, including windows and doors" (ORS 90.320).

34. **D** Oregon Revised Statutes 90.320 (habitability standards) requires the landlord to supply (among other matters) "electrical lighting with wiring and electrical equipment which conform to applicable law at the time of installation and maintained in good working order," "an adequate number of appropriate receptacles for garbage and rubbish in clean condition and good repair at the time of the commencement of the rental agreement," and "working locks for all dwelling entrance doors."

35. **A** Habitability standards of the Oregon Residential Landlord and Tenant Act include premises which are safe, clean and sanitary "at the commencement of the rental agreement" (ORS 90.320). There is no requirement that the landlord continue to maintain the premises clean and sanitary during the rental agreement; only at its commencement. Oregon Revised Statutes 90.320 also requires the landlord to maintain "ventilating, air conditioning ... maintained in good repair ... if supplied or required to be supplied by the landlord." Nothing requires the landlord to supply air conditioning, but if the landlord does, then the landlord must maintain it.

36. **A** Garbage containers and maintenance of air conditioners supplied by the landlord is required of the landlord under the habitability standards, but are not considered essential services. The Oregon Residential Landlord and Tenant Act defines an essential service as "(A) Heat, plumbing, hot and cold running water, gas, electricity, light fixtures, locks for exterior doors, latches for windows and any cooking appliance or refrigerator supplied or required to be supplied by the landlord; and (B) Any other service or habitability obligation imposed by the rental agreement or ORS 90.320, the lack or violation of which creates a serious threat to the tenant's health, safety or property or makes the dwelling unit unfit for occupancy" [ORS 90.100 (9)].

37. **A** The Oregon Residential Landlord and Tenant Act defines an essential service as "(A) Heat, plumbing, hot and cold running water, gas, electricity, light fixtures, locks for exterior doors, latches for windows and any cooking appliance or refrigerator supplied or required to be supplied by the landlord; and (B) Any other service or habitability obligation imposed by the rental agreement or ORS 90.320, the lack or violation of which creates a serious threat to the tenant's health, safety or property or makes the dwelling unit unfit for occupancy" [ORS 90.100 (9)].

38. **D** Oregon Revised Statutes 90.360 gives the tenant various options when the landlord fails to supply an essential service, but the tenant may choose only one of the options.

39. **C** Oregon Revised Statutes 90.365 states the tenant's remedies as "(a) Procure reasonable amounts of the essential service during the period of the landlord's noncompliance and deduct their actual and reasonable cost from the rent; (b) Recover damages based upon the diminution in the fair rental value of the dwelling unit; or (c) If the failure to supply an essential service makes the dwelling unit unsafe or unfit to occupy, procure substitute housing during the period of the landlord's noncompliance, in which case the tenant is excused from paying rent for the period of the landlord's noncompliance. In addition, the tenant may recover as damages from the landlord the actual and reasonable cost or fair and reasonable value of comparable substitute housing in excess of the rent for the dwelling unit ...."

40. **A** Oregon Revised Statutes 90.360 allows the tenant to terminate the rental agreement if the landlord fails to maintain the premises in habitable condition with 30 days notice. If the problem is an essential service, then ORS 90.365 allows the tenant to terminate the rental agreement with 48 hours notice.

41. **A** Oregon Revised Statutes 90.360 provides that a tenant may not terminate the tenancy for lack of an essential service if the problem was caused by the tenant, the tenant's family or other persons on the premises with the tenant's permission. In addition, the tenant must first notify the landlord and

give the landlord the statutory time period in which to remedy the breach.

42. **B** In the event the tenant gives the landlord notice of lack of an essential service and the landlord deliberately refuses or is grossly negligent in failing to supply an essential service within seven days (48 hours if the lack of essential service poses an imminent health or safety hazard), the tenant can (a) procure the essential service and deduct the cost from the rent due or, (b) recover from the landlord damages for to the extent of the diminished rental value of the premises or (c) procure reasonable substitute housing at the landlord's expense, and is not required to pay rent on the landlord's premises during the time the landlord continues to fail to comply (ORS 90.360).

43. **B** If the landlord deliberately neglects or refuses to supply an essential service the tenant may secure the essential service and deduct the cost of it from the rent, among other remedies. Oregon Revised Statutes 90.100 (9) defines an essential service as "(A) Heat, plumbing, hot and cold running water, gas, electricity, light fixtures, locks for exterior doors, latches for windows and any cooking appliance or refrigerator supplied or required to be supplied by the landlord; and (B) Any other service or habitability obligation imposed by the rental agreement or ORS 90.320, the lack or violation of which creates a serious threat to the tenant's health, safety or property or makes the dwelling unit unfit for occupancy."

44. **B** Electricity is defined as an essential service (ORS 90.100 (9). In the case of an essential service, the tenant may give the landlord a notice that the tenancy will terminate in seven days if the landlord fails to correct the problem, or 48 hours if the essential service would cause imminent harm. If the landlord has repairs made within the seven days (or 48 hours), the notice to terminate the tenancy is rescinded. However, if the landlord deliberately neglects or refuses to comply within the seven days (or 48 hours), then the tenant may 1) move out or 2) have the problem corrected and deduct the cost from the rent or, 3) recover from the landlord damages equal to the loss of rental value or, 4) move to alternative quarters, in which case the landlord must pay the rent on the alternative quarters up the fair rental value of the subject property.

45. **B** The Oregon Residential Landlord and Tenant Act provides that it is the landlord's responsibility to see that the property meets certain habitability standards. However, the same section also provides that the landlord and the tenant may agree that the tenant is to perform certain maintenance if the purpose of the agreement is not for the landlord to evade responsibility for maintenance and the tenant receives reasonable consideration. While the landlord may not be responsible for the maintenance in this case, common law provides that if the landlord does the work, the tenant has a right to presume that the work was done properly.

46. **C** The Oregon Residential Landlord and Tenant Act provides that it is the landlord's responsibility to see that the property meets certain habitability standards. These habitability standards include "effective waterproofing and weather protection" (ORS 90.320). However, ORS 90.325 provides that the tenant cannot "deliberately or negligently destroy, deface, damage, impair or remove any part of the premises or knowingly permit any person to do so." Oregon Revised Statutes 90.400 allows the landlord to give the tenant notice to terminate the tenancy for cause if the tenant violates this requirement.

47. **A** The Oregon Residential Landlord and Tenant Act provides that it is the landlord's responsibility to see that the property meets certain habitability standards. These habitability standards include "a water supply ... capable of producing hot and cold running water" (ORS 90.320). However, the same section also provides that the landlord and the tenant may agree that the tenant is to perform certain maintenance if the purpose of the agreement is not for the landlord to evade responsibility for maintenance and the tenant receives consideration.

48. **D** The Oregon Residential Landlord and Tenant Act provides that the tenant may not waive the tenant's rights under the act, therefore the clause in the agreement is void. If there is a lack of an essential service the tenant can (a) procure the essential service and deduct the cost from the rent due or, (b) recover from the landlord damages for to the extent of the diminished rental value of the premises or (c) procure reasonable substitute housing at the landlord's expense, and is not required to pay rent on the landlord's premises during the time the landlord continues to fail to comply (ORS 90.360).

49. **B** Locks and keys for all entrance doors are required under the habitability section of the Oregon Residential Landlord and Tenant Act. Locks and keys would be considered an essential service. Oregon Revised Statutes 90.380 provides damages up to two months rent or twice the actual damages, plus the

tenant's attorney's fees if the landlord knowingly rents property which has been posted as unlawful to occupy. The Oregon Residential Landlord and Tenant Act prohibits a landlord from discriminating in renting because the tenant is physically impaired and has an "assistance animal." Discrimination includes charging an additional nonrefundable fee or an excessive deposit. Tenants who have been illegally discriminated against on this basis may recover damages from the landlord up to $200 plus their attorney's fees.

50. **B** Oregon Revised Statutes 90.325 (9) requires the tenant to "Behave and require other persons on the premises with the consent of the tenant to behave in a manner that will not disturb the peaceful enjoyment of the premises by neighbors." And ORS 90.400 allows the landlord to give the tenant 30 days notice to terminate the tenancy for cause if the tenant violates ORS 90.325.

51. **C** The tenant must "use the parts of the premises ... in a reasonable manner considering the purposes for which they were designed and intended" (ORS 90.325). The garage and driveway were designed and intended for storage, not repair work. However, washing a car is not considered repair work.

52. **B** Oregon Revised Statutes 90.245 states "a rental agreement may not provide that the tenant ... agrees to waive or forego rights or remedies under [the Residential Landlord-Tenant Act].

53. **A** Oregon Revised Statutes 90.340 states "The rental agreement may require that the tenant give actual notice to the landlord of any anticipated extended absence from the premises in excess of seven days no later than the first day of the extended absence." Oregon Revised Statutes 90.245 states "A rental agreement may not provide that the tenant: ... agrees to the exculpation or limitation of any liability arising as a result of the other party's willful misconduct or negligence or to indemnify the other party for that liability or costs connected therewith."

54. **A** Oregon Revised Statutes 90.340 provides "... The rental agreement may require that the tenant give actual notice to the landlord of any anticipated extended absence from the premises in excess of seven days no later than the first day of the extended absence." Oregon Revised Statutes 90.150 permits verbal notices given personally to the landlord or tenant or left on the landlord's or tenant's answering machine.

55. **C** The Oregon Residential Landlord and Tenant Act provides that a landlord may impose reasonable rules which normally take effect immediately (ORS 90.262). The rules must be for the convenience, safety or welfare of the tenants, to preserve the landlord's property, or to make a fair distribution of services. The rules also must be applied to all tenants in a fair manner. An exception is that a rule is not valid without the tenant's agreement if the rule "works a substantial modification of the [tenant's] bargain."

56. **D** Oregon Revised Statutes 90.262 allows the landlord to adopt rules which can go into effect immediately. If the rule "works a substantial modification of the bargain," then the rule does not become effective until the tenant has agreed to it in writing. Rules must be for the convenience, safety or welfare of the tenants, to preserve the landlord's property, or to make a fair distribution of services. Rules must be applied fairly and equally to all tenants.

57. **C** Oregon Revised Statutes 90.262 states that a rule is not enforceable against the tenant unless "(a) Its purpose is to promote the convenience, safety or welfare of the tenants in the premises, preserve the landlord's property from abusive use, or make a fair distribution of services and facilities held out for the tenants generally; (b) It is reasonably related to the purpose for which it is adopted; (c) It applies to all tenants in the premises in a fair manner; (d) It is sufficiently explicit in its prohibition, direction or limitation of the tenant's conduct to fairly inform the tenant of what the tenant must or must not do to comply; (e) It is not for the purpose of evading the obligations of the landlord; and (f) The tenant has written notice of it at the time the tenant enters into the rental agreement, or when it is adopted. (2) If a rule or regulation adopted after the tenant enters into the rental agreement works a substantial modification of the bargain, it is not valid unless the tenant consents to it in writing."

58. **D** Oregon Revised Statutes 90.325 requires the tenant to "Behave and require other persons on the premises with the consent of the tenant to behave in a manner that will not disturb the peaceful enjoyment of the premises by neighbors." Oregon Revised Statutes 90.340 provides "The rental agreement may require that the tenant give actual notice to the landlord of any anticipated extended absence from the premises in excess of seven days ..." Oregon Revised Statutes 90.322 (2) states that "A tenant shall not unreasonably withhold consent from the landlord to enter" for certain purposes. It also states that the landlord must give the tenant 24 hours notice, except in certain cases, one of which is an emergency.

Mobile homes (manufactured dwellings) are covered in this respect the same as other rental property. The landlord may adopt rules which usually can go into effect immediately.

59. **D** Oregon Revised Statutes 90.322 requires 24 hours notice before entering the premises. The statute lists exemptions for emergencies and when the landlord enters under court order.

60. **C** Oregon Revised Statutes 90.322 grants the landlord access to the premises upon giving the tenant 24 hours notice. The landlord need not give the tenant 24 hours notice for purposes of showing the property to prospective buyers, provided the landlord and tenant have agreed that the landlord should have the right to do so and the tenant receives reasonable consideration therefor. There is also an exception for emergency repairs, but if the repairs are not an emergency, then the landlord must still give the 24 hours notice. However, if the repairs were requested by the tenant then the landlord need not give notice to enter the premises for purposes of making the repairs.

61. **C** Oregon Revised Statutes 90.322 (2) states that "A tenant shall not unreasonably withhold consent to the landlord to enter" for certain purposes. It also states that the landlord must give the tenant 24 hours' notice, except in certain cases, one of which is an emergency. Oregon Revised Statutes 90.325 requires the tenant to "Behave and require other persons on the premises with the consent of the tenant to behave in a manner that will not disturb the peaceful enjoyment of the premises by neighbors."

62. **D** Oregon Revised Statutes 90.322 (8) states "If the landlord makes an unlawful entry or a lawful entry in an unreasonable manner or makes repeated demands for entry otherwise lawful but that have the effect of unreasonably harassing the tenant, the tenant may obtain injunctive relief to prevent the reoccurrence of the conduct or may terminate the rental agreement pursuant to ORS 90.360 (1). In addition, the tenant may recover actual damages not less than an amount equal to one week's rent in the case of a week-to-week tenancy or one month's rent in all other cases." Oregon Revised Statutes 90.310 (1) requires the landlord to notify a new tenant if the premises are the subject of a foreclosure action and provides "(2) If the tenant moves as a result of a circumstance that the landlord failed to disclose as required by subsection (1) of this section, the tenant may recover twice the actual damages or twice the monthly rent, whichever is greater, and all prepaid rent, in addition to any other remedy that the law may provide." Oregon Revised Statutes 90.315 requires disclosure if any of a tenant's future utility bills will benefit others in the premises, and provides "If a landlord fails to [disclose that future utility bills will benefit others] ... the tenant may recover from the landlord an amount equal to one month's periodic rent or twice the amount wrongfully charged to the tenant, whichever is greater."

63. **B** Oregon Revised Statutes 90.245 provides up to three months rent as punitive damages in addition to the tenant's actual damages and attorney's fees if the landlord attempts to enforce a provision in a rental agreement which is prohibited. Oregon Revised Statutes 90.315 provides for the greater of twice the tenant's actual damages or one months rent as damages if the landlord fails to disclose that part of a tenant's utility bill will benefit other tenants as well. Oregon Revised Statutes 90.365 allows the tenant to recover damages from the landlord for failure to supply an essential service equal to the diminution of rental value caused by the failure, among other possible remedies the tenant may choose.

64. **C** Oregon Revised Statutes 90.427 (4) states "If the tenant remains in possession without the landlord's consent after expiration of the term of the rental agreement or its termination, the landlord may bring an action for possession. In addition, the landlord may recover from the tenant any actual damages resulting from the tenant holding over, including the value of any rent accruing from the expiration or termination of the rental agreement until the landlord knows or should know that the tenant has relinquished possession to the landlord ...." Oregon Revised Statutes 90.322 (7) provides "If the tenant refuses to allow lawful access, the landlord may obtain injunctive relief to compel access or may terminate the rental agreement pursuant to ORS 90.400 (1) and take possession in the manner provided in ORS 105.105 to 105.168. In addition, the landlord may recover actual damages."

65. **D** Retaliatory conduct is any action adverse to the interests of a tenant which the landlord takes because the tenant exercised any of the tenant's rights listed in ORS 90.385. These include the right to complain about discrimination, the right to form a tenants' union and the right to complain to building and housing code enforcement agencies.

66. **B** Retaliatory conduct means any action against a tenant when the tenant has exercised any of certain rights. These rights include complaining about

habitability standards, complaining about discriminatory conduct by the landlord, and forming or joining a tenants union, among others. Retaliatory conduct subjects the landlord to damages in favor of the tenant. It is not retaliatory conduct, however, if the landlord takes action against a tenant because the tenant complained about a problem which the tenant caused.

67. **D** Oregon Revised Statutes 90.360 states "... if there is a material noncompliance by the landlord with the rental agreement or a noncompliance with ORS 90.320 or 90.730 [the habitability standards], the tenant may deliver a written notice to the landlord ..." The Oregon Residential Landlord and Tenant Act defines "retaliatory conduct" as any act of the landlord adverse to the tenant's interests because the tenant exercised any of several rights under the Act. These rights include the right to file certain complaints and the right to form and join a tenant's association.

68. **D** The Oregon Residential Landlord and Tenant Act defines "retaliatory conduct" as any act of the landlord adverse to the tenant's interests because the tenant exercised any of several rights under the Act. These rights include the right to file certain complaints and the right to form and join a tenant's association.

69. **B** Oregon Revised Statutes 90.385 prohibits the landlord from taking "retaliatory conduct" against the tenant because the tenant exercised certain rights. Among these rights is the right to complain to a governmental agency regarding a "building, health or housing code materially affecting health or safety." Oregon Revised Statutes 90.385 also states "notwithstanding ... this section, a landlord may bring an action for possession if ... the violation of the applicable building or housing code was caused by lack of reasonable care by the tenant ...."

70. **D** Oregon Revised Statutes 90.385 prohibits retaliatory conduct against a tenant for exercising certain rights the tenant has. These rights include the right to form a tenants union, the right to complain to building and housing code enforcement agencies, complaining that the property fails to meet the habitability standards of the Oregon Landlord and Tenant Act, among others.

71. **D** Oregon Revised Statutes 90.427 provides that either the landlord or the tenant may terminate a month-to-month tenancy with 30 days notice to the other, and neither requires a cause. And ORS 90.300 (11) provides "The security deposit or prepaid rent or portion thereof not claimed ... shall be returned to the tenant not later than 31 days after the termination of the tenancy and delivery of possession to the landlord." Electrical lighting is considered an essential service that a landlord must provide.

72. **C** Oregon Revised Statutes 90.340 states "The rental agreement may require that the tenant give actual notice to the landlord of any anticipated extended absence from the premises in excess of seven days ...." In a week-to-week or month-to-month tenancy the tenant must always give notice to terminate. The amount of time depends on whether it is for cause or not, and if for cause, what the cause is.

73. **C** Oregon Revised Statutes 90.425 states "... the specified date by which a tenant, lienholder or owner must contact a landlord to arrange for the disposition of abandoned personal property shall be: (a) for abandoned recreational vehicles, manufactured dwellings or floating homes, not less than 45 days after personal delivery or first class mailing of the notice; or (b) for all other abandoned personal property, not less than five days after personal delivery or eight days after first class mailing of the notice." The statute further provides that if the tenant fails to respond to the notice, and the market value is $500 or less, the landlord may dispose of the property. If it is greater than $500, the landlord must proceed with a public sale.

74. **C** Oregon Revised Statutes 90.425 provides in part that the landlord may "destroy or otherwise dispose of the personal property if the landlord reasonably determines that: (A) for a manufactured dwelling or floating home, the current tax assessed value is $8,000 or less as determined by the county assessor; or (B) for all other personal property, the current fair market value is $500 or less or so low that the cost of storage and conducting a public sale probably exceeds the amount that would be realized from the sale; or (c) consistent with paragraphs (a) and (b) of this subsection, sell certain items and destroy or otherwise dispose of the remaining personal property." It further provides that, after concluding a sale of personal property, the landlord may "deduct from the proceeds of the sale: (A) The reasonable or actual cost of notice, storage and sale; and (B) Unpaid rent."

75. **A** Oregon Revised Statutes 90.420 states "(1) A lien or security interest on behalf of the landlord in the tenant's household goods is not enforceable unless perfected before October 5, 1973" and "(2) Distraint for rent is abolished."

76. **D** Oregon Revised Statutes 90.375 states "If a landlord unlawfully removes or excludes the tenant from the premises, seriously attempts or seriously threatens unlawfully to remove or exclude the tenant from the premises or willfully diminishes or seriously attempts or seriously threatens unlawfully to diminish services to the tenant by interrupting or causing the interruption of heat, running water, hot water, electric or other essential service, the tenant may obtain injunctive relief to recover possession or may terminate the rental agreement and recover an amount up to two months periodic rent or twice the actual damages sustained by the tenant, whichever is greater. If the rental agreement is terminated the landlord shall return all security deposits and prepaid rent recoverable under ORS 90.300. The tenant need not terminate the rental agreement, obtain injunctive relief or recover possession to recover damages under this section."

77. **D** Forcing a tenant out by shutting off services or locking the tenant out is called constructive eviction. Oregon Revised Statutes 90.375 states "If a landlord unlawfully removes or excludes the tenant from the premises, seriously attempts or seriously threatens unlawfully to remove or exclude the tenant from the premises or willfully diminishes or seriously attempts or seriously threatens unlawfully to diminish services to the tenant by interrupting or causing the interruption of heat, running water, hot water, electric or other essential service, the tenant may obtain injunctive relief to recover possession or may terminate the rental agreement and recover an amount up to two months periodic rent or twice the actual damages sustained by the tenant, whichever is greater. If the rental agreement is terminated the landlord shall return all security deposits and prepaid rent recoverable under ORS 90.300. The tenant need not terminate the rental agreement, obtain injunctive relief or recover possession to recover damages under this section."

78. **C** Oregon Revised Statutes 90.600 requires notices of rent increases to be given in writing and ORS 90.400 and 90.427 require notices to terminate rental agreements must also be in writing. Oregon Revised Statutes 90.155 states "where this chapter requires written notice, service or delivery of that written notice shall be executed by one or more of the following methods: (a) Personal delivery to the landlord or tenant; (b) First class mail to the landlord or tenant; or (c) If a written rental agreement so provides, both first class mail and attachment to a designated location …."

79. **B** The phrase "suit for forcible entry and wrongful detainer," or frequently just "forcible entry and detainer," is an older expression for "suit to evict."

80. **A** Oregon Revised Statutes 90.240 provides "Rent may not be increased without a 30-day written notice thereof in the case of a month-to-month tenancy or a seven-day written notice thereof in the case of a week-to-week tenancy." Oregon Revised Statutes 90.300 states "a security deposit or prepaid rent shall not be required or forfeited to the landlord upon the failure of the tenant to maintain a tenancy for a minimum number of months in a month-to-month tenancy."

81. **B** Oregon Revised Statutes 90.245 prohibits a landlord from entering into a rental agreement where the tenant agrees to a limitation of the landlord's liability. If the landlord does so, the provision is not enforceable.

82. **A** Either the tenant or the landlord can give the other notice without cause if the tenancy is periodic. For a month-to-month tenancy, the notice required is 31 days and a ten-day notice is required if the tenant is from week to week. Shorter notices are permitted for certain wrongful acts, i.e., failing to pay the rent. The Residential Landlord and Tenant Act permits periodic tenancies only if they are month-to-month or week-to-week. A lease cannot be terminated without cause.

83. **B** Oregon Revised Statutes 90.400 provides for a 72-hour notice after a seven-day grace period for nonpayment of rent. If the tenancy is month-to-month and the rental agreement provides, the landlord may give a 144-hour notice after a four-day grace period. The notice period is not shortened if the landlord waits longer than seven days before serving it on the tenant.

84. **B** The landlord can terminate the rental agreement for failure to pay rent only after a seven-day grace period and 72 hours notice, or 144 hours notice after a four-day grace period. The landlord can give 24 hours notice if the tenant is harming, or threatening to harm other tenants. Disturbing others generally requires a 30-day notice.

85. **D** Oregon Revised Statutes 90.400 permits the landlord to give the tenant 24 hours notice if "The tenant or someone in the tenant's control intentionally inflicts any substantial damage to the premises or the tenant's pet inflicts substantial damage to the premises on more than one occasion." In addition to giving the tenant notice, if the tenant harms the premises the landlord is entitled to recover for

the damages from the tenant. The landlord can also seek a court order enjoining the tenant from further harming the premises.

86. **A** If a tenant refuses to move after proper notice, the landlord can recover possession by eviction but can only recover damages in the amount of unpaid rent and the landlord's attorney's fees. The landlord must normally give 24 hours notice to enter the premises, including for purposes of showing the premises to prospective new tenants. If the landlord and the tenant enter into a separate agreement for consideration, the tenant can waive the 24 hours notice for showing the property to prospective buyers. Tenants have rights, including the right to form a tenants' union. If the landlord takes any action against a tenant who exercises this right it is called retaliatory conduct and the landlord is liable to the tenant for two months rent as punitive damages.

87. **D** The landlord may give the tenant notice that the tenancy will terminate in ten days unless the tenant removes a pet that is unauthorized. The landlord must ordinarily give the tenant 24 hours notice before entering the premises, but an emergency is excepted. A provision in a rental agreement requiring the tenant to give the landlord notice of any absence in excess of seven days is enforceable. Note that this is an optional provision. If the agreement is silent, then the tenant has no obligation to give the notice.

88. **B** Oregon Revised Statutes 90.400 provides that the landlord may terminate a rental agreement or lease with 24 hours notice for injury to others caused by the tenant or the tenant's pet or others on the premises with the permission of the tenant, or if the tenant has abandoned the premises and the premises are occupied by someone other than the tenant. Nonpayment of rent requires either 72 hours or 144 hours notice.

89. **C** Oregon Revised Statutes 90.405 requires the landlord to give a tenant ten days notice to remove an unpermitted pet or terminate the tenancy. If the tenant commits the same offense within six months the landlord can simply give the tenant ten days notice to terminate the tenancy and does not have to give the tenant the right to reinstate the tenancy by removing the pet. Oregon Revised Statutes 90.400 provides that if the tenant breaches the rental agreement in a manner affecting health or safety the landlord can give the tenant notice that the tenancy will terminate in 30 days if the tenant does not remedy the breach within 14 days. If the same breach occurs within six months, the landlord can simply give the tenant ten days notice and does not have to give the tenant the opportunity to cure the breach.

90. **C** Oregon Revised Statutes 90.405 permits the landlord to give the tenant ten days notice to terminate the rental agreement if the tenant keeps an unauthorized pet. Failing to pay rent by the seventh day after the due date allows the landlord to give the tenant a 72-hour notice. If the tenancy is month to month, the landlord has the option of giving the tenant a 144-hour notice on the fourth day instead.

91. **D** Oregon Revised Statutes 90.415 (11) states "A landlord who accepts rent after the giving of a notice of termination by the landlord or the tenant, other than a nonpayment of rent notice, does not waive the right to terminate on that notice if: (a) The landlord accepts rent prorated to the termination date specified in the notice; or (b) Within six days after receipt of the rent payment, the landlord refunds at least the unused balance of the rent prorated for the period beyond the termination date."

92. **D** Oregon Revised Statutes 90.415 (11) provides in part "A landlord who accepts rent after the giving of a notice of termination by the landlord or the tenant, other than a nonpayment of rent notice, does not waive the right to terminate on that notice if: (a) The landlord accepts rent prorated to the termination date specified in the notice; or (b) Within six days after receipt of the rent payment, the landlord refunds at least the unused balance of the rent prorated for the period beyond the termination date."

93. **A** Oregon Revised Statutes 90.415 (11) provides in part "A landlord who accepts rent after the giving of a notice of termination by the landlord or the tenant, other than a nonpayment of rent notice, does not waive the right to terminate on that notice if: (a) The landlord accepts rent prorated to the termination date specified in the notice; or (b) Within six days after receipt of the rent payment, the landlord refunds at least the unused balance of the rent prorated for the period beyond the termination date."

94. **D** The fact that the landlord wanted the tenant to move so the landlord could move in is irrelevant. If the tenancy is month to month, the landlord need not have a reason for the notice. Oregon Revised Statutes 90.415 (11) provides in part "A landlord who accepts rent after the giving of a notice of termination by the landlord or the tenant, other than a nonpayment of rent notice, does not waive the right to terminate on that notice if: (a) The landlord ac-

cepts rent prorated to the termination date specified in the notice; or (b) Within six days after receipt of the rent payment, the landlord refunds at least the unused balance of the rent prorated for the period beyond the termination date."

95. **B** A landlord has a duty to mitigate. This means that if the premises can be re-rented, the landlord must apply any funds received from the new tenant to the obligation of the old tenant. The old tenant, of course, is responsible for any obligations not paid by the new tenant.

96. **B** Oregon Revised Statutes 90.427 provides "Unless otherwise agreed, rent is uniformly apportionable from day to day," so the tenant will only be responsible for 20 days' rent. If the rent is $975 per month and May has 31 days, then the daily amount is $31.45 ($975 ÷ 31 = $31.4516). Multiplying this by 20 days gives us a prorate of $629 ($31.4516 × 20 = $629.03).

97. **B** Rent is normally prorated on an "actual days" basis. If the rent is due on the first, the presumption is that it is being paid for the coming month (May). Since the tenancy will terminate on May 20, the tenant only owes for 20 days rent. To calculate 20 days rent, first take the monthly rent ($600) and divide it by the number of days in the month (31) to find the daily factor. This comes to $19.35 ($600 ÷ 31 = $19.354838). Now multiply this by the number of days (20) to find the amount of rent the tenant owes. The answer is $387.09 ($19354838 × 20 = $387.09676).

98. **D** Oregon Revised Statutes 90.405 requires the landlord to give a tenant ten days notice to remove an unpermitted pet or terminate the tenancy. Tenants are entitled to 24 hours notice before granting the landlord access except in case of emergency, court order, to allow entrance to workers, or subsequent to an agreement with the landlord to waive the 24 hours notice in order to show the premises to prospective buyers (ORS 90.335). Oregon Revised Statutes 90.410 allows a rental agreement to contain a provision requiring the tenant to give the landlord notice of an absence in excess of seven days. If the agreement contains such a clause, and the tenant fails to give the landlord notice, after seven days the landlord is entitled to assume the premises are abandoned.

99. **C** If a tenant remains in possession without permission ORS 90.427 (4) provides "If the tenant remains in possession without the landlord's consent after expiration of the term of the rental agreement or its termination, the landlord may bring an action for possession. In addition, the landlord may recover from the tenant any actual damages resulting from the tenant holding over, including the value of any rent accruing from the expiration or termination of the rental agreement until the landlord knows or should know that the tenant has relinquished possession to the landlord. Oregon Revised Statutes 90.322 requires the tenant to grant the landlord reasonable access to the premises under prescribed conditions, and if the tenant unlawfully refuses the landlord, ORS 90.920 allows the landlord to obtain an injunction forcing the tenant to allow the landlord access and the landlord may also recover actual damages from the tenant, including attorney's fees.

100. **B** Under the Oregon Residential Landlord and Tenant Act, a landlord may give a tenant 24 hours notice to terminate the tenancy if "(a) The tenant, someone in the tenant's control or the tenant's pet seriously threatens immediately to inflict personal injury, or inflicts any substantial personal injury, upon the landlord, the landlord's agent or other tenants; (b) The tenant, someone in the tenant's control, or the tenant's pet inflicts any substantial personal injury upon a neighbor living in the immediate vicinity of the premises or upon a person other than the tenant on the premises with permission of the landlord or another tenant; (c) The tenant or someone in the tenant's control intentionally inflicts any substantial damage to the premises or the tenant's pet inflicts substantial damage to the premises on more than one occasion; (d) The tenant has vacated the premises, the person in possession is holding contrary to a written rental agreement that prohibits subleasing the premises to another or allowing another person to occupy the premises without the written permission of the landlord, and the landlord has not knowingly accepted rent from the person in possession; or (e) The tenant, someone in the tenant's control or the tenant's pet commits any act that is outrageous in the extreme, on the premises or in the immediate vicinity of the premises. An act that is 'outrageous in the extreme' is an act not described in paragraphs (a) to (c) of this subsection, but is similar in degree and is one that a reasonable person in that community would consider to be so offensive as to warrant termination of the tenancy within 24 hours, considering the seriousness of the act or the risk to others. Such an act is more extreme or serious than an act that warrants a 30-day termination under subsection (1) of this section. An act that is 'outrageous

in the extreme' includes, but is not limited to, the following acts by a person: (A) Prostitution or promotion of prostitution, as described in ORS 167.007 and 167.012; (B) Manufacture or delivery of a controlled substance, as described in ORS 475.005 but not including delivery as described in ORS 475.992 (2)(b); (C) Intimidation, as described in ORS 166.155 and 166.165; or (D) Burglary as described in ORS 164.215 and 164.225." Failing to pay the rent requires a 72-hour notice after a seven-day grace period.

101. **D** Oregon Revised Statutes 90.525 (relating to manufactured housing, floating homes and facilities space rental) provides "no landlord shall impose conditions of rental or occupancy which unreasonably restrict the tenant or prospective tenant in choosing a fuel supplier, furnishings, goods, services or accessories." Oregon Revised Statutes 90.680 states "the landlord shall not exact a commission or fee for the sale of a manufactured dwelling or floating home on a rented space unless the landlord has acted as agent for the seller pursuant to written contract" and "the landlord may not deny the tenant the right to place a "for sale" sign on or in a manufactured dwelling or floating home owned by the tenant. The size, placement and character of such signs shall be subject to reasonable rules of the landlord."

102. **D** Oregon Revised Statutes 90.680 requires the landlord of a mobile home park to allow the tenant to sell the mobile home without having to remove it from the park. This includes the tenant's right to place a "for sale" sign on the dwelling, although the "size, placement and character" of the sign is subject to the landlord's reasonable rules. However, the landlord is entitled to require that the prospective purchaser make application for rent of the space if the purchaser wishes to leave the dwelling in the park and the landlord has the right to reject the purchaser for cause.

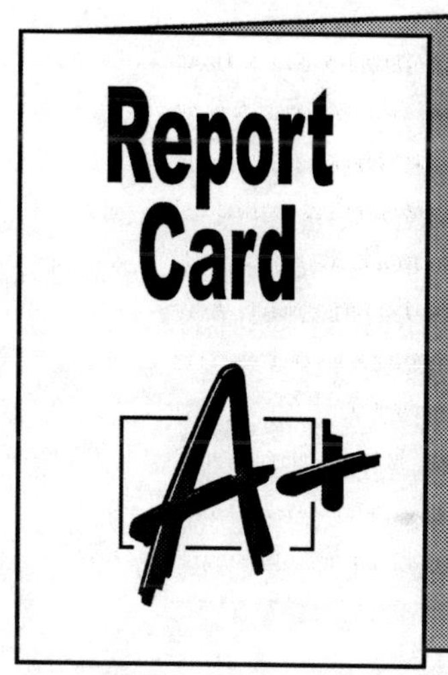

COMMERCIAL LEASING

When people think of property management their minds almost always assume residential properties. While residential property management may account for the majority of property management activity, nonresidential management is no less important. It is especially significant for real estate brokers who specialize in commercial investment property. Being able to manage an office building for a buyer goes hand in glove with commercial brokerage.

There are many differences between managing residential property and commercial property. One difference is the manner in which the agent is typically compensated. In residential management it is customary to collect the rent for the owner, so the property manager normally collects the management fee as a percentage of the rent receipts. In addition, a residential property manager would charge an extra fee for re-renting the property, perhaps half of the new tenant's first month's rent or so.

In commercial management properties are typically leased because businesses need to know they have the right to a location for a period of time. The role of the property manager becomes less a rent collector and more a mere broker of the lease. In the majority of commercial leases the tenant pays the rent directly to the owner. The property manager just brings the parties together, much as a real estate broker brings a buyer and seller together and negotiates the terms of the transaction.

Since the property manager is not collecting the rent, there is nothing from which to collect ongoing management fees. The solution is for the property manager to charge for the negotiation of the lease in more or less the same way that a real estate broker would charge for arranging a sale – a straight percentage of the rent payments over the total term of the lease.

NOTES

As with any compensation arrangement, the amount is negotiable. But there is a problem with charging a commission for arranging a lease. A sale is a transaction that is over and done with. A lease may last for decades. Should the property manager charge the same percentage of the rent over the entire term?

Most owners would object. After all, what would happen if the tenant's circumstances changed and the parties voluntarily terminated the lease early? Or if the owner ended up having to evict the tenant after a few years of a long term lease? For these reasons it is customary to charge a higher percentage of the rent for the first years, diminishing over the later years of the lease.

Renewals are another matter to consider when calculating leasing commissions. The agent normally expects to be paid an additional commission if the parties renew the lease, although the amount is typically considerably less than the original fee.

Lease terms

In commercial (and once in a while even in residential) transactions, there are special terms that are sometimes incorporated into a lease. Brokers and property managers also have special names for certain types of leases.

A ***flat lease*** is a lease where the rental payments are equal throughout the term. It is also sometimes called a ***straight lease*** or ***fixed lease***. In contrast, many leases call for changes in the amount of rent. A ***graduated lease*** (also sometimes called a ***step-up lease***) is a lease where the lease provides for pre-agreed increases in the rent. The part of the lease where this is stipulated is called the ***escalator*** or ***escalation clause***. The rent due under a lease can also be tied to an index (called an ***index lease***), such as the Consumer Price Index. Many times the lease will just provide that the rent will be adjusted annually according to the increase in the owner's operating costs and property taxes.

As mentioned in the first section, there is an implied covenant of quiet enjoyment in all leases and rental agreements. While a lessor of a residential property cannot escape this, owners of commercial properties frequently limit their liability with an ***exculpation clause*** in the agreement.

A ***percentage lease*** is common in retail centers such as shopping malls. The lease payments are usually stipulated as a base, plus a percentage of the tenant's gross sales. The effect of the percentage lease is to make the lessor the "partner" of the lessee so the lessor has an interest in encouraging shoppers to patronize the lessee's business. At the same time, it provides the lessor with funds which can be used to promote the entire shopping center. The more the lessor promotes the shopping center, the greater the number of customers, resulting in greater sales, thereby generating greater rent income to cover the cost of the promotion.

In most cases the percentage portion of the rent is based on the gross sales, rather than the tenant's net income. The reason for this is the difficulty in defining what constitutes expense. Basing the rent on gross sales causes fewer disputes between the landlord and the tenant. Even so, the lease typically has exclusions for certain items. For example, a typical percentage lease would state that income the tenant receives from interest earned on customer accounts is not considered part of gross sales.

When a lease is based on the tenant's gross sales and nothing else, then it is called a ***straight percentage lease***. In most cases the landlord would prefer a base rent, in which case it is called a ***fixed minimum percentage lease***. In a fixed minimum percentage lease the portion of the rent attributable to the percentage is called the ***overage rent***. It is also common to find a ceiling on the gross sales that are subject to the rent percentage calculation.

Percentage leases also frequently contain a ***recapture clause***. This clause allows the landlord to terminate the lease if the tenant's gross sales fall below a stated mini-

NOTES

mum. A landlord desires the recapture clause, not just because it increases the landlord's rent income, but because a tenant who is not performing is hurting all other tenants in the shopping center as well. For this reason a shopping center lease also typically requires each tenant to participate in cooperative advertising.

Shopping centers are very dependent on the existence of one or more ***anchor tenants***. An anchor tenant is any major tenant such as a large department or food store or similar type of business. Without an anchor tenant, the shopping center is likely to wither and die, for it is the anchor tenant which draws the majority of the customers. Because they have great bargaining power, it is common for the anchor tenant to be able to negotiate an ***anchor lease*** at very low rental rates.

The owner of the shopping center typically makes the profit on the smaller tenants. While this may seem undemocratic, the reality is that without the anchor tenant there would be no shopping center in the first place. This is easier to grasp when you consider the process a developer must go through to create a shopping center. Ultimately everything depends on financing, so the first step after identifying the site is to obtain financing commitments. Large shopping centers are typically financed by insurance companies and other large funds. These lenders look first for anchor tenants and will not issue a commitment without first seeing a signed anchor lease.

Which expenses each party will be responsible for during the term of a lease will normally be spelled out in the lease. Real estate agents use the relative terms ***net*** and ***gross*** to describe leases. The more net the lease, the fewer expenses the lessor will pay, and vice-versa.

Investors use the special term ***net, net, net lease*** (or ***triple net lease***) to describe a lease where the tenant pays all of the expenses, including maintenance, insurance and property taxes. The opposite of a net, net, net lease is a ***full-service lease***, where the landlord provides all services, usually including heat, light and janitorial service. Of course, lessors and lessees may negotiate a lease which is anywhere between these two extremes.

When a commercial tenant leases an entire structure, the owner typically desires to lease it on a net, net, net basis, especially if the lease is relatively long term. The usual reason is that the tenant will likely make improvements to the property. The improvements increase the costs, especially the property taxes. Therefore, the owner's inclination is to let the tenant pay such added costs. By the same token, the tenant also prefers a net, net, net lease because the tenant can better control costs such as utilities and janitorial. The result is that both lessor and lessee prefer the net, net, net lease.

On the other hand, if the structure is large and is occupied by various tenants, it is not usually practical to provide individual utility meters and separate janitorial services for each tenant. Apportioning the insurance and property taxes would also be difficult. As a result, such properties are typically leased on a full-service basis.

Many times a lease contains an ***expansion option***. An expansion option is a clause which allows the tenant to lease additional space, usually after a period of time. In reality most landlords would never agree to an expansion option if it requires them to leave premises unrented in case the tenant wishes to exercise the expansion option. However, an expansion option is sometimes used where it gives the tenant the right to additional space from neighboring space when the tenant in that space vacates.

A ***ground lease*** is a lease of the bare land only, usually on a long-term basis and where the tenant typically intends to build a structure on the land. The term of the lease will usually be for a term equal to the projected economic life of the building which the lessee contemplates building. An advantage to the lessee is that the cost of the land can be cheaper this way, and there are potential income tax benefits for both lessor and lessee. If the lessee had purchased the land the only tax write-off would be the cost recov-

Notes

ery on the building because you cannot claim cost recovery on land, whereas with the ground lease the lease payments are also deductible as a business expense. At the same time, using a ground lease can sometimes avoid capital gains tax that the lessor would have had to pay if the lessor had sold the land.

If the lessee wishes to finance the building to be built on ground leased land, there are certain problems which must be addressed. The lender will want to make sure the building is secured as collateral for the loan. Normally a lender would take a note (evidence of the debt) from the borrower, and also a mortgage or trust deed to create a lien on the real property and make it the collateral for the note. In this case, the mortgage or trust deed would have to be a mortgage or trust deed on the leasehold interest, since that is all the borrower holds.

However, an eviction has the effect of extinguishing a lease. Therefore, if the lessee fails to pay the rent, the lessor could evict the tenant and take the property back. If the lender holds a mortgage or trust deed on a leasehold and the leasehold is extinguished, then the lender's mortgage or trust deed is extinguished with it. This leaves the lender with nothing more than an unsecured note. To protect the lender, ground leases where the building must be financed are typically created in such a way as to make the mortgage prior in right to the lease. A simple way to do this is to have the lessor sign the mortgage as well as the lessee. By signing the mortgage, the lessor is agreeing that the lessor's interest is subordinate to the mortgage.

Many times a tenant will desire to install items on the leased premises. Normally items permanently affixed will become part of the real property. However, the law holds that items installed by a tenant remain personal property. Therefore, the tenant may remove the items at the termination of the tenancy. The tenant must do so before the end of the tenancy or they are deemed to be abandoned and become part of the real property. The tenant must also restore the premises and repair any damage caused by their installation and removal.

When items are installed on leased commercial premises we call them ***trade fixtures***. Similarly, items installed on residential property are called ***residential fixtures*** and items installed on agricultural property are called ***agricultural fixtures***.

Note: A sample commercial lease form is reproduced on pages 167-171.

Exercise a

A fixed lease (equal payments) is also called a __straight__ *or* __flat__ *lease. If the payments can increase, it is because there is an* __escalator__ *clause in the lease. If the lease is tied to the CPI, it is called an* __index__ *lease. In shopping centers, it is common to use a* __percentage__ *lease, where the rent is based on the tenant's gross sales. Shopping centers also need an* __anchor__ *tenant to be financially successful. When the tenant pays all of the expenses of the property, we say the lease is* __net__, __net__, __net__. *If the landlord pays all the expenses, then we call it a* __full__ __service__ *lease. When the tenant leases the bare land, it is called a* __ground__ *lease.*

When the tenant installs __fixtures__ *these are called* __trade__ __fixtures__ *in a commercial property,* residential fixtures *in a residential property, and* agricultural fixtures *in an agricultural property. Such items remain the property of the* tenant *provided they are removed prior to the termination of the tenancy and the* tenant *restores the premises.*

KEY TERMS

The key to understanding any new field is the vocabulary used in that field. To maximize your comprehension of the material presented in this chapter, be sure you know the meaning and significance of the following terms. Remember that the majority of test questions primarily test knowledge of vocabulary.

Agricultural fixture
Anchor lease
Anchor tenant
Escalation (escalator) clause
Exculpation clause
Expansion option
Fixed lease
Fixed minimum percentage lease
Flat lease
Full-service lease
Graduated lease
Ground lease
Gross lease
Index lease
Net lease
Net, net, net lease
Overage rent
Percentage lease
Recapture clause
Residential fixture
Step-up lease
Straight lease
Straight percentage lease
Trade fixture
Triple net lease

ANSWERS

To chapter exercises. If you couldn't figure out what to put in the blanks, find the answer here!

Exercise a

A fixed lease (equal payments) is also called a FLAT *or* STRAIGHT *lease. If the payments can increase, it is because there is an* ESCALATION *clause in the lease. If the lease is tied to the* CPI, *it is called an* INDEX *lease. In shopping centers, it is common to use a* PERCENTAGE *lease, where the rent is based on the tenant's gross sales. Shopping centers also need an* ANCHOR *tenant to be financially successful. When the tenant pays all of the expenses of the property, we say the lease is* NET, NET, NET. *If the landlord pays all the expenses, then we call it a* FULL SERVICE *lease. When the tenant leases the bare land, it is called a* GROUND *lease.*

When the tenant installs FIXTURES *these are called* TRADE FIXTURES *in a commercial property,* RESIDENTIAL FIXTURES *in a residential property, and* AGRICULTURAL FIXTURES *in an agricultural property. Such items remain the property of the* TENANT *provided they are removed prior to the termination of the tenancy and the* TENANT *restores the premises.*

PRACTICE QUESTIONS

The following practice questions are representative of the questions you will find on the final examination and on the licensing examinations given by the Oregon Real Estate Agency.

1. You lease property to a tenant with the understanding that the lease payments are to be $3,000 per month the first year, $3,500 per month the second year, and increasing in similar fashion by $500 per month each year during the term of the lease. You have
   (A) a percentage lease.
   (B) a flat lease.
   (C) a net lease.
   (D) a lease with an escalation clause.

2. A graduated lease can best be defined as a lease
   (A) which includes an option to purchase.
   (B) which provides for a possible increase in rent at a stated future time.
   (C) under which the tenant pays all ownership charges, such as property taxes.
   (D) that is passed intact from owner to owner when the property is sold.

3. A graduated lease starts at
   I. an agreed upon payment and increases at set intervals as the lease term matures.
   II. a fixed minimum payment and increases by a portion of the gross sales made each month.
   (A) I only
   (B) II only
   (C) Both I and II
   (D) Neither I nor II

4. A lease which provides for a step-by-step increase in rental payments at regular intervals is called
   (A) a percentage lease.
   (B) an open lease.
   (C) an elevator lease.
   (D) a graduated lease.

5. A lease provided for rent to be adjusted according to the cost of living. This is a
   (A) step-up lease.
   (B) index lease.
   (C) graduated lease.
   (D) percentage lease.

6. An escalation clause in a lease provides for
   (A) adjustment of rental payments to cover contingencies, such as, for example, increased property taxes, insurance or maintenance.
   (B) an extension of the rental term, such as an automatic six-month renewal clause.
   (C) both A and B.
   (D) neither A nor B.

7. A clause may be inserted into a lease allowing rent to increase based upon a formula. This is known as
   (A) an acceleration clause.
   (B) a contingency clause.
   (C) an escalator clause.
   (D) a habendum clause.

8. An escalator clause in an office lease
   I. provides that the rental rate may be increased or decreased.
   II. is used to compensate for inflation and rising operating costs.
   (A) I only
   (B) II only
   (C) Both I and II
   (D) Neither I nor II

9. Which of the following clauses would be of benefit to an owner when costs are rising?
   (A) A gross clause
   (B) An escalation clause
   (C) A percentage clause
   (D) All of the above

10. An escalator clause in a lease may provide for
    (A) periodic maintenance of the equipment in the subject property.
    (B) periodic rent increases negotiated at the time the lease was signed.
    (C) rent increases to match cost increases in specified expenses of the landlord.
    (D) negotiated rent increases at predetermined dates.

11. A percentage lease is a lease
   (A) where rent is based on a percentage of the tenant's receipts.
   (B) which provides for a percentage of rents to be paid to the broker as commission.
   (C) which covers only a certain percentage of property where there are two or more persons sharing the premises.
   (D) which covers the lending of money and interest charged thereon.

12. A percentage lease is a lease
   (A) where the manager receives a commission as a percentage of the gross rents.
   (B) which covers only a certain percentage of the total net leasable area in the building.
   (C) where there are more than just one tenant and each has a percentage of the premises.
   (D) where the rent is based on the tenant's gross sales.

13. When the lessee agrees to pay all the expenses attributable to the property, including the property taxes and insurance, this is commonly referred to as
   (A) a full-service lease.
   (B) a percentage lease.
   (C) a triple-net lease.
   (D) a ground lease.

14. Under a net lease arrangement the tenant
   I. is usually responsible for paying the real estate taxes for the leased property.
   II. has an option to purchase the leased property within a specified time.
   (A) I only
   (B) II only
   (C) Both I and II
   (D) Neither I nor II

15. When a lease requires the lessee to pay taxes, insurance and maintenance costs is a
   (A) gross lease.
   (B) net lease.
   (C) anchor lease.
   (D) percentage lease.

16. A net lease provides
   (A) net income to the lessor.
   (B) the lessor with a participation in the net profits of the lessee.
   (C) that the lessor is responsible for taxes.
   (D) that the lessor is responsible for insurance.

17. What advantage is there to the landlord-owner of commercial property in leasing it to a tenant under a net lease?
   I. The landlord is protected against tax rate increases during the term of the lease because they will be absorbed by the tenant.
   II. The landlord is protected against increases in tax valuation that result from improvements placed on the property by the tenant.
   (A) I only
   (B) II only
   (C) Both I and II
   (D) Neither I nor II

18. Max DeFraude leased his warehouse to Candide L'Innocence. According to the lease, L'Innocence was to pay $1,000 per month, plus expenses for taxes, insurance and maintenance. The lease was a
   (A) net lease.
   (B) gross lease.
   (C) sandwich lease.
   (D) percentage lease.

19. An owner of an improved commercial property sold the land under the building to an investor, but kept ownership of the building and also retained a long term lease on the land. The lease was probably a
   (A) net lease.
   (B) ground lease.
   (C) percentage lease.
   (D) gross lease.

20. The manager of a large shopping center offered an anchor tenant a rental rate significantly below market. Why would the manager do this?
   (A) Because the anchor tenant will take a large space so the owners will make up for the loss on the volume.
   (B) Because it will increase the rents they can charge to other tenants.
   (C) Because of reduced costs with an anchor tenant.
   (D) Because the property manager will be expected to cut the management fees to make up for the loss.

21. An owner had an undeveloped commercial property. The owner wanted a fixed income from it but didn't want to do the development. The owner should consider a
   (A) ground lease.
   (B) reverse annuity mortgage.
   (C) sale-leaseback.
   (D) net lease.

22. Which of the following would be an advantage of a ground lease to the lessee is
(A) a lower cash investment.
(B) freedom from paying property taxes.
(C) interest payments which are deductible.
(D) freedom to sublease.

23. A tenant who is to pay the property taxes on the rental property is probably under
(A) a gross lease. (C) a net lease.
(B) an escalation lease. (D) a percentage lease.

24. Net leases are used least commonly with
(A) apartments. (C) office space.
(B) retail space. (D) industrial property.

25. When a lease requires the landlord to pay operating expenses of the property it is a
(A) net lease. (C) graduated lease.
(B) gross lease. (D) percentage lease.

26. Gross leases are usually encountered when renting or leasing
(A) apartments. (C) office space.
(B) retail space. (D) industrial property.

27. A lease of bare land on which the tenant intends to build a home is best called
(A) a ground lease. (C) a net lease.
(B) a gross lease. (D) a sale-leaseback.

28. Apartments are most commonly rented on a
(A) gross lease.
(B) percentage lease.
(C) net, net, net lease.
(D) lease with an escalation clause.

29. If an owner has a property in a rapidly growing commercial area, which of the following choices would be most advantageous for the owner?
(A) A year-to-year rental based on a flat monthly rent with annual cost of living adjustments tied to the Consumer Price Index.
(B) A straight lease for at least 20 years.
(C) A long term lease with an escalator clause calling for 10% per annum rent increases for the first three years.
(D) A percentage lease based on gross sales which is net of property taxes.

30. An attorney reviewing a lease noticed that it contained the terms "minimum rent" and "gross sales." What kind of lease was this?
(A) Gross (C) Percentage
(B) Triple net (D) Flat

31. A percentage lease is a lease which usually provides for
I. rent tied to a percentage of the assessed value of the building.
II. definite base monthly rent, plus a percentage of the tenant's gross sales over a certain amount.
(A) I only. (C) both I and II.
(B) II only. (D) neither I nor II.

32. A lease whereby the amount of rent is based upon the tenant's volume of business we call it a
(A) ground lease. (C) net lease.
(B) gross lease. (D) percentage lease.

33. A lessor charged rent on a portion of the tenant's gross sales and required that the tenant pay a guaranteed monthly minimum as well. The lease is
(A) an amortized lease.
(B) a net lease.
(C) a percentage lease.
(D) an ad valorem contract.

34. A percentage lease is a lease which calls for
(A) rent as a percentage of the building's value.
(B) a definite periodic rent not to exceed a certain percentage.
(C) a definite monthly rent plus a percentage of the tenant's gross sales.
(D) a graduated amount due monthly not to exceed a certain percentage.

35. In a percentage lease
I. the total annual rent paid by the tenant remains the same throughout the term of the lease.
II. only a specified percentage of the parcel of real estate is covered by the lease.
(A) I only (C) Both I and II
(B) II only (D) Neither I nor II

36. In a percentage lease the amount of the rent is calculated on a percentage of
(A) gross sales. (C) net monthly income.
(B) gross profit. (D) none of the above.

37. The usual basis for determining the rent in a percentage lease is
(A) the tenant's income tax statement
(B) the tenant's net inventory
(C) the tenant's net income
(D) none of the above

38. Which of the following is not an example of a percentage lease.
(A) A fixed minimum rent with percentage added to the minimum
(B) A gradually increasing amount of rent, to step up at specified intervals
(C) A fixed minimum rent with additional rent based on a percentage being payable only after the applicable percentage has earned the minimum
(D) A percentage without any minimum

39. When reviewing the clauses in a lease, you notice there is a percentage rent clause. This means that the lease requires
(A) a periodic payment of a stated percentage of sales.
(B) a percentage increase in the rent on an annual basis.
(C) a periodic payment of a percentage increase in the stated rent.
(D) percentage increase in the rent depending on the taxes and insurance.

40. In a percentage lease
(A) the tenant may occupy only a specified percentage of the premises.
(B) the total annual rental amount remains the same.
(C) the broker earns a commission equal to a percentage of the total rent to be paid.
(D) rent is based on a percentage of the tenant's sales.

41. Bill DePrez is president of Lawn Order, Inc., a landscaping firm. Bill leased premises for the company's use with the understanding that the rent would be $1,500 per month, plus 2% of the company's gross receipts. This arrangement would be considered a
(A) percentage lease. (C) ground lease.
(B) net lease. (D) gross lease.

42. Percentage leases are most often used with
(A) apartments. (C) office space.
(B) retail space. (D) industrial property.

43. Retail establishments in shopping centers typically pay rent based on
(A) their gross annual sales, plus a base amount.
(B) the square footage of the space they occupy.
(C) a pro-rata share of the common areas.
(D) a formula which takes all of the above into account.

44. The landlord would receive the smallest rent during a year under
(A) a straight lease at $600 per month.
(B) a 10% percentage lease when the tenant's gross income is $7,000 per month.
(C) a $550 per month gross lease, linked by an escalator clause to Portland's Consumer Price Index, which rises consistently during the year at a rate of 1% per month.
(D) a lease calling for $300 per month, plus 7% of gross sales receipts, which amount to $52,000 per year.

45. During inflationary times, which of the following would be the least used lease arrangement?
(A) A flat lease (C) An index lease
(B) A percentage lease (D) A gross lease

46. Sometimes a lease will give a tenant an option to renew. This covenant
I. favors the landlord.
II. is called an automatic extension clause.
(A) I only (C) Both I and II
(B) II only (D) Neither I nor II

47. An option to renew clause in a lease is normally to give the
    (A) tenant the option to renegotiate the lease prior to expiration of the term.
    (B) landlord the option to cancel the lease agreement prior to the expiration of the term.
    (C) tenant the option to decrease the amount of space which he leases prior to the expiration of the term.
    (D) tenant the option to renew the lease at a preset level at the expiration of the term.

48. An expansion option in a lease
    I. may pose a problem for an owner.
    II. is not common with fully tenanted, established properties.
    (A) I only
    (B) II only
    (C) Both I and II
    (D) Neither I nor II

97%

ANSWERS

To practice questions. If you chose the wrong letter, here's the right one! The explanations are designed to clarify your understanding.

1. **D** A graduated lease (also called step-up lease) is a lease where there is a pre-agreed periodic increase which is not tied to an index. In contrast, an index lease contains an escalation (escalator) clause which ties the rent payment to some index. Percentage leases tie the rent to the tenant's sales volume. Leases where there are no provisions for rent increases during the term of the lease are called flat leases (also sometimes "straight" or "fixed" leases).
2. **B** A graduated lease is a lease where there is a pre-agreed periodic increase which is not tied to an index. All leases are encumbrances on the title, so if the property is sold, the new owner takes title subject to the lease. When the tenant agrees to pay all expenses attributable to the property, the lease is said to be a net, or net, net, net (triple-net) lease.
3. **A** Graduated leases provide for pre-agreed increases in the periodic rent payments. A percentage lease is one which is tied to a tenant's gross sales.
4. **D** A percentage lease is one which is tied to a tenant's gross sales. "Open" is a term used to describe a real estate loan which is subject to immediate foreclosure because the final due date has arrived and the loan has not been paid in full. The term to describe a clause calling for increases in rent is called an "escalator clause." Graduated leases provide for pre-agreed increases in the periodic rent payments
5. **B** A graduated lease (also called step-up lease) is a lease where there is a pre-agreed periodic increase which is not tied to an index. In contrast, an index lease contains an escalation (escalator) clause which ties the rent payment to some index. Percentage leases tie the rent to the tenant's sales volume.
6. **A** An index lease contains an escalation (escalator) clause which ties the rent payment to some index. When there is a provision for an increase tied to an index, or tied to costs such as property taxes, insurance and maintenance, it is called an index lease.
7. **C** An acceleration clause allows a lender to call the entire loan due in full if the borrower defaults. A contingency clause is a condition required for a contract to be enforceable. An escalator clause is a agreement in a lease which calls for the payments to increase based on some formula or index. A habendum clause is the "to have and to hold" clause in a deed (not generally required in Oregon).
8. **C** An escalator clause provides for lease payments to increase based on some formula or index. The normal purpose of the escalator clause is to cover increases in the landlord's cost of operation, frequently by tying the increase to an index.
9. **B** In a gross lease the lessor pays all the expenses A percentage lease is tied to the tenant's gross sales which may be of some benefit during a time of rising costs, but not as much benefit as an escalation (index) clause. The only type of lease which protects the lessor against rising costs is a lease tied to a cost index.
10. **C** An escalator clause provides for lease payments to increase based on some formula or index.
11. **A** In a percentage lease the rent is a percentage of the tenant's gross sales.
12. **D** In a percentage lease there is usually a base rent (fixed minimum), to which is added an amount according to a formula based on the tenant's gross sales.
13. **C** When the tenant agrees to pay the expenses, the lease is said to be net. There is a special term used in some parts of the country (including Oregon) called a net, net, net lease, or triple-net lease. In a net, net, net lease, the tenant pays all expenses attributable to the property, including maintenance, insurance and property taxes.
14. **A** In net leases, the tenant pays the expenses attributable to the property. In commercial settings (which is usually where net leases are used), this extends even to insurance, maintenance and taxes. A net lease is no more likely to contain an option to purchase than any other lease.
15. **B** In net leases, the tenant pays the expenses attributable to the property. In commercial settings (which is usually where net leases are used), this extends even to insurance, maintenance and taxes. When the expenses paid by the tenant include taxes, insurance and maintenance, some call this a net, net, net lease. The opposite of a net lease is a gross lease (landlord pays expenses). An anchor lease is the lease

of a large retailer in a shopping center. A percentage lease calls for the rent to be a percentage of the tenant's gross sales.

16. **A** A net lease calls for the tenant to pay the expenses attributable to the property. In commercial settings, this usually includes taxes, insurance and maintenance.

17. **C** A net lease calls for the tenant to pay the expenses attributable to the property, usually includes taxes, insurance and maintenance. The advantage to the landlord is that the tenant pays the extra expenses arising from improvements made by the tenant (i.e., increased property taxes). The tenant benefits by being able to control expenses better.

18. **A** When the tenant pays the expenses of the property it is a net lease (i.e., net to the owner). The opposite is a gross lease.

19. **B** A net lease is one where the tenant pays some or all of the expenses of the property. The opposite is a gross lease. In a percentage lease, the rent is tied to the tenant's gross sales. A ground lease is the lease of bare ground only. The idea is that the tenant owns the building, but not the land. The usual purpose is for the landowner to avoid capital gains taxes which would result from a sale, and to create a lease expense which is a tax benefit to the lessee.

20. **B** Anchor tenants in shopping malls get preferential treatment because they attract lots of shoppers. Without the anchor tenant the shopping center would probably never have been built in the first place. Other, smaller tenants ride on the coattails of the anchor tenant, so they pay above market rent in comparison.

21. **B** A ground lease is a lease of bare land, usually for a long term, on which the lessee will build improvements. A reverse annuity mortgage is used on residential property where the borrowers receive the loan proceeds in monthly installments paid by the lender, so the loan balance increases with each payment. In a sale-leaseback an owner sells the property to an investor and then leases it back. A net lease is one where the tenant pays all the expenses associated with the property.

22. **A** By not having to pay for the land the investor on a ground lease can conserve a considerable amount of capital. However, the investor will still have to pay property taxes, either directly or indirectly and there is no automatic right to sublease or assign.

23. **C** A net lease calls for the tenant to pay the expenses attributable to the property. In commercial settings, this usually includes taxes, insurance and maintenance. A gross lease is the opposite of a net lease. An escalator clause calls for the rent payments to increase based on a pre-agreed schedule. A percentage lease ties the rent payments to the tenant's gross sales.

24. **A** In a net lease the tenant to pay the expenses attributable to the property, usually including taxes, insurance and maintenance. The advantage to the landlord is that the tenant pays the extra expenses arising from improvements made by the tenant (i.e., increased property taxes). The tenant benefits by being able to control expenses better. These are more important in commercial settings.

25. **B** In net leases the tenant pays the expenses attributable to the property. The opposite (landlord pays) is a gross lease. A graduated lease calls for the rent to increase according to a pre-agreed schedule. A percentage lease ties the rent payments to the tenant's gross sales.

26. **A** A gross lease is where the landlord pays the expenses, such as property taxes, insurance, maintenance, etc. In commercial settings the tenant generally prefers the opposite (a net lease) in order to maintain control over expenses.

27. **A** A sale leaseback is an arrangement where an owner of property in fee title sells the property (land and buildings) and then leases the entire property back. A net lease is one where the tenant pays some or all of the expenses of the property. The opposite is a gross lease.

28. **A** A gross lease is the opposite of a net lease; that is, the lessor pays all the expenses attributable to the property. In a residential unit these typically include the taxes, insurance and maintenance.

29. **D** If the area is rapidly growing, then it can be presumed that property taxes as well as business activity will increase. The best way for the lessor to protect against increasing taxes, while at the same time participating in the anticipated increase in profits the tenant will make, is to use the percentage lease but make the tenant pay the property taxes (net of taxes).

30. **C** In a percentage lease the rent is a percentage of the tenant's gross sales. Percentage leases are typical in shopping centers. The more the landlord advertises the shopping center, the greater the traffic, and the greater each tenant's sales. Thus it creates a win-win situation. It is very common to establish a minimum monthly rental with the percentage rent on top.

31. **B** Percentage leases usually call for a base amount, plus a percentage of the tenant's gross sales. It is also common for the percentage to be applied to the tenant's sales only above a certain amount, or to use different percentages for different portions of the tenant's gross sales.

32. **D** A ground lease is a long term lease of bare land in order to construct a building on it. A net lease calls for the tenant to pay the expenses attributable to the property, usually including taxes, insurance and maintenance. The opposite of a net lease is a gross lease. In a percentage lease the amount of rent is a percentage of the tenant's gross sales.

33. **C** A percentage lease ties the rent to a percentage of the tenant's gross sales. If there is a base rent it is called a fixed minimum percentage lease. A net lease calls for the tenant to pay expenses attributable to the property. "Ad valorem" means "according to value," and is a term used to describe the fact that property taxes are based on the value of the property.

34. **C** A percentage lease ties the rent to a percentage of the tenant's gross sales. If there is a base rent it is called a fixed minimum percentage lease.

35. **D** In a percentage lease the amount of each period's rent is a percentage of the tenant's gross sales for that period. When the rent never changes, we call it a flat, fixed, or straight lease. A lease which covers only a portion of the premises might describe some subleases.

36. **A** In a percentage lease the amount of each period's rent is a percentage of the tenant's gross sales for that period. It is conceivable to base it on other figures, such as net profit, net income, etc., but this would then make the landlord suffer if the tenant does not control expenses.

37. **D** A percentage lease ties the rent to a percentage of the tenant's gross sales. Net income could be used, but has the disadvantage in that the landlord has no control over the tenant's expenses of operation.

38. **B** Percentage leases tie the rent to a percentage of the tenant's gross sales. If there is a base rent it is called a fixed minimum percentage lease. When a lease calls for pre-agreed increments to the rent without tying the increments to any particular guide, this is called a graduated lease.

39. **A** A percentage lease ties the rent to the tenant's gross sales. A percentage increase on an annual basis is probably an indexed lease. If the rent includes taxes and insurance it is a net lease.

40. **D** A percentage lease ties the rent to a percentage of the tenant's gross sales. A lease where the rent never changes is called a "flat," "fixed," or "straight" lease.

41. **A** Percentage leases are based on the tenant's gross sales, typical of retail space in shopping malls.

42. **B** A percentage lease ties the rent, at least partially, to the tenant's gross sales, so retail property is the only type of property where it is appropriate.

43. **D** The lessor of shopping center space obviously charges more rent the larger the area the tenant occupies. Benefits accruing from adjacent common areas are also considered in setting rental rates. Therefore it is common for shopping center owners to create formulas to determine the amount of rent to charge. These formulas typically include a base rent plus a percentage of the sales, where the base rent and percentage rate are determined by the location and desirability of the space.

44. **C** A straight lease at $600 per month would yield $7,200 per year ($600 times 12 = $7,200). A 10% percentage lease when the tenant's income is $7,000 per month would yield $700 per month, or $8,400 per year ($700 times 12 = $8,400). An easy way to calculate an approximate answer for answer C is to take an average of the high and low monthly rent. The last month's rent would be 112% of the first month's rent (not allowing for compounding), or $616. Since the effects of compounding over a short time like one year are not great, just average the first month's rent and the last month's rent to get the average rent during the year ($550 + $616 = $1,166; $1,166 ÷ 2 = $583). Now take this average monthly rent ($583) times 12 months to find the approximate annual income ($583 × 12 – $6,996). Although this is not an absolutely accurate figure, because we ignored compounding the Consumer Price Index, it is sufficiently accurate to see that it is the lowest of the choices.

45. **A** A long term flat lease would become worthless to the lessor if there is a period of high inflation. To counteract the effects of the inflation, the lessor should insist on an indexed lease.

46. **D** The holder of an option is always the party who benefits from it, since it is up to that party whether or not to exercise it. The clause is called a "option to renew."

47. **D** An option to renew normally has a pre-agreed rate for the renewal lease. Normally, "an agreement to agree is no agreement," but is legally

enforceable to state the new rate as "to be established by neutral appraisal," since the amount can be determined by a disinterested third party.

48. **C** An expansion clause gives the tenant the option to lease additional space for a period of time. This would require the owner to leave the space unrented until the time period expired.

SUCCESSFUL PROPERTY MANAGEMENT

Many owners find it expedient to hire someone to act as their property manager. Increasing urbanization and greater incidence of absentee ownership creates a need for quality property management. In addition, many owners do not have the time to manage their own property, or simply do not have the necessary knowledge of the law or ability to deal with tenants. And finally, even owners who could manage their own property usually find that they are able to negotiate with tenants better if there is a manager for the tenant to deal with.

A property manager becomes successful largely through word of mouth. If you manage a well-run property with satisfied tenants, they will tell other prospective tenants and you will find it easier to fill vacancies. Similarly, owners who are happy with your services will recommend you to other property owners, and your business will multiply.

Property owners expect their managers to maximize the return on their investments. Profits are at their highest when the tenants are satisfied customers because rents can then be maintained at optimum levels and vacancies will be at the lowest. Keeping tenants contented then, is a primary consideration of a successful manager. Of course, maximizing an owner's return on investment also involves complex decisions to maintain the property in good condition while reducing operating costs, as well as countless other factors.

Successful property managers need to understand that lowering costs does not necessarily increase the owner's return on the investment. In business there is a saying, "you have to spend money to make money." Of course, spending the owner's money foolishly is poor management, but at the same time, funds must be budgeted and expended to maintain the property in top condition. Low-paid employees may also seem cost-effective, until you consider the effect on tenant

NOTES

relations and the expense of redoing the work they may do wrong the first time. Demanding top quality for the best price available is a skill owners insist that their managers possess.

Business cycles

The general business cycle is also a matter of concern to a property manager. Every property manager should know that business tends to expand and recede. During a period of expansion, of course, there will be few vacancies and rents can be raised. But management should also prepare for a recession, when vacancies are high. So as to preserve the owner's asset from the negative impact of a recession, a manager must make extra effort to keep expenses low.

The general business cycle goes through four phases – expansion, recession, contraction and revival. During the ***expansion*** period production increases, employment increases and economic growth occurs. Demand is high and market rents increase. The point where demand levels off is called ***recession***.

However, too much demand can cause inflation. To counter inflation the government, through the operation of the Federal Reserve Bank System and other institutions, acts to curtail the availability of money and credit. Interest rates increase, causing demand to slacken. Unemployment rises and the entire economy goes into a downturn. This is called ***contraction***. The period of maximum recession is called ***business contraction***. Ultimately, interest rates are lowered, prices have also lowered due to lack of demand, and consumers are lured back into the market. Thus begins the process of ***revival***.

Real estate markets are also subject to the same wave-like cycles as the general business economy. Extremes of over- and undersupply apply to real estate the same as to any other commodity. However, real estate markets tend to lag behind the rest of the economy, sometimes so much so that it appears that real estate is running counter to the rest of the economy. Much of this is due to the fact that mortgage commitments, particularly for large commercial projects, tend to be made for several months in advance of when the funds will actually be used.

Budgeting and management takeover

Property managers must also be able to handle the tasks involved in taking over the management of a property. When taking on the management of a new property, the manager's first duty is to analyze the regional and neighborhood market in which the property is located.

The regional market includes the entire metropolitan area or general area of the state in which the property is located. Analysis of this market includes demographic and economic information such as population trends, types of employment available in the area and the projections for future growth in the industries that are located in the region.

Analysis of the immediate neighborhood market in which the property is located includes a multitude of factors such as –

- Definition of the boundaries of the neighborhood and the features of the area, such as zoning, recreational areas, traffic counts along arterials, and the like.
- Transportation facilities, including proposed changes, availability of parking.
- Cost, availability and quality of utility services, particularly for industrial properties.
- Economic conditions, types of industries and level of diversification, and the potential for growth

NOTES

- Supply and demand in the rental market, including occupancy rates and the potential for change.
- Current population, their number and density, willingness to lease or rent and their financial strength.

Although all these factors are important, for residential property probably the most important is the makeup of the population. If the population is increasing in number or density and their financial ability is improving, this augurs well for the market. For commercial property, on the other hand, traffic counts, competition in the area, availability of transportation services and other factors are more important.

Following regional and neighborhood market analysis, the property manager must prepare a ***market rent analysis***, also called a ***market rent survey***. This is simply a study of the competition – what other properties there are in the neighborhood and what rents they are able to command. Appraisers define a ***neighborhood*** as an area bordered by natural and man-made barriers in which the land use, economics, transportation and utilities are homogenous. The goal of a neighborhood market rent analysis is to determine the ***market rent*** (also called ***economic rent***) for the property.

Having determined the market rent, the property manager must calculate the projected expenses. Expenses are categorized in two ways. ***Fixed expenses*** are those expenses which will occur regardless of occupancy rates or rental income (e.g., property taxes). ***Variable expenses***, on the other hand, are expenses which increase and decrease as occupancy and income increase and decrease. Many accountants also categorize certain expenses as ***mixed expenses***. For example, fire insurance is completely fixed, because the premium is the same whether the property is full or has vacancies. But if you are charging management fees based on the actual income received, then the owner's management expense is variable. On the other hand, the water bill in most communities is calculated on a base amount, whether any water is used or not, plus an additional amount according to the quantity of water used. Such an expense would have both fixed and variable elements, so it would be called a mixed expense.

Expenses are also categorized as recurring and non-recurring. Most expenses are ***recurring expenses***, that is they recur monthly or yearly. The annual fire insurance premium or the monthly water bill are examples of recurring expenses. Some expenses, on the other hand, are one-time expenses. For example, it might become necessary to replace a refrigerator in an apartment. This would be considered a ***non-recurring expense***. Non-recurring expenses are budgeted as reserves for replacement (see later).

Information on income and expenses is derived both from the marketplace, and from the owner's financial records. Once the manager has determined the market rent and the projected expenses, the manager can prepare a ***projected operating statement***, or ***pro-forma*** to discuss with the owner. The projected operating statement should contain the manager's professional approach to optimizing the owner's investment. Problems to discuss might include abatement of accrued deferred maintenance (rehabilitation), increasing rents and decreasing vacancies and turnover, and the like. A projected operating statement might look something like the example on the next page.

NOTES

Crampington Manor Apartments

Projected Operating Statement (Pro-Forma)

Income			
Potential Gross Income (PGI)		$ 450,000	
Less vacancy and credit loss		– 22,500	
Effective Gross Income (EGI)			$ 427,500
Operating Expenses			
Fixed:			
Property taxes	40,500		
Insurance	10,000		
Total fixed expenses		50,500	
Variable:			
Management (5%)	22,500		
Resident manager (5%)	22,500		
Utilities	24,000		
Maintenance	25,000		
Reserves for replacements	20,000		
Miscellaneous	10,000		
Total variable expenses		129,000	
Total expenses			– 179,500
Net Operating Income (NOI)			$ 248,000

Note above the entry for "reserves for replacements." ***Reserves for replacements*** are also a type of maintenance, but include only large projects which are undertaken only every several years, such as re-roofing, exterior repainting, new carpeting, and the like. Reserves for replacements are also sometimes referred to as non-recurring expenses. The manager must estimate an annual allowance for reserves for replacement on the projected operating statement.

The bottom line in the projected operating statement is the net operating income. This is the amount that should be available to service the debt (***debt service***) and provide a cash return to the owner. The amount left over after debt service is sometimes called the ***net spendable income***.

Another important consideration in the operating statement is the ***break-even point***. In fact, the break-even point is the primary method used by investors to calculate the profitability of the investment. For rental property, the break-even point is the percentage of occupancy necessary to produce enough income to cover all fixed and variable expenses at that occupancy rate. The formula to calculate the break-even point is –

$$\frac{\text{Total Expense Plus Debt Service}}{\text{Potential Gross Income}} = \text{Percent of Occupancy}$$

In addition to the above formula, there are other more sophisticated ways of calculating a break-even point.

An important consideration in analyzing a property is the amount of rentable area and usable area. In an office structure, there are portions which are not usable or rent-

NOTES

able. Property managers refer to the ***construction area*** as the total square footage of the structure as measured from outside dimensions. But the ***rentable area*** is the inside of the structure, including spaces not occupied by tenants such as restrooms, janitor's closets, mechanical equipment rooms, and the like. Rentable area, however, does not include intruding portions of the building structure such as pillars and stairwells. The ***usable area*** of the structure is that portion which tenants can actually occupy. Usable area does not include lobbies, common hallways and restrooms, although hallways contained within the tenant's area are considered part of the usable space.

Property managers and investors consider the ratio of rentable area to usable area an important factor in calculating the profitability of a structure and in setting rent rates. The ratio of rentable area to usable area is sometimes called a ***loss factor***. The loss factor is a measure of the efficiency of space utilization in the building. When there are multiple tenants on the same floor, the loss factor is sometimes called the ***load factor***. For example, if a building has 50,000 square feet of rentable space, but the usable space is only 40,000 square feet, then the rentable/usable ratio, or loss factor, is 125% (50,000 ÷ 40,000 = 1.25). Therefore, if a space is leased to a tenant at $20 per square foot of *rentable space* (for example), the tenant's real cost per square foot of *usable space* is $25.00 ($20.00 × 1.25 = $25.00). If rent rates are calculated on rentable area instead of usable area, then buildings with a high loss factor frequently rent at lower rates per square foot to reflect the fact that tenants do not gain as much benefit for their rent dollar.

When setting rent schedules, the market, of course will be the ultimate determiner of rental rates. Nevertheless, property managers and owners need to consider the minimum rent that they can charge in order to meet the expenses of the property and also provide a reasonable return on the investment. The minimum rent is calculated with the formula –

$$\frac{\text{Operating Expenses} + \text{Debt Service} + \text{Owner's Return}}{\text{Rentable Area}} = \text{Minimum Rent}$$

The results of this calculation will be the minimum rent that the owner can charge. If market rents are lower than the minimum rent, then the owner should not make the investment.

Rehabilitation

Rehabilitation of a property is a common reason an owner hires new management. The term ***rehabilitation*** generally means restoration of the property, but not usually alteration of its design, purpose, function, or utility. If a property requires rehabilitation, the manager must have a clear understanding with the owner as to how the work is to proceed and the source of funds to pay for it.

Government subsidized housing

The federal government has made a major impact in residential rental property through the Section 8 Housing Assistance Payments Program of the Department of Housing and Urban Development (HUD). Under this program, low income tenants receive a rent subsidy. The tenant pays rent in an amount up to 30 percent of the tenant's adjusted monthly income. Housing and Urban Development then pays the owner the difference between the rent paid by the tenant and the market rent as negotiated between the owner or property manager and HUD.

NOTES

To rent a property under the HUD Section 8 Program, the owner must agree to the terms as required by the Program. This is accomplished by a ***Housing Assistance Payments Contract***. In addition to the Housing Assistance Payments Contract, the owner must agree to a lease of the property for a specified period, usually at least one year. The lease is also a standard form required by HUD, and is called the ***HUD Model Lease***.

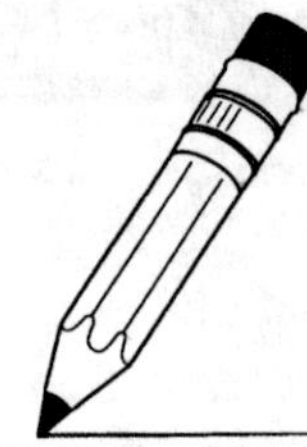

Exercise a

The general business economy goes through cycles *. The period of lowest economic activity is called* business contraction *. The* real estate *economy tends to lag behind the general business economy.*

A regional and neighborhood *market analysis is one of the property manager's first tasks when taking over a new property. In the neighborhood analysis the most important factor is the size and density of the* population *. When taking over a property, a property manager should also prepare a* market *rent survey. Then projected expenses should be analyzed. Expenses are either* fixed *, meaning that they will be incurred regardless of occupancy levels,* variable *which means that they increase and decrease with occupancy levels, or* mixed *which are expenses with the characteristics of both. Most expenses in property management are considered to be* reccurring *expenses because they must be paid periodically. An unusual, one-time expense would be considered a* non-reccurring *such as an expense for* reserves *for* replacements *.*

After determining income and expenses, the property manager should prepare for the owner a projected operating statement *. The manager must also make an allowance for* vacancy *and* credit loss *.*

Subtracting the vacancy *and* credit loss *allowance from the potential gross income leaves the* effective gross *income. By subtracting the operating expenses from this, the* net operating income *is derived. Finally, the* debt service *is subtracted to find the* net spendable *income. These figures are all used to calculate the* break *-* even *point for the property. This is expressed as the* percentage *of occupancy that is necessary to meet all the expenses of the property.*

The total area of a building, measured from the outside, is called the construction *area. The total area inside the building, less portions of the structure which intrude, is called the* rentable *area. The portion which excludes restrooms, maintenance and mechanical rooms is called the* usable *area.*

Restoration of a property without any alteration of its design, purpose, function or utility is called rehabilitation *.*

Subsidized residential rentals are available through the HUD section 8 *Program. Under this program a tenant pays rent up to* 30 *% of the tenant's monthly income, and HUD makes up the rest. To utilize this program an owner must enter into a* housing assistance payments *Contract with HUD, and must lease the property to the tenant on HUD's* model *Lease form.*

KEY TERMS

The key to understanding any new field is the vocabulary used in that field. To maximize your comprehension of the material presented in this chapter, be sure you know the meaning and significance of the following terms. Remember that the majority of test questions primarily test knowledge of vocabulary.

Break-even point
Business contraction
Construction area
Contraction
Debt service
Economic rent
Effective gross income
Expansion
Fixed expenses
Housing Assistance Payments Contract
HUD Model Lease
Load factor
Loss factor
Market rent
Market rent analysis (survey)
Mixed expenses
Neighborhood
Net operating income
Net spendable income
Non-recurring expense
Operating expenses
Potential gross income
Pro-forma
Projected operating statement
Recession
Recurring expenses
Rehabilitation
Rentable area
Reserves for replacements
Revival
Usable area
Variable expenses

ANSWERS

To chapter exercises. If you couldn't figure out what to put in the blanks, find the answer here!

Exercise a

The general business economy goes through __CYCLES__. *The period of lowest economic activity is called* __BUSINESS__ __CONTRACTION__. *The* __REAL__ __ESTATE__ *economy tends to lag behind the general business economy.*

A regional and __NEIGHBORHOOD__ *market analysis is one of the property manager's first tasks when taking over a new property. In the neighborhood analysis the most important factor is the size and density of the* __POPULATION__. *When taking over a property, a property manager should also prepare a* __MARKET__ *rent survey. Then projected expenses should be analyzed. Expenses are either* __FIXED__, *meaning that they will be incurred regardless of occupancy levels,* __VARIABLE__ *which means that they increase and decrease with occupancy levels, or* __MIXED__ *which are expenses with the characteristics of both. Most expenses in property management are considered to be* __RECURRING__ *expenses because they must be paid periodically. An unusual, one-time expense would be considered a* __NON-RECURRING__ *such as an expense for* __RESERVES__ *for* __REPLACEMENTS__.

After determining income and expenses, the property manager should prepare for the owner a projected __OPERATING__ __STATEMENT__. *The manager must also make an allowance for* __VACANCY__ *and* __CREDIT__ __LOSS__.

Subtracting the __VACANCY__ *and* __CREDIT__ __LOSS__ *allowance from the potential gross income leaves the* ___EFFECTIVE___ ___GROSS___ *income. By subtracting the operating expenses from this, the* ___NET___ ___OPERATING___ ___INCOME___ *is derived. Finally, the* ___DEBT___ ___SERVICE___ *is subtracted to find the* ___NET___ ___SPENDABLE___ *income. These figures are all used to calculate the* ___BREAK___ - ___EVEN___ *point for the property. This is expressed as the* ___PERCENTAGE___ *of occupancy that is necessary to meet all the expenses of the property.*

The total area of a building, measured from the outside, is called the ___CONSTRUCTION___ *area. The total area inside the building, less portions of the structure which intrude, is called the* ___RENTABLE___ *area.*

The portion which excludes restrooms, maintenance and mechanical rooms is called the ___USABLE___ *area.*

Restoration of a property without any alteration of its design, purpose, function or utility is called ___REHABILITATION___ .

Subsidized residential rentals are available through the HUD ___SECTION___ ___8___ *Program. Under this program a tenant pays rent up to* ___30___ *% of the tenant's monthly income, and HUD makes up the rest. To utilize this program an owner must enter into a* ___HOUSING___ ___ASSISTANCE___ ___PAYMENTS___ *Contract with HUD, and must lease the property to the tenant on HUD's* ___MODEL___ *Lease form.*

questions & answers

PRACTICE QUESTIONS

The following practice questions are representative of the questions you will find on the final examination and on the licensing examinations given by the Oregon Real Estate Agency.

1. Cycles of the real estate market differ from those of the general business economy in that
   I. the general business economy is usually subject to more extreme oversupply and undersupply.
   II. trends in real estate lag significantly behind trends in the general economy.
   (A) I only (C) Both I and II
   (B) II only (D) Neither I nor II

2. In regard to business cycles,
   (A) during a period of business expansion, vacancies tend to be low.
   (B) during a period of business recession, vacancies tend to increase.
   (C) during a period of business contraction, vacancies are high.
   (D) all of the above are true.

3. With reference to the function of a property manager, which of the following is the responsibility of a property manager?
   (A) Obtain the best possible return on the owner's investment
   (B) Preserve the owner's investment
   (C) Provide financial records and accounts
   (D) All of the above

4. Which one of the following is not among the major responsibilities of a property manager?
   (A) Obtain the highest possible return for the investor
   (B) Preserve the building
   (C) Maintain high occupancy
   (D) Obtain listing for resale

5. Property managers are responsible for
   I. protecting the condition of real estate.
   II. maximizing income from real property.
   (A) I only (C) Both I and II
   (B) II only (D) Neither I nor II

6. The basic goal of the professional real estate manager is to
   (A) maintain the property in as perfect condition as humanly possible.
   (B) return to the property owner in the long term the highest possible net return.
   (C) obtain tenants who will stay for long periods of time.
   (D) keep administration costs to the minimum.

7. Building rules and regulations generally serve to protect which of the following?
   I. The owner's investment
   II. The peaceful enjoyment of all tenants
   (A) I only (C) Both I and II
   (B) II only (D) Neither I nor II

8. A property manager's duties typically include all but which one of the following?
   (A) Collecting rents
   (B) Making minor repairs
   (C) Marketing space
   (D) Investing profits from client's properties

9. A property manager must
   (A) market space in competition with other properties.
   (B) provide the highest level of tenant services, without regard to cost of operation.
   (C) keep rents slightly above the current market level to avoid overcrowding.
   (D) increase gross receipts in a period of rising and continuing vacancies.

10. One of the most effective ways for a property manager to provide income to the owner and to advertise the manager's own abilities is through a well-run building which has
(A) as high or higher rents than other similar buildings.
(B) satisfied tenants served by competent employees.
(C) the most complete and up-to-date accounting reports.
(D) the lowest paid employees.

11. Information for estimating future operating expenses for a property can be obtained
I. from review of operating expenses for comparable properties.
II. from reviewing the owner's past operating expense.
(A) I only
(B) II only
(C) Both I and II
(D) Neither I nor II

12. When completing a budget forecast, the property manager should study past
I. budgets and past income and expense reports.
II. balance sheets.
(A) I only
(B) II only
(C) Both I and II
(D) Neither I nor II

13. Included in the property management budget for a specific property as operating expenses are costs for
I. hazard insurance.
II. the property management fee.
(A) I only
(B) II only
(C) Both I and II
(D) Neither I nor II

14. Which of the following is not an operating expense on a budget as prepared by a property manager?
(A) Janitorial services
(B) Replacement of ceiling
(C) Utilities
(D) Management fees

15. The wages paid to the employees hired to maintain and clean a building are an example of
(A) regularly recurring cost.
(B) periodic cost.
(C) recurring variable cost.
(D) nonrecurring variable cost.

16. The repair of fire damage to an office building is an example of a
(A) regularly recurring cost.
(B) periodic cost.
(C) recurring variable cost.
(D) non-recurring variable cost.

17. An example of a variable operating expense in the operation of a large office complex would be
(A) real property taxes.
(B) fire insurance.
(C) decorating costs.
(D) mortgage payments.

18. An apartment building has fixed costs of $63,000 per year and a variable cost ratio of 30 percent. What is the break-even point for the property expressed in dollars per year?
(A) $44,100
(B) $81,900
(C) $90,000
(D) $210,000

19. In property management, an operating budget
(A) establishes the maximum amount of expenditures a property manager can make.
(B) is the year-end summary of operating costs for a building.
(C) is a projection of anticipated costs for the annual operation of a building.
(D) establishes rental income for a year.

20. Which of the following items would be included in the operating budget of a property manager responsible for management of a condominium complex?
(A) Replacement reserve for cedar shingles on the roof
(B) Replacement reserve for refrigerators and stoves
(C) Vacancy allowance
(D) Painting interiors of owners' units

21. The amount of the mortgage payment applied to the principal is deducted from expenses when computing
I. profit and loss statements.
II. balance sheets.
(A) I only
(B) II only
(C) Both I and II
(D) Neither I nor II

22. Which of the following is not considered in setting rental fees for a tenant in a large office complex?
    (A) Ratio of total space to Rentable space
    (B) Square foot area
    (C) Special services furnished, such as parking, security and utilities
    (D) Cubic foot volume

23. A property manager should be aware of the "break-even" point of any building he or she manages. The break-even point is
    (A) the occupancy level at which gross income for a property equals total fixed and variable operating costs.
    (B) where total profit equals total expenses.
    (C) where rental income equals that obtainable from similar buildings.
    (D) the occupancy level at which gross income for a property equals the debt service of the property.

24. In inflationary times, a property manager would not want a long term lease with rents based upon
    (A) graduated amounts.
    (B) the consumer price index.
    (C) the cost of living index.
    (D) a fixed rate.

25. A long term lease is generally to the owner's advantage in which of the following cases?
    I. When negotiating a commercial lease with an escalation clause
    II. When the owner has made significant alterations in the space to suit the tenant
    (A) I only
    (B) II only
    (C) Both I and II
    (D) Neither I nor II

26. Which of the following should not be a consideration in selecting a tenant?
    (A) The size of space versus the tenant's requirements
    (B) The tenant's ability to pay
    (C) Racial and ethnic backgrounds of the tenants
    (D) Compatibility of the business to other tenants

27. Rehabilitation
    (A) requires a change in design.
    (B) restores a building to new condition.
    (C) increases the risk factor.
    (D) changes property uses.

28. To rehabilitate real property usually means
    (A) design changes must be made to the property.
    (B) the property will be restored to a good condition.
    (C) the use of the property will be changed.
    (D) the property must be replaced to obtain its highest and best use potential.

29. A property manager believes that there will be a shortage of rental units in the near future. The property manager should rent all units
    (A) on long term leases.
    (B) on short term leases.
    (C) at rates based on the Consumer Price Index.
    (D) on triple net leases.

30. When evaluating the data in a neighborhood market survey, a residential property manager will be most concerned with
    (A) opportunity for expansion.
    (B) special utility services.
    (C) traffic counts.
    (D) trends in population composition.

31. A property manager leases office space with dimensions of 30 feet by 40 feet for $29.00 per square foot per year. The rent per month is
    (A) $2,030.00.
    (B) $2,900.00.
    (C) $4,800.00.
    (D) $34,800.00.

32. A commercial property containing 43,000 square feet is rented at $5 per square foot. However, actual rental collections over the past year amounted to only $182,750. What occupancy rate should be used in the budget forecast for the next year?
    (A) 80 percent
    (B) 85 percent
    (C) 82 percent
    (D) 89 percent

33. Which of the following statements concerning property covered by a Housing and Urban Development (HUD) Section 8 Housing Assistance Payments contract is true?
    I. The contract specifies the total rental rate for a housing unit, as well as the portion payable by the family.
    II. The contract serves as a lease between the owner of the project and the tenant.
    (A) I only
    (B) II only
    (C) Both I and II
    (D) Neither I nor II

34. All of the following are major parts of a neighborhood market analysis except
    (A) boundaries and land usage.
    (B) transportation and utilities.
    (C) supply and demand in relation to the economy.
    (D) demographic and economic information on the region in which the neighborhood is located.

ANSWERS

To practice questions. If you chose the wrong letter, here's the right one! The explanations are designed to clarify your understanding.

1. **B** Because real estate takes a long time to develop, a subdivider could put in a subdivision, but by the time it is ready for the market, discover that the market is glutted by then. The opposite is also true. Therefore, real estate tends to more extremes of over- and undersupply. When the economy is overheated and the government acts to slow it down, it always affects lower-priced commodities first.
2. **D** Business expansion and contraction are processes. Business contraction is a condition of maximum recession.
3. **D** The main goal of the property manager is to maximize the owner's return on investment. Preserving the investment is essential to that goal. The license law and the law of agency both require the manager to provide complete accounting to the owner.
4. **D** A property manager's primary goal is to maximize the owner's return on investment. Preserving the premises and maintaining high occupancy at the highest rents possible are essential to that goal. Listing the property for resale has nothing to do with management duties.
5. **C** The main function of a property manager is to maximize the owner's return on investment. Protecting the condition of the property is essential to that goal.
6. **B** A property manager's primary goal is to maximize the owner's return on investment. Maintaining the property in good condition, obtaining and retaining long term tenants, and holding costs to a minimum are all essential to meeting that goal.
7. **C** Professional property managers use rules and regulations primarily to preserve the owner's investment. However, satisfied tenants produce higher rents, so rules are also frequently designed to maintain the tenants' peaceful enjoyment of the premises.
8. **D** An owner generally hires a property manager in order to have a passive investment, therefore the property manager is expected to do everything necessary to run the building profitably. However, the property manager does not ordinarily take the responsibility to reinvest the profits.
9. **A** A property manager's primary goal is to maximize the owner's return on investment. However, a property manager can only operate within market conditions. A property manager cannot be expected to obtain rents that are higher than competing properties, or to raise rents when vacancies are on the increase.
10. **B** Regardless of how much they are paid, competent employees will ensure satisfied customers. If the customers are satisfied, profits will be maximized.
11. **C** While the property manager must base the budget primarily on the market, historical data for the subject property is also of interest.
12. **A** The balance sheet is a statement of net worth. Income and expense (profit and loss) reports are statements of income received and disbursed, and profits retained.
13. **C** There are four kinds of operating expenses: Wages paid to staff, maintenance, administrative, and general operating expenses (e.g., utilities).
14. **B** There are four kinds of operating expenses: Wages paid to staff, maintenance, administrative, and general operating expenses (e.g., utilities). Replacement of major components, such as the roof, appliances, carpeting, etc. are capital outlays, not an expenses.
15. **C** There are four kinds of operating expenses: Wages paid to staff, maintenance, administrative, and general operating expenses (e.g., utilities). Of these, fixed expenses are those which do not change with occupancy. Fixed expenses, in turn, are categorized as regularly recurring costs (e.g., wages of personnel), or periodic costs. Periodic costs are the same as regularly recurring costs, but where the period is longer (e.g., property taxes). Variable expenses are those which are greater with higher occupancy and lower when occupancy drops. Since staff requirements change according to occupancy, wages are variable.
16. **D** Hopefully, the fire is a non-recurring event.
17. **C** Fixed expenses are those which do not change with occupancy. Variable expenses are those which are greater with higher occupancy and lower when occupancy drops. All of the listed expenses do

not change according to occupancy, except decorating costs.

18. **C** Costs are either fixed or variable, so if the variable costs amount to 30% of the total, then the fixed costs must be the remaining 70%. If the fixed costs are stated to be $63,000, and we know that they represent 70% of total costs, then the total costs must be $90,000. You can determine this by dividing the $63,000 by 70% ($63,000 ÷ 0.70 = $90,000). The break-even point is the point at which the expenses equal the income, so the total expenses is the same as the break-even point.

19. **C** In accounting, the word "budget" means a projection. A "statement" is a final accounting of what actually happened and the results.

20. **A** Expenses include all items necessary to operate the premises, but do not include capital expenditures. The vacancy allowance, while it is important, is not included in the operating budget because the operating budget is a projection of how much will be required to operate the premises, not how the funds will be obtained. Replacement reserves for major components, such as a roof, new appliances, etc. are considered capital expenditures, not expenses.

21. **A** The balance sheet is a statement of net worth. For the balance sheet, the remaining principal balance is required, but not the principal or interest payments made. A profit and loss statement, on the other hand, is a statement of funds received, disbursed, and profit retained.

22. **D** Unless the property is a storage facility, cubic footage is usually irrelevant.

23. **A** The break-even point for any business is the point at which all the bills are being paid, but there is no profit yet. For an apartment building, this is the point at which total gross income equals all costs of operation, plus mortgage debt service (principal and interest). Costs of operation include variable expenses (e.g., maintenance, which varies with the percentage of occupancy), and fixed (e.g., property taxes, which remain unaffected by the percentage of occupancy.

24. **D** When costs are going up, the landlord needs a lease arrangement that will cover the increases. A fixed lease would be inadvisable.

25. **C** An owner leasing property on a long term needs to be protected against inflation, hence an escalator (escalation) clause is necessary. Similarly, if the tenant wishes expensive improvements to be made, the owner needs to recover the cost, so a long term lease is needed.

26. **C** The law prohibits discrimination based on various factors, including race and ethnic background.

27. **B** Rehabilitation might require changes in design, might increase the owner's risk, and might even involve changing the use of the property, although none of these is common. Rehabilitation always restores the condition of the structure.

28. **B** When the use of the property is to be changed, this is called renovation. If the property's physical condition is restored, this is rehabilitation.

29. **B** If a shortage of rental units develops, rents will increase in the marketplace. The manager would be advised to rent on short term leases in order not to lock in the current lower rents.

30. **D** While all of these factors are of interest to a property manager, the factor which most affects how the manager can maximize profits is changes in the type of resident in the area. For example, if upscale people are moving into the area, it would make sense to upgrade the apartments.

31. **B** The area to be leased is 1,200 square feet (30 feet × 40 feet = 1,200 square feet). At a price of $29.00 per square foot, this comes to $34,800 per year ($29.00 × 1,200 = $34,800). Therefore, the monthly rent is $2,900.00 ($34,800 ÷ 12 = $2,900.00).

32. **B** If the property is rented at $5 per square foot and there are a total of 43,000 square feet to rent, then the potential gross income is $215,000 ($5 × 43,000 = $215,000). However, if they received only $182,750, then there was clearly a substantial vacancy factor. To determine the percentage of occupancy they experienced, divide the rent actually received ($182,750) by the potential rent ($215,000). This comes to exactly 85% ($182,750 ÷ $215,000 = 0.85). Therefore, if historical trends continue, the property manager should budget for an 85% occupancy rate.

33. **A** Under HUD Section 8, there are two contracts. The Housing Assistance Payments contract is between HUD and the landlord, where the landlord agrees to accept a portion of the rent from HUD. The tenant's right to possession is contained in a lease, a separate document from the Housing Assistance Payments contract.

34. **D** A neighborhood is a local area bordered by natural and man-made barriers such as hills, freeways and differing land use patterns. Neighborhood analysis includes all social, economic, physical and government influences, but does not extend to regional matters.

TRUST ACCOUNTING

Real estate agents have been licensed in Oregon since 1919, but it was not until 1951 that brokers were required to keep clients' funds separate from their own in a clients' trust account. Today the rules relating to handling clients' funds are involved and strict. These days, anyone who deals in the funds of another must adhere to exacting standards of accounting and honesty. Placing clients' funds in your personal or business account is called ***commingling***, and is the fastest way to lose your license. The rules apply to brokers, property managers, and even other persons involved in real estate transactions, such as escrow agents.

While placing clients' funds in your personal or company account is commingling, the opposite, that is, keeping personal funds in a clients' trust account, is also commingling (sometimes called ***reverse commingling***). Since some banks automatically close an account if the balance ever goes to zero, the Administrative Rules make an exception for keeping a nominal amount of personal funds in a clients' trust account in order to keep the account open. And in property management activity you are allowed to leave earned management fees in the account briefly provided you withdraw them monthly, or on some other schedule authorized by the owner.

Under no circumstances can you ever pay funds to yourself from the clients' trust account until the funds have been earned. For sales transactions that means not until the transaction is completely closed.

One of the main reasons for keeping clients' funds in a clients' trust account is that the License Act specifically states that when funds are in an account labeled "clients' trust account" this constitutes prima facie evidence that the funds are not the property of the signer on the account and that they are exempt from execution and garnishment.

NOTES

Thus, if a real estate broker owes money and the creditor obtains a judgment, the judgment creditor cannot reach the funds in the clients' trust account. Furthermore, if a broker dies the clients can easily obtain release of their funds without having to wait until the broker's estate is probated or having to prove that the funds were not part of the broker's personal assets.

When a broker or property manager sets up shop the first step is usually to open a clients' trust account. The statutes require that it be in a federally-insured bank, trust company, savings bank, mutual savings bank, savings and loan association or credit union that maintains a head office or a branch in this state. The Commissioner has no authority outside of Oregon, so the logic of requiring a head office or branch in Oregon is so the Commissioner can obtain account records. Note that in today's financial world there are many depository institutions which do not meet these requirements.

The account can be an interest-bearing account if the parties desire, provided the account does not have a fixed term (e.g., it can be an open savings account, but not a certificate of deposit with an early withdrawal penalty). If an interest-bearing account is used the broker must have a written agreement from all parties with an interest in the funds as to the disposition of the interest. This includes the buyer, the seller, the broker and, if property management is involved, the owner and the tenant. There is no limit to how many clients' trust accounts a broker may have, so when a broker uses an interest-bearing account it is customary to use a separate account for each transaction. If more than one clients' funds are in an interest-bearing account the broker would have significant bookkeeping work keeping track of how much interest belonged to which party. Note that there is no prohibition on the licensee receiving the interest, as long as all parties agree in writing.

Bank service charges and other fees can be a problem with a clients' trust account because the rules do not permit the licensee to allow the bank to apply service charges to a clients' trust account. The reason for this rule is to simplify the bookkeeping and reconciliation tasks for licensees and examiners from the real estate agency, as well as making sure that clients are not charged expenses which should really be a business expense to the licensee. Many banks these days offer free account services as long as the depositor maintains a certain minimum balance, and this is the way most licensees handle the issue. After all, most brokers and property managers have many thousands of dollars in the clients' trust account. The alternative is to ask the bank to charge the licensee's personal or operating account.

When the licensee opens a clients' trust account there are two notices that have to be completed. The first is a notice to the bank which the broker or property manager must fill out and have signed by a bank official (see sample on the next page).

The licensee is required to maintain this form along with other records relating to the clients' trust account for the required six years. (In this case, the six years would run from the termination of the account.)

In addition, the licensee is required to file with the Real Estate Agency a statement indicating the institution(s) and the name(s) and account number(s) of the clients' trust account(s) and giving the Commissioner and the staff of the Real Estate Agency authority to examine the account(s). The statement and the authorization must be on forms which are available from the Real Estate Agency.

A broker's use of a clients' trust account is optional. Most brokers, and all brokers with significant sales activity, maintain at least one clients' trust account. However, if a broker wishes, the funds can be placed in a neutral escrow depository in Oregon. As an additional alternative, they can be placed in the clients' trust account of a cooperating broker in cases where there is more than one broker involved in the transaction.

NOTICE OF CLIENTS' TRUST ACCOUNT

To: (*name of bank*) ______________________________

Under the Oregon Real Estate License Law, I am the real estate broker, principal real estate broker or property manager for (*licensed name of broker or business*) ______________________________

______________________________.

Further, under ORS 696.241, I am required to maintain in Oregon a Clients' Trust Account for the purpose of holding funds belonging to others.

With regard to the account(s) numbered ______________ which is/are designated as a Clients' Trust Account, the account(s) is/are maintained with you as a depository for money belonging to persons other than myself and in my fiduciary capacity as a real estate broker or principal real estate broker established by client agreements in separate documents.

Dated: ______________ (*insert date*)

____

(*signature of broker*)

ACKNOWLEDGMENT OF RECEIPT

I, ______________________________ , a duly authorized representative of (*bank*) ______________________________ , do hereby acknowledge receipt of the above NOTICE OF CLIENTS' TRUST ACCOUNT on (*date*)______________ .

____

(*signature*)

____

(*title*)

Normally, all funds must be deposited by the close of business of the third banking day following receipt from the customer or client. A "banking day" means any day that banks are normally open, but does not include Saturdays, Sundays, or legal holidays. If a principal broker or property manager has other agents associated under his or her license, then all funds received by the associated licensees must be turned over to the principal broker or property manager promptly. The principal licensee must see to it that the funds are deposited to the clients' trust account by the close of business of the third banking day following receipt by the agent of the principal. In other words, if you are a property manager working under another property manager, between the two of you the funds must be in the clients' trust account within three days total. You don't have three days to turn it over to your principal, who then has another three days to get it into the clients' trust account. Note that principal brokers, sole practitioner brokers and property mangers can have clients' trust accounts, but licensees associated with a principal broker or property manager cannot have their own clients' trust accounts.

NOTES

Special property management rules

Property managers handle funds belonging to others as well, usually generating even larger dollar amounts than sales activity. It should come as no surprise, then, that handling clients' funds is subject to even more involved rules for property management activity than for brokerage transactions.

It should also be mentioned that the Administrative Rules define "property manager" as including a broker or principal broker who engages in property management activity. So if a broker or principal broker is managing property, then the special rules for property management clients' trust accounts apply the same as for a property manager licensee.

The first difference is that maintaining a clients' trust account is optional for a sole practitioner broker or for a principal broker, but a property manager has no choice. Property managers must maintain at least one clients' trust account labeled "Clients' Trust Account – Property Management." If a property manager takes refundable deposits, then the property manager will probably also need to have an additional clients' trust account labeled "Clients' Trust Account – Property Management – Security Deposits." The exception is if the property management agreement with the owner provides that the refundable deposits are to be turned over to the owner, then the property manager can deposit them to the regular property management clients' trust account and turn them over to the owner at the end of each accounting period.

In property management it is not uncommon to maintain one clients' trust account for more than one owner, keeping subsidiary ledger accounts to maintain a record of the amounts which belong to each owner. However, if the property manager is not careful, it would be an easy mistake to write a check to pay a bill for an owner even though that owner did not have sufficient funds to pay it. This would be using funds belonging to other owners, and could create a problem. The Administrative Rules prohibit this unless the property manager has formal loan agreements between the owners. In the real world this only happens if the two "owners" are really the same entity, such as different divisions of the same company, or perhaps a husband and wife, each of whom had their own investments. Even then, there must be a separate, dated loan agreement for each transfer; you cannot have a blanket agreement, nor can the loan agreement be contained within the property management agreement.

It is easier to understand accounting procedures for property management when you recognize that everything is based on the management agreement. Each management agreement must be given a unique code to identify it, and a separate ledger card maintained for that agreement. If one owner has given two or more management agreements to the property manager, each agreement must have a separate owner's ledger, even if all the money belongs to the same person. Every receipt and disbursement relating to properties covered under a management agreement must be posted on the ledger for that management agreement.

A property manager must also maintain a receipts and disbursements journal for each property management clients' trust account. "Receipts and disbursements journal" is a fancy accountant's term for a check register. The main difference is that it may have additional columns to record things like the code for the property management agreement for which the funds were received or disbursed – essential if one clients' trust account is used for multiple management agreements. Otherwise, it has the same function, that is, to show each deposit and each check and a running balance. The Administrative Rules require the property manager to post each entry with the date and the amount of the deposit or check, together with from whom it

NOTES

was received or to whom it was paid, and if a check, the number of the check, plus a running balance.

RENT RECEIPTS AND DISBURSEMENTS JOURNAL						
Owner					*Owner No.*	
Address					*Phone*	
Property					*Bus. Phone*	
Spec. Inst.						
Date	*From/To*	*Description*	*Ref. #*	*Debit*	*Credit*	*Balance*

A sample of a rent receipts and disbrusements journal showing the layout. Normally it would be a full page long.

The property manager must also maintain a separate ledger for each tenant. The tenant ledger must have a separate place to post refundable deposits so they are not posted together with rent. Note that the tenant ledger does not have a running balance, except for a balance due column in case the rent is not paid in full – it is just a record of receipts and, occasionally, a disbursement for a refund or return of a security deposit.

TENANT LEDGER						
Tenant					*Owner No.*	
Address					*Tenant Phone*	
Move-in Date		*Deposit Amt.*			*Work Phone*	
SECURITY DEPOSIT SECTION						
Date	*From/To*	*Description*	*Ref. #*	*Debit*	*Credit*	*Balance*
RENT SECTION						
Date	*From/To*	*Description*	*Ref. #*	*Debit*	*Credit*	*Bal. Due*

A sample of a tenant ledger showing the layout. Normally it would be a full page long.

When a property manager receives rent funds they must be deposited to the regular property management clients' trust account, and the date, amount, and source of the funds must be posted to the receipts and disbursements journal and also on the tenant's ledger.

NOTES

Similarly, refundable deposits are normally entered on the receipts and disbursements journal for the security deposit clients' trust account, and also on the tenant ledger.

Many tenants pay their rent in cash, and the property manager is required to give the tenant a receipt for the funds. The receipt must be prenumbered and in duplicate so the tenant can have one copy and the property manager can retain the other. The receipt must show the date and the amount of the funds, name of the tenant from whom the funds were received and what they were for, the name of the property manager who actually received the funds, and the identifying code of the management agreement for the property for which the funds were received.

Reconciliation

Many people do not bother to reconcile their bank accounts but, even those who do not do so at least generally know how to do it. Reconciliation is a pretty simple thing. You take the ending balance from the bank statement, add deposits made since the statement was prepared, subtract checks written that have not yet cleared, and this should equal the amount in your check register. If it does not, then you go through the check register looking for where you added or subtracted wrong, or forgot to write down a check or deposit.

With clients' trust accounts it is the same, except that there are a couple of differences. First, you use a receipts and disbursements journal instead of a check register, although its function is more or less the same. And there is one additional function. You must add up the ledgers for each transaction (for a brokerage clients' trust account), and this must equal the balance showing in the receipts and disbursements journal. In other words, the transaction ledgers show how much you are holding for each transaction, so the totals of the ledgers had better be the amount your register shows you have on hand.

For property management it is the same thing, except that the ledgers are the owners ledgers instead of the transaction ledgers, and there may be much more activity.

We call this the "triple balance" – bank statement, check register, owners' ledgers. Always remember that you're out of balance until all three figures are the same.

To understand better how this works we have provided three samples of simple clients' trust account activity for the month of October. The first is for a property management security deposit clients' trust account, the second is for a rental income property management clients' trust account, and the last is for a brokerage clients' trust account. (Property managers need not complete the brokerage problem.) It is recommend that you go through these samples in class with an instructor. If that is not possible, we have included an answer key showing how each should have come out. If you are studying this on your own you would benefit more by trying to do it first without looking at the answer key.

Property Management – Security Deposit Account

4/10/2002 Received deposit of $500 from Mr. and Mrs. Garvin Sanders by check for property at 799 N.W. 18th Avenue owned by property owner 2001-1, receipt #205

5/5/2002 Received deposit of $600 from Alexander Pope by check for property at 18263 S.E. 42nd Street owned by property owner 2001-1, receipt #206

7/12/2002 Received deposit of $650 from Mr. and Mrs. Adam Suttle by check for property at 1312 Holland Lane owned by property owner 2000-8, receipt #207

7/17/2002 Received deposit of $550 from James Gorin and Mary Abrams in cash for property at 1405 N.E. Sycamore, Unit 2 owned by property owner 2001-2, receipt #208

8/9/2002 Received deposit of $600 from Tim Adamson by check for property at 1405 N.E. Sycamore, Unit 4 owned by property owner 2001-2, receipt #209

8/21/2002 Received deposit of $500 from Beryl Green and Pat Frobisher by check for property at 1105 S.W. Evelyn owned by property owner 2001-1, receipt #210

9/16/2002 Refunded deposit of $500 to Mr. and Mrs. Garvin Sanders by check 2107 for property at 799 N.W. 18th Avenue owned by property owner 2001-1

10/1/2002 Received deposit of $750 from Dan Abrahams and Mike McGuire by check for property at 1405 N.E. Sycamore, Unit 3 owned by property owner 2001-2, receipt #211

Using the transaction information above, fill out the Receipts and Disbursements Journal below and the Tenant Ledgers on pages 114–117. Then reconcile the bank statement on page 118 using the form on pages 119–120. The answers are at the end of this section on pages 136–142.

RECEIPTS AND DISBURSEMENTS JOURNAL – SECURITY DEPOSITS							
Date	From/To	Description	Ref.	Own.	Debit	Credit	Balance
4/10/02	Garvin Sanders	Deposit 799 18th Ave	#205	2001-1		500.00	500.00
5/5/02	Alex Pope	Deposit 18263 42	#206	2001-1		600.00	1100.00
7/12/02	Adam Suttle	Deposit 1312 Holland Lane	#207	2000-8		650.00	1750.00
7/17/02	Gorin/Abrams	1405 NE Sycamore #2	#206	2001-2		550.00	2300.00
8/9/02	Tim Adamson	1405 NE Sycamore #4	#209	2001-2		600.00	2900.00
8/21/02	Green/Frobisher	1105 SW Evelyn	#210	2001-1		500.00	3400.00
9/16/02	Garvin Sanders Refund	799 18th Ave Refund	Check 2107	2001-1	500.00		2900.00
10/1/02	Abrahams/McGuire	1405 NE Sycamore #3	#211	2001-2		750.00	3650.00

TENANT LEDGER

Tenant	Mr. & Mrs. Garvin Sanders	Owner No.	2001-1
Address	799 N.W. 18th Ave	Tenant Phone	
Move-in Date	4/10/2002 Deposit Amt. 500.00	Work Phone	

SECURITY DEPOSIT SECTION

Date	From/To	Description	Ref. #	Debit	Credit	Balance
4/10/02	Garvin Sanders	Deposit	#205		500.00	500.00

RENT SECTION

Date	From/To	Description	Ref. #	Debit	Credit	Bal. Due

TENANT LEDGER

Tenant		Owner No.	
Address		Tenant Phone	
Move-in Date	Deposit Amt.	Work Phone	

SECURITY DEPOSIT SECTION

Date	From/To	Description	Ref. #	Debit	Credit	Balance

RENT SECTION

Date	From/To	Description	Ref. #	Debit	Credit	Bal. Due

TENANT LEDGER

Tenant				*Owner No.*	
Address				*Tenant Phone*	
Move-in Date		*Deposit Amt.*		*Work Phone*	

SECURITY DEPOSIT SECTION

Date	*From/To*	*Description*	*Ref. #*	*Debit*	*Credit*	*Balance*

RENT SECTION

Date	*From/To*	*Description*	*Ref. #*	*Debit*	*Credit*	*Bal. Due*

TENANT LEDGER

Tenant				*Owner No.*	
Address				*Tenant Phone*	
Move-in Date		*Deposit Amt.*		*Work Phone*	

SECURITY DEPOSIT SECTION

Date	*From/To*	*Description*	*Ref. #*	*Debit*	*Credit*	*Balance*

RENT SECTION

Date	*From/To*	*Description*	*Ref. #*	*Debit*	*Credit*	*Bal. Due*

TENANT LEDGER

Tenant				*Owner No.*	
Address				*Tenant Phone*	
Move-in Date		*Deposit Amt.*		*Work Phone*	

SECURITY DEPOSIT SECTION

Date	*From/To*	*Description*	*Ref. #*	*Debit*	*Credit*	*Balance*

RENT SECTION

Date	*From/To*	*Description*	*Ref. #*	*Debit*	*Credit*	*Bal. Due*

TENANT LEDGER

Tenant				*Owner No.*	
Address				*Tenant Phone*	
Move-in Date		*Deposit Amt.*		*Work Phone*	

SECURITY DEPOSIT SECTION

Date	*From/To*	*Description*	*Ref. #*	*Debit*	*Credit*	*Balance*

RENT SECTION

Date	*From/To*	*Description*	*Ref. #*	*Debit*	*Credit*	*Bal. Due*

Tenant Ledger

Tenant				*Owner No.*	
Address				*Tenant Phone*	
Move-in Date		*Deposit Amt.*		*Work Phone*	

Security Deposit Section

Date	*From/To*	*Description*	*Ref. #*	*Debit*	*Credit*	*Balance*

Rent Section

Date	*From/To*	*Description*	*Ref. #*	*Debit*	*Credit*	*Bal. Due*

Tenant Ledger

Tenant				*Owner No.*	
Address				*Tenant Phone*	
Move-in Date		*Deposit Amt.*		*Work Phone*	

Security Deposit Section

Date	*From/To*	*Description*	*Ref. #*	*Debit*	*Credit*	*Balance*

Rent Section

Date	*From/To*	*Description*	*Ref. #*	*Debit*	*Credit*	*Bal. Due*

Bank of America

P.O. Box 3977
Seattle, WA 98124-2477

E 11-2

PROPERTY MANAGEMENT, INC.
CLIENTS TRUST ACCT - SEC DEPOSITS
12345 LOIS LANE
WILLAMETTE OR 97200-0000

Your Bank of America Business Checking Statement

Statement Period:
October 1 through October 31, 2002
Account Number: 28534-19731

At Your Service
1.800.873.2632
503.275.2222 in Portland
1.800.845.8893 TTY device access only
www.bankofamerica.com

Customer Service
10101 SW Washington Sq Rd
Portland, OR 97223-4460

Bank of America appreciates your business and we enjoy serving you.

With our free Online Banking service, you can check balances, transfer funds, pay bills and more. See www.bankofamerica.com for details.

❑ Summary of Your Business Checking Account

Beginning Balance on 10/01/02	$3,400.00
Total Deposits and Other Credits	0.00
Total Checks, Withdrawals Transfers, Acount Fees	0.00
Ending Balance	$3,400.00

❑ Bank of America News

Introducing the new Alaska Airlines Visa Business Card from Bank of America for small businesses. Turn your everyday business expenses into travel rewards. This new card gives you expense management tools, convenience and travel rewards like no other business card. Earn 5,000 bonus miles after your first purchase. Call 1.888.600.4000 today to apply.

❑ Deposits

❑ Checks Paid

* Gap in check sequence

❑ Bank of America: In Balance

To assist you in reconciling your account, we have provided the following summary information. A reconciliation worksheet is provided on the reverse of this page.

Mark off each deposit, withdrawal and check shown on this statement in your checkbook register.

Make sure that all transfers are written in your checkbook register, including automatic deposits, automatic payments, ATM and Bank of America Check Card transactions or transfers you made between accounts

• Your ending balance from this statement.. **$3,400.00**

OR 007866.001.1031

Oregon

Clients' Trust Account Reconciliation

Name of trust account: Clients Trust Acct. Security Deposits

Bank: Bank of America

Account number: 28534-19731 Date prepared: ~

Prepared by: Me For month of: October 2002

Part I

Ending balance from bank statement as of 10-31-02 $ 3 400.00

Plus Deposits made and posted to ledgers but not posted on bank statement (outstanding deposits), from Schedule A on reverse 750.00

Subtotal $ 4150.00

Less Checks written and posted to ledgers but not posted on bank statement (outstanding checks), from Schedule B on reverse 500.00

Subtotal $ 3650.00

Plus or minus adjustments, from Schedule C on reverse 0.0

Reconciled bank balance (Total for Part I) as of 10-31-02 $ 3650.00

Part II

Check Register or Receipts and Disbursements Journal Balance as of 10-31-02 $ 3650.00

Part III

Total of Ledger Cards (Schedule D on reverse) as of 10-31-02 $

Must be the same date — Must be the same

Part IV

The totals in Parts I, II and III above must be the same and as of the same date. If any figures are not the same, enter the explanation below and take corrective action to bring books into balance.

Trust accounts must be balanced monthly and all records kept for six years. Retain this completed and signed form with the rest of your records.

Page 1

Schedule A (Deposits not yet posted on bank statement)

Date	Reference	Description	Amount
10/1/02	#211	Abrahams / McGuire	750.00
Total for Schedule A (Enter here and in Part I of the reconciliation			750.00

Schedule B (Outstanding checks)

Date	Ref.	Check #	Description	Amount
10/30/02		C2107	Sanders	500.00
Total for Schedule B (Enter here and in Part I of the reconciliation				500.00

Schedule C (Other adjustments)

Date	Ref.	Check #	Description	Amount
Total for Schedule C (Enter here and in Part I of the reconciliation				

Schedule D (Ledger Cards)

Reference	Description	Amount
Total for Schedule D (Enter here and in Part III of the reconciliation		3650.00

Property Management – Rental Account

October 1 – October 31

10/1/2002 Received rent of $850 from James Gorin and Mary Abrams by check for property at 1405 N.E. Sycamore, Unit 2 owned by property owner 2001-2, receipt #211

10/1/2002 Received rent of $950 from Alexander Pope by check for property at 18263 S.E. 42nd Street owned by property owner 2001-1, receipt #212

10/1/2002 Received $900 rent from Mr. and Mrs. Garvin Sanders by check for property at 799 N.W. 18th Avenue owned by property owner 2001-1, receipt #213

10/2/2002 Received rent of $800 from Mr. and Mrs. Adam Suttle in cash for property at 1312 Holland Lane owned by property owner 2000-8, receipt #214

10/3/2002 Received rent of $1,000 from Tim Adamson by check for property at 1405 N.E. Sycamore, Unit 4 owned by property owner 2001-2, receipt #215

10/4/2002 Received rent of #950 from Beryl Green and Pat Frobisher by check for property at 1105 S.W. Evelyn owned by property owner 2001-1, receipt #216

10/5/2002 Paid mortgage payment of $542 to Mortgage Lenders, Inc. for property at 18263 S.E. 42nd Street owned by property owner 2001-1 by check #2132

10/5/2002 Paid mortgage payment of $1,356 to Fidelity Mortgage Company for property at 1405 N.E. Sycamore, owned by property owner 2001-4 by check #2133

10/5/2002 Paid mortgage payment of $352 to United Lenders for property at 1105 S.W. Evelyn owned by property owner 2001-1 by check #2134

10/5/2002 Paid mortgage payment of $451 to Federal Savings Bank for property at 1816 Hamster Lane owned by property owner 2001-1 by check #2135

10/6/2002 Paid Property Managers, Inc. $85 for cleaning Unit 1 of property at 1405 N.E. Sycamore, owned by property owner 2001-2, by check #2136

10/30/2002 Received rent of $750 from Dan Abrahams and Mike McGuire by check for property at 1405 Sycamore, Unit 3 owned by property owner 2001-2, receipt #217

10/31/2002 Paid management fees for October, 2002 to Property Managers, Inc. in the amount of $462 by check #2137, of which $80 was for owner 2000-8, $252 was for owner 2001-1, and $130 was for owner 2001-2.

10/31/2002 Disbursed $500 to Sandra McCulloch, owner of property at 1405 N.E. Sycamore, property owner 2001-2, by check #2138

Using the transaction information above, fill out the Receipts and Disbursements Journal on the next page and the owners ledgers on pages 122–123, and the Tenant Ledgers on pages 114–117 (this completes the tenant ledgers that were started in the previous exercise). Then reconcile the bank statement on pages 124–125 using the form on pages 126–127. The answers are at the end of this section on pages 136–146.

RECEIPTS AND DISBURSEMENTS JOURNAL – RENTAL INCOME

Date	From/To	Description	Ref.	Own.	Debit	Credit	Balance
10/1		Brought forward					$2,100.00
10/1	Gorin/Abrams	Rent	#211	2001-2		850.00	2950.00

OWNER RENT RECEIPTS AND DISBURSEMENTS LEDGER

Owner	Barry Dunthorpe	*Owner No.*	2000-8
Address	14561 Countryland Lane	*Phone*	314-4123
Property	1312 Holland Lane	*Bus. Phone*	
Spec. Inst.	Maintain minimum $200 for repairs		

Date	From/To	Description	Ref. #	Debit	Credit	Balance
10/1/2002		Balance forward				$300.00

Owner Rent Receipts and Disbursements Ledger

Owner	Sandra McCulloch				*Owner No.*	2001-1
Address	1512 Winding Drive				*Phone*	216-2154
Property	42nd, 18th, Evelyn, Hamster				*Bus. Phone*	
Spec. Inst.	Maintain minimum $500 for repairs					
Date	*From/To*	*Description*	*Ref. #*	*Debit*	*Credit*	*Balance*
10/1/2000		Balance forward				$700.00

Owner Rent Receipts and Disbursements Ledger

Owner	Jameson Investment Company				*Owner No.*	2001-2
Address	2100 West Brunel Parkway				*Phone*	
Property	1405 N.E. Sycamore				*Bus. Phone*	234-1205
Spec. Inst.	Maintain minimum $1,000 for repairs					
Date	*From/To*	*Description*	*Ref. #*	*Debit*	*Credit*	*Balance*
10/1/2002		Balance forward				$1,100.00

Bank of America

P.O. Box 3977
Seattle, WA 98124-2477

E 11-2

PROPERTY MANAGEMENT, INC.
CLIENTS TRUST ACCT - RENT ACCOUNT
12345 LOIS LANE
WILLAMETTE OR 97200-0000

Your Bank of America Business Checking Statement

Statement Period:
October 1 through October 31, 2002
Account Number: 28621-32424

At Your Service
1.800.873.2632
503.275.2222 in Portland
1.800.845.8893 TTY device access only
www.bankofamerica.com

Customer Service
10101 SW Washington Sq Rd
Portland, OR 97223-4460

Bank of America appreciates your business and we enjoy serving you.

With our free Online Banking service, you can check balances, transfer funds, pay bills and more. See www.bankofamerica.com for details.

❑ Summary of Your Business Checking Account

Beginning Balance on 10/01/02	$2,100.00
Total Deposits and Other Credits	$6,200.00
Total Checks, Withdrawals Transfers, Acount Fees	$2,786.00
Ending Balance	$5,514.00

❑ Bank of America News

Introducing the new Alaska Airlines Visa Business Card from Bank of America for small businesses. Turn your everyday business expenses into travel rewards. This new card gives you expense management tools, convenience and travel rewards like no other business card. Earn 5,000 bonus miles after your first purchase. Call 1.888.600.4000 today to apply.

❑ Deposits

	Date Posted	Amount
	10/2	$ 850.00
	10/2	950.00
	10/2	900.00
	10/4	1,000.00
	10/4	$ 800.00
	10/7	950.00
	10/31	750.00
Total of 7 Deposits		**$ 6,200.00**

❑ Checks Paid

* Gap in check sequence

Date Paid	Number	Amount
10/08	2132	$ 542.00
10/08	2133	1,356.00
10/09	2134	352.00
10/9	*2136	$ 85.00
10/10	*2135	451.00
Total of 5 Checks Paid		**$ 2,786.00**

Continued on page 2

Bank of America

PROPERTY MANAGEMENT, INC.

Statement Period: October 1 through October 31, 2002
Account Number **28621-32424**

❑ **Account Activity**

❑ **Daily Account Balance**

Date	Amount	Date	Amount	Date	Amount
10/01	$ 2,100.00	10/07	7,550.00	10/10	4,764.00
10/02	4,800.00	10/08	5,652.00	10/31	5,514.00
10/04	6,600.00	10/09	5,215.00		

❑ **Bank of America: In Balance**

To assist you in reconciling your account, we have provided the following summary information.
A reconciliation worksheet is provided on the reverse of this page.

Mark off each deposit, withdrawal and check shown on this statement in your checkbook register.

Make sure that all transfers are written in your checkbook register, including automatic deposits, automatic payments, ATM and Bank of America Check Card transactions or transfers you made between accounts

• Your ending balance from this statement........ **$5,514.00**

OR 007866.001.1031 Oregon Page 2 of 2

Clients' Trust Account Reconciliation

Name of trust account ______________________________

____

Bank ______________________________

Account number ______________ Date prepared ______________

Prepared by ______________ For month of ______________

Part I

Ending balance from bank statement as of ______________ $ ______________

Plus Deposits made and posted to ledgers but not posted on bank statement (outstanding deposits), from Schedule A on reverse ______________

Subtotal $ ______________

Less Checks written and posted to ledgers but not posted on bank statement (outstanding checks), from Schedule B on reverse ______________

Subtotal $ ______________

Plus or minus adjustments, from Schedule C on reverse ______________

Reconciled bank balance (Total for Part I) as of ______________ $ ______________

Part II

Check Register or Receipts and Disbursements Journal

Balance as of ______________ $ ______________

Part III

Total of Ledger Cards (Schedule D on reverse) as of ______________ $ ______________

Must be the same date

Must be the same

Part IV

The totals in Parts I, II and III above must be the same and as of the same date. If any figures are not the same, enter the explanation below and take corrective action to bring books into balance.

____

____

____

____

____

____

____

____

____

Trust accounts must be balanced monthly and all records kept for six years. Retain this completed and signed form with the rest of your records.

Page 1

Schedule A (Deposits not yet posted on bank statement)

Date	*Reference*	*Description*	*Amount*
Total for Schedule A (Enter here and in Part I of the reconciliation			

Schedule B (Outstanding checks)

Date	*Ref.*	*Check #*	*Description*	*Amount*
Total for Schedule B (Enter here and in Part I of the reconciliation				

Schedule C (Other adjustments)

Date	*Ref.*	*Check #*	*Description*	*Amount*
Total for Schedule C (Enter here and in Part I of the reconciliation				

Schedule D (Ledger Cards)

Reference	*Description*	*Amount*
Total for Schedule D (Enter here and in Part III of the reconciliation		

Brokerage – Sales Account

October 1 – October 31

Balance at beginning of month $17,000 includes funds for transaction 2002-35 (Williams to Marison, $5,000) and 2002-39 (Jameson Investment Company to Birdwell, $9,500).

10/3/2002 Received $2,500 earnest money in form of check from Aaron and Maria King on purchase of property at 13213 West Ash Street from Bill Hightower for $329,000, transaction number 2002-45 assigned

10/3/2002 Received $2,000 in form of check to redeem note for transaction 2002-44 from Mustafa Alqaran on purchase of land on Sanders Road from Ben and Susan Schmidt for $56,000. Original transaction date 9/25/2002

10/10/2002 Received $5,000 earnest money in form of check from Darren Smith and Jill Owens on purchase of property at 132 Baker Street for $220,000 from Gerald and Candice Baker, transaction number 2002-46 assigned

10/10/2002 Transferred $2,500 by check number 3124 to Transamerica Title Insurance Company to close transaction 2002-42, James Oldham seller to Edelberto Ramirez for property at 1221 S.E. 42nd Street, original purchase date 9/7/2002, price $435,000 earnest money of $2,500 received by check on 9/7.

10/11/2002 Received $2,000 earnest money from Bill Marks and James Gavin in cash on purchase of property at Rt. 1, Box 342 for $289,000 from Donald and Sherry Marquam, transaction number 2002-47 assigned and receipt 304 issued.

10/13/2002 Received $150 by check from Daniel Bellini, out-of-town seller of vacant property at 3421 S.E. Lafayette Street, to cover lawn care expense during listing

10/14/2002 Aaron and Maria King forfeit earnest money on transaction 2002-45, agreement on listing is to split 50/50 between agent and seller. Check 3125 written for $1,250 to Bill Hightower; check 3126 written for $1,250 to company.

10/26/2002 Transferred $2,000 earnest money by check number 3127 to Fidelity National Title Insurance Company to close transaction 2002-44, Ben and Susan Schmidt to Mustafa Alqaran for purchase of land on Sanders Road

10/28/2002 Received $3,000 earnest money in form of check from Mary Loeb and Jane Loeb on purchase of property at 12310 Lower Ferry Road for $285,000 from Phillip and Theresa Cantrell, transaction number 2002-48 assigned

The Receipts and Disbursements Journal below and the ledger cards on pages 129–131 have been completed based on the transaction information above. Using the form on pages 134–135, reconcile the bank statement on page 132–133 . The answers are at the end of this section on pages 147-148.

RECEIPTS AND DISBURSEMENTS JOURNAL						
Date	*From/To*	*Description*	*Ref. #*	*Debit*	*Credit*	*Balance*
10/1/2002		Balance forward				$17,000.00
10/3	Aaron & Maria King	EM check 2002-45			2,500.00	19,500.00
10/3	Mustafa Alqaran	Redeem note 2002-44			2,000,00	21,500.00
10/10	D. Smith/J. Owens	EM check 2002-46			5,000.00	26,500.00
10/10	Transamerica	EM 2002-42	C3124	2,500.00		25,000.00
10/11	B. Marks/J. Gavin	EM 2002-47	R304		2,000.00	27,500.00
10/13	Daniel Bellini	Yard maint Lafayette			150.00	27,650.00
10/14	Bill Hightower (seller)	Forfeit EM 2002-45	C3125	1,250.00		25,750.00
10/14	Real Estate Brokers, Inc.	Forfeit EM 2002-45	C3126	1,250.00		24,500.00
10/26	Fidelity National	EM 2002-44	C3127	2,000.00		22,500.00
10/28	Mary/Jane Loeb	EM 2002-48			3,000.00	25,500.00

Sale Ledger						
Seller	James Oldham				*Transaction #*	2002-42
Buyer	Edelberto Ramirez				*Sales Price*	$435,000
Address	1221 S.E. 42nd Street					
Date	*From/To*	*Description*	*Ref. #*	*Debit*	*Credit*	*Balance*
9/7	Ramirez	EM			2,500.00	2,500.00
10/10	Transamerica TI	EM	C3124	2,500.00		0.00

Sale Ledger						
Seller	Ben and Susan Schmidt				*Transaction #*	2002-44
Buyer	Mustafa Alqaran				*Sales Price*	$56,000
Address	Sanders Road					
Date	*From/To*	*Description*	*Ref. #*	*Debit*	*Credit*	*Balance*
9/25	Mustafa Alqaran	EM note				0.00
10/3	Mustafa Alqaran	Note redeemed			2,000.00	2,000.00
10/26	Fidelity National TI	E.M. to escrow	C3127	2,000.00		0.00

Sale Ledger						
Seller	Bill Hightower				*Transaction #*	2002-45
Buyer	Aaron & Maria King				*Sales Price*	$329,000
Address	13213 West Ash Street					
Date	*From/To*	*Description*	*Ref. #*	*Debit*	*Credit*	*Balance*
10/3	A. & M. King	EM			2,500.00	2,500.00
10/14	Bill Hightower	Forfeited E.M.	C3125	1,250.00		1,250.00
10/14	Us	Forfeited E.M.	C3126	1,250.00		0.00

SALE LEDGER						
Seller	Gerald and Candice Baker				*Transaction #*	2002-46
Buyer	Darren Smith and Jill Owens				*Sales Price*	$220,000
Address	132 Baker Street					
Date	*From/To*	*Description*	*Ref. #*	*Debit*	*Credit*	*Balance*
10/10	D. Smith/J. Owens	EM.			5,000.00	5,000.00

SALE LEDGER						
Seller	Donald and Sherry Marquam				*Transaction #*	2002-47
Buyer	Bill Marks and James Gavin				*Sales Price*	$289,000
Address	Rt. 1, Box 342					
Date	*From/To*	*Description*	*Ref. #*	*Debit*	*Credit*	*Balance*
10/11	B. Marks/J. Gavin	EM.			2,000.00	2,000.00

SALE LEDGER						
Seller	Phillip and Theresa Cantrell				*Transaction #*	2002-48
Buyer	Mary Loeb and Jane Loeb				*Sales Price*	$285,000
Address	12310 Lower Ferry Road					
Date	*From/To*	*Description*	*Ref. #*	*Debit*	*Credit*	*Balance*
10/28	M. and J. Loeb	EM.		3,000.00		3,000.00

SALE LEDGER						
Seller				Transaction #		
Buyer				Sales Price		
Address						
Date	From/To	Description	Ref. #	Debit	Credit	Balance

SALE LEDGER						
Seller				Transaction #		
Buyer				Sales Price		
Address						
Date	From/To	Description	Ref. #	Debit	Credit	Balance

SALE LEDGER						
Seller				Transaction #		
Buyer				Sales Price		
Address						
Date	From/To	Description	Ref. #	Debit	Credit	Balance

Bank of America

P.O. Box 3977
Seattle, WA 98124-2477

E 11-2

REAL ESTATE BROKERS, INC.
CLIENTS TRUST ACCOUNT
12345 LOIS LANE
WILLAMETTE OR 97200-0000

Your Bank of America Business Checking Statement

Statement Period:
October 1 through October 31, 2002
Account Number: 24321-12436

At Your Service
1.800.873.2632
503.275.2222 in Portland
1.800.845.8893 TTY device access only
www.bankofamerica.com

Customer Service
10101 SW Washington Sq Rd
Portland, OR 97223-4460

Bank of America appreciates your business and we enjoy serving you.

❑ Summary of Your Business Checking Account

Beginning Balance on 10/01/02	$17,000.00
Total Deposits and Other Credits	$14,650.00
Total Checks, Withdrawals Transfers, Acount Fees	$5,000.00
Ending Balance	$26,650.00

❑ Bank of America News

❑ Deposits

Date Posted	Amount
10/4	$ 2,500.00
10/4	2,000.00
10/11	5,000.00
10/11	2,000.00
10/15	$ 150.00
10/29	3,000.00
Total of 6 Deposits	**$ 14,650.00**

❑ Checks Paid

* Gap in check sequence

Date Paid	Number	Amount
10/15	3124	$ 2,500.00
10/16	3125	1,250.00
10/16	3126	$ 1,250.00
Total of 3 Checks Paid		**$ 5,000.00**

Continued on page 2
OR 007866.001.1031

Oregon

Bank of America

REAL ESTATE BROKERS, INC.

Statement Period: October 1 through October 31, 2002
Account Number **24321-12436**

❑ **Account Activity**

❑ **Daily Account Balance**

Date	Amount	Date	Amount	Date	Amount
10/01	$ 17,000.00	10/11	28,500.00	10/16	23,650.00
10/04	21,500.00	10/15	26,150.00	10/29	26,650.00

❑ **Bank of America: In Balance**

To assist you in reconciling your account, we have provided the following summary information. A reconciliation worksheet is provided on the reverse of this page.

Mark off each deposit, withdrawal and check shown on this statement in your checkbook register.

Make sure that all transfers are written in your checkbook register, including automatic deposits, automatic payments, ATM and Bank of America Check Card transactions or transfers you made between accounts

• Your ending balance from this statement........ **$26,650.00**

Clients' Trust Account Reconciliation

Name of trust account: Clients Trust Account – Sales

Bank: Bank of America

Account number: 24321- 12436 Date prepared: Nov 5

Prepared by: Me For month of: October 02

Part I

Ending balance from bank statement as of 10-31-02 — $ 26,650.00

Plus Deposits made and posted to ledgers but not posted on bank statement (outstanding deposits), from Schedule A on reverse — 0.0

Subtotal — $ 26,650.00

Less Checks written and posted to ledgers but not posted on bank statement (outstanding checks), from Schedule B on reverse — 2001.00

Subtotal — $ 24,650.00

Plus or minus adjustments, from Schedule C on reverse — 0.0

Reconciled bank balance (Total for Part I) as of 10-31-02 — $ 24,650.00

Part II

Check Register or Receipts and Disbursements Journal Balance as of 10-31-02 — $ 25,500.00

Part III

Total of Ledger Cards (Schedule D on reverse) as of 10-31-02 — $ 10,000.00

Must be the same date — Must be the same

Part IV

The totals in Parts I, II and III above must be the same and as of the same date. If any figures are not the same, enter the explanation below and take corrective action to bring books into balance.

Trust accounts must be balanced monthly and all records kept for six years. Retain this completed and signed form with the rest of your records.

Page 1

Schedule A (Deposits not yet posted on bank statement)

Date	*Reference*	*Description*	*Amount*
Total for Schedule A (Enter here and in Part I of the reconciliation			

Schedule B (Outstanding checks)

Date	*Ref.*	*Check #*	*Description*	*Amount*
Total for Schedule B (Enter here and in Part I of the reconciliation				

Schedule C (Other adjustments)

Date	*Ref.*	*Check #*	*Description*	*Amount*
Total for Schedule C (Enter here and in Part I of the reconciliation				

Schedule D (Ledger Cards)

Reference	*Description*	*Amount*
Total for Schedule D (Enter here and in Part III of the reconciliation		

Answers to Reconciliation Problems

Starting below and continuing for the next several pages are the solutions to the three reconciliation problems in this section. Be sure you have completed the problems and checked your work here to make sure you have filled out all the ledgers correctly and that you understand proper trust account balancing procedures.

RECEIPTS AND DISBURSEMENTS JOURNAL – SECURITY DEPOSITS							
Date	*From/To*	*Description*	*Ref.*	*Own.*	*Debit*	*Credit*	*Balance*
4/10/2002	Mr. & Mrs. Sanders	Deposit	R205	01-1		500.00	500.00
5/5	Alexander Pope	Deposit	R206	01-3		600.00	1,100.00
7/12	Mr. & Mrs. Suttle	Deposit	R207	00-8		650.00	1,750.00
7/17	Gorin/Abrams	Deposit	R208	01-4		550.00	2,300.00
8/9	Tim Anderson	Deposit	R209	01-4		600.00	2,900.00
8/21	Green/Frobisher	Deposit	R210	01-1		500.00	3,400.00
10/30	Mr. & Mrs. Sanders	Refund	C2107	01-1	500.00		2,900.00
10/30	Abrahams/McGuire	Deposit	R211	01-4		750.00	3,650.00

TENANT LEDGER

Tenant	Mr. and Mrs. Garvin Sanders			Owner No.	2001-01
Address	799 N.W. 18th Avenue			Tenant Phone	
Move-in Date	4/10/2002	Deposit Amt.	500.00	Work Phone	

SECURITY DEPOSIT SECTION

Date	From/To	Description	Ref. #	Debit	Credit	Balance
4/10	Mr. & Mrs. Sanders	Deposit	R205		500.00	500.00
10/30	Mr. & Mrs. Sanders	Refund	C2107	500.00		0.00

RENT SECTION

Date	From/To	Description	Ref. #	Debit	Credit	Bal. Due
10/1	Mr. & Mrs. Sanders	Rent	R213		900.00	0.00

TENANT LEDGER

Tenant	Alexander Pope			Owner No.	2001-03
Address	18263 S.E. 42nd Street			Tenant Phone	
Move-in Date	5/5/2002	Deposit Amt.	600.00	Work Phone	

SECURITY DEPOSIT SECTION

Date	From/To	Description	Ref. #	Debit	Credit	Balance
5/5	Alexander Pope	Deposit	R206		600.00	600.00

RENT SECTION

Date	From/To	Description	Ref. #	Debit	Credit	Bal. Due
10/1	Alexander Pope	Rent	R212		950.00	0.00

TENANT LEDGER

Tenant	Mr. and Mrs. Adam Suttle			*Owner No.*	2000-8
Address	1312 Holland Lane			*Tenant Phone*	
Move-in Date	7/12/2002	*Deposit Amt.*	650.00	*Work Phone*	

SECURITY DEPOSIT SECTION

Date	*From/To*	*Description*	*Ref. #*	*Debit*	*Credit*	*Balance*
7/12	Mr. & Mrs. Suttle	Deposit	R207		650.00	650.00

RENT SECTION

Date	*From/To*	*Description*	*Ref. #*	*Debit*	*Credit*	*Bal. Due*
10/2	Mr. and Mrs. Suttle	Rent	R214		800.00	0.00

TENANT LEDGER

Tenant	James Gorin and Mary Abrams			*Owner No.*	2001-4
Address	1405 N.E. Sycamore #2			*Tenant Phone*	
Move-in Date	7/17/2002	*Deposit Amt.*	550.00	*Work Phone*	

SECURITY DEPOSIT SECTION

Date	*From/To*	*Description*	*Ref. #*	*Debit*	*Credit*	*Balance*
7/17	Gorin/Abrams	Deposit	R208		550.00	550.00

RENT SECTION

Date	*From/To*	*Description*	*Ref. #*	*Debit*	*Credit*	*Bal. Due*
10/1	Gorin/Abrams	Rent	R211		850.00	0.00

Tenant Ledger						
Tenant	Tim Adamson				*Owner No.*	2001-4
Address	1405 N.E. Sycamore #4				*Tenant Phone*	
Move-in Date	8/9/2002	*Deposit Amt.*	600.00		*Work Phone*	
Security Deposit Section						
Date	*From/To*	*Description*	*Ref. #*	*Debit*	*Credit*	*Balance*
8/9	Tim Adamson	Deposit	R209		600.00	600.00
Rent Section						
Date	*From/To*	*Description*	*Ref. #*	*Debit*	*Credit*	*Bal. Due*
10/3	Tim Adamson	Rent	R215		1,000.00	0.00

Tenant Ledger						
Tenant	Beryl Green and Pat Frobisher				*Owner No.*	2001-01
Address	1105 S.W. Evelyn				*Tenant Phone*	
Move-in Date	8/21/2002	*Deposit Amt.*	600.00		*Work Phone*	
Security Deposit Section						
Date	*From/To*	*Description*	*Ref. #*	*Debit*	*Credit*	*Balance*
8/21	Green/Frobisher	Deposit	R210		500.00	500.00
Rent Section						
Date	*From/To*	*Description*	*Ref. #*	*Debit*	*Credit*	*Bal. Due*
10/4	Green/Frobisher	Rent	R217		950.00	0.00

TENANT LEDGER

Tenant	Dan Abrahams and Mike McGuire			*Owner No.*	2001-4
Address	1405 N.E. Sycamore #3			*Tenant Phone*	
Move-in Date	10/30/2002	*Deposit Amt.*	750.00	*Work Phone*	

SECURITY DEPOSIT SECTION

Date	*From/To*	*Description*	*Ref. #*	*Debit*	*Credit*	*Balance*
10/30	Abrahams/McGuire	Deposit	R211		750.00	750.00

RENT SECTION

Date	*From/To*	*Description*	*Ref. #*	*Debit*	*Credit*	*Bal. Due*
10/30	Abrahams/McGuire	Rent	R211		750.00	0.00

TENANT LEDGER

Tenant				*Owner No.*	
Address				*Tenant Phone*	
Move-in Date		*Deposit Amt.*		*Work Phone*	

SECURITY DEPOSIT SECTION

Date	*From/To*	*Description*	*Ref. #*	*Debit*	*Credit*	*Balance*

RENT SECTION

Date	*From/To*	*Description*	*Ref. #*	*Debit*	*Credit*	*Bal. Due*

Clients' Trust Account Reconciliation

Name of trust account: Clients' Trust Account – Property Management – Security Deposits

Bank: Bank of America

Account number: 28534--19731 Date prepared: November 4,2002

Prepared by: Joe Manager For month of: October, 2002

Part I

Ending balance from bank statement as of 10/31/2002	$ 3,400.00
Plus Deposits made and posted to ledgers but not posted on bank statement (outstanding deposits), from Schedule A on reverse	750.00
Subtotal	$ 4,150.00
Less Checks written and posted to ledgers but not posted on bank statement (outstanding checks), from Schedule B on reverse	500.00
Subtotal	$ 3,650.00
Plus or minus adjustments, from Schedule C on reverse	0.00
Reconciled bank balance (Total for Part I) as of 10/31/2002	$ 3,650.00

Part II

Check Register or Receipts and Disbursements Journal Balance as of 10/31/2002	$ 3,650.00

Part III

Total of Ledger Cards (Schedule D on reverse) as of 10/31/2002	$ 3,650.00

Must be the same date — Must be the same

Part IV

The totals in Parts I, II and III above must be the same and as of the same date. If any figures are not the same, enter the explanation below and take corrective action to bring books into balance.

Trust accounts must be balanced monthly and all records kept for six years. Retain this completed and signed form with the rest of your records.

Page 1

Schedule A (Deposits not yet posted on bank statement)

Date	Reference	Description	Amount
10/30	R211	Abrahams/McGuire	750.00
Total for Schedule A (Enter here and in Part I of the reconciliation			750.00

Schedule B (Outstanding checks)

Date	Ref.	Check #	Description	Amount
10/30		C2107	Mr. and Mrs. Sanders	500.00
Total for Schedule B (Enter here and in Part I of the reconciliation				500.00

Schedule C (Other adjustments)

Date	Ref.	Check #	Description	Amount
Total for Schedule C (Enter here and in Part I of the reconciliation				

Schedule D (Ledger Cards)

Reference	Description	Amount
	Alexander Pope	600.00
	Mr. and Mrs. Adam Suttle	650.00
	James Gorin/Mary Abrams	550.00
	Tim Adamson	600.00
	Beryl Green and Pat Frobisher	500.00
	Dan Abrahams and Mike Mcguire	750.00
Total for Schedule D (Enter here and in Part III of the reconciliation		3,650.00

To balance the rental income clients' trust account, you will need to use the tenant ledgers on pages 89–92.

RECEIPTS AND DISBURSEMENTS JOURNAL – RENTAL INCOME

Date	From/To	Description	Ref.	Own.	Debit	Credit	Balance
10/1		Brought forward					$2,100.00
10/1	Gorin/Abrams	Rent	R211	01-2		850.00	2,950.00
10/1	Alexander Pope	Rent	R212	01-1		950.00	3,900.00
10/1	Mr. & Mrs. Sanders	Rent	R213	01-1		900.00	4,800.00
10/2	Mr. & Mrs. Suttle	Rent	R214	00-8		800.00	5,600.00
10/3	Tim Adamson	Rent	R215	01-2		1,000.00	6,600.00
10/4	Green/Frobisher	Rent	R216	01-1		950.00	7,550.00
10/5	Mortgage Lenders	Mtg payment	C2132	01-1	542.00		7008.00
10/5	Fidelity Mortgage	Mtg payment	C2133	01-2	1,356.00		5,652.00
10/5	United Lenders	Mtg payment	C2134	01-1	352.00		5,300.00
10/5	Federal Savings	Mtg payment	C2135	01-1	451.00		4,849.00
10/6	Property Mgmt, Inc.	Cleaning Unit 1	C2136	01-2	85.00		4,764.00
10/30	Abrahams/McGuire	Rent	R217	01-2		750.00	5,514.00
10/31	Sandra McCulloch	Disbursal	C2137	01-1	500.00		5,014.00
10/31	Property Mgmt, Inc.	Management fees	C2138		462.00		4,552.00

OWNER RENT RECEIPTS AND DISBURSEMENTS LEDGER

Owner	Barry Dunthorpe	*Owner No.*	2000-8
Address	14561 Countryland Lane	*Phone*	314-4123
Property	1312 Holland Lane	*Bus. Phone*	
Spec. Inst.	Maintain minimum $200 for repairs		

Date	From/To	Description	Ref. #	Debit	Credit	Balance
10/1/2002		Balance forward				$300.00
10/2	Mr. & Mrs. Suttle	Rent	R214		800.00	1,100.00
10/31	Property Mgmt. Inc.	Management fee	C2138	80.00		1,020.00

OWNER RENT RECEIPTS AND DISBURSEMENTS LEDGER						
Owner	Sandra McCulloch				*Owner No.*	2001-1
Address	1512 Winding Drive				*Phone*	216-2154
Property	42nd, 18th, Evelyn, Hamster				*Bus. Phone*	
Spec. Inst.	Maintain minimum $500 for repairs					
Date	*From/To*	*Description*	*Ref. #*	*Debit*	*Credit*	*Balance*
10/1/2000		Balance forward				$700.00
10/1	Alexander Pope	Rent	R212		950.00	1,650.00
10/1	Mr. & Mrs. Sanders	Rent	R213		900.00	2,550.00
10/4	Green/Frobisher	Rent	R216		950.00	3,500.00
10/5	Mortgage Lenders	Mtg Payment	C2132	542.00		2,958.00
10/5	United Lenders	Mtg Payment	C2134	352.00		2,606.00
10/5	Federal Savings	Mtg Payment	C2135	451.00		2,155.00
10/31	Owner	Disbursal	C2137	500.00		1,655.00
10/31	Property Mgmt. Inc.	Management fee	C2138	252.00		1,403.00

OWNER RENT RECEIPTS AND DISBURSEMENTS LEDGER						
Owner	Jameson Investment Company				*Owner No.*	2001-2
Address	2100 West Brunel Parkway				*Phone*	
Property	1405 N.E. Sycamore				*Bus. Phone*	234-1205
Spec. Inst.	Maintain minimum $1,000 for repairs					
Date	*From/To*	*Description*	*Ref. #*	*Debit*	*Credit*	*Balance*
10/1/2002		Balance forward				$1,100.00
10/1	Gorin/Abrams	Rent	R211		850.00	1,950.00
10/3	Tim Adamson	Rent	R215		1,000.00	2,950.00
10/5	Fidelity Mortgage	Mtg Payment	C2133	1,356.00		1,594.00
10/6	Property Mgmt, Inc.	Cleaning Unit 1	C2136	85.00		1,509.00
10/30	Abrahams/McGuire	Rent	R217		750.00	2,259.00
10/31	Property Mgmt, Inc.	Management fee	C2138	130.00		2,129.00

Clients' Trust Account Reconciliation

Name of trust account: Clients' Trust Account – Property Management – Rent Account

Bank: Bank of America

Account number: 28621--32424 Date prepared: November 4,2002

Prepared by: Joe Manager For month of: October, 2002

Part I

Ending balance from bank statement as of 10/31/2002	$	5,514.00
Plus Deposits made and posted to ledgers but not posted on bank statement (outstanding deposits), from Schedule A on reverse		0.00
Subtotal	$	5,514.00
Less Checks written and posted to ledgers but not posted on bank statement (outstanding checks), from Schedule B on reverse		962.00
Subtotal	$	4,552.00
Plus or minus adjustments, from Schedule C on reverse		0.00
Reconciled bank balance (Total for Part I) as of 10/31/2002	$	4,552.00

Part II

Check Register or Receipts and Disbursements Journal Balance as of 10/31/2002	$	4,552.00

Part III

Total of Ledger Cards (Schedule D on reverse) as of 10/31/2002	$	4,552.00

Must be the same date — Must be the same

Part IV

The totals in Parts I, II and III above must be the same and as of the same date. If any figures are not the same, enter the explanation below and take corrective action to bring books into balance.

Trust accounts must be balanced monthly and all records kept for six years. Retain this completed and signed form with the rest of your records.

Schedule A (Deposits not yet posted on bank statement)

Date	Reference	Description	Amount
Total for Schedule A (Enter here and in Part I of the reconciliation			

Schedule B (Outstanding checks)

Date	Ref.	Check #	Description	Amount
10/31	2001-1	C2137	Sandra McCulloch	500.00
10/31		C2138	Property Management, Inc.	462.00
Total for Schedule B (Enter here and in Part I of the reconciliation				962.00

Schedule C (Other adjustments)

Date	Ref.	Check #	Description	Amount
Total for Schedule C (Enter here and in Part I of the reconciliation				

Schedule D (Ledger Cards)

Reference	Description	Amount
2000-8	Barry Dunthorpe	1,020.00
2001-1	Sandra McCulloch	1,403.00
2001-2	Jameson Investment Co.	2,129.00
Total for Schedule D (Enter here and in Part III of the reconciliation		4,552.00

Clients' Trust Account Reconciliation

Name of trust account: Real Estate Brokers, Inc., Clients' Trust Account

Bank: Bank of America

Account number: 24321-12436 — Date prepared: November 4,2002

Prepared by: Joe Broker — For month of: October, 2002

Part I

Ending balance from bank statement as of 10/31/2002	$ 26,650.00
Plus Deposits made and posted to ledgers but not posted on bank statement (outstanding deposits), from Schedule A on reverse	0.00
Subtotal	$ 26,650.00
Less Checks written and posted to ledgers but not posted on bank statement (outstanding checks), from Schedule B on reverse	2,000.00
Subtotal	$ 24,650.00
Plus or minus adjustments, from Schedule C on reverse	0.00
Reconciled bank balance (Total for Part I) as of 10/31/2002	$ 24,650.00

Part II

Check Register or Receipts and Disbursements Journal Balance as of 10/31/2002	$ 25,500.00

Part III

Total of Ledger Cards (Schedule D on reverse) as of 10/31/2002	$ 10,000.00

Must be the same date — Must be the same

Part IV

The totals in Parts I, II and III above must be the same and as of the same date. If any figures are not the same, enter the explanation below and take corrective action to bring books into balance.

Trust accounts must be balanced monthly and all records kept for six years. Retain this completed and signed form with the rest of your records.

Page 1

Schedule A (Deposits not yet posted on bank statement)

Date	*Reference*	*Description*	*Amount*
Total for Schedule A (Enter here and in Part I of the reconciliation			

Schedule B (Outstanding checks)

Date	*Ref.*	*Check #*	*Description*	*Amount*
10/26	02-44	C3127	Fidelity National Title Insurance	2,000.00
Total for Schedule B (Enter here and in Part I of the reconciliation				2,000.00

Schedule C (Other adjustments)

Date	*Ref.*	*Check #*	*Description*	*Amount*
Total for Schedule C (Enter here and in Part I of the reconciliation				

Schedule D (Ledger Cards)

Reference	*Description*	*Amount*
2002-46	Baker to Owens	5,000.00
2002-46	Marquam to Marks/Gavin	2,000.00
2002-48	Cantrell to Loeb/Loeb	3,000.00
Total for Schedule D (Enter here and in Part III of the reconciliation		10,000.00

Forms

On the following pages are forms for residential and commercial property management. The residential forms are published by the Multi Family Housing Council of Oregon and are reproduced here with their kind permission. Persons interested in membership or ordering forms can contact their Salem office at 800-378-7129. They also have an office in the Portland area which can be reached at 503-245-1721.

The Multi Family Housing Council publishes an extensive list of forms for landlords in Oregon. The forms reproduced in this section are the most commonly used. There is a complete list of forms available from the Multi Family Housing Council on the next page. They will be happy to send you at no charge a sample packet of all their current forms.

Membership dues in the Multi Family Housing Council of Oregon are based on the number of units owned or managed, plus a base fee.

A sample commercial lease form is reproduced on pages 167-171. This form is provided here for educational purposes only. Reading through it after studying the previous sections will help your understanding of legal and financial concepts used in leasing commercial property. In actual practice most commercial leases are drafted by the attorney for the lessor.

Forms available from Multi Family Housing Council

Forms in *italic* are reproduced in this section.

1 *Rental agreement*
1a Application
1c Co-signer agreement
2 Reservation deposit
3 Move-in/Move-out accounting
4 Tenant's 30-day notice
5 Notice of rent increase
6 Termination – landlord to tenant
7 Maintenance request and log
7a Maintenance request
7b Maintenance request activity
8 Nonpayment of rent notice
9 Confirmation of termination
10 Pet/Aid animal addendum
11 Notice of pet violation
12 Notice of violation/disturbance
13 Smoke detector addendum
13d Smoke detector door hanger
14 24-hour notice of eviction
14a 24-hour unauthorized occupant
15 Notice of entry
15a Permission to show for sale
16 Partial payment of rent receipt
17 Notice of termination with cause
17a Rental agreement/Rule violation
17b Termination due to prior non-compliance
18 Applicant screening checklist
19 Notice of abandoned property
19a Waiver of notice of abandoned property
19s Notice of abandoned property/structure
20 Abandoned property accounting
21 Notice of parking violation
21b Abandoned vehicle towing notification
22 Applicant screening disclosure
23 Applicant screening charge receipt
24 Criminal activity and disturbances addendum
26 Employee termination notice
27 Applicant/Tenant work for rent credit agreement
28 Service of notice addendum
29 Utility building addendum
30 Mold addendum
31 Facility statement policy
32 Facility rental agreement
33 RV rental agreement
34 Applicant acceptance or denial
35 Emergency contact disclosure
36 Notice of proposed rule change
37 General addendum (blank)
38s Facility storage agreement
40 Landlord's lead-based paint disclosure
41 Seller's lead-based paint disclosure
42 Request for reasonable accommodation

RENTAL AGREEMENT SINGLE-FAMILY, MULTIFAMILY FORM 1

1 PREMISES: Name of property (if applicable) complete address
Name ______
Address: ______
City, State, Zip: ______

2 TYPE OF TENANCY, RENT AMOUNT AND DUE DATE
A. ☐ Week-to-week Beginning: ______ due on ______ of the week in the amount of $ ______
B. ☐ Month-to-month Beginning: ______ due on ______ of the month in the amount of $ ______
C. ☐ Fixed term lease Beginning: ______ due on ______ of the month in the amount of $ ______
Total amount of the lease: $ ______ payable in monthly payments of $ ______ due on ______
Failure to complete the term of the lease will result in a charge of ☐ the balance owed on the lease or ☐ a charge of $ ______

3A. PARTIES: OWNER/AGENT: Name, mailing address for payment of rent and/or service of notice, demand or process:
______
______
Service of notices pursuant to Section 11 of the Terms and Conditions on the reverse side. The location for the posting of notices by the tenant to the landlord if other than the address indicated above is ______
Landlord telephone number (General) ______ (Emergency) ______ (Fax) ______

3B. PARTIES: OCCUPANTS: The following individuals, hereafter referred to as "tenant" are authorized to occupy the dwelling unit. Wherever the term "tenant" is used, the term shall apply in the singular or plural. Unauthorized occupants may result in the termination of the rental agreement.

	Name	Date of Birth	Social Security Number
1.			
2.			
3.			
4.			
5.			
6.			

4. IN CASE OF EMERGENCY: The tenant may contact the landlord at the address or phone number provided in Section 3(A). In case of emergency, the landlord may contact the following parties (name, address, phone number)
______
The tenant is responsible to keep the landlord advised of any change in information for emergency contact.

5. APPLIANCES INCLUDED:
☐ Range ______
☐ Refrigerator ______
☐ Washer ______
☐ Dryer ______
☐ Microwave ______
☐ Dishwasher ______
☐ Garbage Disposal ______
☐ Other ______

6. PETS: Pets are strictly prohibited unless hereby authorized
☐ Pets are accepted subject to addendum
Assistance animals are allowed with a properly documented Request for Reasonable Accommodations.

7. MAINTENANCE AND REPAIR CHARGES: Repairs and/or maintenance of tenant-caused damages and/or cleaning above normal wear and tear will be billed as subcontracted by the landlord and/or up to $ ______ per hour. Charges not paid within 15 days of billing will result in a deduction from the security deposit (if any) and the requirement to reimburse the security deposit being held.

8. SMOKING: ☐ Smoking is not permitted in or around the dwelling.
☐ Smoking is permitted in the dwelling, subject to issues regarding disabilities of others in or around the premises.
☐ Smoking is permitted only in designated areas as follows: ______
______
Any and all damage to the dwelling or premises caused by smoking materials will be charged to the tenant and are not considered normal wear and tear.

9. VEHICLES: The number of vehicles allowed on-site is ______
☐ Permit required # ______ ☐ Assigned parking space # ______

Make / Model / License # / State	Make / Model / License # / State

 Tenant's Name and Address: ______ Initials ______

If applicable, Real Estate Broker Approval: ______ Date: ______

1. OREGON LANDLORD/TENANT LAW: Landlord and tenant agree to abide by all state, federal, local laws or adopted rules and regulations. Tenant agrees not to permit or allow any acts to be done in, on, or within the immediate vicinity of the premises that violate any law, rule or regulation.
2. REQUEST FOR REASONABLE ACCOMMODATION: Any request for reasonable accommodations as required by the federal or state Fair Housing law, shall be made by the tenant in writing to the landlord specifying the request and the nature of the accommodation requested.
3. RENT: Rents are due and payable on the first of the rental period, unless other wise indicated. If rent is not paid by the fourth day of the rental period, a late fee in the amount stated in Section 15 will be assessed. If more than one person signs this agreement, all parties are obligated to the full amount of funds due and commitments made regarding tenancy, Payments made by tenants that are returned as non-negotiable may result in the application of a late fee, other penalties and the requirement that subsequent payments be made by money order or cashier's check.
4. ASSIGNMENT OR SUBLETTING: Subleasing is prohibited. The tenant agrees that only those listed as occupant(s)/tenants in Section 3B will occupy the dwelling unit. Any person not named as an occupant (tenant) who remains on the premises more than fourteen (14) days and/or nights in a calendar year must have the written permission of the landlord. The landlord may assess a per day guest fee.
5. CHANGE IN OCCUPANCY: If one tenant vacates the dwelling unit, any remaining tenants must notify the landlord within three (3) days of the change in occupancy. The remaining and/or additional tenants may be subject to the landlord's screening procedures. Failure to report any change in occupants of the dwelling unit may result in the termination of the rental agreement and penalties for rental agreement violations. The security deposit shall stay with the unit until the last tenant has vacated the unit. Tenants are responsible for inter-tenant agreements regarding the security deposit or fees.
6. CONTROL OF COMMON AREAS: The landlord and any person identified as the "person in charge" pursuant to ORS 164.205(5) shall retain control over any and all common areas. Common areas are shared facilities such as laundry rooms, swimming pools, courtyards and other areas of general use. If identified, the landlord may implement exclusion rules for these areas which restrict access and activity by visitors and/or guests. Exclusion rules shall be posted or made a part of this agreement as well as reported to law enforcement agencies in the area. Tenants are responsible for the activities and actions of visitors and guests.
7. PERSONAL PROPERTY: The tenant agrees not to destroy, damage, deface, or remove any part of the premises or permit any person to do so and to assume all liability for damages, other than ordinary wear and tear or those caused by the landlord. The landlord will not be liable for responsible for loss or damages to articles or property belonging to the tenant(s). The tenant SHALL MAINTAIN FIRE AND THEFT INSURANCE for their personal property.
8. LOSS RECOVERY: The tenant agrees that the landlord has the right to recover from the tenant any loss caused by fire, vandalism or other acts of misuse by the tenant, animals of the tenant or guests of the tenant. The landlord reserves the right to assign such right of recover to their insurance carrier.
9. USE OF PREMISES: (a) At the commencement of the rental agreement, the tenant accepts that the unit and its premises are safe for reasonable and foreseeable uses. Any unsafe condition shall be noted on the Move-in/Out Addendum.
(b) Tenant is to use the premises for a dwelling unit and not conduct any commercial activity or services for compensation in or on the premises without the written consent of the landlord. Day care shall be considered a business.
(c) Tenant will behave and require other person(s) on the premises with the consent of the tenant to behave in a manner that will not disturb the peaceful enjoyment of others. Tenant shall restrict all sound or noise so as not to be heard outside the unit. Tenants and their guests shall not be permitted to play or loiter in halls, stairways, entrance of buildings or other common areas except in those areas designated by the landlord.
(d) Alcoholic beverages shall not be served or consumed in the common areas without written permission of the landlord.
(e) Tenant or their guests shall not be permitted to operate recreational vehicles or equipment in common areas except as designated by the landlord.
(f) Tenant agrees to keep all areas of the premises under their control in every part clean, safe, sanitary and free from the accumulation of debris, filth, rubbish, garbage, rodents and vermin. To the extent that the tenant is responsible for causing a problem, the tenant shall cooperate, to a reasonable extent, in assisting the landlord in any reasonable efforts to remedy the problem. Garbage and other items shall be disposed of in a proper manner,. Medical waste such as needles, blood products and related articles are to be disposed of as "medical waste" as required by law. Patios, porches and stairways are to be kept clean and orderly and are not to be used for general storage. The landlord's definition of clean shall be the final definition.
(g) Tenant shall use all electrical, plumbing, sanitary, heating, ventilating, air conditioning, and other facilities or appliances on the premises in a reasonable manner. Telephone wiring and services within the unit shall be the responsibility of the tenant.
(h) Tenant shall immediately report, in writing, all malfunctions of equipment, failure of essential services, or need for repair. Damage caused by the tenant such as stoppage of waste pipes or overflow of toilets, bathtubs or defective faucets, as well as any damage to the building or furnishings other than ordinary wear and tear, shall be paid by the tenant.
(i) Tenant shall not tamper with the exterior lights, furnace, refrigerator or other appliances or make any alterations of any nature on or to the premises. Hooks, nails, screws or other attachments shall not be installed in any ceilings. Attachments, including, but not limited to signs, that affect the exterior appearance of the unit shall require the written consent of the landlord.
(j) Locks may not be tampered with or changed without the written consent of the landlord. Entrance doors to the building, if designated, shall be kept locked. Entrance doors and windows of the tenants' dwelling unit shall be kept locked. Tenant shall immediately notify the landlord in writing if locks or latches fail to operate properly.
(k) In the event of severe temperature changes, tenant shall take reasonable measures to prevent pipes from freezing including but not limited to maintaining adequate heat, covering any foundation vents and disconnecting exterior hoses.
(l) Landlord shall not be liable for damages of any kind caused by the lack of heat, refrigeration or other services arising out of any accident, act of God or occurrence beyond the control of the landlord. The tenant shall be limited to the rights and remedies specified by law.

RENTAL AGREEMENT SINGLE-FAMILY, MULTIFAMILY FORM 1

10. LANDSCAPING MAINTENANCE:

☐ The tenant shall be responsible to properly and adequately cultivate and maintain lawn, shrubbery and grounds. Failure to maintain landscaping in a condition acceptable to the landlord shall result in the tenant being charged for necessary work in addition to other penalties.

☐ Landscaping will be maintained by the landlord or the landlord's subcontractor. Tenant agrees that access to the premises may be made without notice to the tenant ____________ (initials indicate acceptance).

☐ Property is a multi-unit property with common areas maintained by the landlord. No notice is provided by landlord to tenant for maintenance.

In any or all circumstances, the landlord may elect to use pesticides or insecticides as necessary.

11. WINDOWS AND DOORS:

☐ The property is equipped with a screen and/or storm door.

☐ The property is equipped with screens on the following windows: ____

____

The tenant is hereby notified that neither windows nor screens are considered safety devices. It is the responsibility of the tenant to prevent occupants and/or guests from falling out of or otherwise being injured by windows, doors or any other portion of the property including railings, stairs, balconies or fencing. If the tenant wishes to install window guards, written permission shall be obtained from the landlord regarding installation requirements.

12. AGENT DISCLOSURE AND SECURITY DEPOSIT DISCLOSURE:

1) ☐ Property is managed by an employe of the landlord and is authorized to act on behalf of the owner or agent.
2) ☐ Agent is a Real Estate licensee and is authorized to act on behalf of the owner.
3) Pursuant to the management contract between the owner and licensee the Security Deposit is:
   a. ☐ Transferred to the owner whose name and address is:
   ____
   b. ☐ Held by the real estate licensee in non interest-bearing Clients' Trust Account; or
   c. ☐ Held by the real estate licensee in an interest-bearing Clients' Trust Account and the interest is transferred to:
      1. ☐ The State of Oregon Low-Income Housing Trust account; or
      2. ☐ Payable to the property management agent; or
      3. ☐ Payable to the owner; or
      4. ☐ Payable to the tenant, per federal or state law, if applicable.

13. UTILITY PAYMENT RESPONSIBILITY:

"X" Indicates responsibility for payment. Note: Garbage service: If single can, tenant shall be limited to one 30 gallon can picked up weekly, including recycling. If dumpster service, the tenant is limited to the equivalenty of **one 30 gallon can**. Garbage is limited to solid waste and does not include furniture or other non-waste related items. **Additional amounts will be billed to the tenant.**	WATER	SEWER	ELECTRIC	GAS	BASIC CABLE	INTERNET ACCESS	OIL	GARBAGE (See note)	OTHER
A. Paid by landlord and included in rent.									
B. Paid by the tenant. Account number to be listed if required by landlord.									
C. Paid by the tenant and may directly benefit other tenants and/or landlord.									
D. The landlord has elected to bill the tenant separately from the rent according to the formula identified in Section E.									
E. Utility billing formula:									

14. RECYCLING: The landlord identifies the availability of recycling as follows:

☐ Provided on-site, information available from the landlord regarding materials, requirements and location.

☐ Provided by the hauler. Information available from the hauler.

☐ Not provided and is the responsibility of the tenant.

 Tenant's Name and Address: ________________________________ Initials ________

SINGLE FAMILY, MULTIFAMILY TERMS AND CONDITIONS (07/02)	Page 2 of 3

(m) Tenant shall not store combustibles, gasoline or other flammable liquids inside the unit, on the sidewalk, porches or patios except as permitted by the Fire Department and insurance regulations. Tenant shall use smoking materials with caution and properly dispose of ashes and materials. Bar-b-ques and similar equipment shall not be operated within 10 feet of the building or as restricted by rule.
(n) No animals, aquariums, water beds, pianos or organs are allowed without the written consent of the landlord. Food for animal(s) shall not be located outside the dwelling unit.
(o) The tenant shall maintain a permanent source of heat. Heat shall be maintained at not less than 55 degrees or more than 72 degrees. Any damage caused by the lack of heat shall be charged to the tenant.
10. RIGHT OF ACCESS: (a) Tenant shall not unreasonably withhold consent to the landlord to enter the premises or the dwelling unit to inspect, make necessary or agreed repairs, decorations, alterations or improvements, or to show the unit to prospective tenants or purchasers.
(b) Landlord may enter without consent in an emergency and shall provide tenant with a post-entry notice of the entry and its purpose.
(c) Landlord may issue a 24-hour notice of entry for necessary inspections or repairs pursuant to ORS 90.322(f).
11. NOTICES: (a) Notices shall be either actual (verbal or fax) or written as provided by law.
(b) All written notices under the rental agreement or Oregon statute shall be deemed served when
(1) personally served to the other named party, OR
(2) mailed by first class mail and the effective date is extended by three days, OR
(3) mailed by first class mail and attachment as further identified:
(A) A notice served by first class mail and attachment from the landlord to the tenant shall be deemed served on the day and at the time it is both mailed by first class mail to the tenant at the premises and attached in a secure manner to the main entrance door of that portion of the premises to which the tenant has possession.
(B) A notice from the tenant to the landlord served by first class mail and attachment to the address disclosed in Section 3A. If the address for the landlord is a post office box, is not available for posting 24 hours a day, is not available to the tenant or reasonably located for access to the tenant, the tenant can mail the notice by first class mail without amending the effective date by three days.
(c) The tenant shall notify the landlord in writing of any post office box or telephone number to be used by the tenant.
(d) The tenant agrees to provide the landlord a forwarding address at the time of termination.
(e) Tenant shall notify landlord of any anticipated absence from the premises in excess of seven (7) days, not later than the first day of absence.
12. TERMS AND CONDITIONS:
(a) Week-to-week tenancy.
1. The landlord reserves the right to raise the rent with a seven (7) day notice.
2. Termination by either the landlord or tenant requires a written notice of not less than ten (10) days.
(b) Month-to-month tenancy.
1. The landlord reserves the right to raise the rent with a 30-day written notice.
2. Termination by either the landlord or the tenant requires a written notice of not less than 30 days.
3. If the tenancy is for the land and the tenant owns the structure, this agreement may be terminated by the landlord with a 180-day notice and by the tenant with a 30-day notice of termination.
(c) Fixed term tenancy
1. The landlord reserves the right to raise the rent with a 30-day notice.
2. Either the landlord or the tenant shall give a minimum 30-day written notice of the intent not to renew the lease.
3. Failure of either party to give a notice of intent not to renew will allow the rental agreement to automatically convert to a month-to-month tenancy with all terms and conditions of the agreement continued unless otherwise agreed to in writing.
(d) In the event landlord must bring an action to enforce any provisions of this agreement, the Landlord/Tenant Act or other statutes the landlord shall be entitled to, in addition to costs, reasonable attorney's fees and/or prevailing party fees.
(e) At the time of termination of tenancy, any goods, chattels, motor vehicles, or other property left on the premises shall be considered abandoned property and disposed of as provided by Oregon law. Any expenses incurred by the landlord shall be charged to the tenant.
13. SECURITY DEPOSIT: During tenancy or at the termination of tenancy, the security deposit, if any, shall be used to secure the performance of the rental agreement including, but limited to, cleaning and damage above ordinary wear and tear, pet damage, nonpayment of rent, utilities, fees assessed or other charges during tenancy, and/or failure to give notice as required by this agreement or statute. The landlord shall provide a written accounting of the use of the security deposit within 31 days of termination of tenancy or delivery of possession to the landlord.
14. APPLICATION OF FEES: Upon termination of tenancy and delivery of possession, landlord shall first apply designated fees collected, if any, to the related landlord expense. Such fees collected will be applied to items considered normal wear and tear. The landlord's definition of normal wear and tear shall be what would result in a reasonable occupancy and use of the premises. Any outstanding balance due, if any, will be deducted from the security deposit. If funds are outstanding by the tenant at the time of termination of tenancy, the landlord may take such actions necessary to collect the identified funds.
15. TERMINATION RIGHTS AND RESPONSIBILITIES:
(a) If rent is more than four (4) days past due, the landlord may issue a 144-hour notice, terminate the rental agreement and take possession according to law.
(b) If rent is more than seven (7) days past due, the landlord may issue a 72-hour notice, terminate the rental agreement and take possession according to law.

RENTAL AGREEMENT SINGLE-FAMILY, MULTIFAMILY — FORM 1

15. FINANCIAL TERMS:
a. Stated rent $ ______
b. Additional monthly rent charges for ______ $ ______
c. **Total monthly rent:** $ ______
d. Fees chargeable during tenancy:
  1. Return check charge: $ ______ (Limited to not more than $25.00)
  2. Smoke detector tampering fee: $ ______
  3. Late fee of $ ______ will be assessed if rent is received at the place of payment after the ______ of the rental period.
  4. Fee for service of notice for violation of the rental agreement, statute or rules/regulations, first occurrence $ ______ , each additional notice shall be increased by $ ______ .
  5. If an eviction is necessary, the landlord will charge a fee of $ ______ for each trip related to the action in addition to filing fees, prevailing party fees, and attorney fees.

e. Other charges for ______ in the amount of $ ______
f. Other: ______

* Additional rent or security deposits may be charged for the allowance for pets, smokers, co-signers, or other as indicated.

16. MOVE-IN ACCOUNTING:

CHARGES:
a. Rent from ______ to ______ $ ______
b. Rent from ______ to ______ $ ______
c. Security deposit: $ ______
d. Fee for reasonably anticipated landlord's expenses [Pursuant to ORS 90.302(1)]
  1. Initial contract processing fee: $ ______
  2. Fee to be used at move-out for items considered normal wear & tear. Expenses incurred which exceed this amount will be deducted from the security deposit: $ ______

TOTAL DUE $ ______

CREDITS:
a. ☐ Reservation deposit $ ______
b. ☐ Special program for ______ month $ ______
c. ☐ Other ______ $ ______

TOTAL CREDITS $ ______
TOTAL AMOUNT DUE ______ $ ______
Payment agreement, if any ______ .

Memo: If move-in is during the month and a full month's rent is required upon move-in, the pro-ration of of the next month's in the amount of $ ______ will be due on the first of the next month as follows: ______

17. ADDENDUM(S) made a part of this agreement and agreed to by landlord and tenant:
A. ☐ Additional Rules and Regulations
B. ☐ Pet/Aid Animal Addendum
C. ☐ Smoke Detector/Alarm Addendum
D. ☐ Move-In/Out Inspection Addendum
E. ☐ Landscaping Addendum
F. ☐ Reasonable Accommodation Addendum
G. ☐ Co-Signer Agreement
H. ☐ Water Bed Addendum
I. ☐ Common Area/Illegal Activity Addendum
J. ☐ Pre-1978 Construction Lead-Based Paint Addendum and Handbook delivered prior to the signing of this agreement
K. ☐ Other ______
L. ☐ Other ______

18. Date : ______ I (we) have read and agreed to all pages of this rental agreement and the terms and conditions on the reverse side of applicable pages.

Tenant (x): ______ Tenant (x): ______
Tenant (x): ______ Tenant (x): ______
Tenant (x): ______ Tenant (x): ______

Tenants are individually and jointly liable for the rental agreement. A violation by one will be considered a violation by all and may result in a termination of the rental agreement.

19. Landlord or landlord's agent : ______

Page 3 of 3 Tenant's Name and Address: ______ Initials ______

If the tenant, someone in the tenant's control, or the tenant's pet threatens to inflict or actually inflicts personal injury upon the landlord or other tenants, inflicts injury upon any person on the premises with the consent of another tenant or the landlord, inflicts injury upon another located in the immediate vicinity of the property, intentionally inflicts substantial damage to the premises or commits any act which is outrageous in the extreme, including illegal activity, a 24-hour notice to terminate the tenancy may be served upon the tenant.
(d) Upon any material noncompliance of this agreement, the landlord may issue a 30-day notice and if the breach is not remedied within 14 days, the rental agreement may be terminated and the landlord may take possession pursuant to Oregon law.
(e) Any omission, misstatement or falsification by the tenant on the application or the rental agreement may be grounds for termination of the tenancy at the option of the landlord.
(f) Nothing in this agreement shall limit the right of the tenant or the landlord to terminate this agreement as provided by law.
(g) If at some future date a portion of this rental agreement should be ruled unenforceable by the courts, it shall only affect that portion of the rental agreement and all other provisions of the rental agreement shall remain in force.
(h) Any interference by a tenant or guest of a tenant with management of the property may be considered a material noncompliance and result in termination of tenancy.

16. SATELLITE DISH INSTALLATION POLICY

(a) As required by federal law, satellite dishes may be allowed but <u>cannot</u> be attached to any portion of the landlord's property.
(b) Federal law allows the installation of direct broadcast satellite antennas or dishes of one meter or less in diameter.
(c) Satellite dishes may only be installed inside the tenant's unit or on a porch, patio, deck, banded to a balcony or other portion to which the tenant has possession.
(d) No satellite dish may be installed on the exterior of the building, roof or area under control of the landlord.
(e) The tenant shall be aware that not all areas of the property may receive acceptable satellite broadcast signals.
(f) Tenants are responsible for any injury or damage to people or property cause by the installation of a satellite dish.
(g) If the landlord has installed a central satellite dish for use by all tenants, then individually tenant satellite dishes are prohibited.
(h) The policies applicable to satellite dishes are regulated by federal law which may change periodically and may cause adaptations to this agreement.

17. VEHICLES: The use of designated and off-street parking shall be limited to vehicles in drivable condition which are properly licensed and insured. No vehicle repair, including changing of oil, shall be made without the written consent of the landlord. Unauthorized vehicles, vehicles not in drivable condition or vehicles parked in other than designated spaces or parked in a location posted as "no parking" may be towed <u>without notice</u> at the vehicle owner's expense. Vehicles with visible damage to the interior or exterior which are determined to be unsightly may be prohibited from parking in or around the premises.

18. MOLD AND MILDEW

(a) In order to reduce the incidence of mold and mildew, protect your health and protect the dwelling unit, the tenant agrees to maintain the premises in a manner that prevents the occurrence of an infestation of mold or mildew in the dwelling unit by reducing or eliminating the sources of moisture.
(b) If the dwelling contains excess moisture due to the tenant's lifestyle or activities, the tenant may be required to obtain and maintain a product or product(s) which reduce moisture in the unit.
(c) To uphold this responsibility by complying with the following list of responsibilities, the tenant(s) agrees:

- To keep the dwelling clean at all times, free of dirt and debris, especially those things that can harbor mold or mildew spores.
- To clean bathroom, kitchen surfaces and walls with products which reduce or inhibit growth of mold or mildew.
- To clean and dry any visible moisture on windows, walls and other surfaces, including personal property, as soon as the condition occurs.
- To agree to use bathroom fans while bathing or showering, kitchen fans while cooking and utility area fans whenever water is being used. Continued use of fans for more than 30 minutes following activity.
- To agree to report to the landlord when any exhaust fan does not operate.
- To agree to use all reasonable care to close all windows and other openings in the premises to prevent outdoor water from penetrating the dwelling unit.
- To open multiple windows, weather permitting, at least twice a week for one hour each time to allow cross ventilation of the dwelling.
- To keep any fish tanks covered, if allowable under the rental agreement and/or pet addendum.
- To maintain connections and operation of the applicable heating source and to keep thermostats at no more than 72 degrees and no less than 55 degrees at all times. No non-vented kerosene space heaters are to be used indoors.
- To allow a minimum of a six-inch space between furniture and walls for air ventilation.
- To notify landlord immediately of any circumstance involving excess moisture or water leakage such as plumbing leaks or drips, sweating pipes or toilet tanks as well as overflows in the bathroom, kitchen or laundry facilities (if applicable), especially in cases where the overflow may have permeated walls, carpeting or flooring coverings or cabinets. Excess water shall be immediately removed to prevent further damage.
- To notify the landlord of any mold growth on surfaces inside the dwelling unit that cannot be removed or controlled by the tenant.

Multifamily Housing Council of Oregon
2765 19th Street SE
Salem, OR 973

TENANT'S 30 DAY NOTICE — FORM 4

DATE: ________ TENANT(S) ________

UNIT ADDRESS: ________

CITY ________ STATE ________ ZIP ________

Pursuant to Oregon Landlord/Tenant law, I/We the undersigned hereby give 30-days notice of intent to terminate tenancy and vacate the unit. Possession will be delivered to landlord on ________

☐ The unit may be shown during the hours of ________ to ________

Daytime number ________ Evening number ________

Note: ORS 90.427(4) If the tenant remains in possession without the landlord's consent after expiration of the rental agreement or its termination, the landlord may bring an action for possession. In such case the landlord may recover from the tenant any actual damages resulting from the tenant holding over, including the value of any rent accrued up to the expiration or termination of the rental agreement until the landlord knows or should know that the tenant has relinquished possession to the landlord.

Tenant(s) ________ Tenant(s) ________

Tenant(s) ________ Tenant(s) ________

Date management received notice: Tenant(s) ________

Distribution: Original - Landlord; Second Copy - Tenant Mail

Multifamily Housing Council of Oregon
2765 19th Street SE
Salem, OR 973

NOTICE OF RENT INCREASE — FORM 5

DATE: ________ TENANT(S) ________

UNIT ADDRESS: ________

CITY ________ STATE ________ ZIP ________

Pursuant to Oregon Landlord/Tenant law, this is to inform you that your rent will be increased $ ________ from $ ________ to $ ________ .

☐ This notice has been served personally. The rent increase will be effective 12:01 am ________ .

☐ This notice has been served by first class mail and the effective date is extended by four days including the date mailed. The rent increase is effective 12:01 am ________ .

☐ The written rental agreement calls for service by attachment and mail by either the landlord or tenant. This notice has been served by such service and the rent increase will be effective 12:01 am ________ .

OWNER/AGENT: ________

ADDRESS: ________ TELEPHONE: ________

Distribution: Original - Landlord; Second Copy - Tenant Mail; Third Copy - Tenant Post

Multifamily Housing Council
of Oregon
2765 19th Street SE
Salem, OR 973

TERMINATION OF TENANCY FROM LANDLORD TO TENANT

FORM 6

DATE: ____________ **TENANT(S)**____ **et al.**
(and all others)

UNIT ADDRESS: ____

CITY ____________________ **STATE** ____________________ **ZIP** ____________________

Pursuant to Oregon Landlord/Tenant law, this is your ____________ notice of the landlord's intention to terminate your tenancy.

☐ This notice has been served personally. Your rental agreement will terminate at midnight ____________________ .

☐ This notice has been served by first class mail and the effective date is extended by four days including the date mailed. Your rental agreement will terminate at midnight ____________ .

☐ The written rental agreement calls for service by attachment and mail by either the landlord or tenant. This notice has been served by such service and the rental agreement will terminate at midnight ____________________ .

OWNER/AGENT: ____

ADDRESS: ____

TELEPHONE: ____

Distribution: Original - Landlord; Second Copy - Tenant Mail; Third Copy - Tenant Post

Multifamily Housing Council of Oregon
2765 19th Street
Salem, OR 97

NONPAYMENT OF RENT NOTICE

FORM 8

DATE: ________ **TENANT(S)** ________________ **et al.** (and all parties unkown)

ADDRESS: ________________

CITY ________________ **STATE** ________ **ZIP** ________

This is to inform you that your **rent in the amount of $** ________ is now past due. You may avoid the termination of your tenancy by paying the rent amount due by the date and time indicated.

☐ If checked, payment must be paid by money order or certified funds due to the return of previous checks.

TENANCY AND NOTICE:

1. ☐ Tenancy is a week-to-week and rent is at least four days past due. This is your 72-hour written notice to pay your past due rent.
2. ☐ Tenancy is a month-to-month or a fixed-term lease* and rent is at least four days past due. This is your 144-hour notice to pay your past due rent.
3. ☐ Tenancy is a month-to-month or a fixed-term lease* and rent is at least seven (7) days past due. This is your 72-hour notice to pay your past due rent.

* If rent is unpaid on a fixed-term lease and an eviction is fuiled terminating the rental agreement, a penalty for early lease termination may be assessed as provided for in your rental agreement.

Statement of Account

Past due rent:	$ ________*
Late charges	$ ________
NSF Fee	$ ________
Other ________	$ ________
Other ________	$ ________
Total outstanding	$ ________

*You may avoid termination by paying the past due rent. However, you are responsible for the total amount due.

TYPE OF SERVICE:

Option A

☐ This notice has been served personally at ________ am/pm on ________ (date). Rent will be considered timely if payment is received at the place of payment by ________ am/pm on ________ (date). Your written rental agreement and this notice require the payment to be received at the following location: ________________

This location is either

1. On the premises or
2. Where all previous rent payments have been made in person and
3. The location is available to the tenant for payment throughout the period of the notice.

Option B

☐ This notice has been served personally and does not meet the requirements of Option A. Rent will be considered timely if personally delivered or mailed to the landlord by midnight on ________ (date).

Option C

☐ This notice has been served by first class mail. Therefore, the time limit for the payment of your rent has been extended by four days including the date mailed. Rent will be considered timely if personally delivered or if mailed to the landlord by midnight on ________ (date).

Option D

☐ Your rental agreement allows for service of this notice by attachment to the main entrance door of the tenant's dwelling unit and mailing by first class mail. Rent will be considered timely if personally delivered or if mailed to the landlord by 11:59 pm on ________ (date).

Pursuant to ORS 90.400(2) if your rent is not paid in full, within the time indicated, your rental agreement will be terminated and the landlord will proceed to take possession by filing an eviction. If rent is mailed, mailing must be by first class mail. Unless otherwise indicated, rent is to be paid at the location identified on the rental agreement.

☐ Alternate location for payment is: ________________

WARNING FOR FACILITY TENANCIES (Mobile, manufactured or floating home park)

☐ This tenancy is located within a facility. Pursuant to ORS 90.630(13), if the tenant receives three or more nonpayment of rent notices in at least three of the preceding 12 months, the landlord may terminate the tenancy with a 30-day notice of termination (with no right to correct the cause) upon the occurrence of a third notice of nonpayment of rent.

This is the ☐ First notice; ☐ Second notice; ☐ Third notice of Nonpayment of Rent.

OWNER/AGENT: ________________

ADDRESS: ________________

TELEPHONE: ________________

Distribution: Original - Landlord; Second Copy - Tenant Mail; Third Copy - Tenant Post

Multifamily Housing Council of Oregon
2765 19th Street
Salem, OR 9

CONFIRMATION OF TERMINATION

FORM 9

DATE: ________ **TENANT NAME(S)** ________________________

UNIT ADDRESS: ________________________

CITY ________________ **STATE** ________ **ZIP** ________

☐ The landlord acknowledges receipt of your notice of termination which is effective as of:
Date and time ________________________

☐ The landlord has terminated your rental agreement with a notice given on ________ which is effective as of:
Date and time ________________________

Rent due for the period ________ to ________ will be $ ________ × ________ = $ ________
Per day rent / Number of days / Amount due

Rent due for the period ________ to ________ will be $ ________ × ________ = $ ________
Per day rent / Number of days / Amount due

Other outstanding monies due:

Amount Purpose

____

____

____

This (these) amount(s) which total $ ________ is/are due on or before ________ .

When you move, please take care of the following:

1. Have necessary meters read on move-out date.
2. Pay all outstanding utility bills.
3. Cancel newspaper delivery, if any.
4. Return keys to the landlord.
5. Complete move-out inspection ☐ with landlord ☐ without landlord.
6. Provide a forwarding address to the post office.
7. Provide a forwarding address to the landlord for return of the accounting of the security deposit and any unused funds which will be be forwarded to you within 31 days following termination of occupancy.
8. Other ________________________

OWNER/AGENT: ________________________

Multifamily Housing Council
of Oregon
2765 19th Street SE
Salem, OR 973

NOTICE OF VIOLATION/DISTURBANCE

FORM 12

DATE: ____________ TENANT NAME(S) ____________________________

UNIT ADDRESS: ____________________________

CITY ____________________________ STATE ____________ ZIP ____________

You are hereby given formal notice that on ____________________________

The following disturbances or other violations of the rental agreement have occurred:

____

____

____

____

____

____

____

You are advised that all such actions must cease immediately in order to protect the rights of others.

If you fail to comply, law enforcement or health officers may be notified and if necessary called to insure the abatement of such disturbances.

The landlord reserves the right to issue a notice of termination or immediate removal of those on the premises who are not authorized by the rental agreement.

OWNER/AGENT: ____________________________

ADDRESS: ____________________________

Distribution: Original - Landlord; Second Copy - Tenant Mail; Third Copy - Tenant Post

Multifamily Housing Council of Oregon
2765 19th Street SE
Salem, OR 973

24 HOUR NOTICE OF EVICTION

FORM 14

DATE: ______________ TENANT(S)____ et al. *(and all others)*

UNIT ADDRESS: ____

CITY ______________________ STATE ______________ ZIP ______________

Pursuant to ORS 90.400(3), this notice is to inform you that your occupancy will terminate and you must vacate the premises by the date and time indicated. If you fail to vacate the premises, legal action will be taken. This notice is given because:

☐ You, someone in your control, or your pet/animal seriously threatened immediately to inflict personal injury, or inflicted any substantial personal injury upon the landlord, the landlord's agent or other tenants.

☐ You, someone in your control, or your pet/animal inflicted substantial personal injury upon a neighbor living in the immediate vicinity or upon a person other than a tenant on the premises with the permission of the landlord or of another tenant.

☐ You, or somone in your control intentionally inflicted substantial damage to the premises.

☐ You, or someone in your control or your pet/animal has committed an act which is outrageous in the extreme on the premises or in the immediate vicinity of the premises.

☐ A pet/animal has inflicted substantial damage to the premises on more than one occasion. The cause for this termination notice is based upon the acts the pet/animal. You may cure the cause and avoid termination of the tenancy by removing the pet/animal from the premises prior to the end of the notice period.

☐ The pet/animal, for which a previous 24 hour termination notice has been given, has returned to the premises. Your rental agreement will terminate due to this action. Pursuant to ORS 90.400(4) the tenant shall not have a right to cure this subsequent violation.

☐ Pursuant to ORS 90.380(2) this notice is to inform you that your occupancy will terminate and you must vacate the premises due to circumstances not caused by the landlord which has rendered the dwelling unit unsafe to occupy.

SERVICE OF NOTICE AND EFFECTIVE DATE:

☐ This notice has been served personally.
Your rental agreement will terminate: (date/time) ______________________

☐ .This notice has been served by first class mail and the effective date is extended by four days including the date mailed.
Your rental agreement will terminate: (date/time) ______________________

☐ The written rental agreement allows for service by attachment and mail by either the landlord or tenant. This notice has been served by such notice.
Your rental agreement will terminate: (date/time) ______________________

SPECIFICS OF VIOLATIONS:

Date of occurrence: ______________ Time: ______________ Location: ______________

Persons involved in occurrence: ____

Details: ____

____

____

OWNER/AGENT: ____

ADDRESS: ____

TELEPHONE: ____

Distribution: Original - Landlord; Second Copy - Tenant Mail; Third Copy - Tenant Post

Multifamily Housing Council
of Oregon
2765 19th Street SE
Salem, OR 973

24 HOUR NOTICE OF EVICTION UNAUTHORIZED OCCUPANT

FORM 14a

DATE: ____________ OCCUPANT NAME(S)____________________________

UNIT ADDRESS:____________________________

CITY ____________________________ STATE ____________ ZIP ____________

Pursuant to ORS 90.400 (3)(d), this is to inform you:

- that the authorized tenant has vacated the premises;
- that the person(s) in possession is holding possession contrary to a written rental agreement that prohibits subleasing the premises without the written permission of the landlord; and
- the landlord has not knowingly accepted rent from the person(s) in possession.

This is your notice to vacate the premises by the date specified below:

DATE SERVED: ____________ TIME SERVED: ____________

- This notice has been served personally.
  You must vacate as of midnight ____________________

or

- This notice has been served by first class mail and the effective date is extended by four days including the date mailed
  You must vacate as of midnight ____________________

If you fail to vacate the premises by the date indicated, legal action will be taken against you
.

OWNER/AGENT: ____________________________

ADDRESS:____________________________

Distribution: Original - Office; Second Copy - Tenant

Multifamily Housing Council
of Oregon
2765 19th Street SE
Salem, OR 973

NOTICE OF TERMINATION WITH CAUSE

FORM 17

DATE: ____________ TENANT(S)____ et al.
and all others

UNIT ADDRESS: ____

CITY ______________________________ STATE ________________ ZIP ____________

Pursuant to ORS 90.400 (1) or ORS 90.630, you are hereby notified that you are in material noncompliance with your rental agreement or there is a noncompliance with ORS 90.325 materially affecting health and safety in the following manner:

____

____

____

____

____

You are hereby required to make the following remedies:

____

____

____

____

____

If you fail to remedy this (these) violation(s) by the date indicated below, your rental agreement will terminate on the date indicated. If you comply, your rental agreement will not terminate.

☐ This notice has been served personally. If you fail to remedy the violation by midnight on (date) ____________ your rental agreement will terminate as of midnight on (date) ____________

☐ This notice has been served by first class mail and the effective date is extended by four days including the date mailed. If you fail to remedy the violation by midnight on (date) ____________ your rental agreement will terminate as of midnight (date) ____________ .

☐ The written rental agreement calls for service by attachment and mail by either the landlord or tenant. This notice is served in that manner. If you fail to remedy the violation(s) by midnight on (date) ____________ your rental agreement will terminate as of midnight on (date) ____________ .

Non-subsidized contracts: Reoccurrence of any of the above listed violation(s) within a six month period will allow termination of your rental agreement with a ten day notice of termination without further opportunity to correct the violation.

Subsidized contracts: Reoccurrence of any of the above listed violation(s) within a six month period will allow termination of your rental agreement as provided in your subsidized housing contract. Pursuant to 24 CFR 99.511 (2)(ii), if a judicial proceeding for eviction is instituted, the tenant may present a defense in the proceeding. Other information as required by your subsidized contract : ____________

Manufactured dwellings or floating homes located within a facility: Reoccurrence of any of the above listed violation(s) within a six month period will allow termination of your rental agreement with a 20 day notice of termination without further opportunity to correct the violation.

OWNER/AGENT: ____

ADDRESS: ____

TELEPHONE: ____

Distribution: Original - Landlord; Second Copy - Tenant Mail; Third Copy - Tenant Post

Multifamily Housing Council
of Oregon
2765 19th Street SE
Salem, OR 973

RENTAL AGREEMENT OR RULE VIOLATION NOTICE

FORM 17A

DATE: ____________ **TENANT NAME(S)**____ (and all parties unkown)

UNIT/SPACE ADDRESS: ____

CITY ______________________________ **STATE** ____________ **ZIP** ____________

With a desire to maintain the rental property and prevent disturbances to other residents,

- ☐ A recent inspection was done on the dwelling unit/space and the following items need your immediate attention.
- ☐ Information has been received which requires your prompt attention and resolution.

☐ This notice has been served personally. If you fail to remedy the violation by midnight on (date) ______________ , your rental agreement will terminate as of midnight on (date) ______________ .

☐ This notice has been served by first class mail and the effective date is extended by four days including the date mailed. If you fail to remedy the violation by midnight on (date) ______________ , your rental agreement will terminate as of midnight on (date) ______________ .

☐ The written rental agreement allows for service by attachment and mail by either the landlord or tenant. This notice has been served by being posted and mailed. If you fail to remedy the violations by midnight on (date) ______________ your rental agreement will terminate as of midnight on (date) ______________ .

ANIMALS

- ☐ Animals – noisy pets inside or outside the unit or animals observed running loose.
  Animals are to be kept quiet and leashed.
- ☐ Animal food is outside the dwelling unit.
  Remove all food to prevent ants, mice and other rodents or vermin.

MAINTENANCE

- ☐ General cleanup necessary inside and outside the unit.
  Clean as necessary. If there is a question regarding the acceptable standard of cleanliness, contact the landlord immediately.
- ☐ Lawn and/or yard not properly maintained.
  Mow, water weed and/or remove debris.
- ☐ Unapproved items are stored on the exterior of the dwelling.
  Remove items or store them properly.
- ☐ Structure is a mobile or manufactured dwelling and is required to be maintained according to published standards. Tenant is required to complete required maintenance necessary to meet specifications. Acceptance of rent by the landlord will not be considered a waiver of this requirement. If conditions prevent or hinder such activity to bring the structure into compliance, contact the landlord for a written extension.

RENTAL AGREEMENT, RULE OR REGULATION OR STATUTE VIOLATION

- ☐ Vehicles: Inoperable or unauthorized vehicle(s) on the property.
  Remove or bring vehicles into compliance.
- ☐ Tenant or guests observed working on vehicles on the rented property.
  Stop any work on vehicles on the rented property. Any damage caused by such activity will be billed to the tenant.
- ☐ Unauthorized person(s) residing in the unit beyond the time authorized in the rental agreement.
  Unauthorized person(s) must meet with the landlord to complete a rental application, be processed as a potential tenant and/or vacate the unit.
- ☐ Unauthorized person(s) residing in the unit beyond the time authorized in the rental agreement.
  Current occupancy exceeds occupancy limitations, unauthorized occupants must vacate the unit or the rental agreement will be terminated.
- ☐ Tenant or guests are violating the following rule, regulation or statute: ______________________
  Compliance with rules, regulations and statutes are required for continuation of tenancy.

UNPAID FEES OR PENALTIES

- ☐ Fees or penalties in the amount of $ ______________ have been assessed for ______________ .
  Pay the outstanding fees or penalties designated.

If you have any questions or a concern about any of the items noted, please contact the landlord to resolve the concerns in a prompt and timely manner. Failure to comply within the designated time will result in the termination of your rental agreement, Any subsequent violation during the next six months may result in the termination of tenancy with less than a 30 day notice.

OWNER/AGENT: ______________________________ **TELEPHONE:** ______________

ADDRESS: ____

Distribution: Original - Landlord; Second Copy - Tenant; Third Copy - File

Multifamily Housing Council of Oregon
2765 19th Street SE
Salem, OR 973

Notice of Termination with Cause Due to Repeated Noncompliance FORM 17b

DATE: ____________ **TENANT NAME(S)**____ (and all parties unkown)

UNIT/SPACE ADDRESS: ____

CITY ______________________________ **STATE** ______________ **ZIP** ______________

☐ This notice has been served personally. Your rental agreement will terminate as of midnight on (date) ____________ .

☐ This notice has been served by first class mail and the effective date is extended by four days including the date mailed. Your rental agreement will terminate as of midnight on (date) ____________ .

☐ The written rental agreement allows for service by attachment and mail by either the landlord or tenant. Your rental agreement will terminate as of midnight on (date) ____________ .

YOU HAVE NOT COMPLIED OR HAVE VIOLATED YOUR RENTAL AGREEMENT AFTER THE FIRST NOTICE WAS GIVEN

☐ The rental agreement is a non-facility tenancy. Pursuant to ORS 90.400 you were previously given a notice of noncompliance on ____________ . You were notified that if you did not correct the listed violations within the given time period, your rental agreement would terminate. According to our records you have not complied as required. Pursuant to ORS 90.400 (1)(d) YOUR RENTAL AGREEMENT WILL TERMINATE as indicated above. This date is the same as designated as the termination date on the first notice of violation and is not less than that period of time.

YOU HAVE VIOLATED A PREVIOUSLY GIVEN NOTICE WITHIN A SIX MONTH PERIOD

☐ Pursuant to ORS 90.400 or 90.630, you are hereby notified that the same act or omission which constituted a prior notice of noncompliance has reoccurred. The first notice was given (date) ____________ . Pursuant to statute, if you commit the same act or omission within six months the landlord may terminate your rental agreement. Due to the reoccurrence of the violation notice given, YOUR RENTAL AGREEMENT WILL TERMINATE as indicated above.

Second violation termination dates:

☐ Residential properties: not less than 10 day notice to terminate – ORS 90.400

☐ Facility properties: not less than 20 day notice to terminate – ORS 90.630

OWNER/AGENT: ______________________________ **TELEPHONE:** ______________

ADDRESS: ____

Distribution: Original - Landlord; Second Copy - Tenant; Third Copy - File

LEASE

THIS LEASE is entered into between ____
____ (lessor)
and ____
____ (lessee)
covering premises located in ____________________ County, Oregon, described as:

☐ See Exhibit ___ for floor plans of premises covered by this lease. Except as further provided in this lease agreement, lessee shall have exclusive possession of premises.

☐ See Exhibit ___ for floor plans and description of common areas. Lessee and lessee's customers, invitees and guests shall have right of use of the common areas in common with all other tenants and not exclusively. Lessee and lessee's customers, guests and invitees shall use common areas in a manner to ensure the use of the common areas by other tenants without hindrance.

☐ See Exhibit ___ for description of parking areas. Lessee shall have exclusive use of parking spaces as follows ____
____
____.
Lessee shall have common usage of parking spaces as follows ____________________
____.
Lessee and lessee's customers, guests and invitees shall use parking spaces in a manner to ensure use of parking areas by other tenants without hindrance.

☐ Lessee shall be entitled to signage on the premises which complies with all applicable laws as follows ____
____.

All references to square footage in the above descriptions shall be based on standards established by the Building Owners and Managers Association (BOMA).

[If additional space is required to describe the leased premises, or any other provision of this lease, attach addendum]

LESSOR AND LESSEE AGREE to the following terms and conditions:

Term: The term of this lease shall begin at 12:01 AM on ____________, ________ and end at 12:00 PM on ____________, ________.

Premises: Lessor leases the above premises to lessee complete with all easements and other rights appurtenant thereto.

Rent: Lessee agrees to pay to the order of lessor the sum of $ ________ on the ________ of each ________ during the term of this lease beginning on ____________, ________, which shall be known as the base rent. All such payments to be made to lessor at ____
____
______________________________ unless lessor shall notify lessee otherwise.

The following provisions for calculation of rent will apply if checked:

☐ Common area expenses: In addition to the base rent above, lessee shall pay ☐ the sum of $ ______________ ☐ a sum equal to one-twelfth lessor's annual expense of the common areas as lessee's prorata share thereof; the initial amount of which shall be $ __________ , which amount shall be adjusted annually on the anniversary date of this lease.

☐ Index and escalation: During the term of this lease the rent shall increase based on ☐ the index of building operations as maintained by the Building Owners and Managers Association (BOMA) ☐ the following index or formula: ____
____
____ .
Such increase will apply with the rent payment due __________________ , __________ and again on the rent payment due at the beginning of each fiscal year thereafter.

☐ Percentage rent: In addition to the base rent stated above, lessee shall pay to lessor additional rent each month ☐ equal to _______ % of lessee's gross sales during the preceding month ☐ based on the following formula: ______________________________________ . Lessee shall maintain adequate records of sales and make such records available to lessor's inspection during reasonable business hours. Such records shall be maintained for a period of not less than one year after each accounting period. For purposes of this provision, the term gross sales shall mean the revenue received by lessee from the sale of goods or services on the leased premises and shall include such sales made by sublessees, agents, licensees, concessionaires, and all others conducting business on the premises whether independently or for the benefit of lessee. Such sales amounts shall be reduced by credits granted by lessee for returns and damaged merchandise. Gross sales shall not include sales of assets other than inventory maintained by lessee for resale. Receipts by lessee for interest earned on credit accounts carried by lessee shall not be considered part of gross income. Gross sales shall not be reduced by lessee's costs of operation, including, but not limited to interest or carrying charges on inventory and merchant credit card discounts.

☐ Property tax: In addition to the base rent stated above, lessee shall pay a sum with each rent payment equal to one-twelfth the annual property taxes on the leased premises. Each year not later than the first of December lessor shall notify less of the amount of the taxes for the coming year which shall be used for calculation of the tax figure to be added to each payment commencing with the rent payment next due thereafter and continuing for the following eleven months. If the leased premises are less than 100% of the total property, such additional payment shall be based on ________ % of the annual property tax.

☐ Insurance: In addition to the base rent stated above, lessee shall pay an initial amount of $ ______________ to cover lessor's cost of insurance. This amount shall be increased to one-twelfth lessor's annual insurance premium. If the leased premises are less than 100% of the total property, such additional payment shall be based on _______ % of the annual insurance premium. Lessor shall notify lessee of the new premium amount each year upon receipt of premium statement from lessor's insurance carrier and the increase shall apply to the rent payment next following and for the next eleven payments thereafter.

☐ Maintenance and operating expenses: Within 30 days of the end of the first fiscal year of this lease lessor shall notify lessee of lessor's increase in operating expenses. Beginning with the rent payment next following lessee shall pay an additional amount in addition to the base rent stated above equal to one-twelfth the increase. Maintenance and operating expenses includes all costs of operations except property taxes and insurance premiums. If the leased premises are less than 100% of the total space, the additional amount shall be _______ % of the total increase.

☐ Security deposit: Lessee shall tender to lessor prior to the inception of this lease a security deposit in the amount of $ ______________ to secure the performance of lessee's obligations under this lease, including the obligation to pay rent, the obligation to surrender the premises at the conclusion of this lease, and any and all other obligations of lessee. If lessor applies the deposit or any portion of it to cure any default of lessee during the term of this lease, lessee shall, on demand by lessor, deposit replacement funds with lessor to ensure the continual availability of the entire deposit. Within 60 days after the termination of this lease, and provided lessee has performed all covenants and conditions of this lease, lessor shall return the deposit to lessee. All interest or benefits accruing from the deposit funds shall be the property of the ____________________ .

☐ Option to renew: As long as the lessee is not in default of any of the provisions of this lease, lessee shall have the option to renew this lease for an additional term of ____________ years, provided that lessee notifies lessor of intention to exercise the option to renew within 60 days of the end date of this lease. The rental for such renewal shall be the amount then in force under the terms of this lease, plus any automatic increases or escalations accruing by the end of this lease. All provisions for adjustments to rent or escalations of the amount of rent shall continue under the same terms as set for in this lease.

☐ Expansion option: Lessee shall have the option to lease additional space as described in Exhibit ____ provided tenant notifies lessor of lessee's intent to exercise this option not later than ______________ , ________ . If this option is exercised the rent shall be increased by a prorata percentage based on the rent currently in effect under this lease based on square footage of the original premises and the square footage of the additional premises.

☐ Non-competition: During the term of this lease lessor shall not lease premises in the same complex or in any other premises owned or managed by lessor within ____________________ miles of the premises if the potential lessee's occupancy of the premises would be of substantially the same nature or business as lessee's use of these premises as provided below.

Use of premises: Lessee shall use and occupy the premises for ______________________________

____

____

and no other purpose without permission of lessor in writing.

Utilities: All utilities shall be in the name of and the responsibility of the tenant except

____

____.

Maintenance: Lessee acknowledges that the premises are in good order and condition with no defects. During the term of this lease lessor shall, at lessor's expense, maintain the foundation, roof and structural portions of the building, heating, ventilating and air conditioning equipment, and plumbing and electrical systems. Lessor shall also maintain all common areas, sidewalks and parking areas not under lessee's exclusive control. Lessee shall, at its sole cost and expense, maintain all portions of the leased premises not to be maintained by lessor in good and sanitary condition, including all necessary replacements, the same as when received, ordinary wear and tear excepted.

Alterations: Lessee shall not make any alteration of the leased premises or any part thereof without first securing permission of lessor in writing. Unless agreed otherwise in writing, all additions permitted by lessor and made by lessee shall, at the termination of this lease, be presumed to become a part of the real property and belong to lessor. All additions or alterations permitted by lessor and made by lessee shall be made in conformance with all local and state laws and ordinances. Prior to commencing any such work lessor shall have to right to post a notice of non-responsibility as provided by ORS 87.030.

Applicable law: During the term of this lease lessee shall comply with all laws, statutes, ordinances and requirements of all government agencies having jurisdiction over the property and the activity of the lessee therein.

Entry and inspection: Lessor and lessor's agents may enter the premises immediately and without notice to lessee in the event of emergency. In all other cases lessor and lessor's agents shall have the right to inspect the premises during reasonable hours and lessee shall not interfere with this right provided lessor gives lessee reasonable notice. Notwithstanding, lessor and lessor's agents shall not enter the premises except during such times as lessee is present. Within 60 days of the termination of this lease lessor and lessor's agents shall have the right to place signs on the premises advertising the availability of the space and to show the premises to prospective tenants. Such showings shall be upon reasonable notice and only when lessee is present.

Insurance: During the term of this lease lessee shall maintain in full force and effect a public liability insurance policy covering all damages for injuries or death of any person on the leased premises in an amount not less than $ ______________ . Lessee shall also maintain at all times tenant's insurance covering liability to lessor for damage to the premises caused by lessee, lessee's customers, invitees or guests in the same amount. In the event lessee employs others on the premises lessee shall maintain worker's compensation insurance covering their activities. Lessee shall cause lessor's name to be listed on said policies as an additional insured party with a certificate of insurance issued to lessor. Said certificates or policies shall contain a provision that the policies shall not be canceled or amended without prior notice to lessor and a subrogation clause in favor of lessor. If lessee should fail to maintain such insurance lessor may obtain replacement insurance to protect lessor's interests and the cost thereof shall be charged to the lessee the same as rent due.

Liability of lessor: Lessee shall look solely to lessor's equity in the property of which the premises are a part for the satisfaction of lessee's remedies in the event of a breach of the lease by lessor. If lessor conveys the property to another, lessor's liability for the performance of its agreements in the lease shall end on the day of the conveyance and lessor shall look solely to the purchaser for performance of the agreement thereafter.

Destruction of the premises: If the premises are damaged or destroyed by fire or other casualty or force majeure to the extent that rebuilding cannot be completed within 120 days from the date of the loss, lessee may terminate this lease by notice to lessor within 30 days of the date of the loss. In all other cases the lease shall continue and lessee's obligations hereunder shall be reduced proportionate to the extent of the premises rendered unusable and the lessee's business on the premises is interfered with. If the premises can be rebuilt within 120 days lessor shall commence such reconstruction with all deliberate speed and in a manner so as to minimize interference with lessee's business and occupancy of the premises. If the premises are completely destroyed, this lease shall terminate fully.

Eminent domain: If the premises, or any part or interest therein, is taken by any government agency under eminent domain action and the taking materially affects lessee's occupancy and use of the premises, lessee shall have the option of terminating this lease upon notice to lessor within 30 days of the vesting of title resulting from such taking. Rent for the time period between the last scheduled payment of rent and the date of the taking shall be apportioned prorata. Lessee shall not be entitled to any portion of the amounts paid for the taking of the premises, but lessor and lessee shall cooperate if lessee wishes to file a claim in the eminent domain action for lessee's loss of business, trade fixtures, and moving expenses.

Indemnification of lessor: Lessee shall hold and save lessor harmless from and indemnify lessor against any and all injury, loss, damages, liability or expenses, including, but not limited to, attorney's fees and costs of investigation and discovery resulting from any act or failure to act by lessee or lessee's customers, invitees or guests on the premises.

Possession: In the event lessor cannot or does not deliver the premises to lessee by the date of commencement of this lease, lessor shall not be liable to lessee for any damages caused thereby, nor shall this lease terminate, but lessee shall not be liable for rent until such time as possession is delivered. Notwithstanding, if lessor cannot or does not deliver the premises to lessee within 30 days of the commencement date of this lease, lessee may terminate this lease.

Assignment and sublease: Lessee shall not assign this lease or sublet the premises or any part thereof without the permission of lessor in writing. Such permission shall not be unreasonably withheld. If lessee should assign this lease or sublease the premises or any part thereof without permission of lessor in writing, lessor may terminate this lease for cause. In the event lessor shall agree to assignment of this lease or sublease of the premises, such assignment or sublease shall not be construed as a novation and lessee's obligations hereunder shall not be extinguished. All profits from a sublease shall inure to the benefit of the ________________________.

Successors and assigns: This lease is binding upon and inures to the benefit of the parties and their successors and assigns in interest, whether by operation of law or contract.

Waiver: No failure to enforce any provision of this lease by either party shall be deemed a waiver of the provision.

Subordination: Lessee agrees that in the event lessor should desire to secure financing or otherwise encumber the premises lessee will subordinate this lease to said encumbrance(s) and sign all documents convenient thereto.

Holding over: Any holding over by lessee after the end date of this lease as provided above shall be as a tenant from month to month and not otherwise. If lessee shall remain in possession after this lease has been terminated for cause, whether the termination was by action of the lessor or of the lessee, lessee shall be deemed a tenant at sufferance and not otherwise.

Lessor's remedies: In the event of default by lessee in the payment of rent or other charges, or any other provision or requirement of this lease, lessor may give notice to lessee of such default and if lessee does not cure the default within ______ days, lessor may accelerate the total amount of rent due under this lease and/or terminate this lease upon ______ days notice to lessee. Upon such termination lessee shall quit and surrender the premises to lessor and lessee's obligations under this lease shall not be deemed extinguished thereby. If lessor has terminated this lease as provided in this section and lessee has not quit and surrendered the premises to lessor within the time period above stated, lessor may retake possession of the premises by any lawful means. Nothing in this section shall be deemed a waiver of any other remedies available to lessor at law.

Environmental issues: Lessee shall occupy the premises in compliance with all applicable federal, state and local laws with regard to environmental safety and hazards. Lessee indemnifies lessor for costs of cleanup or mitigation, or any other expense incurred by lessor as a result of any act of lessee during lessee's possession of the premises. Lessee's obligations to lessor under this provision shall remain in force as long as lessor may be liable under the Comprehensive Environmental Response Compensation and Liability Act or any other federal, state or local law, including liabilities to third parties and successors in interest.

Lessor makes the following disclosure:

"Radon gas is a naturally occurring radioactive gas that, when it has accumulated in a building in sufficient quantities, may present health risks to persons who are exposed to it over time. Levels of radon that exceed federal and state guidelines have been found in buildings in ______________ . Additional information regarding radon and radon testing may be obtained from your county public health unit."

Representations: In agreeing to the terms and conditions of the lease lessor affirms that lessor has not relied on any representations of lessor or lessor's agents not herein expressed.

Attorney's fees: In the event suit or action is brought upon this lease or any provisions contained herein the prevailing party therein shall be entitled to costs and attorney's fees incurred in the action, including any appeal thereof. ☐ The parties agree that prior to commencing suit or action at law under this agreement any dispute shall be submitted to binding arbitration to be held in the state of Oregon and the decision of the arbitrator therein shall be deemed the same as a judgment or decree of a court and enforceable as provided by Oregon law, and the prevailing party shall be entitled to costs and attorney's fees in connection with such arbitration.

Entire agreement and severability: This lease contains the entire agreement between the parties and may be modified only by amendments in writing signed by the parties. If any portion of this agreement is deemed unenforceable the remainder of its provisions remain in full force and effect.

Notice: Any notice by lessee to lessor shall be deemed effective when placed in the U.S. mails, postage prepaid, addressed to ______________________ . Any notice by lessor to lessee shall be deemed effective when placed in the U.S. mails, postage prepaid, addressed to______________________ .

In witness whereof, the parties have signed this lease this ________ day of ________ , ________

______________________	______________________
Lessor	Lessee
______________________	______________________
Lessor	Lessee

Oregon Case Law

In the following section are landmark cases decided by the Oregon Supreme Court and the Oregon Court of Appeals relating to landlord and tenant issues.

In reading this section it is important to understand the difference between statutes and court decisions. Statutes are passed by the Oregon Legislature and signed into law by the Governor. A statute, however, is subject to interpretation by the courts. The courts also have the authority to declare a statute unconstitutional.

When a landlord or a tenant brings suit against the other the case is filed in a county court. The court hears all the arguments, testimony, and observes the evidence presented, then renders its decision. This decision establishes a precedent – that is, if a similar case is presented in the future, the court must render the same decision.

The losing party may appeal the decision of the county court to the Oregon Court of Appeals. It is important to note that the Court of Appeals does not retry the case. Its sole function is to decided if the trial court erred in interpreting the law. Thus, any evidence or testimony must be presented at the original trial.

The loser in the Court of Appeals may file a further appeal to the Oregon Supreme Court. In the majority of cases the Supreme Court will refuse to hear the cases, allowing the decision of the Court of Appeals to stand.

A decision rendered by a county court is binding only on that court. Thus we frequently find differences in the way landlord-tenant laws are interpreted in each of Oregon's 36 counties. But once a decision is rendered in the Court of Appeals or the Supreme Court it establishes the precedent statewide and is binding on all county courts.

Court cases make dry reading material. To make it more interesting we have presented the case first, as though you were reading the pleadings of the parties in court. At the end you are given the opportunity to decide how the case should be decided, using your knowledge of landlord and tenant law learned in previous sections. At the end of this section is a summary of what the Court of Appeals or the Supreme Court decided in each case. You can compare your decision to theirs to see if you agree.

Cases

1

An owner of an older house leased it to tenants. At the start of the lease the owner was aware that the wiring was old, including the service panel, which was an older fuse-type panel instead of circuit breakers. Prior to leasing the property the owner had done some electrical repair work inside the house himself.

The tenants soon discovered that the condition of the wiring caused fuses to blow repeatedly. When they complained to the owner he came out and repaired a service pole outside the house, but did not make any repairs inside the house. He did, however, point out to the tenants that there was a gallon jar in the basement full of fuses for them to use. The tenants then pointed out that he must have had a problem with the wiring in the past if he kept so many fuses on hand. The owner responded by suggesting that they could alleviate the problem by using larger fuses or using a penny in place of a fuse. The tenants told the owner they thought that would be a foolish thing to do.

A short time later a fire occurred and the tenants lost a substantial amount of personal property. It was determined that the fire was caused by using fuses rated too high for the wiring. The tenants sued for the loss of their personal property. The landlord claimed that the wiring was adequate under the habitability standards of the Residential Landlord-Tenant Act and that the fire was caused by the tenants' failure to use the right size fuses.

If you were the judge, how would you decide this case?

2

A tenant rented a house on a month-to-month basis over a period of several years. As a result of storm damage the chimney had a crack in it. On October 1, one year after the beginning of the rental the tenant notified the landlord by letter of the crack in the chimney, complaining that it was a fire hazard. The tenant sent similar letters to the landlord one year later, two years later, and three years later. Shortly after the last letter the landlord received notice from the tax assessor that the assessed value of the property would be increased by a substantial amount. At that point the landlord decided to sell the property.

While the property was for sale the tenant refused to allow the landlord to enter the house to show it to buyers. However, she, herself, made two offers to buy the house from the landlord; the first with 5% down payment and the balance on a contract, and the second for cash. The price offered was approximately two thirds of the new assessed valuation. The landlord did not accept either offer.

By the end of December the house had not sold. The landlord notified the tenant on December 29 that the rent would increase effective February 1 to an amount equal to 1% of the new assessed valuation per month, stating that as his reasoning in his letter of notice.

On February 5 the tenant sent a rent check to the landlord in an amount equal to 1% of the previous year's assessed value, along with a letter explaining that the new assessed valuation was "illegal and contrary to law" because there had been no "proof of actual and substantial improvements." The letter further reminded the landlord of the defective chimney and advised the landlord to have it inspected by the local fire marshal.

The landlord returned the check with a letter demanding the full, new rental amount. The letter did not mention the chimney. On February 11 the tenant had the chimney repaired herself. And three days after having the chimney repaired, she filed a complaint with the Oregon Bureau of Labor that the landlord had discriminated against her because of her sex.

On February 22 the landlord served the tenant with a 30-day notice to vacate the premises for failure to pay rent. On February 28 the tenant filed a complaint with the local building inspector that the wiring was unsafe. The property was inspected by the city, which sent the landlord a "Notice of Violation of City Ordinance."

On March 28 the landlord filed a forcible entry and detainer action to recover possession. The tenant counterclaimed for "mental distress" and also that the landlord's eviction was retaliatory conduct because she had filed the complaint with the city about the electrical problems.

If you were the judge, how would you decide this case?

3

A tenant rented an apartment and paid a "cleaning deposit" in the amount of $50. On August 6 the tenant moved out after giving proper notice and delivered possession to the landlord. Upon moving out the tenant requested return of the deposit and provided the landlord's wife with her new phone number. The landlord responded that he would first have to view the premises and, after having done so, he would prepare a written statement and allow the tenant to inspect the premises with him to discuss any damages.

On August 9 the landlord called the tenant and stated that there were damages, but that the landlord would refund $12 if the tenant would come to the landlord's house where the landlord would give the tenant the $12 refund and an accounting. The tenant later informed the landlord's wife that she thought she was entitled to the full $50 and that she had consulted an attorney and wanted the landlord to contact her attorney.

The tenant subsequently never received any refund or accounting from the landlord and filed suit for twice the amount of the deposit, in reliance on the Residential Landlord-Tenant Act which provides for twice the amount of the deposit as damages in the event the landlord does not refund or account for withheld deposits. The trial court found in favor of the landlord and the tenant appealed.

If you were the judge, how would you decide this case?

4

A tenant in an apartment building went to visit her neighbor in the apartment next door. The adjoining apartment had a patio in front surrounded by a fence. It had been raining and there was water standing on the patio high enough that it made it difficult to enter the apartment without stepping in the water. The water was deep enough that it would have overflowed the ordinary pair of oxford shoes that the visitor was wearing. The visitor did manage to enter the apartment, but on leaving she slipped and fell, causing injuries.

The visiting tenant sued the owner and the property manager for personal injury damages. At trial it was determined that the standing water problem was known to the host tenant before she rented the apartment, which had been several years earlier. At no time during the host tenant's occupancy did she notify the owner or the manager of the problem. However, evidence was presented that both the owner and the manager were aware of the problem in spite of the lack of notice. It was also evident that the visiting tenant was aware of the problem.

The Residential Landlord-Tenant Act includes "floors, walls, ceilings, stairways and railings maintained in good repair" as part of the habitability standards. It also provides "the remedies provided by this chapter shall be so administered that an aggrieved party may recover appropriate damages." However, at common law a landlord has no obligation to a tenant or the tenant's guests for matters known to the tenant at the start of the tenancy.

Whether the visitor was entitled to damages revolves around several issues. First, is the patio a "floor" within the meaning of the language of the habitability standards? Second, is the visitor entitled to damages under the Residential Landlord-Tenant Act as an "aggrieved party," or does "aggrieved party" mean only the landlord or the tenant? And finally, since both the host and the visitor were aware of the problem, should the visitor be entitled to damages because she failed to take sufficient care in leaving the premises, given the fact that the problem was obvious and an ordinary person would have done so?

If you were the judge, how would you decide this case?

5

A tenant rented a house from a landlord. From the beginning of the tenancy the tenant complained to the landlord about deficiencies in the house, including that the roof leaked and that the wood stove, the only source of heat for the first floor, spewed smoke every time it was used. The tenant also complained that the smoke alarm did not work, window locks were broken, there were missing covers on electrical switches, and the foundation was rotting.

Because the landlord did nothing to remedy these problems the tenant decided to withhold rent. When the landlord stopped receiving the rent he filed a forcible entry and detainer action, asking for restitution of possession, plus judgment against the tenant for unpaid rent and his costs and attorney's fees.

The tenant answered the landlord's FED action by asserting counterclaims for loss of rent value due to the deficiencies which she claimed violated the habitability standards of the Residential Landlord-

Tenant Act. However, in spite of her claims, she also paid the full amount of rent into the court, although there was evidence that she had to borrow the money to do so, and that she did so only when prompted to do so by the judge.

The landlord argued that the tenant's counterclaims were baseless and that she was not due any reduction in rent. The landlord claimed that the leaks in the roof were trivial and that the wood stove smoked only because the tenant used it incorrectly. He denied completely the rest of the tenants allegations. Neither the tenant nor the landlord offered any evidence as to the alleged deficiencies in the property other than by their testimony.

If you were the judge, how would you decide this case?

6

A landlord rented a residential property to tenants on a month-to-month basis. When the tenants later surrendered possession the landlord discovered that they had caused substantial damage to the premises. The landlord sued for waste in the amount it cost to repair the premises, plus loss of rent for the time it took to conclude the repairs.

The landlord's case was filed more than one year after the termination of the tenancy. The Residential Landlord-Tenant Act provides a one-year statute of limitations – "An action arising under a rental agreement or ORS chapter 90 shall be commenced within one year" (ORS 12.125). However, the landlord maintained, as a point of law, that his suit for waste depended on the tenants' common-law duties and not under the rental agreement or the Residential Landlord-Tenant Act. Therefore, the landlord argued, he should be entitled to the more liberal statute of limitations for waste, which allows six years.

If you were the judge, how would you decide this case?

7

A manager in a mobile home park was facing efforts of tenants to form a tenants' union. In attempting to quash these efforts the manager had engaged in baiting tenants involved in forming the union. At one point he told a tenant who was one of the ringleaders "hit me and then I'll evict you."

Another tenant, who was also one of the leaders, lived in the park with her 17-year old son. On July 19 the manager received complaints that the tenant's son was playing loud music and creating a disturbance. When the manager approached the mobile home he found the son sitting on the tenant's car, with a stereo speaker in the window of the mobile home facing outward. The manager told the son to turn the music down. The son responded that if the manager came onto their space he would hit him. The manager ignored the son, proceeded to the mobile home, and disconnected the speaker from the stereo. The son then hit the manager over the head with a hockey stick. The mother was not at home when this occurred.

On July 23 the manager served the tenant with a 24-hour notice of termination of her rental agreement "because you or someone in your control inflicted substantial personal injury upon the landlord." The manager then filed an FED action to recover possession.

At the FED hearing the tenant argued that her 17-year old son was not someone in her control. She also argued that the manager had entered her space unlawfully and without notice, in violation of the Residential Landlord-Tenant Act. She also complained that the manager was attempting to evict her because of her activity in forming the tenants' union.

If you were the judge, how would you decide this case?

8

A property owner rented a house to a tenant. At the commencement of the tenancy there was a concealed hole in the front lawn. Both the owner and the tenant were aware of the hole. The tenant never made any demands that the owner fill in or repair the hole, and the owner never did anything about it or provide warnings of its existence.

Several months later a visitor to the premises fell into the hole while out trick or treating with her children on Halloween. The porch light was on at the time of the incident. There was no sidewalk up to the front door, so the visitor and her children had no choice but to cross the lawn. The visitor sued the tenant and the owner for personal injury damages.

If you were the judge, how would you decide this case?

9

A tenant leased commercial premises at a rate of $3,150 per month beginning on November

1 and ending September 30, 35 months later. The tenant paid the rent at the agreed rate for one year and then stopped making payments. After several months without receiving rent the landlord filed a forcible entry and detainer action to recover possession. At the FED hearing the court awarded possession to the landlord. Three weeks after gaining possession the landlord filed suit for unpaid rent to the end of the lease, 22 months then remaining, times the monthly rent, for a total complaint of $69,300, plus the landlord's costs and attorney's fees. The lease contained a provision that in the event of a suit the prevailing party would be entitled to costs and attorney's fees.

At trial the court awarded judgment in favor of the landlord against the tenant for $69,300, plus the landlord's costs and attorney's fees. The tenant appealed to the Court of Appeals, arguing that the FED action terminated the lease, and therefore all the tenant's obligations to the landlord thereafter.

If you were the judge, how would you decide this case?

10

A couple rented a house from a landlord which had a fireplace. Two years after the beginning of the tenancy heat transmitting through the bricks caused a fire which destroyed the house. According to testimony, at the time of the fire neither the tenants nor the landlord knew that the chimney was defective.

Tenants sued for damages under the Residential Landlord-Tenant Act, claiming violation of habitability standards. Specifically, the tenants claimed the landlord had a duty to provide "safety from fire hazards" [ORS 90.320 (j)], and that the habitability standards also required this as a continuing obligation of the landlord. The landlord argued that he should have no liability for matters which were latent (concealed from view) and of which he had no knowledge.

If you were the judge, how would you decide this case?

Final decisions

1

The Oregon Supreme Court agreed that the wiring might have been adequate under the Residential Landlord-Tenant Act, or at least that the tenants did not claim that it was not, so the presumption was that it was adequate.

However, the Court found that the owner had induced the tenants to use fuses of too high amperage for the circuits. The Court further found that, while the lessor may not have had a duty to make repairs, if the lessor does make repairs the lessor is responsible for damages caused by failure to make the repairs properly. The owner admitted to having repaired the wiring, thus the owner was liable for the condition of the wiring, even though the repairs were done before the start of the tenancy. Therefore, the Court found in favor of the tenants for the value of their lost property and ordered judgment against the owner.

Conradi v. Helvogt, 278 Or 229, 563 P2d 707 (1977)

2

At the FED hearing the judge denied the tenant's counterclaims and awarded possession to the landlord. The tenant appealed to the Court of Appeals.

In reviewing the case the Court of Appeals noted that nothing in the Residential Landlord-Tenant Act specified damages for mental distress. The Court further noted that in most, if not all cases, the Act expresses damages in ways which are readily converted to dollar amounts, such as "two months rent" and "an amount equal to twice the amount wrongfully withheld." The Court further noted that in any court case there is likely to be emotional distress, and the landlord could therefore just as easily claim damages. The Court stated "the result would be a balancing act to determine which of the two became more distressed as a result of the dispute." Therefore, the Court decided that the tenant's claim of damages for emotional distress was unfounded under the Residential Landlord-Tenant Act.

As to the tenant's counterclaim of retaliatory conduct when the landlord raised the rent because the tenant complained to the city about the wiring, the Court noted that the rent increase was made on December 29, but the complaint to the city was not made until February 22. Therefore, the Court dismissed the tenant's counterclaim noting that the landlord could not retaliate against an action the tenant had not yet taken.

Ficker v. Diefenbach, 34 Or App 241, 578 P2d 467 (1978)

3

The Court of Appeals noted the precise language of the Residential Landlord-Tenant Act requires the landlord to provide the tenant with the refund or an accounting, or partial refund and accounting for the difference within 30 days after the termination of the tenancy. (At the time of this case the statute required only 30 days, where it now requires 31 days, but that fact is irrelevant to the resolution of the case.) The Court noted that the legislature gave the landlord the duty of providing a specific written accounting before he could claim all or part of a security deposit. In this case the landlord did not provide the required accounting. The landlord's wife merely stated that the tenant could go to the landlord's home to get the written accounting. The Court stated that they did not feel the tenant had a duty to go get the accounting; the statute stated that it was the landlord's duty to provide it to the tenant. Since the landlord did not do so, the Court reversed the trial court and found in favor of the tenant for twice the amount of the deposit.

Ellsworth v. Gladden, 36 Or App 385, 584 P2d 774 (1978)

4

At trial the defendant owner and property manager filed a motion to dismiss the case on the grounds that the landlord is not liable to the tenant or the tenant's guests for conditions that existed at the start of the tenancy. The court agreed with this argument and granted the motion. The visitor appealed and the Oregon Court of Appeals affirmed the trial court's decision.

The visitor then appealed to the Oregon Supreme Court which agreed to review the case. With one justice strongly dissenting, the majority ruled that the patio was a "floor" within the meaning of the statute, principally because it was within the control of the tenant in the unit. Therefore, the landlord had a duty to maintain it. The majority also agreed that the visitor was an "aggrieved party," and therefore entitled to damages. And finally, the majority agreed that the landlord's duty to maintain the floor existed in spite of the fact that it was pre-existing and known to the tenant. The Court reversed the decision of the Court of Appeals and remanded the case to the original trial court for determination of the amount of the damages and judgment.

Humbert v. Sellars, 300 Or 113, 708 P2d 344 (1985)

5

At the conclusion of the FED hearing the judge ruled against the tenant on the tenant's counterclaims. The judge admitted that the property had deficiencies, but in his judgment they were not substantial enough to constitute a violation of the habitability standards of the Residential Landlord-Tenant Act. The judge also found in favor of the landlord for the amount of rent due. The amount due was judged to be $2,000, and this was the amount the tenant had tendered to the court, so the judge ordered it turned over to the landlord. The judge also entered judgment against the tenant for the landlord's costs and attorney's fees.

The tenant appealed from this decision to the Court of Appeals. In its review of the case the Court of Appeals ruled that the tenant had paid the full amount of rent into court and was therefore entitled to retain possession. The landlord argued that this was ridiculous because any tenant could stop paying rent and then allege any counterclaims to retain possession for months while the landlord has to hire attorneys and might still not recover possession, all the time having to go without rent income. The Court of Appeals pointed out, however, that while the judge at the hearing had ruled against the tenant on the counterclaims, there was evidence that the property did have deficiencies and that the tenant's counterclaims were brought in good faith. As for the fact that the tenant had to borrow the money to pay into court and did so only when prompted to do so by the judge, the Court of Appeals noted that the Residential Landlord-Tenant Act provides the remedy of withholding rent and paying it to a court to force a landlord to remedy habitability problems. The Court noted that the statute does not deny the tenant this right merely because she had to borrow the money or because she did so only because the judge prompted her to. The fact that the amount she tendered was adequate to pay the rent due the landlord was all that was necessary for her to retain possession. Therefore, the judge's order of possession to the landlord was reversed.

As for the award of attorney's fees to the landlord, the Court of Appeals noted that the Residential Landlord-Tenant Act provides for costs and attorney's fees to the "prevailing party." In this case the landlord prevailed on the rent due and the tenant prevailed on possession. Therefore, neither party "prevailed" and the award of costs and attorney's fees was improper.

Amatisto v. Paz, 82 Or App 341, 728 P2d 42 (1986)

6

The trial judge dismissed the landlord's complaint as untimely under the statute of limitations. The landlord appealed to the Court of Appeals, which affirmed the trial court's decision. The landlord then appealed to the Oregon Supreme Court.

The Supreme Court ruled that the landlord's right to damages for waste under the more liberal six-year statute of limitations applied only to tenants for years. However, it further ruled that a month-to-month tenant was a tenant "for years" in the sense that each month was a definite term, therefore the landlord was entitled to the longer statute of limitations. The Court added that a month-to-month tenant would be considered "for years" only in actions brought by a landlord for waste. The Court remanded the case to the trial court for determination of the amount of the landlord's damages and judgment.

Vollertsen v. Lamb, 302 Or 489, 732 P2d 486 (1987)

7

The FED hearing was held before a jury which found against the tenant and ordered restitution of possession to the landlord on the grounds that the actions of the son were at least "outrageous in the extreme," for which the Residential Landlord-Tenant Act allows a 24-hour notice of termination. The jury noted that the landlord did enter the premises wrongfully, but that the actions of the son justified the 24-hour notice. The tenant appealed to the Court of Appeals.

In its review the Court of Appeals pointed out that whether her son was in her control was irrelevant. The Residential Landlord-Tenant Act allows a landlord to give the tenant a 24-hour notice if the "tenant" or "someone in the tenant's control" harms the landlord or does acts which are "outrageous in the extreme." The Court noted that the son was a "tenant" under the statute, which defines a tenant as "a person entitled under a rental agreement to occupy … ." Therefore, the son was a tenant, so whether he was under his mother's control made no difference. The Court of Appeals affirmed the decision of the jury and ordered restitution of possession to the landlord.

Portland Mobile Home Park v. Wojtyna, 85 Or App 368, 736 P2d 604 (1987)

8

At trial the owner filed a motion to dismiss the case on the grounds that the property owner has no liability to third parties for defects in the property that existed at the time the property was rented, either under common law or under the Residential Landlord-Tenant Act, unless the defect related to the habitability standards of the Act. The owner maintained that the hole in the ground was not a habitability issue. The court agreed and dismissed the case.

The visitor appealed to the Court of Appeals, which affirmed the trial court's decision. The visitor then filed for review by the Oregon Supreme Court, which was granted.

In its decision the justices agreed that the hole in the lawn was not an issue that came within the scope of the habitability standards of the Residential Landlord-Tenant Act because it was part of the grounds. The Residential Landlord-Tenant Act required of the grounds only that they be "at the time of the commencement of the rental agreement in every part clean, sanitary and free from all accumulations of debris, filth, rubbish, garbage, rodents and vermin, and all areas under control of the landlord kept in every part clean, sanitary and free from all accumulations of debris, filth, rubbish, garbage, rodents and vermin." (Note, the statutory language has since been changed by the addition of "safe for normal and reasonably foreseeable uses" to the requirement for "grounds.")

However, the justices ruled that the decision of the trial court to dismiss the case was improper because the visitor did have a claim under common-law negligence. The case was remanded to the trial court for determination of the amount of the damages and judgment. Note that since "safe" has been added to the requirements under the Residential Landlord-Tenant Act, the visitor would also have a claim under that statute if the case were filed today.

Bellikka v. Green, 306 Or 630, 762 P2d 997 (1988)

9

The Court of Appeals noted that the Oregon Supreme Court has recognized the dual nature of a lease as a conveyance of an estate in real property as well as a contract, at least as far as the obligations of a tenant who abandons the premises and the duty of the landlord to mitigate damages. The Court also noted that the Oregon statute says that the "tenancy" is terminated by the tenant's failure to pay rent, but does not state that the "lease" is also thereby terminated. Therefore, the Court reasoned that the tenant who fails to pay rent in timely fashion forfeits the tenant's leasehold estate, but does not thereby escape liability for the damages suffered by the landlord as a result. The Court further found that the landlord was the prevailing party, and was therefore entitled to costs and attorney's fees.

Although the Court did not address the issue, it is presumed that the landlord would have a duty to mitigate. The judgment against the tenant for $69,300 plus costs and attorney's fees would therefore be offset if the landlord is successful in re-leasing the premises before the end date of the tenant's lease.

Sunset Fuel and Engineering Co. v. Compton, 97 Or App 244, 775 P2d 901 (1989)

10

At trial the landlord moved to dismiss the tenant's claim on the grounds that the Residential Landlord-Tenant Act did not specifically require a landlord to be liable for matters unknown and unknowable by the landlord. The court granted this motion and the tenants appealed to the Court of Appeals.

The Court of Appeals reversed the trial court and remanded the case for determination of the amount of the damages and judgment. The landlord then appealed to the Oregon Supreme Court.

The Supreme Court ruled that the text and context of the Residential Landlord-Tenant Act (habitability requirements) do not specifically require the tenant to prove that the landlord had knowledge of an unhabitable condition in order to prevail on their claim for damages under the statute. The fact that the premises were found to be unhabitable is sufficient for the landlord to be liable for damages. The justices affirmed the decision of the Court of Appeals and ordered the case back to the trial court for determination of the amount of the damages and judgment.

Davis v. Campbell, 327 Or 584, 965 P2d 1017 (1998)

Appendix

On the following pages you will find sections from Oregon Revised Statutes and Oregon Administrative Rules relating to property management –

ORS Chapter 90 – The Residential Landlord-Tenant Act.

ORS Chapter 91 – Tenancy

ORS Chapter 105 – Property Rights

Students can obtain the full text of any Oregon statute and any Oregon administrative rule at most public libraries or on the internet.

The Oregon Real Estate Agency uses all three of the above sections from Oregon Revised Statutes as sources for exam material, especially for the property manager license exam, and also for the Oregon portion of the brokers exam.

Students should also be aware that the text portions of each section in this book (especially Section 2 on the Residential Landlord and Tenant Act) were written as summaries of these statutes, not as replacements for studying them in detail. State examinations are constantly being changed and updated, so students preparing for license examinations should study these statutes thoroughly.

Chapter 90 – Residential Landlord and Tenant
2003 Edition
GENERAL PROVISIONS

90.100 Definitions. Subject to additional definitions contained in this chapter that apply to specific sections or parts thereof, and unless the context otherwise requires, in this chapter:

(1) "Accessory building or structure" means any portable, demountable or permanent structure, including but not limited to cabanas, ramadas, storage sheds, garages, awnings, carports, decks, steps, ramps, piers and pilings, that is:

(a) Owned and used solely by a tenant of a manufactured dwelling or floating home; or

(b) Provided pursuant to a written rental agreement for the sole use of and maintenance by a tenant of a manufactured dwelling or floating home.

(2) "Action" includes recoupment, counterclaim, setoff, suit in equity and any other proceeding in which rights are determined, including an action for possession.

(3) "Applicant screening charge" means any payment of money required by a landlord of an applicant prior to entering into a rental agreement with that applicant for a residential dwelling unit, the purpose of which is to pay the cost of processing an application for a rental agreement for a residential dwelling unit.

(4) "Building and housing codes" include any law, ordinance or governmental regulation concerning fitness for habitation, or the construction, maintenance, operation, occupancy, use or appearance of any premises or dwelling unit.

(5) "Conduct" means the commission of an act or the failure to act.

(6) "Dealer" means any person in the business of selling, leasing or distributing new or used manufactured dwellings or floating homes to persons who purchase or lease a manufactured dwelling or floating home for use as a residence.

(7) "Domestic violence" has the meaning given that term in ORS 135.230.

(8) "Drug and alcohol free housing" means a rental agreement as described in ORS 90.243.

(9) "Dwelling unit" means a structure or the part of a structure that is used as a home, residence or sleeping place by one person who maintains a household or by two or more persons who maintain a common household. "Dwelling unit" regarding a person who rents a space for a manufactured dwelling or recreational vehicle or regarding a person who rents moorage space for a floating home as defined in ORS 830.700, but does not rent the home, means the space rented and not the manufactured dwelling, recreational vehicle or floating home itself.

(10) "Essential service" means:

(a) For a tenancy not consisting of rental space for a manufactured dwelling, floating home or recreational vehicle owned by the tenant and not otherwise subject to ORS 90.505 to 90.840:

(A) Heat, plumbing, hot and cold running water, gas, electricity, light fixtures, locks for exterior doors, latches for windows and any cooking appliance or refrigerator supplied or required to be supplied by the landlord; and

(B) Any other service or habitability obligation imposed by the rental agreement or ORS 90.320, the lack or violation of which creates a serious threat to the tenant's health, safety or property or makes the dwelling unit unfit for occupancy.

(b) For a tenancy consisting of rental space for a manufactured dwelling, floating home or recreational vehicle owned by the tenant or that is otherwise subject to ORS 90.505 to 90.840:

(A) Sewage disposal, water supply, electrical supply and, if required by applicable law, any drainage system; and

(B) Any other service or habitability obligation imposed by the rental agreement or ORS 90.730, the lack or violation of which creates a serious threat to the tenant's health, safety or property or makes the rented space unfit for occupancy.

(11) "Facility" means:

(a) A place where four or more manufactured dwellings are located, the primary purpose of which is to rent space or keep space for rent to any person for a fee; or

(b) A moorage of contiguous dwelling units that may be legally transferred as a single unit and are owned by one person where four or more floating homes are secured, the primary purpose of which is to rent space or keep space for rent to any person for a fee.

(12) "Facility purchase association" means a group of three or more tenants who reside in a facility and have organized for the purpose of eventual purchase of the facility.

(13) "Fee" means a nonrefundable payment of money.

(14) "First class mail" does not include certified or registered mail, or any other form of mail that may delay or hinder actual delivery of mail to the recipient.

(15) "Fixed term tenancy" means a tenancy that has a fixed term of existence, continuing to a specific end-

ing date and terminating on that date without requiring further notice to effect the termination.
(16) "Floating home" has the meaning given that term in ORS 830.700. As used in this chapter, "floating home" includes an accessory building or structure.
(17) "Good faith" means honesty in fact in the conduct of the transaction concerned.
(18) "Hotel or motel" means "hotel" as that term is defined in ORS 699.005.
(19) "Informal dispute resolution" means, but is not limited to, consultation between the landlord or landlord's agent and one or more tenants, or mediation utilizing the services of a third party.
(20) "Landlord" means the owner, lessor or sublessor of the dwelling unit or the building or premises of which it is a part. "Landlord" includes a person who is authorized by the owner, lessor or sublessor to manage the premises or to enter into a rental agreement.
(21) "Landlord's agent" means a person who has oral or written authority, either express or implied, to act for or on behalf of a landlord.
(22) "Last month's rent deposit" means a type of security deposit, however designated, the primary function of which is to secure the payment of rent for the last month of the tenancy.
(23) "Manufactured dwelling" means a residential trailer, a mobile home or a manufactured home as those terms are defined in ORS 446.003 (26). "Manufactured dwelling" includes an accessory building or structure. "Manufactured dwelling" does not include a recreational vehicle.
(24) "Manufactured dwelling park" has the meaning given that term in ORS 446.003.
(25) "Month-to-month tenancy" means a tenancy that automatically renews and continues for successive monthly periods on the same terms and conditions originally agreed to, or as revised by the parties, until terminated by one or both of the parties.
(26) "Organization" includes a corporation, government, governmental subdivision or agency, business trust, estate, trust, partnership or association, two or more persons having a joint or common interest, and any other legal or commercial entity.
(27) "Owner" includes a mortgagee in possession and means one or more persons, jointly or severally, in whom is vested:
(a) All or part of the legal title to property; or
(b) All or part of the beneficial ownership and a right to present use and enjoyment of the premises.
(28) "Person" includes an individual or organization.
(29) "Premises" means a dwelling unit and the structure of which it is a part and facilities and appurtenances therein and grounds, areas and facilities held out for the use of tenants generally or whose use is promised to the tenant.
(30) "Prepaid rent" means any payment of money to the landlord for a rent obligation not yet due. In addition, "prepaid rent" means rent paid for a period extending beyond a termination date.
(31) "Recreational vehicle" has the meaning given that term in ORS 446.003.
(32) "Rent" means any payment to be made to the landlord under the rental agreement, periodic or otherwise, in exchange for the right of a tenant and any permitted pet to occupy a dwelling unit to the exclusion of others. "Rent" does not include security deposits, fees or utility or service charges as described in ORS 90.315 (4) and 90.510 (8).
(33) "Rental agreement" means all agreements, written or oral, and valid rules and regulations adopted under ORS 90.262 or 90.510 (6) embodying the terms and conditions concerning the use and occupancy of a dwelling unit and premises. "Rental agreement" includes a lease. A rental agreement shall be either a week-to-week tenancy, month-to-month tenancy or fixed term tenancy.
(34) "Roomer" means a person occupying a dwelling unit that does not include a toilet and either a bathtub or a shower and a refrigerator, stove and kitchen, all provided by the landlord, and where one or more of these facilities are used in common by occupants in the structure.
(35) "Screening or admission criteria" means a written statement of any factors a landlord considers in deciding whether to accept or reject an applicant and any qualifications required for acceptance. "Screening or admission criteria" includes, but is not limited to, the rental history, character references, public records, criminal records, credit reports, credit references and incomes or resources of the applicant.
(36) "Security deposit" means any refundable payment or deposit of money, however designated, the primary function of which is to secure the performance of a rental agreement or any part of a rental agreement, but does not mean a fee.
(37) "Sexual assault" has the meaning given that term in ORS 147.450.
(38) "Squatter" means a person occupying a dwelling unit who is not so entitled under a rental agreement or who is not authorized by the tenant to occupy that

dwelling unit. "Squatter" does not include a tenant who holds over as described in ORS 90.427 (4).
(39) "Stalking" means the behavior described in ORS 173.732.
(40) "Statement of policy" means the summary explanation of information and facility policies to be provided to prospective and existing tenants under ORS 90.510.
(41) "Surrender" means an agreement, express or implied, as described in ORS 90.148 between a landlord and tenant to terminate a rental agreement that gave the tenant the right to occupy a dwelling unit.
(42) "Tenant" means a person, including a roomer, entitled under a rental agreement to occupy a dwelling unit to the exclusion of others, including a dwelling unit owned, operated or controlled by a public housing authority. "Tenant" also includes a minor, as defined and provided for in ORS 109.697. As used in ORS 90.505 to 90.840, "tenant" includes only a person who owns and occupies as a residence a manufactured dwelling or a floating home in a facility and persons residing with that tenant under the terms of the rental agreement.
(43) "Transient lodging" means a room or a suite of rooms.
(44) "Transient occupancy" means occupancy in transient lodging that has all of the following characteristics:
(a) Occupancy is charged on a daily basis and is not collected more than six days in advance;
(b) The lodging operator provides maid and linen service daily or every two days as part of the regularly charged cost of occupancy; and
(c) The period of occupancy does not exceed 30 days.
(45) "Vacation occupancy" means occupancy in a dwelling unit, not including transient occupancy in a hotel or motel, that has all of the following characteristics:
(a) The occupant rents the unit for vacation purposes only, not as a principal residence;
(b) The occupant has a principal residence other than at the unit; and
(c) The period of authorized occupancy does not exceed 45 days.
(46) "Victim" means a person who is the subject of domestic violence, sexual assault or stalking. "Victim" includes a parent or guardian of a minor who is the subject of domestic violence, sexual assault or stalking.
(47) "Week-to-week tenancy" means a tenancy that has all of the following characteristics:
(a) Occupancy is charged on a weekly basis and is payable no less frequently than every seven days;
(b) There is a written rental agreement that defines the landlord's and the tenant's rights and responsibilities under this chapter; and
(c) There are no fees or security deposits, although the landlord may require the payment of an applicant screening charge, as provided in ORS 90.295.

90.105 Short title. This chapter shall be known and may be cited as the "Residential Landlord and Tenant Act."

90.110 Exclusions from application of this chapter. Unless created to avoid the application of this chapter, the following arrangements are not governed by this chapter:
(1) Residence at an institution, public or private, if incidental to detention or the provision of medical, geriatric, educational, counseling, religious or similar service, but not including residence in off-campus nondormitory housing.
(2) Occupancy of a dwelling unit for no more than 90 days by a purchaser prior to the scheduled closing of a real estate sale or by a seller following the closing of a sale, in either case as permitted under the terms of an agreement for sale of a dwelling unit or the property of which it is a part. The occupancy by a purchaser or seller described in this subsection may be terminated only pursuant to ORS 91.130. A tenant who holds but has not exercised an option to purchase the dwelling unit is not a purchaser for purposes of this subsection.
(3) Occupancy by a member of a fraternal or social organization in the portion of a structure operated for the benefit of the organization.
(4) Transient occupancy in a hotel or motel.
(5) Occupancy by a squatter.
(6) Vacation occupancy.
(7) Occupancy by an employee of a landlord whose right to occupancy is conditional upon employment in and about the premises. However, the occupancy by an employee as described in this subsection may be terminated only pursuant to ORS 91.120.
(8) Occupancy by an owner of a condominium unit or a holder of a proprietary lease in a cooperative.
(9) Occupancy under a rental agreement covering premises used by the occupant primarily for agricultural purposes.

90.115 Territorial application. This chapter applies to, regulates and determines rights, obligations and remedies under a rental agreement, wherever made, for a dwelling unit located within this state.

90.120 Applicability of other statutory lien, tenancy and rent provisions; applicability of ORS 90.100 to 90.450 and 90.505 to 90.840. (1) The provisions of ORS 87.152 to 87.212, 91.010 to 91.110, 91.130, 91.210 and 91.220 do not apply to the rights and obligations of landlords and tenants governed by this chapter.
(2) Any provisions of this chapter which reasonably apply only to the structure that is used as a home, residence or sleeping place shall not apply to a manufactured dwelling, recreational vehicle or floating home where the tenant owns the manufactured dwelling, recreational vehicle or floating home but rents the space on which it is located.
(3) The provisions of ORS 90.505 to 90.840 apply only if:
(a) The tenant owns the manufactured dwelling or floating home;
(b) The tenant rents the space on which the dwelling or home is located; and
(c) The space is in a facility.
(4) Residential tenancies for recreational vehicles and for manufactured dwellings and floating homes that are not subject to ORS 90.505 to 90.840 shall be subject to ORS 90.100 to 90.450. Tenancies described in this subsection include tenancies for:
(a) A recreational vehicle, located inside or outside of a facility, if the tenant owns or rents the vehicle;
(b) A manufactured dwelling or floating home, located inside or outside of a facility, if the tenant rents both the dwelling or home and the space; and
(c) A manufactured dwelling or floating home, located outside a facility, if the tenant owns the dwelling or home and rents the space.

90.125 Administration of remedies; enforcement. (1) The remedies provided by this chapter shall be so administered that an aggrieved party may recover appropriate damages. The aggrieved party has a duty to mitigate damages.
(2) Any right or obligation declared by this chapter is enforceable by action unless the provision declaring it specifies a different and limited effect.

90.130 Obligation of good faith. Every duty under this chapter and every act which must be performed as a condition precedent to the exercise of a right or remedy under this chapter imposes an obligation of good faith in its performance or enforcement.

90.135 Unconscionability. (1) If the court, as a matter of law, finds:
(a) A rental agreement or any provision thereof was unconscionable when made, the court may refuse to enforce the agreement, enforce the remainder of the agreement without the unconscionable provision, or limit the application of any unconscionable provision to avoid an unconscionable result; or
(b) A settlement in which a party waives or agrees to forego a claim or right under this chapter or under a rental agreement was unconscionable when made, the court may refuse to enforce the settlement, enforce the remainder of the settlement without the unconscionable provision, or limit the application of any unconscionable provision to avoid an unconscionable result.
(2) If unconscionability is put into issue by a party or by the court upon its own motion the parties shall be afforded a reasonable opportunity to present evidence as to the setting, purpose and effect of the rental agreement or settlement to aid the court in making the determination.

90.140 Types of payments landlord may require or accept; written evidence of payment. (1) A landlord may require or accept the following types of payments:
(a) Applicant screening charges, pursuant to ORS 90.295;
(b) Deposits to secure the execution of a rental agreement, pursuant to ORS 90.297;
(c) Security deposits, pursuant to ORS 90.300;
(d) Fees, pursuant to ORS 90.302;
(e) Rent, as defined in ORS 90.100;
(f) Prepaid rent, as defined in ORS 90.100;
(g) Utility or service charges, pursuant to ORS 90.315 (4) or 90.510 (8);
(h) Late charges or fees, pursuant to ORS 90.260; and
(i) Damages, for noncompliance with a rental agreement or ORS 90.325, pursuant to ORS 90.400 (11) or as provided elsewhere in this chapter.
(2) A tenant who requests a writing that evidences the tenant's payment is entitled to receive that writing from the landlord as a condition for making the payment. The writing may be a receipt, statement of the tenant's account or other acknowledgement of the tenant's payment. The writing must include the amount paid, the date of payment and information identifying the landlord or the rental property. If the tenant makes the payment by mail, deposit or a method other than in person and requests the writing, the landlord shall within a reasonable time provide the tenant with the writing in a manner consistent with ORS 90.150.

90.145 Tenant or applicant who conducts repairs, routine maintenance or cleaning services not employee of landlord; restrictions. (1) A tenant who occupies or an applicant who will occupy a dwelling unit and who conducts repairs, routine maintenance or cleaning services on that dwelling unit in exchange for a reduction in rent pursuant to a written or oral agreement with the landlord shall not be considered to be an employee of the landlord.

(2) A person described in subsection (1) of this section shall not conduct electrical or plumbing installation, maintenance or repair unless properly licensed or certified under ORS chapter 479 or 693.

(3) Nothing in this section diminishes the obligations of a landlord to maintain the dwelling unit in a habitable condition under ORS 90.320 or 90.730.

(4) Any work performed by a tenant or applicant under this section shall be in compliance with ORS chapters 447 and 479. However, a tenant or applicant shall not be required to secure a certificate of registration under ORS 447.010 to 447.156 and 447.992.

90.147 Delivery of possession. For the purposes of this chapter, delivery of possession occurs:

(1) From the landlord to the tenant, when the landlord gives actual notice to the tenant that the tenant has the right under a rental agreement to occupy the dwelling unit to the exclusion of others. The right to occupy may be implied by actions such as the landlord's delivery of the keys to the dwelling unit; and

(2) From the tenant to the landlord at the termination of the tenancy, when:

(a) The tenant gives actual notice to the landlord that the tenant has relinquished any right to occupy the dwelling unit to the exclusion of others. Relinquishment of the right to occupy may be implied by actions such as the tenant's return of the keys to the dwelling unit;

(b) After the expiration date of an outstanding termination of tenancy notice or the end of a term tenancy, the landlord reasonably believes under all the circumstances that the tenant has relinquished or no longer claims the right to occupy the dwelling unit to the exclusion of others; or

(c) The landlord reasonably knows of the tenant's abandonment of the dwelling unit.

90.148 Landlord acts that imply acceptance of tenant abandonment or relinquishment of right to occupy. The surrender of a dwelling unit may be implied from the landlord's acceptance of a tenant's abandonment or relinquishment of the right to occupy. The landlord's acceptance may be demonstrated by acts of the landlord that are inconsistent with the existence of the tenancy. A landlord's receipt of the keys to the dwelling unit or a landlord's reasonable efforts to mitigate the landlord's damages by attempting to rent the dwelling unit to a new tenant shall not constitute acts inconsistent with the existence of the tenancy. Reasonable efforts to mitigate damages include preparing the unit for rental.

Note: 90.148 was added to and made a part of ORS chapter 90 by legislative action but was not added to any smaller series therein. See Preface to Oregon Revised Statutes for further explanation.

SERVICE OR DELIVERY OF NOTICES

90.150 Service or delivery of actual notice. When this chapter requires actual notice, service or delivery of that notice shall be executed by one or more of the following methods:

(1) Verbal notice that is given personally to the landlord or tenant or left on the landlord's or tenant's telephone answering device;

(2) Written notice that is personally delivered to the landlord or tenant, left at the landlord's rental office, sent by facsimile to the landlord's residence or rental office or to the tenant's dwelling unit, or attached in a secure manner to the main entrance of the landlord's residence or tenant's dwelling unit;

(3) Written notice that is delivered by first class mail to the landlord or tenant. If the notice is mailed, the notice shall be considered served three days after the date the notice was mailed; or

(4) Any other method reasonably calculated to achieve actual receipt of notice, as agreed to and described in a written rental agreement.

90.155 Service or delivery of written notice. (1) Except as provided in ORS 90.300, 90.425 and 90.675, where this chapter requires written notice, service or delivery of that written notice shall be executed by one or more of the following methods:

(a) Personal delivery to the landlord or tenant;

(b) First class mail to the landlord or tenant; or

(c) If a written rental agreement so provides, both first class mail and attachment to a designated location. In order for a written rental agreement to provide for mail and attachment service of written notices from the landlord to the tenant, the agreement must also provide for such service of written notices from the tenant to the landlord. Mail and attachment service of written notices shall be executed as follows:

(A) For written notices from the landlord to the tenant, the first class mail notice copy shall be addressed to the tenant at the premises and the second notice copy shall be attached in a secure manner to

the main entrance to that portion of the premises of which the tenant has possession; and
(B) For written notices from the tenant to the landlord, the first class mail notice copy shall be addressed to the landlord at an address as designated in the written rental agreement and the second notice copy shall be attached in a secure manner to the landlord's designated location, which shall be described with particularity in the written rental agreement, reasonably located in relation to the tenant and available at all hours.
(2) If a notice is served by mail, the minimum period for compliance or termination of tenancy, as appropriate, shall be extended by three days, and the notice shall include the extension in the period provided.
(3) A landlord or tenant may utilize alternative methods of notifying the other so long as the alternative method is in addition to one of the service methods described in subsection (1) of this section.
(4) Notwithstanding ORS 90.510 (4), after 30 days' written notice, a landlord may unilaterally amend a rental agreement for a manufactured dwelling or floating home that is subject to ORS 90.505 to 90.840 to provide for service or delivery of written notices by mail and attachment service as provided by subsection (1)(c) of this section.

90.160 Calculation of notice periods. (1) Notwithstanding ORCP 10 and not including the seven-day and four-day waiting periods provided in ORS 90.400 (2), where there are references in this chapter to periods and notices based on a number of days, those days shall be calculated by consecutive calendar days, not including the initial day of service, but including the last day until midnight of that last day. Where there are references in this chapter to periods or notices based on a number of hours, those hours shall be calculated in consecutive clock hours, beginning immediately upon service.
(2) Notwithstanding subsection (1) of this section, for 72-hour or 144-hour nonpayment notices under ORS 90.400 (2) that are served pursuant to ORS 90.155 (1)(c), the time period described in subsection (1) of this section begins at 11:59 PM the day the notice is both mailed and attached to the premises. The time period shall end 72 hours or 144 hours, as the case may be, after the time started to run at 11:59 p.m.

Content of Agreements

90.240 Terms and conditions of rental agreement; rent obligation and payment. (1) A landlord and a tenant may include in a rental agreement terms and conditions not prohibited by this chapter or other rule of law including rent, term of the agreement and other provisions governing the rights and obligations of the parties.
(2) The terms of a fixed term tenancy, including the amount of rent, may not be unilaterally amended by the landlord or tenant.
(3) The landlord shall provide the tenant with a copy of any written rental agreement and all amendments and additions thereto.
(4) Notwithstanding ORS 90.245 (1), the parties to a rental agreement to which ORS 90.100 to 90.459 apply may include in the rental agreement a provision for informal dispute resolution.
(5) In absence of agreement, the tenant shall pay as rent the fair rental value for the use and occupancy of the dwelling unit.
(6) Except as otherwise provided by this chapter:
(a) Rent is payable without demand or notice at the time and place agreed upon by the parties. Unless otherwise agreed, rent is payable at the dwelling unit, periodic rent is payable at the beginning of any term of one month or less and otherwise in equal monthly or weekly installments at the beginning of each month or week, depending on whether the tenancy is month-to-month or week-to-week. Rent may not be considered to be due prior to the first day of each rental period. Rent may not be increased without a 30-day written notice thereof in the case of a month-to-month tenancy or a seven-day written notice thereof in the case of a week-to-week tenancy.
(b) If a rental agreement does not create a week-to-week tenancy, as defined in ORS 90.100, or a fixed term tenancy, the tenancy shall be a month- to-month tenancy.
(7) Except as provided by ORS 90.427 (4), a tenant is responsible for payment of rent until the earlier of:
(a) The date that a notice terminating the tenancy expires;
(b) The date that the tenancy terminates by its own terms;
(c) The date that the tenancy terminates by surrender;
(d) The date that the tenancy terminates as a result of the landlord failing to use reasonable efforts to rent the dwelling unit to a new tenant as provided under ORS 90.410 (3);
(e) The date when a new tenancy with a new tenant begins;
(f) Thirty days after delivery of possession without prior notice of termination of a month-to-month tenancy; or

(g) Ten days after delivery of possession without prior notice of termination of a week-to-week tenancy.

90.243 Qualifications for drug and alcohol free housing; "program of recovery" defined. (1) A dwelling unit qualifies as drug and alcohol free housing if:

(a)(A) For premises consisting of more than eight dwelling units, the dwelling unit is one of at least eight contiguous dwelling units on the premises that are designated by the landlord as drug and alcohol free housing dwelling units and that are each occupied or held for occupancy by at least one tenant who is a recovering alcoholic or drug addict and is participating in a program of recovery; or

(B) For premises consisting of eight or fewer dwelling units, the dwelling unit is one of at least four contiguous dwelling units on the premises that are designated by the landlord as drug and alcohol free housing dwelling units and that are each occupied or held for occupancy by at least one tenant who is a recovering alcoholic or drug addict and is participating in a program of recovery;

(b) The landlord is a nonprofit corporation incorporated pursuant to ORS chapter 65 or a housing authority created pursuant to ORS 456.055 to 456.235;

(c) The landlord provides for the designated drug and alcohol free housing dwelling units:

(A) A drug and alcohol free environment, covering all tenants, employees, staff, agents of the landlord and guests;

(B) Monitoring of the tenants for compliance with the requirements of paragraph (d) of this subsection;

(C) Individual and group support for recovery; and

(D) Access to a specified program of recovery; and

(d) The rental agreement for the designated drug and alcohol free housing dwelling unit is in writing and includes the following provisions:

(A) That the dwelling unit is designated by the landlord as a drug and alcohol free housing dwelling unit;

(B) That the tenant may not use, possess or share alcohol, illegal drugs, controlled substances or prescription drugs without a medical prescription, either on or off the premises;

(C) That the tenant may not allow the tenant's guests to use, possess or share alcohol, illegal drugs, controlled substances or prescription drugs without a medical prescription, on the premises;

(D) That the tenant shall participate in a program of recovery, which specific program is described in the rental agreement;

(E) That on at least a quarterly basis the tenant shall provide written verification from the tenant's program of recovery that the tenant is participating in the program of recovery and that the tenant has not used alcohol or illegal drugs;

(F) That the landlord has the right to require the tenant to take a test for drug or alcohol usage promptly, and at the landlord's discretion and expense; and

(G) That the landlord has the right to terminate the tenant's tenancy in the drug and alcohol free housing for noncompliance with the requirements described in this paragraph, pursuant to ORS 90.400 (1) and (9) or 90.630.

(2) A dwelling unit qualifies as drug and alcohol free housing despite the premises not having the minimum number of qualified dwelling units required by subsection (1)(a) of this section if:

(a) The premises are occupied but have not previously qualified as drug and alcohol free housing;

(b) The landlord designates certain dwelling units on the premises as drug and alcohol free dwelling units;

(c) The number of designated drug and alcohol free housing dwelling units meets the requirement of subsection (1)(a) of this section;

(d) When each designated dwelling unit becomes vacant, the landlord rents that dwelling unit to, or holds that dwelling unit for occupancy by, at least one tenant who is a recovering alcoholic or drug addict and is participating in a program of recovery and the landlord meets the other requirements of subsection (1) of this section; and

(e) The dwelling unit is one of the designated drug and alcohol free housing dwelling units.

(3) The failure by a tenant to take a test for drug and alcohol usage as requested by the landlord pursuant to subsection (1)(d)(F) of this section may be considered evidence of drug or alcohol use.

(4) As used in this section, "program of recovery" means a verifiable program of counseling and rehabilitation treatment services, including a written plan, to assist recovering alcoholics or drug addicts to recover from their addiction to alcohol or illegal drugs while living in drug and alcohol free housing. A "program of recovery" includes Alcoholics Anonymous, Narcotics Anonymous and similar programs.

90.245 Prohibited provisions in rental agreements; remedy. (1) A rental agreement may not provide that the tenant:

(a) Agrees to waive or forego rights or remedies under this chapter;

(b) Authorizes any person to confess judgment on a claim arising out of the rental agreement; or
(c) Agrees to the exculpation or limitation of any liability arising as a result of the other party's willful misconduct or negligence or to indemnify the other party for that liability or costs connected therewith.
(2) A provision prohibited by subsection (1) of this section included in a rental agreement is unenforceable. If a landlord deliberately uses a rental agreement containing provisions known by the landlord to be prohibited and attempts to enforce such provisions, the tenant may recover in addition to the actual damages of the tenant an amount up to three months' periodic rent.

90.250 Receipt of rent without obligation to maintain premises prohibited. A rental agreement, assignment, conveyance, trust deed or security instrument may not permit the receipt of rent free of the obligation to comply with ORS 90.320 (1) or 90.730.

90.255 Attorney fees. In any action on a rental agreement or arising under this chapter, reasonable attorney fees at trial and on appeal may be awarded to the prevailing party together with costs and necessary disbursements, notwithstanding any agreement to the contrary. As used in this section, "prevailing party" means the party in whose favor final judgment is rendered.

90.260 Late rent payment charge or fee; restrictions; calculation. (1) A landlord may impose a late charge or fee, however designated, only if:
(a) The rent payment is not received by the fourth day of the weekly or monthly rental period for which rent is payable; and
(b) There exists a written rental agreement that specifies:
(A) The tenant's obligation to pay a late charge on delinquent rent payments;
(B) The type and amount of the late charge, as described in subsection (2) of this section; and
(C) The date on which rent payments are due and the date or day on which late charges become due.
(2) The amount of any late charge shall not exceed:
(a) A reasonable flat amount, charged once per rental period. "Reasonable amount" means the customary amount charged by landlords for that rental market;
(b) A reasonable amount, charged on a per-day basis, beginning on the fifth day of the rental period for which rent is delinquent. This daily charge may accrue every day thereafter until the rent, not including any late charge, is paid in full, through that rental period only. The per-day charge may not exceed six percent of the amount described in paragraph (a) of this subsection; or
(c) Five percent of the periodic rent payment amount, charged once for each succeeding five-day period, or portion thereof, for which the rent payment is delinquent, beginning on the fifth day of that rental period and continuing and accumulating until that rent payment, not including any late charge, is paid in full, through that rental period only.
(3) In periodic tenancies, a landlord may change the type or amount of late charge by giving 30 days' written notice to the tenant.
(4) A landlord shall not deduct a previously imposed late charge from a current or subsequent rental period rent payment, thereby making that rent payment delinquent for imposition of a new or additional late charge or for termination of the tenancy for nonpayment pursuant to ORS 90.400 (2).
(5) A landlord may charge simple interest on an unpaid late charge at the rate allowed for judgments pursuant to ORS 82.010 (2) and accruing from the date the late charge is imposed.
(6) Nonpayment of a late charge alone shall not constitute grounds for termination of a rental agreement for nonpayment of rent pursuant to ORS 90.400 (2), but shall constitute grounds for termination of a rental agreement for cause pursuant to ORS 90.400 (1) or 90.630 (1). A landlord may note the imposition of a late charge on a notice of nonpayment of rent pursuant to ORS 90.400 (2), so long as the notice states or otherwise makes clear that the tenant may cure the nonpayment notice by paying only the delinquent rent, not including any late charge, within the allotted time.
(7) A late charge includes an increase or decrease in the regularly charged periodic rent payment imposed because a tenant does or does not pay that rent by a certain date.

90.262 Use and occupancy rules and regulations; adoption; enforceability; restrictions. (1) A landlord, from time to time, may adopt a rule or regulation, however described, concerning the tenant's use and occupancy of the premises. It is enforceable against the tenant only if:
(a) Its purpose is to promote the convenience, safety or welfare of the tenants in the premises, preserve the landlord's property from abusive use, or make a fair distribution of services and facilities held out for the tenants generally;
(b) It is reasonably related to the purpose for which it is adopted;

(c) It applies to all tenants in the premises in a fair manner;
(d) It is sufficiently explicit in its prohibition, direction or limitation of the tenant's conduct to fairly inform the tenant of what the tenant must or must not do to comply;
(e) It is not for the purpose of evading the obligations of the landlord; and
(f) The tenant has written notice of it at the time the tenant enters into the rental agreement, or when it is adopted.
(2) If a rule or regulation adopted after the tenant enters into the rental agreement works a substantial modification of the bargain, it is not valid unless the tenant consents to it in writing.
(3) If adopted, an occupancy guideline for a dwelling unit shall not be more restrictive than two people per bedroom and shall be reasonable. Reasonableness shall be determined on a case-by-case basis. Factors to be considered in determining reasonableness include, but are not limited to:
(a) The size of the bedrooms;
(b) The overall size of the dwelling unit; and
(c) Any discriminatory impact on those identified in ORS 659A.421.
(4) As used in this section:
(a) "Bedroom" means a habitable room that:
(A) Is intended to be used primarily for sleeping purposes;
(B) Contains at least 70 square feet; and
(C) Is configured so as to take the need for a fire exit into account.
(b) "Habitable room" means a space in a structure for living, sleeping, eating or cooking. Bathrooms, toilet compartments, closets, halls, storage or utility space and similar areas are not included.

90.263 Vehicle tags. A landlord may not require that a tenant display a nonremovable tag, sticker or other device on a motor vehicle that might reveal or indicate to the public the premises where the tenant resides.
Note: 90.263 was added to and made a part of ORS chapter 90 by legislative action but was not added to any smaller series therein. See Preface to Oregon Revised Statutes for further explanation.

90.265 Interest in alternative energy device installed by tenant. (1) An alternative energy device installed in a dwelling unit by a tenant with the landlord's written permission is not a fixture in which the landlord has a legal interest, except as otherwise expressly provided in a written agreement between the landlord and tenant.
(2) As a condition to a grant of written permission referred to in subsection (1) of this section, a landlord may require a tenant to do one or more of the following:
(a) Provide a waiver of the landlord's liability for any injury to the tenant or other installer resulting from the tenant's or installer's negligence in the installation of the alternative energy device;
(b) Secure a waiver of the right to a lien against the property of the landlord from each contractor, subcontractor, laborer and material supplier who would obtain the right to a lien when the tenant installs or causes the installation of the alternative energy device; or
(c) Post a bond or pay a deposit in an amount not to exceed the cost of restoring the premises to its condition at the time of installation of the alternative energy device.
(3) Nothing in this section:
(a) Authorizes the installation of an alternative energy device in a dwelling unit without the landlord's written permission; or
(b) Limits a landlord's right to recover damages and obtain injunctive relief as provided in ORS 90.400 (11).
(4) As used in this section, "alternative energy device" has the meaning given that term in ORS 469.160.

FEES AND DEPOSITS

90.295 Applicant screening charge; limitations; notice upon denial of tenancy; refund; remedies. (1) A landlord may require payment of an applicant screening charge solely to cover the costs of obtaining information about an applicant as the landlord processes the application for a rental agreement. This activity is known as screening, and includes but is not limited to checking references and obtaining a consumer credit report or tenant screening report. The landlord must provide the applicant with a receipt for any applicant screening charge.
(2) The amount of any applicant screening charge shall not be greater than the landlord's average actual cost of screening applicants. Actual costs may include the cost of using a tenant screening company or a consumer credit reporting agency, and may include the reasonable value of any time spent by the landlord or the landlord's agents in otherwise obtaining information on applicants. In any case, the applicant screening charge may not be greater than the customary amount charged by tenant screening companies or consumer credit reporting agencies for a comparable level of screening.

(3) A landlord may not require payment of an applicant screening charge unless prior to accepting the payment the landlord:
(a) Adopts written screening or admission criteria;
(b) Gives written notice to the applicant of:
(A) The amount of the applicant screening charge;
(B) The landlord's screening or admission criteria;
(C) The process that the landlord typically will follow in screening the applicant, including whether the landlord uses a tenant screening company, credit reports, public records or criminal records or contacts employers, landlords or other references; and
(D) The applicant's rights to dispute the accuracy of any information provided to the landlord by a screening company or credit reporting agency; and
(c) Gives actual notice to the applicant of an estimate, made to the best of the landlord's ability at that time, of the approximate number of rental units of the type, and in the area, sought by the applicant that are, or within a reasonable future time will be, available to rent from that landlord. The estimate shall include the approximate number of applications previously accepted and remaining under consideration for those units. A good faith error by a landlord in making an estimate under this paragraph does not provide grounds for a claim under subsection (8) of this section.
(4) Regardless of whether a landlord requires payment of an applicant screening charge, if a landlord denies an application for a rental agreement by an applicant and that denial is based in whole or in part on a tenant screening company or consumer credit reporting agency report on that applicant, the landlord shall give the applicant actual notice of that fact at the same time that the landlord notifies the applicant of the denial. Unless written notice of the name and address of the screening company or credit reporting agency has previously been given, the landlord shall promptly give written notice to the applicant of the name and address of the company or agency that provided the report upon which the denial is based.
(5) Except as provided in subsection (4) of this section, a landlord need not disclose the results of an applicant screening or report to an applicant, with respect to information that is not required to be disclosed under the federal Fair Credit Reporting Act. A landlord may give to an applicant a copy of that applicant's consumer report, as defined in the Fair Credit Reporting Act.
(6) Unless the applicant agrees otherwise in writing, a landlord may not require payment of an applicant screening charge when the landlord knows or should know that no rental units are available at that time or will be available within a reasonable future time.
(7) If a landlord requires payment of an applicant screening charge but fills the vacant rental unit before screening the applicant or does not conduct a screening of the applicant for any reason, the landlord must refund the applicant screening charge to the applicant within a reasonable time.
(8) The applicant may recover from the landlord the amount of any applicant screening charge paid, plus $100, if:
(a) The landlord fails to comply with this section and does not within a reasonable time accept the applicant's application for a rental agreement; or
(b) The landlord does not conduct a screening of the applicant for any reason and fails to refund an applicant screening charge to the applicant within a reasonable time.

90.297 Prohibition on charging deposit or fee to enter rental agreement; exceptions; deposit allowed for securing execution of rental agreement; remedy.
(1) Except as provided in ORS 90.295 and in this section, a landlord may not charge a deposit or fee, however designated, to an applicant who has applied to a landlord to enter a rental agreement for a dwelling unit.
(2) A landlord may charge a deposit, however designated, to an applicant for the purpose of securing the execution of a rental agreement, after approving the applicant's application but prior to entering into a rental agreement. The landlord must give the applicant a written statement describing the terms of the agreement to execute a rental agreement and the conditions for refunding or retaining the deposit.
(a) If a rental agreement is executed, the landlord shall either apply the deposit toward the moneys due the landlord under the rental agreement or refund it immediately to the tenant.
(b) If a rental agreement is not executed due to a failure by the applicant to comply with the agreement to execute, the landlord may retain the deposit.
(c) If a rental agreement is not executed due to a failure by the landlord to comply with the agreement to execute, within four days the landlord shall return the deposit to the applicant either by making the deposit available to the applicant at the landlord's customary place of business or by mailing the deposit by first class mail to the applicant.
(3) If a landlord fails to comply with this section, the applicant or tenant, as the case may be, may recover

from the landlord the amount of any fee or deposit charged, plus $100.

90.300 Security deposits; deposit changes; claims payable from deposit; last month's rent; prepaid rent; accounting. (1) As used in this section, "security deposit" includes any last month's rent deposit.

(2) Except as otherwise provided in this section, a landlord may require the payment of a security deposit. A security deposit or prepaid rent shall be held by the landlord for the tenant who is a party to the rental agreement. The claim of a tenant to the security deposit or prepaid rent shall be prior to the claim of any creditor of the landlord, including a trustee in bankruptcy. The holder of the landlord's interest in the premises at the time of termination of the tenancy is responsible to the tenant for any security deposit or prepaid rent and is bound by this section.

(3)(a) A landlord may not change the rental agreement to require the payment of a new or increased security deposit during the first year after the tenancy has begun, except that an additional deposit may be required if the landlord and tenant agree to modify the terms and conditions of the rental agreement to permit a pet or for other cause and the additional deposit relates to that modification. This paragraph does not prevent the collection of a security deposit that was provided for under an initial rental agreement but remained unpaid at the time the tenancy began.

(b) If a landlord requires a new or increased security deposit after the first year of the tenancy, the landlord shall allow the tenant at least three months to pay that deposit.

(4) The landlord may claim all or part of the security deposit only if the security deposit was made for any or all of the purposes provided by subsection (5) of this section.

(5) The landlord may claim from the security deposit only the amount reasonably necessary:

(a) To remedy the tenant's defaults in the performance of the rental agreement including, but not limited to, unpaid rent; and

(b) To repair damages to the premises caused by the tenant, not including ordinary wear and tear.

(6) A security deposit or prepaid rent shall not be required or forfeited to the landlord upon the failure of the tenant to maintain a tenancy for a minimum number of months in a month-to-month tenancy.

(7) Any last month's rent deposit shall be applied to the rent due for the last month of the tenancy:

(a) Upon either the landlord or tenant giving to the other a notice of termination, pursuant to this chapter, other than a notice of termination under ORS 90.400 (2);

(b) Upon agreement by the landlord and tenant to terminate the tenancy; or

(c) Upon termination pursuant to the provisions of a written rental agreement for a term tenancy.

(8) Any portion of a last month's rent deposit not applied as provided under subsection (7) of this section shall be accounted for and refunded as provided under subsections (10) to (12) of this section. Unless the tenant and landlord agree otherwise, a last month's rent deposit shall not be applied to rent due for any period other than the last month of the tenancy. A last month's rent deposit shall not operate to limit the amount of rent charged unless a written rental agreement provides otherwise.

(9) Upon termination of the tenancy, a landlord shall account for and refund to the tenant the unused balance of any prepaid rent not previously refunded to the tenant as required by ORS 90.380 and 105.120 (4)(b) or any other provision of this chapter, in the same manner as required for security deposits by this section. The landlord may claim from the remaining prepaid rent only the amount reasonably necessary to pay the tenant's unpaid rent.

(10) In order to claim all or part of any prepaid rent or security deposit, within 31 days after the termination of the tenancy and delivery of possession the landlord shall give to the tenant a written accounting that states specifically the basis or bases of the claim. The landlord shall give a separate accounting for security deposits and for prepaid rent.

(11) The security deposit or prepaid rent or portion thereof not claimed in the manner provided by subsections (9) and (10) of this section shall be returned to the tenant not later than 31 days after the termination of the tenancy and delivery of possession to the landlord.

(12) The landlord shall give the written accounting as required by subsection (10) of this section or shall return the security deposit or prepaid rent as required by subsection (11) of this section by personal delivery or by first class mail.

(13) If a security deposit or prepaid rent secures a tenancy for a space for a tenant owned and occupied manufactured dwelling or floating home, whether or not in a facility, and the dwelling or home is abandoned as described in ORS 90.425 (2) or 90.675 (2), the

31-day period described in subsections (10 and (11) of this section commences on the earliest of:
(1) Waiver of the abandoned property process under ORS 90.425 (24) or 90.675 (22);
(c) Destruction or other disposition of the manufactured dwelling or floating home under ORS 90.425 (1)(b) or 90.675 (10)(b); or
(d) Sale of the manufactured dwelling or floating home pursuant to ORS 90.425 (10)(a) or 90.675 (10)(a).
(14) If the landlord fails to comply with subsection (11) of this section or if the landlord in bad faith fails to return all or any portion of any prepaid rent or security deposit due to the tenant under this chapter or the rental agreement, the tenant may recover the money due in an amount equal to twice the amount:
(a) Withheld without a written accounting under subsection (10) of this section; or
(b) Withheld in bad faith.
(15) This section does not preclude the landlord or tenant from recovering other damages under this chapter.

90.302 Fees allowed for certain landlord expenses; accounting not required. (1) Except as specifically provided otherwise in this chapter, a landlord may require the payment of a fee, if the fee is related to and designated as being charged for a specific reasonably anticipated landlord expense. A landlord shall provide a receipt for the fee, and the receipt or a written rental agreement shall describe the anticipated landlord expense to be covered by the fee and describe the landlord's duties under subsection (4) of this section.
(2) Except as provided in subsection (3) of this section, a landlord shall not charge a fee more than once, at the beginning of or during the tenancy.
(3) A landlord may charge a fee more than once, at the beginning of or during the tenancy, for:
(a) A late rent payment, pursuant to ORS 90.260;
(b) A dishonored check, pursuant to ORS 30.701 (5);
(c) Removal or tampering with a properly functioning smoke alarm or smoke detector, as provided in ORS 90.325 (7), if a written rental agreement provides for a fee for that removal or tampering; and
(d) Any other noncompliance by the tenant with a written rental agreement that provides for a fee for that noncompliance, provided that the fee shall not be excessive.
(4) A landlord shall not be required to account for or return to the tenant any fee. Upon termination of a tenancy and delivery of possession, a landlord shall first apply any fee to the related landlord expense as reasonably assessed against the tenant, before applying the tenant's security deposit, if any, to that expense.
(5) Nonpayment of a fee shall not constitute grounds for termination of a rental agreement for nonpayment of rent pursuant to ORS 90.400 (2), but shall constitute grounds for termination of a rental agreement for cause pursuant to ORS 90.400 (1) or 90.630 (1).
(6) This section shall not apply to attorney fees awarded pursuant to ORS 90.255 or to applicant screening charges paid pursuant to ORS 90.295.
Note: Section 15, chapter 577, Oregon Laws 1997, provides:
Sec. 15. The amendments to ORS 90.302, 90.315 (4) and 90.510 (8) by sections 14, 16 and 26 of this Act apply only to tenancies, whether periodic or fixed term, that are entered into on or after October 1, 1997, or are extended or renewed after that date.

Landlord Rights and Obligations

90.305 Disclosure of certain matters; retention of rental agreement; inspection of agreement. (1) The landlord shall disclose to the tenant in writing at or before the commencement of the tenancy the name and address of:
(a) The person authorized to manage the premises; and
(b) An owner of the premises or a person authorized to act for and on behalf of the owner for the purpose of service of process and receiving and receipting for notices and demands.
(2) The information required to be furnished by this section shall be kept current and this section extends to and is enforceable against any successor landlord, owner or manager.
(3) A person who is authorized to manage the premises, or to enter into a rental agreement, and fails to comply with subsection (1) of this section becomes an agent of each person who is a landlord for service of process and receiving and receipting for notices and demands.
(4)(a) A landlord shall retain a copy of each rental agreement at the resident manager's office or at the address provided to the tenant under subsection (1)(a) of this section.
(b) A tenant may request to see the rental agreement and, within a reasonable time, the landlord shall make the agreement available for inspection. At the request of the tenant and upon payment of a reasonable charge, not to exceed the lesser of 25 cents per page or the actual copying costs, the landlord shall provide the tenant with a copy of the rental agreement. This subsection shall not diminish the landlord's obligation to

furnish the tenant an initial copy of the rental agreement and any amendments under ORS 90.240 (3).

90.310 Disclosure of legal proceedings; tenant remedies for failure to disclose; liability of manager. (1) If at the time of the execution of a rental agreement for a dwelling unit in premises containing no more than four dwelling units the premises are subject to any of the following circumstances, the landlord shall disclose that circumstance to the tenant in writing before the execution of the rental agreement:

(a) Any outstanding notice of default under a trust deed, mortgage or contract of sale, or notice of trustee's sale under a trust deed;

(b) Any pending suit to foreclose a mortgage, trust deed or vendor's lien under a contract of sale;

(c) Any pending declaration of forfeiture or suit for specific performance of a contract of sale; or

(d) Any pending proceeding to foreclose a tax lien.

(2) If the tenant moves as a result of a circumstance that the landlord failed to disclose as required by subsection (1) of this section, the tenant may recover twice the actual damages or twice the monthly rent, whichever is greater, and all prepaid rent, in addition to any other remedy that the law may provide.

(3) This section shall not apply to premises managed by a court appointed receiver.

(4) A manager who has complied with ORS 90.305 shall not be liable for damages under this section if the manager had no knowledge of the circumstances that gave rise to a duty of disclosure under subsection (1) of this section.

90.315 Utility or service payments; additional charges; responsibility for utility or service; remedies. (1) As used in this section, "utility or service" includes but is not limited to electricity, natural or liquid propane gas, oil, water, hot water, heat, air conditioning, cable television, direct satellite or other video subscription service, Internet access or usage, sewer service and garbage collection and disposal.

(2) The landlord shall disclose to the tenant in writing at or before the commencement of the tenancy any utility or service that the tenant pays directly to a utility or service provider that benefits, directly, the landlord or other tenants. A tenant's payment for a given utility or service benefits the landlord or other tenants if the utility or service is delivered to any area other than the tenant's dwelling unit.

(3) If the landlord knowingly fails to disclose those matters required under subsection (2) of this section, the tenant may recover twice the actual damages sustained or one month's rent, whichever is greater.

(4)(a) Except for tenancies covered by ORS 90.505 to 90.840, if a written rental agreement so provides, a landlord may require a tenant to pay to the landlord a utility or service charge that has been billed by a utility or service provider to the landlord for utility or service provided directly to the tenant's dwelling unit or to a common area available to the tenant as part of the tenancy. A utility or service charge that shall be assessed to a tenant for a common area must be described in the written rental agreement separately and distinctly from such a charge for the tenant's dwelling unit. Unless the method of allocating the charges to the tenant is described in the tenant's written rental agreement, the tenant may require that the landlord give the tenant a copy of the provider's bill as a condition of paying the charges.

(b) A utility or service charge shall include only the value or cost of the utility or service as billed to the landlord by the provider as described in this subsection, except that a landlord may add an additional amount to that value or cost if:

(A) The utility or service charge to which the additional amount is added is for cable television, direct satellite or other video subscription service or for Internet access or usage;

(B) The additional amount added to the utility or service charge of each tenant is not more than 10 percent of the charge to that tenant for cable television, direct satellite or other video subscription service or Internet access or usage;

(C) The total of the utility or service charge plus the additional amount is less than the typical periodic cost that the tenant would incur if the tenant contracted for the cable television, direct satellite or other video subscription service or the Internet access or usage directly with the provider; and

(D) The written rental agreement providing for the utility or service charge describes the additional amount separately and distinctly from the charge itself and any bill or notice from the landlord to the tenant regarding the charge lists the additional amount separately and distinctly from the utility or service charge.

(c) A landlord shall not require an existing tenant to modify a rental agreement, or terminate the tenancy of the tenant for refusing to modify a rental agreement, to obligate the tenant to pay an additional amount for cable television, direct satellite or other

video subscription service or Internet access or usage as provided in paragraph (b) of this subsection.
(d) A utility or service charge, including any additional amount added pursuant to paragraph (b) of this subsection, shall not be considered to be rent or a fee. Nonpayment of a utility or service charge shall not constitute grounds for termination of a rental agreement for nonpayment of rent pursuant to ORS 90.400 (2), but shall constitute grounds for termination of a rental agreement for cause pursuant to ORS 90.400 (1).
(e) If a landlord fails to comply with paragraph (a), (b) or (c) of this subsection, the tenant may recover from the landlord an amount equal to one month's periodic rent or twice the amount wrongfully charged to the tenant, whichever is greater.
(5)(a) If a tenant, under the rental agreement, is responsible for a utility or service and is unable to obtain the service prior to moving into the premises due to a nonpayment of an outstanding amount due by a previous tenant or the owner, the tenant may either:
(A) Pay the outstanding amount and deduct the amount from the rent;
(B) Enter into a mutual agreement with the landlord to resolve the lack of service; or
(C) Immediately terminate the rental agreement by giving the landlord actual notice and the reason for the termination.
(b) If the tenancy terminates, the landlord shall return all moneys paid by the tenant as deposits, rent or fees within four days after termination.
(6) If a tenant, under the rental agreement, is responsible for a utility or service and is unable to obtain the service after moving into the premises due to a nonpayment of an outstanding amount due by a previous tenant or the owner, the tenant may either:
(a) Pay the outstanding amount and deduct the amount from the rent; or
(b) Terminate the rental agreement by giving the landlord actual notice 72 hours prior to the date of termination and the reason for the termination. The tenancy shall not terminate if the landlord restores service or the availability of service during the 72 hours. If the tenancy terminates, the tenant may recover actual damages from the landlord resulting from the shutoff and the landlord shall return:
(A) Within four days after termination, all rent and fees; and
(B) All of the security deposit owed to the tenant under ORS 90.300.
(7) If a landlord, under the rental agreement, is responsible for a utility or service and the utility or service is shut off due to a nonpayment of an outstanding amount, the tenant may either:
(a) Pay the outstanding balance and deduct the amount from the rent; or
(b) Terminate the rental agreement by giving the landlord actual notice 72 hours prior to the date of termination and the reason for the termination. The tenancy shall not terminate if the landlord restores service during the 72 hours. If the tenancy terminates, the tenant may recover actual damages from the landlord resulting from the shutoff and the landlord shall return:
(A) Within four days after termination, all rent prepaid for the month in which the termination occurs prorated from the date of termination or the date the tenant vacates the premises, whichever is later, and any other prepaid rent; and
(B) All of the security deposit owed to the tenant under ORS 90.300.
(8) If a landlord fails to return to the tenant the moneys owed as provided in subsection (5), (6) or (7) of this section, the tenant shall be entitled to twice the amount wrongfully withheld.
(9) This section does not preclude the tenant from pursuing any other remedies under this chapter.
Note: See note under 90.302.
90.318 Criteria for landlord provision of certain recycling services. (1) In a city or the county within the urban growth boundary of a city that has implemented multifamily recycling service, a landlord who has five or more residential dwelling units on a single premises or five or more manufactured dwellings in a single facility shall at all times during tenancy provide to all tenants:
(a) A separate location for containers or depots for at least four principal recyclable materials or for the number of materials required to be collected under the residential on-route collection program, whichever is less, adequate to hold the reasonably anticipated volume of each material;
(b) Regular collection service of the source separated recyclable materials; and
(c) Notice at least once a year of the opportunity to recycle with a description of the location of the containers or depots on the premises and information about how to recycle. New tenants shall be notified of the opportunity to recycle at the time of entering into a rental agreement.

(2) As used in this section, "recyclable material" and "source separate" have the meaning given those terms in ORS 459.005.

90.320 Landlord to maintain premises in habitable condition; agreement with tenant to maintain premises. (1) A landlord shall at all times during the tenancy maintain the dwelling unit in a habitable condition. For purposes of this section, a dwelling unit shall be considered unhabitable if it substantially lacks:

(a) Effective waterproofing and weather protection of roof and exterior walls, including windows and doors;

(b) Plumbing facilities which conform to applicable law in effect at the time of installation, and maintained in good working order;

(c) A water supply approved under applicable law, which is:

(A) Under the control of the tenant or landlord and is capable of producing hot and cold running water;

(B) Furnished to appropriate fixtures;

(C) Connected to a sewage disposal system approved under applicable law; and

(D) Maintained so as to provide safe drinking water and to be in good working order to the extent that the system can be controlled by the landlord;

(d) Adequate heating facilities which conform to applicable law at the time of installation and maintained in good working order;

(e) Electrical lighting with wiring and electrical equipment which conform to applicable law at the time of installation and maintained in good working order;

(f) Buildings, grounds and appurtenances at the time of the commencement of the rental agreement in every part safe for normal and reasonably foreseeable uses, clean, sanitary and free from all accumulations of debris, filth, rubbish, garbage, rodents and vermin, and all areas under control of the landlord kept in every part safe for normal and reasonably foreseeable uses, clean, sanitary and free from all accumulations of debris, filth, rubbish, garbage, rodents and vermin;

(g) Except as otherwise provided by local ordinance or by written agreement between the landlord and the tenant, an adequate number of appropriate receptacles for garbage and rubbish in clean condition and good repair at the time of the commencement of the rental agreement, and the landlord shall provide and maintain appropriate serviceable receptacles thereafter and arrange for their removal;

(h) Floors, walls, ceilings, stairways and railings maintained in good repair;

(i) Ventilating, air conditioning and other facilities and appliances, including elevators, maintained in good repair if supplied or required to be supplied by the landlord;

(j) Safety from fire hazards, including a working smoke alarm or smoke detector, with working batteries if solely battery-operated, provided only at the beginning of any new tenancy when the tenant first takes possession of the premises, as provided in ORS 479.270, but not to include the tenant's testing of the smoke alarm or smoke detector as provided in ORS 90.325 (6); or

(k) Working locks for all dwelling entrance doors, and, unless contrary to applicable law, latches for all windows, by which access may be had to that portion of the premises which the tenant is entitled under the rental agreement to occupy to the exclusion of others and keys for such locks which require keys.

(2) The landlord and tenant may agree in writing that the tenant is to perform specified repairs, maintenance tasks and minor remodeling only if:

(a) The agreement of the parties is entered into in good faith and not for the purpose of evading the obligations of the landlord;

(b) The agreement does not diminish the obligations of the landlord to other tenants in the premises; and

(c) The terms and conditions of the agreement are clearly and fairly disclosed and adequate consideration for the agreement is specifically stated.

(3) Any provisions of this section that reasonably apply only to a structure that is used as a home, residence or sleeping place shall not apply to a manufactured dwelling, recreational vehicle or floating home where the tenant owns the manufactured dwelling, recreational vehicle or floating home, rents the space and, in the case of a dwelling or home, the space is not in a facility. Manufactured dwelling or floating home tenancies in which the tenant owns the dwelling or home and rents space in a facility shall be governed by ORS 90.730, not by this section.

90.322 Landlord or agent access to premises; manner of entry; denial of entry; remedies. (1) A landlord or, to the extent provided in this section, a landlord's agent may enter into the tenant's dwelling unit or any portion of the premises under the tenant's exclusive control in order to inspect the premises, make necessary or agreed repairs, decorations, alterations or improvements, supply necessary or agreed services, perform agreed yard maintenance or grounds keeping or exhibit the dwelling unit to prospective or actual purchasers, mortgagees, tenants, workers or contractors. The right of access of the landlord or landlord's agent is limited as follows:

(a) A landlord or landlord's agent may enter upon the premises under the tenant's exclusive control not including the dwelling unit without consent of the tenant and without notice to the tenant, for the purpose of serving notices required or permitted under this chapter, the rental agreement or any provision of applicable law.

(b) In case of an emergency, a landlord may enter the dwelling unit or any portion of the premises under a tenant's exclusive control without consent of the tenant, without notice to the tenant and at any time. "Emergency" includes but is not limited to a repair problem that, unless remedied immediately, is likely to cause serious damage to the premises. If a landlord makes an emergency entry in the tenant's absence, the landlord shall give the tenant actual notice within 24 hours after the entry, and the notice shall include the fact of the entry, the date and time of the entry, the nature of the emergency and the names of the persons who entered.

(c) If the tenant requests repairs or maintenance in writing, the landlord or landlord's agent, without further notice, may enter upon demand, in the tenant's absence or without the tenant's consent, for the purpose of making the requested repairs until the repairs are completed. The tenant's written request may specify allowable times. Otherwise, the entry must be at a reasonable time. The authorization to enter provided by the tenant's written request expires after seven days, unless the repairs are in progress and the landlord or landlord's agent is making a reasonable effort to complete the repairs in a timely manner. If the person entering to do the repairs is not the landlord, upon request of the tenant, the person must show the tenant written evidence from the landlord authorizing that person to act for the landlord in making the repairs.

(d) A landlord and tenant may agree that the landlord or the landlord's agent may enter the dwelling unit and the premises without notice at reasonable times for the purpose of showing the premises to a prospective buyer, provided that the agreement:

(A) Is executed at a time when the landlord is actively engaged in attempts to sell the premises;

(B) Is reflected in a writing separate from the rental agreement and signed by both parties; and

(C) Is supported by separate consideration recited in the agreement.

(e)(A) If a written agreement requires the landlord to perform yard maintenance or grounds keeping for the premises:

(i) A landlord and tenant may agree that the landlord or landlord's agent may enter for that purpose upon the premises under the tenant's exclusive control not including the dwelling unit, without notice to the tenant, at reasonable times and with reasonable frequency. The terms of the right of entry must be described in the rental agreement or in a separate written agreement.

(ii) A tenant may deny consent for a landlord or landlord's agent to enter upon the premises pursuant to this paragraph if the entry is at an unreasonable time or with unreasonable frequency. The tenant must assert the denial by giving actual notice of the denial to the landlord or landlord's agent prior to, or at the time of, the attempted entry.

(B) As used in this paragraph:

(i) "Yard maintenance or grounds keeping" includes, but is not limited to, weeding, mowing grass and pruning trees and shrubs.

(ii) "Unreasonable time" refers to a time of day, day of the week or particular time that conflicts with the tenant's reasonable and specific plans to use the premises.

(f) In all other cases, unless there is an agreement between the landlord and the tenant to the contrary regarding a specific entry, the landlord shall give the tenant at least 24 hours' actual notice of the intent of the landlord to enter and the landlord or landlord's agent may enter only at reasonable times. The landlord or landlord's agent may not enter if the tenant, after receiving the landlord's notice, denies consent to enter. The tenant must assert this denial of consent by giving actual notice of the denial to the landlord or the landlord's agent or by attaching a written notice of the denial in a secure manner to the main entrance to that portion of the premises or dwelling unit of which the tenant has exclusive control, prior to or at the time of the attempt by the landlord or landlord's agent to enter.

(2) A landlord shall not abuse the right of access or use it to harass the tenant. A tenant shall not unreasonably withhold consent from the landlord to enter.

(3) This section does not apply to tenancies consisting of a rental of space in a facility for a manufactured dwelling or floating home under ORS 90.505 to 90.840.

(4) If a tenancy consists of rented space for a manufactured dwelling or floating home that is owned

by the tenant, but the tenancy is not subject to ORS 90.505 to 90.840 because the space is not in a facility, this section shall allow access only to the rented space and not to the dwelling or home.
(5) A landlord has no other right of access except:
(a) Pursuant to court order;
(b) As permitted by ORS 90.410 (2); or
(c) When the tenant has abandoned or relinquished the premises.
(6) If a landlord is required by a governmental agency to enter a dwelling unit or any portion of the premises under a tenant's exclusive control, but the landlord fails to gain entry after a good faith effort in compliance with this section, the landlord shall not be found in violation of any state statute or local ordinance due to the failure.
(7) If the tenant refuses to allow lawful access, the landlord may obtain injunctive relief to compel access or may terminate the rental agreement pursuant to ORS 90.400 (1) and take possession in the manner provided in ORS 105.105 to 105.168. In addition, the landlord may recover actual damages.
(8) If the landlord makes an unlawful entry or a lawful entry in an unreasonable manner or makes repeated demands for entry otherwise lawful but that have the effect of unreasonably harassing the tenant, the tenant may obtain injunctive relief to prevent the reoccurrence of the conduct or may terminate the rental agreement pursuant to ORS 90.360 (1). In addition, the tenant may recover actual damages not less than an amount equal to one week's rent in the case of a week-to-week tenancy or one month's rent in all other cases.

TENANT OBLIGATIONS

90.325 Tenant duties. The tenant shall:
(1) Use the parts of the premises including the living room, bedroom, kitchen, bathroom and dining room in a reasonable manner considering the purposes for which they were designed and intended;
(2) Keep all areas of the premises under control of the tenant in every part as clean, sanitary and free from all accumulations of debris, filth, rubbish, garbage, rodents and vermin, as the condition of the premises permits and to the extent that the tenant is responsible for causing the problem. The tenant shall cooperate to a reasonable extent in assisting the landlord in any reasonable effort to remedy the problem;
(3) Dispose from the dwelling unit all ashes, garbage, rubbish and other waste in a clean, safe and legal manner. With regard to needles, syringes and other infectious waste, as defined in ORS 459.386, the tenant may not dispose of these items by placing them in garbage receptacles or in any other place or manner except as authorized by state and local governmental agencies;
(4) Keep all plumbing fixtures in the dwelling unit or used by the tenant as clean as their condition permits;
(5) Use in a reasonable manner all electrical, plumbing, sanitary, heating, ventilating, air conditioning and other facilities and appliances including elevators in the premises;
(6) Test at least once every six months and replace batteries as needed in any smoke alarm or smoke detector provided by the landlord and notify the landlord in writing of any operating deficiencies as described in ORS 479.275;
(7) Not remove or tamper with a properly functioning smoke alarm or smoke detector, including removing any working batteries, as provided in ORS 479.300;
(8) Not deliberately or negligently destroy, deface, damage, impair or remove any part of the premises or knowingly permit any person to do so; and
(9) Behave and require other persons on the premises with the consent of the tenant to behave in a manner that will not disturb the peaceful enjoyment of the premises by neighbors.

90.340 Occupancy of premises as dwelling unit only; notice of tenant absence. Unless otherwise agreed, the tenant shall occupy the dwelling unit only as a dwelling unit. The rental agreement may require that the tenant give actual notice to the landlord of any anticipated extended absence from the premises in excess of seven days no later than the first day of the extended absence.

TENANT REMEDIES

90.360 Effect of landlord noncompliance with rental agreement or obligation to maintain premises; generally. (1)(a) Except as provided in this chapter, if there is a material noncompliance by the landlord with the rental agreement or a noncompliance with ORS 90.320 or 90.730, the tenant may deliver a written notice to the landlord specifying the acts and omissions constituting the breach and that the rental agreement will terminate upon a date not less than 30 days after delivery of the notice if the breach is not remedied in seven days in the case of an essential service or 30 days in all other cases, and the rental agreement shall terminate as provided in the notice subject to paragraphs (b) and (c) of this subsection. However, in the case of a week- to-week tenancy, the rental agreement will terminate upon a date

not less than seven days after delivery of the notice if the breach is not remedied.
(b) If the breach is remediable by repairs, the payment of damages or otherwise and if the landlord adequately remedies the breach before the date specified in the notice, the rental agreement shall not terminate by reason of the breach.
(c) If substantially the same act or omission that constituted a prior noncompliance of which notice was given recurs within six months, the tenant may terminate the rental agreement upon at least 14 days' written notice specifying the breach and the date of termination of the rental agreement. However, in the case of a week-to-week tenancy, the tenant may terminate the rental agreement upon at least seven days' written notice specifying the breach and date of termination of the rental agreement.
(2) Except as provided in this chapter, the tenant may recover damages and obtain injunctive relief for any noncompliance by the landlord with the rental agreement or ORS 90.320 or 90.730. The tenant shall not be entitled to recover damages for a landlord noncompliance with ORS 90.320 or 90.730 if the landlord neither knew nor reasonably should have known of the condition that constituted the noncompliance and:
(a) The tenant knew or reasonably should have known of the condition and failed to give actual notice to the landlord in a reasonable time prior to the occurrence of the personal injury, damage to personal property, diminution in rental value or other tenant loss resulting from the noncompliance; or
(b) The condition was caused after the tenancy began by the deliberate or negligent act or omission of someone other than the landlord or a person acting on behalf of the landlord.
(3) The remedy provided in subsection (2) of this section is in addition to any right of the tenant arising under subsection (1) of this section.
(4) The tenant may not terminate or recover damages under this section for a condition caused by the deliberate or negligent act or omission of the tenant or other person on the premises with the tenant's permission or consent.
(5) If the rental agreement is terminated, the landlord shall return all security deposits and prepaid rent recoverable by the tenant under ORS 90.300.
90.365 Failure of landlord to supply essential services; remedies. (1) If contrary to the rental agreement or ORS 90.320 or 90.730 the landlord intentionally or negligently fails to supply any essential service, the tenant may give written notice to the landlord specifying the breach and that the tenant may seek substitute services, diminution in rent damages or substitute housing. After allowing the landlord a reasonable time and reasonable access under the circumstances to supply the essential service, the tenant may:
(a) Procure reasonable amounts of the essential service during the period of the landlord's noncompliance and deduct their actual and reasonable cost from the rent;
(b) Recover damages based upon the diminution in the fair rental value of the dwelling unit; or
(c) If the failure to supply an essential service makes the dwelling unit unsafe or unfit to occupy, procure substitute housing during the period of the landlord's noncompliance, in which case the tenant is excused from paying rent for the period of the landlord's noncompliance. In addition, the tenant may recover as damages from the landlord the actual and reasonable cost or fair and reasonable value of comparable substitute housing in excess of the rent for the dwelling unit. For purposes of this paragraph, substitute housing is comparable if it is of a quality that is similar to or less than the quality of the dwelling unit with regard to basic elements including cooking and refrigeration services and, if warranted, upon consideration of factors such as location in the same area as the dwelling unit, the availability of substitute housing in the area and the expense relative to the range of choices for substitute housing in the area. A tenant may choose substitute housing of relatively greater quality, but the tenant's damages shall be limited to the cost or value of comparable substitute housing.
(2) If contrary to the rental agreement or ORS 90.320 or 90.730 the landlord fails to supply any essential service, the lack of which poses an imminent and serious threat to the tenant's health, safety or property, the tenant may give written notice to the landlord specifying the breach and that the rental agreement shall terminate in not less than 48 hours unless the breach is remedied within that period. If the landlord adequately remedies the breach before the end of the notice period, the rental agreement shall not terminate by reason of the breach. As used in this subsection and subsection (3) of this section, "imminent and serious threat to the tenant's health, safety or property" shall not include the presence of radon, asbestos or lead-based paint or the future risk of flooding or seismic hazard, as defined by ORS 455.447.

(3)(a) If contrary to the rental agreement or ORS 90.320 or 90.730 the landlord intentionally or negligently fails to supply any essential service, the tenant may give notice to the landlord as provided in paragraph (b) of this subsection and may cause to be done in a workmanlike manner the work necessary to provide the essential service and, after submitting to the landlord receipts or an agreed upon itemized statement, deduct from the rent the actual and reasonable cost or the fair and reasonable value of the work not exceeding:
(A) $1,000, if the lack of the essential service poses an imminent and serious threat to the tenant's health, safety or property and the work is performed by a licensed or registered professional; or
(B) $500, if the lack of the essential service is significant but does not pose an imminent and serious threat to the tenant's health, safety or property or if work is not performed by a licensed or registered professional.
(b) The notice required by this subsection shall specify the breach and that the tenant may use the remedy specified in paragraph (a) of this subsection if the landlord fails to supply the essential service within the following periods:
(A) If the lack of the essential service poses an imminent and serious threat to the tenant's health, safety or property, the notice shall be written or actual and shall be given to the landlord at least 48 hours before the tenant causes the necessary work to be done to supply the essential service. If the notice is actual, the tenant shall also give the landlord written notice as promptly after the actual notice as conditions permit.
(B) In all other cases, the notice shall be written and given to the landlord at least:
(i) Seventy-two hours before the tenant causes the necessary work to be done to correct a substantial lack of a cooking or refrigeration service; or
(ii) Seven days before the tenant causes the necessary work to be done to correct a substantial lack of any other essential service.
(c) A tenant who conducts repairs pursuant to this subsection shall not be considered to be an employee of the landlord.
(d) The landlord and tenant may agree, at any time, to allow the tenant to exceed the monetary limits of this subsection when making reasonable repairs. The landlord may specify people to do all work under this section if the tenant's rights under this section are not diminished.
(4) For purposes of subsections (1) and (3) of this section, a landlord shall not be considered to be intentionally or negligently failing to supply an essential service if:
(a) The landlord substantially supplies the essential service; or
(b) The landlord is making a reasonable and good faith effort to supply the essential service and the failure is due to conditions beyond the landlord's control.
(5) This section shall not be construed to require a landlord to supply a cooking appliance or a refrigerator if the landlord did not supply or agree to supply a cooking appliance or refrigerator to the tenant.
(6) If the tenant proceeds under this section, the tenant may not proceed under ORS 90.360 (1) as to that breach.
(7) Rights of the tenant under this section do not arise if the condition was caused by the deliberate or negligent act or omission of the tenant or a person on the premises with the tenant's consent.
(8) Service or delivery of actual or written notice shall be as provided by ORS 90.150 and 90.155, including the addition of three days to the notice period if written notice is delivered by first class mail.
(9) Any provisions of this section that reasonably apply only to a structure that is used as a home, residence or sleeping place shall not apply to a manufactured dwelling, recreational vehicle or floating home if the tenant owns the manufactured dwelling, recreational vehicle or floating home and rents the space.
90.370 Tenant counterclaims in action by landlord for possession or rent. (1)(a) In an action for possession based upon nonpayment of the rent or in an action for rent when the tenant is in possession, the tenant may counterclaim for any amount, not in excess of the jurisdictional limits of the court in which the action is brought, that the tenant may recover under the rental agreement or this chapter, provided that the tenant must prove that prior to the filing of the landlord's action the landlord reasonably had or should have had knowledge or had received actual notice of the facts that constitute the tenant's counterclaim.
(b) In the event the tenant counterclaims, the court at the landlord's or tenant's request may order the tenant to pay into court all or part of the rent accrued and thereafter accruing, and shall determine the amount due to each party. The party to whom a net amount is owed shall be paid first from the money paid into court, and shall be paid the balance by the other party. The court may at any time release

money paid into court to either party if the parties agree or if the court finds such party to be entitled to the sum so released. If no rent remains due after application of this section and unless otherwise agreed between the parties, a judgment shall be entered for the tenant in the action for possession.

(2) In an action for rent when the tenant is not in possession, the tenant may counterclaim as provided in subsection (1) of this section but is not required to pay any rent into court.

(3) If the tenant does not comply with an order to pay rent into the court as provided in subsection (1) of this section, the tenant shall not be permitted to assert a counterclaim in the action for possession.

(4) If the total amount found due to the tenant on any counterclaims is less than any rent found due to the landlord, and the tenant retains possession solely because the tenant paid rent into court under subsection (1) of this section, no attorney fees shall be awarded to the tenant unless the tenant paid at least the balance found due to the landlord into court no later than the commencement of the trial.

(5) When a tenant is granted a continuance for a longer period than two days, and has not been ordered to pay rent into court under subsection (1) of this section, the tenant shall be ordered to pay rent into court under ORS 105.140 (2).

90.375 Effect of unlawful ouster or exclusion; willful diminution of services. If a landlord unlawfully removes or excludes the tenant from the premises, seriously attempts or seriously threatens unlawfully to remove or exclude the tenant from the premises or willfully diminishes or seriously attempts or seriously threatens unlawfully to diminish services to the tenant by interrupting or causing the interruption of heat, running water, hot water, electric or other essential service, the tenant may obtain injunctive relief to recover possession or may terminate the rental agreement and recover an amount up to two months' periodic rent or twice the actual damages sustained by the tenant, whichever is greater. If the rental agreement is terminated the landlord shall return all security deposits and prepaid rent recoverable under ORS 90.300. The tenant need not terminate the rental agreement, obtain injunctive relief or recover possession to recover damages under this section.

90.380 Effect of rental of dwelling in violation of building or housing codes; remedy. (1) As used in this section, "posted" means that a governmental agency has attached a copy of the agency's written determination in a secure manner to the main entrance of the dwelling unit or to the premises or building of which the dwelling unit is a part.

(2)(a) If a governmental agency has posted a dwelling unit as unsafe and unlawful to occupy due to the existence of conditions that violate state or local law and materially affect health or safety to an extent that, in the agency's determination, the tenant must vacate the unit and another person may not take possession of the unit, a landlord may not continue a tenancy or enter into a new tenancy for the dwelling unit until the landlord corrects the conditions that led to the agency's determination.

(b) If a landlord knowingly violates paragraph (a) of this subsection, the tenant may immediately terminate the tenancy by giving the landlord actual notice of the termination and the reason for the termination and may recover from the landlord either two months' periodic rent or up to twice the actual damages sustained by the tenant as a result of the violation, whichever is greater. The tenant need not terminate the tenancy to recover damages under this section.

(3)(a) If a governmental agency has given a written notice to a landlord that a dwelling unit has been determined to be unlawful, but not unsafe, to occupy due to the existence of conditions that violate state or local law and materially affect health or safety to an extent that, in the agency's determination, although the unit is safe for an existing tenant to occupy, another person may not take possession of the unit, the landlord may not enter into a new tenancy for the dwelling unit until the landlord corrects the conditions that led to the agency's determination.

(b) If a landlord knowingly violates paragraph (a) of this subsection, the tenant may recover from the landlord either two months' periodic rent or up to twice the actual damages sustained by the tenant as a result of the violation, whichever is greater.

(c) Notwithstanding paragraph (b) of this subsection, a landlord is not liable to a tenant for a violation of paragraph (a) of this subsection if, prior to the commencement of the tenancy, the landlord discloses to the tenant that the dwelling unit has been determined to be unlawful to occupy.

(d) A disclosure described in paragraph (c) of this subsection must be in writing, include a description of the conditions that led to the agency's determination and state that the landlord is obligated to correct

the conditions before entering into a new tenancy. The landlord shall attach a copy of the agency's notice to the disclosure. The notice copy may provide the information required by this paragraph to be disclosed by the landlord to the tenant.
(e) A disclosure described in paragraph (c) of this subsection does not release the landlord from the duties imposed by this chapter, including the duty to maintain the dwelling unit in a habitable condition pursuant to ORS 90.320 or 90.730. A tenant who enters into a tenancy after the landlord's disclosure does not waive the tenant's other remedies under this chapter. The disclosure does not prevent the governmental agency that made the determination from imposing on the landlord any penalty authorized by law for entering into the new tenancy.
(4)(a) If a governmental agency has made a determination regarding a dwelling unit and has posted or given notice for conditions described in subsection (2)(a) or (3)(a) of this section, a landlord may not accept from an applicant for that dwelling unit a deposit to secure the execution of a rental agreement pursuant to ORS 90.297 unless, before accepting the deposit, the landlord discloses to the applicant as provided by subsection (3)(c) of this section that the dwelling unit has been determined to be unlawful to occupy.
(b) If a landlord knowingly violates paragraph (a) of this subsection or fails to correct the conditions leading to the agency's determination before the date a new tenancy is to begin as provided by the agreement to secure the execution of a rental agreement, an applicant may terminate the agreement to secure the execution of the rental agreement by giving the landlord actual notice of the termination and the reason for termination. As a result of a termination, the applicant may recover from the landlord an amount equal to twice the deposit. If an applicant recovers damages for a violation pursuant to this paragraph, the applicant may not recover any amounts under ORS 90.297.
(5) If, after a landlord and a tenant have entered into a tenancy, a governmental agency posts a dwelling unit as unsafe and unlawful to occupy due to the existence of conditions that violate state or local law, that materially affect health or safety and that:
(a) Were not caused by the tenant, the tenant may immediately terminate the tenancy by giving the landlord actual notice of the termination and the reason for the termination; or
(b) Were not caused by the landlord or by the landlord's failure to maintain the dwelling, the landlord may terminate the tenancy by giving the tenant 24 hours' written notice of the termination and the reason for the termination, after which the landlord may take possession in the manner provided in ORS 105.105 to 105.168.
(6) If the tenancy is terminated, as a result of conditions as described in subsections (2), (4) and (5) of this section, within 14 days of the notice of termination the landlord shall return to the applicant or tenant:
(a) All of the deposit to secure the execution of a rental agreement, security deposit or prepaid rent owed to the applicant under this section or to the tenant under ORS 90.300; and
(b) All rent prepaid for the month in which the termination occurs, prorated, if applicable, to the date of termination or the date the tenant vacates the premises, whichever is later.
(7) If conditions at premises that existed at the outset of the tenancy and that were not caused by the tenant pose an imminent and serious threat to the health or safety of occupants of the premises within six months from the beginning of the tenancy, the tenant may immediately terminate the rental agreement by giving the landlord actual notice of the termination and the reason for the termination. In addition, if the landlord knew or should have reasonably known of the existence of the conditions, the tenant may recover either two months' periodic rent or twice the actual damages sustained by the tenant as a result of the violation, whichever is greater. The tenant need not terminate the rental agreement to recover damages under this section. Within four days of the tenant's notice of termination, the landlord shall return to the tenant:
(a) All of the security deposit or prepaid rent owed to the tenant under ORS 90.300; and
(b) All rent prepaid for the month in which the termination occurs, prorated to the date of termination or the date the tenant vacates the premises, whichever is later.
(8)(a) A landlord shall return the money due the applicant or tenant under subsections (6) and (7) of this section either by making the money available to the applicant or tenant at the landlord's customary place of business or by mailing the money by first class mail to the applicant or tenant.
(b) The applicant or tenant has the option of choosing the method for return of any money due under this section. If the applicant or tenant fails to choose one of these methods at the time of giving the notice of ter-

mination, the landlord shall use the mail method, addressed to the last-known address of the applicant or tenant and mailed within the relevant four-day or 14-day period following the applicant's or tenant's notice.
(9) If the landlord fails to comply with subsection (8) of this section, the applicant or tenant may recover the money due in an amount equal to twice the amount due.

90.385 Retaliatory conduct by landlord prohibited; tenant remedies and defenses; action for possession in certain cases. (1) Except as provided in this section, a landlord may not retaliate by increasing rent or decreasing services, by serving a notice to terminate the tenancy or by bringing or threatening to bring an action for possession after:
(a) The tenant has complained to, or expressed to the landlord in writing an intention to complain to, a governmental agency charged with responsibility for enforcement of any of the following concerning a violation applicable to the tenancy:
(A) A building, health or housing code materially affecting health or safety;
(B) Laws or regulations concerning the delivery of mail; or
(C) Laws or regulations prohibiting discrimination in rental housing;
(b) The tenant has made any complaint to the landlord that is in good faith and related to the tenancy;
(c) The tenant has organized or become a member of a tenants' union or similar organization;
(d) The tenant has testified against the landlord in any judicial, administrative or legislative proceeding;
(e) The tenant successfully defended an action for possession brought by the landlord within the previous six months except if the tenant was successful in defending the action only because:
(A) The termination notice by the landlord was not served or delivered in the manner required by ORS 90.155; or
(B) The period provided by the termination notice was less than that required by the statute upon which the notice relied to terminate the tenancy; or
(f) The tenant has performed or expressed intent to perform any other act for the purpose of asserting, protecting or invoking the protection of any right secured to tenants under any federal, state or local law.
(2) As used in subsection (1) of this section, "decreasing services" includes:
(a) Unreasonably restricting the availability of or placing unreasonable burdens on the use of common areas or facilities by tenant associations or tenants meeting to establish a tenant organization; and
(b) Intentionally and unreasonably interfering with and substantially impairing the enjoyment or use of the premises by the tenant.
(3) If the landlord acts in violation of subsection (1) of this section the tenant is entitled to the remedies provided in ORS 90.375 and has a defense in any retaliatory action against the tenant for possession.
(4) Notwithstanding subsections (1) and (3) of this section, a landlord may bring an action for possession if:
(a) The complaint by the tenant was made to the landlord or an agent of the landlord in an unreasonable manner or at an unreasonable time or was repeated in a manner having the effect of unreasonably harassing the landlord. A determination whether the manner, time or effect of a complaint was unreasonable shall include consideration of all related circumstances preceding or contemporaneous to the complaint;
(b) The violation of the applicable building or housing code was caused primarily by lack of reasonable care by the tenant or other person in the household of the tenant or upon the premises with the consent of the tenant;
(c) The tenant is in default in rent; or
(d) Compliance with the applicable building or housing code requires alteration, remodeling or demolition which would effectively deprive the tenant of use of the dwelling unit.
(5) For purposes of this section, a complaint made by another on behalf of a tenant is considered a complaint by the tenant.
(6) For the purposes of subsection (4)(c) of this section, a tenant who has paid rent into court pursuant to ORS 90.370 shall not be considered to be in default in rent.
(7) The maintenance of an action under subsection (4) of this section does not release the landlord from liability under ORS 90.360 (2).

90.390 Discrimination against tenant or applicant; tenant defense. (1) A landlord may not discriminate against a tenant in violation of local, state or federal law, including ORS 346.630, 346.660, 346.690, 659A.145 and 659A.421.
(2) If the tenant can prove that the landlord has in fact acted in violation of subsection (1) of this section the tenant has a defense in any discriminatory action brought by the landlord against the tenant for possession, unless the tenant is in default in rent.
(3) A tenant may prove a landlord's discrimination in violation of ORS 659A.145 or 659A.421 by demonstrat-

ing that a racially neutral housing policy has a disparate adverse impact on members of a protected class as described in ORS 659A.424.

(4) A landlord may not discriminate against an applicant because the applicant was in fact a defendant in an action for possession pursuant to ORS 105.105 to 105.168 that prior to the application was dismissed in favor of the defendant or that resulted in final judgment for the defendant. If the landlord knowingly acts in violation of this subsection, the applicant may recover actual damages or $200, whichever is greater.

LANDLORD REMEDIES

90.400 Effect of tenant noncompliance with rental agreement or statute; failure to pay rent; damage to persons or property; false information; drug or alcohol violations. (1)(a) Except as provided in this chapter, if there is a material noncompliance by the tenant with the rental agreement, a noncompliance with ORS 90.325 materially affecting health and safety, a material noncompliance with a rental agreement regarding a program of recovery in drug and alcohol free housing or a failure to pay a late charge pursuant to ORS 90.260 or a utility or service charge pursuant to ORS 90.315 (4), the landlord may deliver a written notice to the tenant terminating the tenancy for cause as provided in this subsection. The notice shall specify the acts and omissions constituting the breach and shall state that the rental agreement will terminate upon a date not less than 30 days after delivery of the notice. If the breach is remediable by repairs, payment of damages, payment of a late charge or utility or service charge, change in conduct or otherwise, the notice shall also state that the tenant can avoid termination by remedying the breach within 14 days.

(b) If the breach is not remedied in 14 days, the rental agreement shall terminate as provided in the notice subject to paragraphs (c) and (d) of this subsection.

(c) If the tenant adequately remedies the breach before the date for remedying the breach as specified in the notice, the rental agreement shall not terminate.

(d) If substantially the same act or omission that constituted a prior noncompliance of which notice was given pursuant to paragraph (a) of this subsection recurs within six months after the date specified in that notice as the date for remedying the prior noncompliance, the landlord may terminate the rental agreement upon at least 10 days' written notice specifying the breach and the date of termination of the rental agreement. The tenant does not have a right to cure this subsequent breach. The date of termination specified in the 10-day notice given pursuant to this paragraph may not be sooner than the date of termination specified in the 30-day notice of the prior noncompliance given pursuant to paragraph (a) of this subsection. A landlord may not terminate a rental agreement pursuant to this paragraph if the only breach is a failure to pay the current month's rent.

(e) In the case of a week-to-week tenancy, the notice periods in:

(A) Paragraph (a) of this subsection shall be changed from 30 days to seven days and from 14 days to four days;

(B) Paragraph (b) of this subsection shall be changed from 14 days to four days; and

(C) Paragraph (d) of this subsection shall be changed from 10 days to four days.

(f) This subsection does not apply to a tenancy governed by ORS 90.505 to 90.840.

(2) The landlord may immediately terminate the rental agreement for nonpayment of rent and take possession of the dwelling unit in the manner provided in ORS 105.105 to 105.168 after written notice, as follows:

(a) In the case of a week-to-week tenancy, by delivering to the tenant at least 72 hours' written notice of nonpayment and the landlord's intention to terminate the rental agreement if the rent is not paid within that period. The landlord shall give this notice no sooner than on the fifth day of the rental period, including the first day the rent is due.

(b) In the case of all other tenancies, by delivering to the tenant:

(A) At least 72 hours' written notice of nonpayment and the landlord's intention to terminate the rental agreement if the rent is not paid within that period. The landlord shall give this notice no sooner than on the eighth day of the rental period, including the first day the rent is due; or

(B) At least 144 hours' written notice of nonpayment and the landlord's intention to terminate the rental agreement if the rent is not paid within that period. The landlord shall give this notice no sooner than on the fifth day of the rental period, including the first day the rent is due.

(c) The notices described in this subsection shall also specify the date and time by which the tenant must pay the rent to cure the nonpayment of rent.

(d) Payment by a tenant who has received a nonpayment of rent notice under this subsection is timely if mailed to the landlord within the period of the notice unless:

(A) The nonpayment of rent notice is served on the tenant:
(i) By personal delivery as provided in ORS 90.155 (1)(a); or
(ii) By first class mail and attachment as provided in ORS 90.155 (1)(c).
(B) A written rental agreement and the nonpayment of rent notice expressly state that payment is to be made at a specified location that is either on the premises or at a place where the tenant has made all previous rent payments in person; and
(C) The place so specified is available to the tenant for payment throughout the period of the notice.
(3) Except as provided in subsection (4) of this section, the landlord, after at least 24 hours' written notice specifying the acts and omissions constituting the cause and specifying the date and time of the termination, may immediately terminate the rental agreement and take possession in the manner provided in ORS 105.105 to 105.168, if:
(a) The tenant, someone in the tenant's control or the tenant's pet seriously threatens to inflict substantial personal injury, or inflicts any substantial personal injury, upon a person on the premises other than the tenant;
(b) The tenant or someone in the tenant's control recklessly endangers a person on the premises other than the tenant by creating a serious risk of substantial personal injury;
(c) The tenant, someone in the tenant's control or the tenant's pet inflicts any substantial personal injury upon a neighbor living in the immediate vicinity of the premises;
(d) The tenant or someone in the tenant's control intentionally inflicts any substantial damage to the premises or the tenant's pet inflicts substantial damage to the premises on more than one occasion;
(e)(A) The tenant intentionally provided substantial false information on the application for the tenancy within the past year;
(B) The false information was with regard to a criminal conviction of the tenant that would have been material to the landlord's acceptance of the application; and
(C) The landlord terminates the rental agreement within 30 days after discovering the falsity of the information;
(f) The tenant has vacated the premises, the person in possession is holding contrary to a written rental agreement that prohibits subleasing the premises to another or allowing another person to occupy the premises without the written permission of the landlord, and the landlord has not knowingly accepted rent from the person in possession; or
(e) The tenant, someone in the tenant's control or the tenant's pet commits any act that is outrageous in the extreme, on the premises or in the immediate vicinity of the premises. An act that is "outrageous in the extreme" is an act not described in paragraphs (a) to (e) of this subsection, but is similar in degree and is one that a reasonable person in that community would consider to be so offensive as to warrant termination of the tenancy within 24 hours, considering the seriousness of the act or the risk to others. Such an act is more extreme or serious than an act that warrants a 30-day termination under subsection (1) of this section. An act that is "outrageous in the extreme" includes, but is not limited to, the following acts by a person:
(A) Prostitution or promotion of prostitution, as described in ORS 167.007 and 167.012;
(B) Manufacture or delivery of a controlled substance, as described in ORS 475.005 but not including:
(i) The medical use of marijuana in compliance with ORS 475.300 to 475.346;
(ii) Possession of, or delivery for no consideration of, one avoirdupois ounce of marijuana as described in ORS 475.992 (2)(b) or (4)(f); or
(iii) Possession of prescription drugs.
(C) Intimidation, as described in ORS 166.155 and 166.165; or
(D) Burglary as described in ORS 164.215 and 164.225.
(4) If the cause for a termination notice given pursuant to subsection (3)(a), (c), (d) or (g) of this section is based upon the acts of the tenant's pet, the tenant may cure the cause and avoid termination of the tenancy by removing the pet from the premises prior to the end of the notice period. The notice shall describe the right of the tenant to cure the cause. If the tenant returns the pet to the premises at any time after having cured the violation, the landlord, after at least 24 hours' written notice specifying the subsequent presence of the offending pet, may terminate the rental agreement and take possession in the manner provided in ORS 105.105 to 105.168. The tenant shall not have a right to cure this subsequent violation.
(5) Someone is in the tenant's control, as that phrase is used in subsection (3) of this section, when that person enters or remains on the premises with the tenant's permission or consent after the tenant rea-

sonably knows or should know of that person's act or likelihood to commit any act of the type described in subsection (3)(a) to (d) and (g) of this section.
(6) The landlord's 24 hours' written notice given under subsection (3)(f) of this section is not an admission by the landlord that the individual occupying the premises is a lessee or sublessee of the landlord.
(7) With regard to "acts outrageous in the extreme" as described in subsection (3)(g) of this section, an act can be proven to be outrageous in the extreme even if it is one that does not violate a criminal statute. In addition, notwithstanding the reference in subsection (3) of this section to existing criminal statutes, the landlord's standard of proof in an action for possession under this subsection remains the civil standard, proof by a preponderance of the evidence.
(8) If a good faith effort by a landlord to terminate a tenancy pursuant to subsection (3)(g) of this section and to recover possession of the rental unit pursuant to ORS 105.105 to 105.168 fails by decision of the court, the landlord shall not be found in violation of any state statute or local ordinance requiring the landlord to remove that tenant upon threat of fine, abatement or forfeiture as long as the landlord continues to make a good faith effort to terminate the tenancy.
(9) If a tenant living for less than two years in drug and alcohol free housing uses, possesses or shares alcohol, illegal drugs, controlled substances or prescription drugs without a medical prescription, the landlord may deliver a written notice to the tenant terminating the tenancy for cause as provided in this subsection. The notice shall specify the acts constituting the drug or alcohol violation and shall state that the rental agreement will terminate in not less than 48 hours after delivery of the notice, at a specified date and time. The notice shall also state that the tenant can cure the drug or alcohol violation by a change in conduct or otherwise within 24 hours after delivery of the notice. If the tenant cures the violation within the 24-hour period, the rental agreement does not terminate. If the tenant does not cure the violation within the 24-hour period, the rental agreement shall terminate as provided in the notice. If substantially the same act that constituted a prior drug or alcohol violation of which notice was given reoccurs within six months, the landlord may terminate the rental agreement upon at least 24 hours' written notice specifying the violation and the date and time of termination of the rental agreement. The tenant shall not have a right to cure this subsequent violation.
(10) Except as provided in this chapter, a landlord may pursue any one or more of the remedies listed in this section, simultaneously or sequentially.
(11) Except as provided in this chapter, the landlord may recover damages and obtain injunctive relief for any noncompliance by the tenant with the rental agreement or ORS 90.325 or 90.740.

90.405 Effect of tenant keeping unpermitted pet. (1) If the tenant, in violation of the rental agreement, keeps on the premises a pet capable of causing damage to persons or property, the landlord may deliver a written notice specifying the violation and stating that the tenancy will terminate upon a date not less than 10 days after the delivery of the notice unless the tenant removes the pet from the premises prior to the termination date specified in the notice. If the pet is not removed by the date specified, the tenancy shall terminate and the landlord may take possession in the manner provided in ORS 105.105 to 105.168.
(2) For purposes of this section, "a pet capable of causing damage to persons or property" means an animal that, because of the nature, size or behavioral characteristics of that particular animal or of that breed or type of animal generally, a reasonable person might consider to be capable of causing personal injury or property damage, including but not limited to, water damage from medium or larger sized fish tanks or other personal injury or property damage arising from the environment in which the animal is kept.
(3) If substantially the same act that constituted a prior noncompliance of which notice was given under subsection (1) of this section recurs within six months, the landlord may terminate the rental agreement upon at least 10 days' written notice specifying the breach and the date of termination of the rental agreement.
(4) This section shall not apply to any tenancy governed by ORS 90.505 to 90.840.

90.410 Effect of tenant failure to give notice of absence; absence; abandonment. (1) If the rental agreement requires the tenant to give actual notice to the landlord of an anticipated extended absence in excess of seven days as permitted by ORS 90.340 and the tenant willfully fails to do so, the landlord may recover actual damages from the tenant.
(2) During any absence of the tenant in excess of seven days, the landlord may enter the dwelling unit at times reasonably necessary.
(3) If the tenant abandons the dwelling unit, the landlord shall make reasonable efforts to rent it for a fair rental. If the landlord rents the dwelling unit for

a term beginning before the expiration of the rental agreement, the rental agreement terminates as of the date of the new tenancy. If the landlord fails to use reasonable efforts to rent the dwelling unit at a fair rental or if the landlord accepts the abandonment as a surrender, the rental agreement is deemed to be terminated by the landlord as of the date the landlord knows or should know of the abandonment. If the tenancy is from month to month or week to week, the term of the rental agreement for this purpose is deemed to be a month or a week, as the case may be.

90.415 Landlord waiver of right to terminate tenancy; exceptions. (1) Except as otherwise provided in this section, a landlord waives the right to terminate a rental agreement for a particular breach if the landlord:

(a) During two or more separate rental periods, accepts rent with knowledge of the default by the tenant; or

(b) Accepts performance by a tenant that varies from the terms of the rental agreement.

(2) For purposes of subsection (1)(a) of this section, a landlord has not accepted rent if within six days after receipt of the rent payment, the landlord refunds the rent.

(3) A landlord does not waive the right to terminate as described in subsection (1)(a) of this section if the termination is pursuant to ORS 90.400 (3).

(4) A landlord does not waive the right to terminate as described in subsection (1) of this section if the landlord and tenant agree otherwise after the breach has occurred.

(5) If a tenancy consists of rented space for a manufactured dwelling or floating home as described in ORS 90.505, a landlord does not waive the right to terminate as described in subsection (1) of this section if:

(a) The breach or default at issue concerns:

(A) Disrepair or deterioration of the manufactured dwelling or floating home pursuant to ORS 90.632; or

(B) A failure to maintain the space, as provided by ORS 90.740 (2), (4)(b) and (4)(h); or

(b) The breach or default at issue concerns the tenant's conduct and, following the breach or default, but prior to acceptance of rent or performance as described in subsection (1) of this section, the landlord gives written notice to the tenant regarding the breach or default that:

(A) Describes specifically the conduct that constitutes the breach or default, either as a separate and distinct breach or default, a series or group of breaches or defaults or a continuous or ongoing breach or default;

(B) States that the tenant is required to discontinue the conduct or correct the breach or default; and

(C) States that a reoccurrence of the conduct that constitutes a breach or default may result in a termination of the tenancy pursuant to ORS 90.630. For a continuous or ongoing breach or default, the landlord's notice remains effective for 12 months.

(6) Prior to giving a nonpayment of rent termination notice pursuant to ORS 90.400 (2), a landlord who accepts partial rent for a rental period does not waive the right to terminate for nonpayment if:

(a) The landlord accepted the partial rent before the landlord gave any notice of intent to terminate under ORS 90.400 (2) based on the tenant's agreement to pay the balance by a time certain; and

(b) The tenant does not pay the balance of the rent as agreed.

(7) A landlord who accepts partial rent under subsection (6) of this section may proceed to serve a notice under ORS 90.400 (2) to terminate the tenancy if the balance of the rent is not paid, provided:

(a) The notice is served no earlier than it would have been permitted under ORS 90.400 (2) had no rent been accepted; and

(b) The notice permits the tenant to avoid termination of the tenancy for nonpayment of rent by paying the balance within 72 hours or 144 hours, as the case may be, or by any date to which the parties agreed, whichever is later.

(8) After giving a nonpayment of rent termination notice pursuant to ORS 90.400 (2), a landlord who accepts partial rent for a rental period does not waive the right to terminate for nonpayment if the landlord and tenant agree in writing that the acceptance does not constitute waiver.

(9) A written agreement under subsection (8) of this section may provide that the landlord may proceed to terminate the rental agreement and take possession in the manner provided by ORS 105.105 to 105.168 without serving a new notice under ORS 90.400 (2) in the event the tenant fails to pay the balance of the rent by a time certain.

(10) A landlord's acceptance of partial rent for a rental period does not waive the right to terminate the rental agreement if the entire amount of the partial payment was from funds paid under the United States Housing Act of 1937 (42 U.S.C. 1437f) or any state low income rental housing fund administered by the Housing and Community Services Department.

(11) A landlord who accepts rent after the giving of a notice of termination by the landlord or the tenant, other than a nonpayment of rent notice, does not waive the right to terminate on that notice if:
(a) The landlord accepts rent prorated to the termination date specified in the notice; or
(b) Within six days after receipt of the rent payment, the landlord refunds at least the unused balance of the rent prorated for the period beyond the termination date.
(12) A landlord who has served a notice of termination for cause under ORS 90.400 (1), 90.630 or 90.632 does not waive the right to terminate on that notice by accepting rent for the rental period and beyond the period covered by the notice if within six days after the end of the remedy or correction period described in the applicable statute, the landlord refunds the rent for the period beyond the termination date.
(13) A landlord who has served a notice of termination for cause under ORS 90.400 (1), 90.630 or 90.632 and who has commenced proceedings under ORS 105.105 to 105.168 to recover possession of the premises does not waive the right to terminate on that notice:
(a) By accepting rent for any period beyond the expiration of the notice during which the tenant remains in possession provided:
(A) The landlord notifies the tenant in writing, in or after the service of the notice of termination for cause, that acceptance of rent while a termination action is pending will not waive the right to terminate on that notice; and
(B) The rent does not cover a period extending beyond the date of its acceptance.
(b) By serving a notice of nonpayment of rent under ORS 90.400 (2).
(14) A landlord and tenant may by written agreement provide that monthly rent shall be paid in regular installments of less than a month pursuant to a schedule specified in the agreement. Those installment rent payments are not partial rent, as that term is used in this section.
(15) Unless otherwise agreed, a landlord does not waive the right to terminate as described in subsection (1) of this section by accepting:
(a) A last month's rent deposit collected at the beginning of the tenancy, even if the deposit covers a period beyond a termination date; or
(b) Rent distributed pursuant to a court order releasing money paid into court as provided by ORS 90.370 (1).
(16) Notwithstanding subsections (2), (11) and (12) of this section, if a tenancy consists of rented space for a manufactured dwelling or floating home as described in ORS 90.505, the period for the landlord to refund rent under subsection (2), (11) or (12) of this section is seven days.
(17) When a landlord must refund rent under this section, the refund shall be made to the tenant or other payer by personal delivery or first class mail and may be in the form of the tenant's or other payer's check or any other form of check or money.

90.420 Enforceability of landlord liens; distraint for rent abolished. (1) A lien or security interest on behalf of the landlord in the tenant's household goods is not enforceable unless perfected before October 5, 1973.
(2) Distraint for rent is abolished.

90.420 Enforceability of landlord liens; distraint for rent abolished. (1) A lien or security interest on behalf of the landlord in the tenant's household goods is not enforceable unless perfected before October 5, 1973.
(2) Distraint for rent is abolished.

90.425 Disposition of personal property abandoned by tenant; notice; sale; limitation on landlord liability; tax cancellation; storage agreements; hazardous property. (1) As used in this section:
(a) "Current market value" means the amount in cash, as determined by the county assessor, that could reasonably be expected to be paid for a manufactured dwelling or floating home by an informed buyer to an informed seller, each acting without compulsion in an arm's length transaction occurring on the assessment date for the tax year or on the date of a subsequent reappraisal by the county assessor.
(b) "Dispose of the personal property" means that, if reasonably appropriate, the landlord may throw away the property or may give it without consideration to a nonprofit organization or to a person unrelated to the landlord. The landlord may not retain the property for personal use or benefit.
(c) "Goods" includes those goods left inside a recreational vehicle, manufactured dwelling or floating home or left upon the rental space outside a recreational vehicle, manufactured dwelling or floating home, whether the recreational vehicle, dwelling or home is located inside or outside of a facility.
(d) "Lienholder" means any lienholder of an abandoned recreational vehicle, manufactured dwelling or floating home, if the lien is of record or the lienholder is actually known to the landlord.

(e) "Of record" means:
(A) For a manufactured dwelling or recreational vehicle, that a security interest has been properly recorded with the Department of Transportation pursuant to ORS 802.200 (1)(a)(A) and 803.097 for a dwelling or vehicle registered and titled by the department pursuant to ORS 820.500.
(B) For a floating home, that a security interest has been properly recorded with the State Marine Board pursuant to ORS 830.740 to 830.755 for a home registered and titled with the board pursuant to ORS 830.715.
(f) "Owner" means any owner of an abandoned recreational vehicle, manufactured dwelling or floating home, if different from the tenant and either of record or actually known to the landlord.
(g) "Personal property" means goods, vehicles and recreational vehicles and includes manufactured dwellings and floating homes not located in a facility. "Personal property" does not include manufactured dwellings and floating homes located in a facility and therefore subject to being stored, sold or disposed of as provided under ORS 90.675.
(2) A landlord may not store, sell or dispose of abandoned personal property except as provided by this section. This section governs the rights and obligations of landlords, tenants and any lienholders or owners in any personal property abandoned or left upon the premises by the tenant or any lienholder or owner in the following circumstances:
(a) The tenancy has ended by termination or expiration of a rental agreement or by relinquishment or abandonment of the premises and the landlord reasonably believes under all the circumstances that the tenant has left the personal property upon the premises with no intention of asserting any further claim to the premises or to the personal property;
(b) The tenant has been absent from the premises continuously for seven days after termination of a tenancy by a court order that has not been executed; or
(c) The landlord receives possession of the premises from the sheriff following restitution pursuant to ORS 105.161.
(3) Prior to selling or disposing of the tenant's personal property under this section, the landlord must give a written notice to the tenant that shall be:
(a) Personally delivered to the tenant; or
(b) Sent by first class mail addressed and mailed to the tenant at:
(A) The premises;
(B) Any post-office box held by the tenant and actually known to the landlord; and
(C) The most recent forwarding address if provided by the tenant or actually known to the landlord.
(4)(a) In addition to the notice required by subsection (3) of this section, in the case of an abandoned recreational vehicle, manufactured dwelling or floating home, a landlord shall also give a copy of the notice described in subsection (3) of this section to:
(A) Any lienholder of the recreational vehicle, manufactured dwelling or floating home;
(B) Any owner of the recreational vehicle, manufactured dwelling or floating home;
(C) The tax collector of the county where the manufactured dwelling or floating home is located; and
(D) The assessor of the county where the manufactured dwelling or floating home is located.
(b) The landlord shall give the notice copy required by this subsection by personal delivery or first class mail, except that for any lienholder, mail service shall be both by first class mail and by certified mail with return receipt requested.
(c) A notice to lienholders under paragraph (a)(A) of this subsection must be sent to each lienholder at each address:
(A) Actually known to the landlord;
(B) Of record; and
(C) Provided to the landlord by the lienholder in a written notice that identifies the personal property subject to the lien and that was sent to the landlord by certified mail with return receipt requested within the preceding five years. The notice must identify the personal property by describing the physical address of the property.
(5) The notice required under subsection (3) of this section shall state that:
(a) The personal property left upon the premises is considered abandoned;
(b) The tenant or any lienholder or owner must contact the landlord by a specified date, as provided in subsection (6) of this section, to arrange for the removal of the abandoned personal property;
(c) The personal property is stored at a place of safekeeping, except that if the property includes a manufactured dwelling or floating home, the dwelling or home shall be stored on the rented space;
(d) The tenant or any lienholder or owner, except as provided by subsection (18) of this section, may arrange for removal of the personal property by contacting the landlord at a described telephone number or address on or before the specified date;

(e) The landlord shall make the personal property available for removal by the tenant or any lienholder or owner, except as provided by subsection (18) of this section, by appointment at reasonable times;
(f) If the personal property is considered to be abandoned pursuant to subsection (2)(a) or (b) of this section, the landlord may require payment of removal and storage charges, as provided by subsection (7)(d) of this section, prior to releasing the personal property to the tenant or any lienholder or owner;
(g) If the personal property is considered to be abandoned pursuant to subsection (2)(c) of this section, the landlord may not require payment of storage charges prior to releasing the personal property;
(h) If the tenant or any lienholder or owner fails to contact the landlord by the specified date, or after that contact, fails to remove the personal property within 30 days for recreational vehicles, manufactured dwellings and floating homes or 15 days for all other personal property, the landlord may sell or dispose of the personal property. If the landlord reasonably believes that the personal property will be eligible for disposal pursuant to subsection (10)(b) of this section and the landlord intends to dispose of the property if it is not claimed, the notice shall state that belief and intent; and
(i) If the personal property includes a recreational vehicle, manufactured dwelling or floating home and if applicable, there is a lienholder or owner that has a right to claim the recreational vehicle, dwelling or home, except as provided by subsection (18) of this section.
(6) For purposes of subsection (5) of this section, the specified date by which a tenant, lienholder or owner must contact a landlord to arrange for the disposition of abandoned personal property shall be:
(a) For abandoned recreational vehicles, manufactured dwellings or floating homes, not less than 45 days after personal delivery or mailing of the notice; or
(b) For all other abandoned personal property, not less than five days after personal delivery or eight days after mailing of the notice.
(7) After notifying the tenant as required by subsection (3) of this section, the landlord:
(a) Shall store any abandoned manufactured dwelling or floating home on the rented space and shall exercise reasonable care for the dwelling or home;
(b) Shall store all other abandoned personal property of the tenant, including goods left inside a recreational vehicle, manufactured dwelling or floating home or left upon the rented space outside a recreational vehicle, dwelling or home, in a place of safekeeping and shall exercise reasonable care for the personal property, except that the landlord may:
(A) Promptly dispose of rotting food; and
(B) Allow an animal control agency to remove any abandoned pets or livestock. If an animal control agency will not remove the abandoned pets or livestock, the landlord shall exercise reasonable care for the animals given all the circumstances, including the type and condition of the animals, and may give the animals to an agency that is willing and able to care for the animals, such as a humane society or similar organization;
(c) Except for manufactured dwellings and floating homes, may store the abandoned personal property at the dwelling unit, move and store it elsewhere on the premises or move and store it at a commercial storage company or other place of safekeeping; and
(d) Is entitled to reasonable or actual storage charges and costs incidental to storage or disposal, including any cost of removal to a place of storage. In the case of an abandoned manufactured dwelling or floating home, the storage charge shall be no greater than the monthly space rent last payable by the tenant.
(8) If a tenant, lienholder or owner, upon the receipt of the notice provided by subsection (3) or (4) of this section or otherwise, responds by actual notice to the landlord on or before the specified date in the landlord's notice that the tenant, lienholder or owner intends to remove the personal property from the premises or from the place of safekeeping, the landlord must make that personal property available for removal by the tenant, lienholder or owner by appointment at reasonable times during the 15 days or, in the case of a recreational vehicle, manufactured dwelling or floating home, 30 days following the date of the response, subject to subsection (18) of this section. If the personal property is considered to be abandoned pursuant to subsection (2)(a) or (b) of this section, but not pursuant to subsection (2)(c) of this section, the landlord may require payment of removal and storage charges, as provided in subsection (7)(d) of this section, prior to allowing the tenant, lienholder or owner to remove the personal property. Acceptance by a landlord of such payment does not operate to create or reinstate a tenancy or create a waiver pursuant to ORS 90.415.
(9) Except as provided in subsections (18) to (20) of this section, if the tenant, lienholder or owner of a

recreational vehicle, manufactured dwelling or floating home does not respond within the time provided by the landlord's notice, or the tenant, lienholder or owner does not remove the personal property within the time required by subsection (8) of this section or by any date agreed to with the landlord, whichever is later, the tenant's, lienholder's or owner's personal property is conclusively presumed to be abandoned. The tenant and any lienholder or owner that have been given notice pursuant to subsection (3) or (4) of this section shall, except with regard to the distribution of sale proceeds pursuant to subsection (12) of this section, have no further right, title or interest to the personal property and may not claim or sell the property.

(10) If the personal property is presumed to be abandoned under subsection (9) of this section, the landlord then may:

(a) Sell the personal property at a public or private sale, provided that prior to the sale of a recreational vehicle, manufactured dwelling or floating home:

(A) The landlord may seek to transfer the certificate of title and registration to the personal property by complying with the requirements of the appropriate state agency; and

(B) The landlord shall:

(i) Place a notice in a newspaper of general circulation in the county in which the recreational vehicle, manufactured dwelling or floating home is located. The notice shall state:

(I) That the recreational vehicle, manufactured dwelling or floating home is abandoned;

(II) The tenant's and owner's name, if of record or actually known to the landlord;

(III) The address and any space number where the recreational vehicle, manufactured dwelling or floating home is located, and if actually known to the landlord, the plate, registration or other identification number as noted on the certificate of title;

(IV) Whether the sale is by private bidding or public auction;

(V) Whether the landlord is accepting sealed bids and, if so, the last date on which bids will be accepted; and

(VI) The name and telephone number of the person to contact to inspect the recreational vehicle, manufactured dwelling or floating home;

(ii) At a reasonable time prior to the sale, give a copy of the notice required by sub-subparagraph (i) of this subparagraph to the tenant and to any lienholder and owner, by personal delivery or first class mail, except that for any lienholder, mail service shall be by first class mail with certificate of mailing;

(iii) Obtain an affidavit of publication from the newspaper to show that the notice required under sub-subparagraph (i) of this subparagraph ran in the newspaper at least one day in each of two consecutive weeks prior to the date scheduled for the sale or the last date bids will be accepted; and

(iv) Obtain written proof from the county that all property taxes on the manufactured dwelling or floating home have been paid or, if not paid, that the county has authorized the sale, with the sale proceeds to be distributed pursuant to subsection (13) of this section;

(b) Destroy or otherwise dispose of the personal property if the landlord determines that:

(A) For a manufactured dwelling or floating home, the current market value of the property is $8,000 or less as determined by the county assessor; or

(B) For all other personal property, the reasonable current fair market value is $500 or less or so low that the cost of storage and conducting a public sale probably exceeds the amount that would be realized from the sale; or

(c) Consistent with paragraphs (a) and (b) of this subsection, sell certain items and destroy or otherwise dispose of the remaining personal property.

(11)(a) A public or private sale authorized by this section shall:

(A) For a recreational vehicle, manufactured dwelling or floating home, be conducted consistent with the terms listed in subsection (10)(a)(B)(i) of this section. Every aspect of the sale including the method, manner, time, place and terms must be commercially reasonable; or

(B) For all other personal property, be conducted under the provisions of ORS 79.0610.

(b) If there is no buyer at a sale of a manufactured dwelling or floating home, the personal property is considered to be worth $8,000 or less, regardless of current market value, and the landlord shall destroy or otherwise dispose of the personal property.

(12) Notwithstanding ORS 446.155 (1) and (2), unless a landlord intentionally misrepresents the condition of a manufactured dwelling or floating home, the landlord is not liable for the condition of the dwelling or home to:

(a) A buyer of the dwelling or home at a sale, pursuant to subsection (10)(a) of this section, with or without consideration; or

(b) A person or nonprofit organization to whom the landlord gives the dwelling or home pursuant to subsection (1)(b), (10)(b) or (11)(b) of this section.
(13)(a) The landlord may deduct from the proceeds of the sale:
(A) The reasonable or actual cost of notice, storage and sale; and
(B) Unpaid rent.
(b) If the sale was of a manufactured dwelling or floating home, after deducting the amounts listed in paragraph (a) of this subsection, the landlord shall remit the remaining proceeds, if any, to the county tax collector to the extent of any unpaid property taxes owed on the dwelling or home.
(c) If the sale was of a recreational vehicle, manufactured dwelling or floating home, after deducting the amounts listed in paragraphs (a) and (b) of this subsection, if applicable, the landlord shall remit the remaining proceeds, if any, to any lienholder to the extent of any unpaid balance owed on the lien on the recreational vehicle, dwelling or home.
(d) After deducting the amounts listed in paragraphs (a), (b) and (c) of this subsection, if applicable, the landlord shall remit to the tenant or owner the remaining proceeds, if any, together with an itemized accounting.
(e) If the tenant or owner cannot after due diligence be found, the remaining proceeds shall be deposited with the county treasurer of the county in which the sale occurred, and if not claimed within three years shall revert to the general fund of the county available for general purposes.
(14) The county tax collector shall cancel all unpaid property taxes owed on a manufactured dwelling or floating home, as provided under ORS 311.790, only under circumstances described in paragraph (a), (b), (c) or (d) of this subsection:
(a) The landlord disposes of the manufactured dwelling or floating home after a determination described in subsection (10)(b) of this section.
(b) There is no buyer of the manufactured dwelling or floating home at a sale described under subsection (11) of this section.
(c)(A) There is a buyer of the manufactured dwelling or floating home at a sale described under subsection (11) of this section;
(B) The current market value of the manufactured dwelling or floating home is $8,000 or less; and
(C) The proceeds of the sale are insufficient to satisfy the unpaid property taxes owed on the dwelling or home after distribution of the proceeds pursuant to subsection (13) of this section.
(d)(A) The landlord buys the manufactured dwelling or floating home at a sale described under subsection (11) of this section;
(B) The current market value of the manufactured dwelling or floating home is more than $8,000;
(C) The proceeds of the sale are insufficient to satisfy the unpaid property taxes owed on the manufactured dwelling or floating home after distribution of the proceeds pursuant to subsection (13) of this section; and
(D) The landlord disposes of the manufactured dwelling or floating home.
(15) The landlord is not responsible for any loss to the tenant, lienholder or owner resulting from storage of personal property in compliance with this section unless the loss was caused by the landlord's deliberate or negligent act. In the event of a deliberate and malicious violation, the landlord is liable for twice the actual damages sustained by the tenant, lienholder or owner.
(16) Complete compliance in good faith with this section shall constitute a complete defense in any action brought by a tenant, lienholder or owner against a landlord for loss or damage to such personal property disposed of pursuant to this section.
(17) If a landlord does not comply with this section:
(a) The tenant is relieved of any liability for damage to the premises caused by conduct that was not deliberate, intentional or grossly negligent and for unpaid rent and may recover from the landlord up to twice the actual damages sustained by the tenant;
(b) A lienholder or owner aggrieved by the noncompliance may recover from the landlord the actual damages sustained by the lienholder or owner. ORS 90.255 does not authorize an award of attorney fees to the prevailing party in any action arising under this paragraph; and
(c) A county tax collector aggrieved by the noncompliance may recover from the landlord the actual damages sustained by the tax collector, if the noncompliance is part of an effort by the landlord to defraud the tax collector. ORS 90.255 does not authorize an award of attorney fees to the prevailing party in any action arising under this paragraph.
(18) In the case of an abandoned recreational vehicle, manufactured dwelling or floating home, the provisions of this section regarding the rights and responsibilities of a tenant to the abandoned vehicle,

dwelling or home shall also apply to any lienholder except that the lienholder may not sell or remove the vehicle, dwelling or home unless:
(a) The lienholder has foreclosed its lien on the recreational vehicle, manufactured dwelling or floating home;
(b) The tenant or a personal representative or designated person described in subsection (20) of this section has waived all rights under this section pursuant to subsection (24) of this section; or
(c) The notice and response periods provided by subsections (6) and (8) of this section have expired.
(19)(a) In the case of an abandoned manufactured dwelling or floating home but not including a dwelling or home abandoned following a termination pursuant to ORS 90.429 and except as provided by subsection (20)(d) and (e) of this section, if a lienholder makes a timely response to a notice of abandoned personal property pursuant to subsections (6) and (8) of this section and so requests, a landlord shall enter into a written storage agreement with the lienholder providing that the dwelling or home may not be sold or disposed of by the landlord for up to 12 months. A storage agreement entitles the lienholder to store the personal property on the previously rented space during the term of the agreement, but does not entitle anyone to occupy the personal property.
(b) The lienholder's right to a storage agreement arises upon the failure of the tenant, owner or, in the case of a deceased tenant, the personal representative, designated person, heir or devisee to remove or sell the dwelling or home within the allotted time.
(c) To exercise the right to a storage agreement under this subsection, in addition to contacting the landlord with a timely response as described in paragraph (a) of this subsection, the lienholder must enter into the proposed storage agreement within 60 days after the landlord gives a copy of the agreement to the lienholder. The landlord shall give a copy of the proposed storage agreement to the lienholder in the same manner as provided by subsection (4)(b) of this section. The landlord may include a copy of the proposed storage agreement with the notice of abandoned property required by subsection (4) of this section. A lienholder enters into a storage agreement by signing a copy of the agreement provided by the landlord and personally delivering or mailing the signed copy to the landlord within the 60-day period.
(d) The storage agreement may require, in addition to other provisions agreed to by the landlord and the lienholder, that:
(A) The lienholder make timely periodic payment of all storage charges, as described in subsection (7)(d) of this section, accruing from the commencement of the 45-day period described in subsection (6) of this section. A storage charge may include a utility or service charge, as described in ORS 90.510 (8), if limited to charges for electricity, water, sewer service and natural gas and if incidental to the storage of personal property. A storage charge may not be due more frequently than monthly;
(B) The lienholder pay a late charge or fee for failure to pay a storage charge by the date required in the agreement, if the amount of the late charge is no greater than for late charges described in the rental agreement between the landlord and the tenant; and
(C) The lienholder maintain the personal property and the space on which the personal property is stored in a manner consistent with the rights and obligations described in the rental agreement between the landlord and the tenant.
(e) During the term of an agreement described under this subsection, the lienholder shall have the right to remove or sell the property, subject to the provisions of its lien. Selling the property includes a sale to a purchaser who wishes to leave the dwelling or home on the rented space and become a tenant, subject to any conditions previously agreed to by the landlord and tenant regarding the landlord's approval of a purchaser or, if there was no such agreement, any reasonable conditions by the landlord regarding approval of any purchaser who wishes to leave the dwelling or home on the rented space and become a tenant. The landlord also may condition approval for occupancy of any purchaser of the property upon payment of all unpaid storage charges and maintenance costs.
(f)(A) If the lienholder violates the storage agreement, the landlord may terminate the agreement by giving at least 90 days' written notice to the lienholder stating facts sufficient to notify the lienholder of the reason for the termination. Unless the lienholder corrects the violation within the notice period, the agreement terminates as provided and the landlord may sell or dispose of the dwelling or home without further notice to the lienholder.
(B) After a landlord gives a termination notice pursuant to subparagraph (A) of this paragraph for failure of the lienholder to pay a storage charge and the lienholder corrects the violation, if the lienholder again violates the storage agreement by failing to pay a sub-

sequent storage charge, the landlord may terminate the agreement by giving at least 30 days' written notice to the lienholder stating facts sufficient to notify the lienholder of the reason for termination. Unless the lienholder corrects the violation within the notice period, the agreement terminates as provided and the landlord may sell or dispose of the property without further notice to the lienholder.
(C) A lienholder may terminate a storage agreement at any time upon at least 14 days' written notice to the landlord and may remove the property from the rented space if the lienholder has paid all storage charges and other charges as provided in the agreement.
(g) Upon the failure of a lienholder to enter into a storage agreement as provided by this subsection or upon termination of an agreement, unless the parties otherwise agree or the lienholder has sold or removed the manufactured dwelling or floating home, the landlord may sell or dispose of the property pursuant to this section without further notice to the lienholder.
(20) If the personal property consists of an abandoned manufactured dwelling or floating home and is considered abandoned as a result of the death of a tenant who was the only tenant and who owned the dwelling or home, this section applies, except as follows:
(a) Any personal representative named in a will or appointed by a court to act for the deceased tenant or any person designated in writing by the tenant to be contacted by the landlord in the event of the tenant's death has the same rights and responsibilities regarding the abandoned dwelling or home as a tenant.
(b) The notice required by subsection (3) of this section shall be:
(A) Sent by first class mail to the deceased tenant at the premises; and
(B) Personally delivered or sent by first class mail to any personal representative or designated person if actually known to the landlord.
(c) The notice described in subsection (5) of this section shall refer to any personal representative or designated person, instead of the deceased tenant, and shall incorporate the provisions of this subsection.
(d) If a personal representative, designated person or other person entitled to possession of the property, such as an heir or devisee, responds by actual notice to a landlord within the 45-day period provided by subsection (6) of this section and so requests, the landlord shall enter into a written storage agreement with the representative or person providing that the dwelling or home may not be sold or disposed of by the landlord for up to 90 days or until conclusion of any probate proceedings, whichever is later. A storage agreement entitles the representative or person to store the personal property on the previously rented space during the term of the agreement, but does not entitle anyone to occupy the personal property. If such an agreement is entered, the landlord may not enter a similar agreement with a lienholder pursuant to subsection (19) of this section until the agreement with the personal representative or designated person ends.
(e) If a personal representative or other person requests that a landlord enter into a storage agreement, subsection (19)(c), (d) and (f)(C) of this section apply, with the representative or person having the rights and responsibilities of a lienholder with regard to the storage agreement.
(f) During the term of an agreement described under paragraph (d) of this subsection, the representative or person shall have the right to remove or sell the dwelling or home, including a sale to a purchaser or a transfer to an heir or devisee where the purchaser, heir or devisee wishes to leave the dwelling or home on the rented space and become a tenant, subject to any conditions previously agreed to by the landlord and tenant regarding the landlord's approval for occupancy of a purchaser, heir or devisee or, if there was no such agreement, any reasonable conditions by the landlord regarding approval for occupancy of any purchaser, heir or devisee who wishes to leave the dwelling or home on the rented space and become a tenant. The landlord also may condition approval for occupancy of any purchaser, heir or devisee of the dwelling or home upon payment of all unpaid storage charges and maintenance costs.
(g) If the representative or person violates the storage agreement, the landlord may terminate the agreement by giving at least 30 days' written notice to the representative or person stating facts sufficient to notify the representative or person of the reason for the termination. Unless the representative or person corrects the violation within the notice period, the agreement terminates as provided and the landlord may sell or dispose of the dwelling or home without further notice to the representative or person.
(h) Upon the failure of a representative or person to enter into a storage agreement as provided by this subsection or upon termination of an agreement, unless the parties otherwise agree or the representative or person has sold or removed the manufactured

dwelling or floating home, the landlord may sell or dispose of the property pursuant to this section without further notice to the representative or person.

(21) If a governmental agency determines that the condition of a manufactured dwelling, floating home or recreational vehicle abandoned under this section constitutes an extreme health or safety hazard under state or local law and the agency determines that the hazard endangers others in the facility and requires quick removal of the property, the landlord may sell or dispose of the property pursuant to this subsection. The landlord shall comply with all provisions of this section, except as follows:

(a) The date provided in subsection (6) of this section by which a tenant, lienholder, owner, personal representative or designated person must contact a landlord to arrange for the disposition of the property shall be not less than 15 days after personal delivery or mailing of the notice required by subsection (3) of this section.

(b) The date provided in subsections (8) and (9) of this section by which a tenant, lienholder, owner, personal representative or designated person must remove the property shall be not less than seven days after the tenant, lienholder, owner, personal representative or designated person contacts the landlord.

(c) The notice required by subsection (3) of this section shall be as provided in subsection (5) of this section, except that:

(A) The dates and deadlines in the notice for contacting the landlord and removing the property shall be consistent with this subsection;

(B) The notice shall state that a governmental agency has determined that the property constitutes an extreme health or safety hazard and must be removed quickly; and

(C) The landlord shall attach a copy of the agency's determination to the notice.

(d) If the tenant, a lienholder, owner, personal representative or designated person does not remove the property within the time allowed, the landlord or a buyer at a sale by the landlord under subsection (11) of this section shall promptly remove the property from the facility.

(e) A landlord is not required to enter into a storage agreement with a lienholder, owner, personal representative or designated person pursuant to subsection (19) of this section.

(22) In the case of an abandoned recreational vehicle, manufactured dwelling or floating home that is owned by someone other than the tenant, the provisions of this section regarding the rights and responsibilities of a tenant to the abandoned vehicle, dwelling or home shall also apply to that owner, with regard only to the vehicle, dwelling or home, and not to any goods left inside or outside the vehicle, dwelling or home.

(23) In the case of an abandoned motor vehicle, the procedure authorized by ORS 98.830 and 98.835 for removal of abandoned motor vehicles from private property may be used by a landlord as an alternative to the procedures required in this section.

(24)(a) A landlord may sell or dispose of a tenant's abandoned personal property without complying with the provisions of this section if, after termination of the tenancy or no more than seven days prior to the termination of the tenancy, the following parties so agree in a writing entered into in good faith:

(A) The landlord;

(B) The tenant, or for an abandonment as the result of the death of a tenant who was the only tenant, the personal representative, designated person or other person entitled to possession of the personal property, such as an heir or devisee, as described in subsection (20) of this section; and

(C) In the case of a manufactured dwelling, floating home or recreational vehicle, any owner and any lienholder.

(b) A landlord may not, as part of a rental agreement, require a tenant, a personal representative, a designated person or any lienholder or owner to waive any right provided by this section.

(25) Until personal property is conclusively presumed to be abandoned under subsection (9) of this section, a landlord does not have a lien pursuant to ORS 87.152 for storing the personal property.

Note: The 2003 Legislative Session enacted amendments to ORS 90.425 with an operative date of May 1, 2005. The foregoing is the text of the statute that is in effect until then. The text of the statute that will become effective on May 1, 2005 is included below.

90.425 Disposition of personal property abandoned by tenant; notice; sale; tax cancellation; storage agreements; hazardous property. (1) As used in this section:

(a) "Current market value" means the amount in cash, as determined by the county assessor, that could reasonably be expected to be paid for a manu-

factured dwelling or floating home by an informed buyer to an informed seller, each acting without compulsion in an arm's length transaction occurring on the assessment date for the tax year or on the date of a subsequent reappraisal by the county assessor.
(b) "Dispose of the personal property" means that, if reasonably appropriate, the landlord may throw away the property or may give it without consideration to a nonprofit organization or to a person unrelated to the landlord. The landlord may not retain the property for personal use or benefit.
(c) "Goods" includes those goods left inside a recreational vehicle, manufactured dwelling or floating home or left upon the rental space outside a recreational vehicle, manufactured dwelling or floating home, whether the recreational vehicle, dwelling or home is located inside or outside of a facility.
(d) "Lienholder" means any lienholder of an abandoned recreational vehicle, manufactured dwelling or floating home, if the lien is of record or the lienholder is actually known to the landlord.
(e) "Of record" means:
(A) For a recreational vehicle that is not a manufactured structure as defined in ORS 446.561, that a security interest has been properly recorded with the Department of Transportation pursuant to ORS 802.200 (1)(a)(A) and 803.097.
(B) For a manufactured dwelling or recreational vehicle that is a manufactured structure as defined in ORS 446.551, that a security interest has been properly recorded for the manufactured dwelling or recreational vehicle in the records of the Department of Consumer and Business Services pursuant to ORS 446.611 or on a certificate of title issued by the Department of Transportation prior to July 1, 2004.
(C) For a floating home, that a security interest has been properly recorded with the State Marine Board pursuant to ORS 830.740 to 830.755 for a home registered and titled with the board pursuant to ORS 830.715.
(f) "Owner" means any owner of an abandoned recreational vehicle, manufactured dwelling or floating home, if different from the tenant and either of record or actually known to the landlord.
(g) "Personal property" means goods, vehicles and recreational vehicles and includes manufactured dwellings and floating homes not located in a facility. "Personal property" does not include manufactured dwellings and floating homes located in a facility and therefore subject to being stored, sold or disposed of as provided under ORS 90.675.

(2) A landlord may not store, sell or dispose of abandoned personal property except as provided by this section. This section governs the rights and obligations of landlords, tenants and any lienholders or owners in any personal property abandoned or left upon the premises by the tenant or any lienholder or owner in the following circumstances:
(a) The tenancy has ended by termination or expiration of a rental agreement or by relinquishment or abandonment of the premises and the landlord reasonably believes under all the circumstances that the tenant has left the personal property upon the premises with no intention of asserting any further claim to the premises or to the personal property;
(b) The tenant has been absent from the premises continuously for seven days after termination of a tenancy by a court order that has not been executed; or
(c) The landlord receives possession of the premises from the sheriff following restitution pursuant to ORS 105.165.
(3) Prior to selling or disposing of the tenant's personal property under this section, the landlord must give a written notice to the tenant that must be:
(a) Personally delivered to the tenant; or
(b) Sent by first class mail addressed and mailed to the tenant at:
(A) The premises;
(B) Any post-office box held by the tenant and actually known to the landlord; and
(C) The most recent forwarding address if provided by the tenant or actually known to the landlord.
(4)(a) In addition to the notice required by subsection (3) of this section, in the case of an abandoned recreational vehicle, manufactured dwelling or floating home, a landlord shall also give a copy of the notice described in subsection (3) of this section to:
(A) Any lienholder of the recreational vehicle, manufactured dwelling or floating home;
(B) Any owner of the recreational vehicle, manufactured dwelling or floating home;
(C) The tax collector of the county where the manufactured dwelling or floating home is located; and
(D) The assessor of the county where the manufactured dwelling or floating home is located.
(b) The landlord shall give the notice copy required by this subsection by personal delivery or first class mail, except that for any lienholder, mail service shall be both by first class mail and by certified mail with return receipt requested.
(c) A notice to lienholders under paragraph (a)(A)

of this subsection must be sent to each lienholder at each address:
(A) Actually known to the landlord;
(B) Of record; and
(C) Provided to the landlord by the lienholder in a written notice that identifies the personal property subject to the lien and that was sent to the landlord by certified mail with return receipt requested within the preceding five years. The notice must identify the personal property by describing the physical address of the property.
(5) The notice required under subsection (3) of this section must state that:
(a) The personal property left upon the premises is considered abandoned;
(b) The tenant or any lienholder or owner must contact the landlord by a specified date, as provided in subsection (6) of this section, to arrange for the removal of the abandoned personal property;
(c) The personal property is stored at a place of safekeeping, except that if the property includes a manufactured dwelling or floating home, the dwelling or home shall be stored on the rented space;
(d) The tenant or any lienholder or owner, except as provided by subsection (18) of this section, may arrange for removal of the personal property by contacting the landlord at a described telephone number or address on or before the specified date;
(e) The landlord shall make the personal property available for removal by the tenant or any lienholder or owner, except as provided by subsection (18) of this section, by appointment at reasonable times;
(f) If the personal property is considered to be abandoned pursuant to subsection (2)(a) or (b) of this section, the landlord may require payment of removal and storage charges, as provided by subsection (7)(d) of this section, prior to releasing the personal property to the tenant or any lienholder or owner;
(g) If the personal property is considered to be abandoned pursuant to subsection (2)(c) of this section, the landlord may not require payment of storage charges prior to releasing the personal property;
(h) If the tenant or any lienholder or owner fails to contact the landlord by the specified date, or after that contact, fails to remove the personal property within 30 days for recreational vehicles, manufactured dwellings and floating homes or 15 days for all other personal property, the landlord may sell or dispose of the personal property. If the landlord reasonably believes that the personal property will be eligible for disposal pursuant to subsection (10)(b) of this section and the landlord intends to dispose of the property if it is not claimed, the notice shall state that belief and intent; and
(i) If the personal property includes a recreational vehicle, manufactured dwelling or floating home and if applicable, there is a lienholder or owner that has a right to claim the recreational vehicle, dwelling or home, except as provided by subsection (18) of this section.
(6) For purposes of subsection (5) of this section, the specified date by which a tenant, lienholder or owner must contact a landlord to arrange for the disposition of abandoned personal property is:
(a) For abandoned recreational vehicles, manufactured dwellings or floating homes, not less than 45 days after personal delivery or mailing of the notice; or
(b) For all other abandoned personal property, not less than five days after personal delivery or eight days after mailing of the notice.
(7) After notifying the tenant as required by subsection (3) of this section, the landlord:
(a) Shall store any abandoned manufactured dwelling or floating home on the rented space and shall exercise reasonable care for the dwelling or home;
(b) Shall store all other abandoned personal property of the tenant, including goods left inside a recreational vehicle, manufactured dwelling or floating home or left upon the rented space outside a recreational vehicle, dwelling or home, in a place of safekeeping and shall exercise reasonable care for the personal property, except that the landlord may:
(A) Promptly dispose of rotting food; and
(B) Allow an animal control agency to remove any abandoned pets or livestock. If an animal control agency will not remove the abandoned pets or livestock, the landlord shall exercise reasonable care for the animals given all the circumstances, including the type and condition of the animals, and may give the animals to an agency that is willing and able to care for the animals, such as a humane society or similar organization;
(c) Except for manufactured dwellings and floating homes, may store the abandoned personal property at the dwelling unit, move and store it elsewhere on the premises or move and store it at a commercial storage company or other place of safekeeping; and
(d) Is entitled to reasonable or actual storage charges and costs incidental to storage or disposal, including any cost of removal to a place of storage. In the case

of an abandoned manufactured dwelling or floating home, the storage charge shall be no greater than the monthly space rent last payable by the tenant.
(8) If a tenant, lienholder or owner, upon the receipt of the notice provided by subsection (3) or (4) of this section or otherwise, responds by actual notice to the landlord on or before the specified date in the landlord's notice that the tenant, lienholder or owner intends to remove the personal property from the premises or from the place of safekeeping, the landlord must make that personal property available for removal by the tenant, lienholder or owner by appointment at reasonable times during the 15 days or, in the case of a recreational vehicle, manufactured dwelling or floating home, 30 days following the date of the response, subject to subsection (18) of this section. If the personal property is considered to be abandoned pursuant to subsection (2)(a) or (b) of this section, but not pursuant to subsection (2)(c) of this section, the landlord may require payment of removal and storage charges, as provided in subsection (7)(d) of this section, prior to allowing the tenant, lienholder or owner to remove the personal property. Acceptance by a landlord of such payment does not operate to create or reinstate a tenancy or create a waiver pursuant to ORS 90.415.
(9) Except as provided in subsections (18) to (20) of this section, if the tenant, lienholder or owner of a recreational vehicle, manufactured dwelling or floating home does not respond within the time provided by the landlord's notice, or the tenant, lienholder or owner does not remove the personal property within the time required by subsection (8) of this section or by any date agreed to with the landlord, whichever is later, the tenant's, lienholder's or owner's personal property is conclusively presumed to be abandoned. The tenant and any lienholder or owner that have been given notice pursuant to subsection (3) or (4) of this section shall, except with regard to the distribution of sale proceeds pursuant to subsection (13) of this section, have no further right, title or interest to the personal property and may not claim or sell the property.
(10) If the personal property is presumed to be abandoned under subsection (9) of this section, the landlord then may:
(a) Sell the personal property at a public or private sale, provided that prior to the sale of a recreational vehicle, manufactured dwelling or floating home:
(A) The landlord may seek to transfer the certificate of title and registration to the personal property by complying with the requirements of the appropriate state agency; and
(B) The landlord shall:
(i) Place a notice in a newspaper of general circulation in the county in which the recreational vehicle, manufactured dwelling or floating home is located. The notice shall state:
(I) That the recreational vehicle, manufactured dwelling or floating home is abandoned;
(II) The tenant's and owner's name, if of record or actually known to the landlord;
(III) The address and any space number where the recreational vehicle, manufactured dwelling or floating home is located, and any plate, registration or other identification number for a recreational vehicle or floating home noted on the certificate of title, if actually known to the landlord;
(IV) Whether the sale is by private bidding or public auction;
(V) Whether the landlord is accepting sealed bids and, if so, the last date on which bids will be accepted; and
(VI) The name and telephone number of the person to contact to inspect the recreational vehicle, manufactured dwelling or floating home;
(ii) At a reasonable time prior to the sale, give a copy of the notice required by sub-subparagraph (i) of this subparagraph to the tenant and to any lienholder and owner, by personal delivery or first class mail, except that for any lienholder, mail service must be by first class mail with certificate of mailing;
(iii) Obtain an affidavit of publication from the newspaper to show that the notice required under sub-subparagraph (i) of this subparagraph ran in the newspaper at least one day in each of two consecutive weeks prior to the date scheduled for the sale or the last date bids will be accepted; and
(iv) Obtain written proof from the county that all property taxes on the manufactured dwelling or floating home have been paid or, if not paid, that the county has authorized the sale, with the sale proceeds to be distributed pursuant to subsection (13) of this section;
(b) Destroy or otherwise dispose of the personal property if the landlord determines that:
(A) For a manufactured dwelling or floating home, the current market value of the property is $8,000 or less as determined by the county assessor; or
(B) For all other personal property, the reasonable current fair market value is $500 or less or so low that the cost of storage and conducting a public sale

probably exceeds the amount that would be realized from the sale; or

(c) Consistent with paragraphs (a) and (b) of this subsection, sell certain items and destroy or otherwise dispose of the remaining personal property.

(11)(a) A public or private sale authorized by this section must:

(A) For a recreational vehicle, manufactured dwelling or floating home, be conducted consistent with the terms listed in subsection (10)(a)(B)(i) of this section. Every aspect of the sale including the method, manner, time, place and terms must be commercially reasonable; or

(B) For all other personal property, be conducted under the provisions of ORS 79.0610.

(b) If there is no buyer at a sale of a manufactured dwelling or floating home, the personal property is considered to be worth $8,000 or less, regardless of current market value, and the landlord shall destroy or otherwise dispose of the personal property.

(12) Notwithstanding ORS 446.155 (1) and (2), unless a landlord intentionally misrepresents the condition of a manufactured dwelling or floating home, the landlord is not liable for the condition of the dwelling or home to:

(a) A buyer of the dwelling or home at a sale pursuant to subsection (10)(a) of this section, with or without consideration; or

(b) A person or nonprofit organization to whom the landlord gives the dwelling or home pursuant to subsection (1)(b), (10)(b) or (11)(b) of this section.

(13)(a) The landlord may deduct from the proceeds of the sale:

(A) The reasonable or actual cost of notice, storage and sale; and

(B) Unpaid rent.

(b) If the sale was of a manufactured dwelling or floating home, after deducting the amounts listed in paragraph (a) of this subsection, the landlord shall remit the remaining proceeds, if any, to the county tax collector to the extent of any unpaid property taxes owed on the dwelling or home.

(c) If the sale was of a recreational vehicle, manufactured dwelling or floating home, after deducting the amounts listed in paragraphs (a) and (b) of this subsection, if applicable, the landlord shall remit the remaining proceeds, if any, to any lienholder to the extent of any unpaid balance owed on the lien on the recreational vehicle, dwelling or home.

(d) After deducting the amounts listed in paragraphs (a), (b) and (c) of this subsection, if applicable, the landlord shall remit to the tenant or owner the remaining proceeds, if any, together with an itemized accounting.

(e) If the tenant or owner cannot after due diligence be found, the remaining proceeds shall be deposited with the county treasurer of the county in which the sale occurred. If not claimed within three years the deposited proceeds revert to the general fund of the county available for general purposes.

(14) The county tax collector shall cancel all unpaid property taxes owed on a manufactured dwelling or floating home, as provided under ORS 311.790, only under one of the following circumstances:

(a) The landlord disposes of the manufactured dwelling or floating home after a determination described in subsection (10)(b) of this section.

(b) There is no buyer of the manufactured dwelling or floating home at a sale described under subsection (11) of this section.

(c)(A) There is a buyer of the manufactured dwelling or floating home at a sale described under subsection (11) of this section;

(B) The current market value of the manufactured dwelling or floating home is $8,000 or less; and

(C) The proceeds of the sale are insufficient to satisfy the unpaid property taxes owed on the dwelling or home after distribution of the proceeds pursuant to subsection (13) of this section.

(d)(A) The landlord buys the manufactured dwelling or floating home at a sale described under subsection (11) of this section;

(B) The current market value of the manufactured dwelling or floating home is more than $8,000;

(C) The proceeds of the sale are insufficient to satisfy the unpaid property taxes owed on the manufactured dwelling or floating home after distribution of the proceeds pursuant to subsection (13) of this section; and

(D) The landlord disposes of the manufactured dwelling or floating home.

(15) The landlord is not responsible for any loss to the tenant, lienholder or owner resulting from storage of personal property in compliance with this section unless the loss was caused by the landlord's deliberate or negligent act. In the event of a deliberate and malicious violation, the landlord is liable for twice the actual damages sustained by the tenant, lienholder or owner.

(16) Complete compliance in good faith with this section shall constitute a complete defense in any action

brought by a tenant, lienholder or owner against a landlord for loss or damage to such personal property disposed of pursuant to this section.
(17) If a landlord does not comply with this section:
(a) The tenant is relieved of any liability for damage to the premises caused by conduct that was not deliberate, intentional or grossly negligent and for unpaid rent and may recover from the landlord up to twice the actual damages sustained by the tenant;
(b) A lienholder or owner aggrieved by the noncompliance may recover from the landlord the actual damages sustained by the lienholder or owner. ORS 90.255 does not authorize an award of attorney fees to the prevailing party in any action arising under this paragraph; and
(c) A county tax collector aggrieved by the noncompliance may recover from the landlord the actual damages sustained by the tax collector, if the noncompliance is part of an effort by the landlord to defraud the tax collector. ORS 90.255 does not authorize an award of attorney fees to the prevailing party in any action arising under this paragraph.
(18) In the case of an abandoned recreational vehicle, manufactured dwelling or floating home, the provisions of this section regarding the rights and responsibilities of a tenant to the abandoned vehicle, dwelling or home shall also apply to any lienholder except that the lienholder may not sell or remove the vehicle, dwelling or home unless:
(a) The lienholder has foreclosed its lien on the recreational vehicle, manufactured dwelling or floating home;
(b) The tenant or a personal representative or designated person described in subsection (20) of this section has waived all rights under this section pursuant to subsection (24) of this section; or
(c) The notice and response periods provided by subsections (6) and (8) of this section have expired.
(19)(a) In the case of an abandoned manufactured dwelling or floating home but not including a dwelling or home abandoned following a termination pursuant to ORS 90.429 and except as provided by subsection (20)(d) and (e) of this section, if a lienholder makes a timely response to a notice of abandoned personal property pursuant to subsections (6) and (8) of this section and so requests, a landlord shall enter into a written storage agreement with the lienholder providing that the dwelling or home may not be sold or disposed of by the landlord for up to 12 months. A storage agreement entitles the lienholder to store the personal property on the previously rented space during the term of the agreement, but does not entitle anyone to occupy the personal property.
(b) The lienholder's right to a storage agreement arises upon the failure of the tenant, owner or, in the case of a deceased tenant, the personal representative, designated person, heir or devisee to remove or sell the dwelling or home within the allotted time.
(c) To exercise the right to a storage agreement under this subsection, in addition to contacting the landlord with a timely response as described in paragraph (a) of this subsection, the lienholder must enter into the proposed storage agreement within 60 days after the landlord gives a copy of the agreement to the lienholder. The landlord shall give a copy of the proposed storage agreement to the lienholder in the same manner as provided by subsection (4)(b) of this section. The landlord may include a copy of the proposed storage agreement with the notice of abandoned property required by subsection (4) of this section. A lienholder enters into a storage agreement by signing a copy of the agreement provided by the landlord and personally delivering or mailing the signed copy to the landlord within the 60-day period.
(d) The storage agreement may require, in addition to other provisions agreed to by the landlord and the lienholder, that:
(A) The lienholder make timely periodic payment of all storage charges, as described in subsection (7)(d) of this section, accruing from the commencement of the 45-day period described in subsection (6) of this section. A storage charge may include a utility or service charge, as described in ORS 90.510 (8), if limited to charges for electricity, water, sewer service and natural gas and if incidental to the storage of personal property. A storage charge may not be due more frequently than monthly;
(B) The lienholder pay a late charge or fee for failure to pay a storage charge by the date required in the agreement, if the amount of the late charge is no greater than for late charges described in the rental agreement between the landlord and the tenant; and
(C) The lienholder maintain the personal property and the space on which the personal property is stored in a manner consistent with the rights and obligations described in the rental agreement between the landlord and the tenant.
(e) During the term of an agreement described under this subsection, the lienholder has the right to remove or sell the property, subject to the provisions

of the lien. Selling the property includes a sale to a purchaser who wishes to leave the dwelling or home on the rented space and become a tenant, subject to any conditions previously agreed to by the landlord and tenant regarding the landlord's approval of a purchaser or, if there was no such agreement, any reasonable conditions by the landlord regarding approval of any purchaser who wishes to leave the dwelling or home on the rented space and become a tenant. The landlord also may condition approval for occupancy of any purchaser of the property upon payment of all unpaid storage charges and maintenance costs.

(f)(A) If the lienholder violates the storage agreement, the landlord may terminate the agreement by giving at least 90 days' written notice to the lienholder stating facts sufficient to notify the lienholder of the reason for the termination. Unless the lienholder corrects the violation within the notice period, the agreement terminates as provided and the landlord may sell or dispose of the dwelling or home without further notice to the lienholder.

(B) After a landlord gives a termination notice pursuant to subparagraph (A) of this paragraph for failure of the lienholder to pay a storage charge and the lienholder corrects the violation, if the lienholder again violates the storage agreement by failing to pay a subsequent storage charge, the landlord may terminate the agreement by giving at least 30 days' written notice to the lienholder stating facts sufficient to notify the lienholder of the reason for termination. Unless the lienholder corrects the violation within the notice period, the agreement terminates as provided and the landlord may sell or dispose of the property without further notice to the lienholder.

(C) A lienholder may terminate a storage agreement at any time upon at least 14 days' written notice to the landlord and may remove the property from the rented space if the lienholder has paid all storage charges and other charges as provided in the agreement.

(g) Upon the failure of a lienholder to enter into a storage agreement as provided by this subsection or upon termination of an agreement, unless the parties otherwise agree or the lienholder has sold or removed the manufactured dwelling or floating home, the landlord may sell or dispose of the property pursuant to this section without further notice to the lienholder.

(20) If the personal property consists of an abandoned manufactured dwelling or floating home and is considered abandoned as a result of the death of a tenant who was the only tenant and who owned the dwelling or home, this section applies, except as follows:

(a) Any personal representative named in a will or appointed by a court to act for the deceased tenant or any person designated in writing by the tenant to be contacted by the landlord in the event of the tenant's death has the same rights and responsibilities regarding the abandoned dwelling or home as a tenant.

(b) The notice required by subsection (3) of this section must be:

(A) Sent by first class mail to the deceased tenant at the premises; and

(B) Personally delivered or sent by first class mail to any personal representative or designated person if actually known to the landlord.

(c) The notice described in subsection (5) of this section must refer to any personal representative or designated person, instead of the deceased tenant, and must incorporate the provisions of this subsection.

(d) If a personal representative, designated person or other person entitled to possession of the property, such as an heir or devisee, responds by actual notice to a landlord within the 45-day period provided by subsection (6) of this section and so requests, the landlord shall enter into a written storage agreement with the representative or person providing that the dwelling or home may not be sold or disposed of by the landlord for up to 90 days or until conclusion of any probate proceedings, whichever is later. A storage agreement entitles the representative or person to store the personal property on the previously rented space during the term of the agreement, but does not entitle anyone to occupy the personal property. If such an agreement is entered, the landlord may not enter a similar agreement with a lienholder pursuant to subsection (19) of this section until the agreement with the personal representative or designated person ends.

(e) If a personal representative or other person requests that a landlord enter into a storage agreement, subsection (19)(c), (d) and (f)(C) of this section applies, with the representative or person having the rights and responsibilities of a lienholder with regard to the storage agreement.

(f) During the term of an agreement described under paragraph (d) of this subsection, the representative or person shall have the right to remove or sell the dwelling or home, including a sale to a purchaser or a transfer to an heir or devisee where the purchaser, heir or devisee wishes to leave the dwelling or home on the rented space and become a tenant, subject to any conditions previously agreed to by the landlord and tenant regarding the landlord's approval for occupancy of a purchaser, heir or devisee or, if there was no such agreement, any reasonable conditions by the landlord regarding approval for occupancy of any purchaser, heir or devisee who wishes to leave the dwelling or home on the rented space and become a tenant. The landlord also may condition approval for occupancy of any purchaser, heir or devisee of the dwelling or home upon payment of all unpaid storage charges and maintenance costs.

(g) If the representative or person violates the storage agreement, the landlord may terminate the agreement by giving at least 30 days' written notice to the representative or person stating facts sufficient to notify the representative or person of the reason for the termination. Unless the representative or person corrects the violation within the notice period, the agreement terminates as provided and the landlord may sell or dispose of the dwelling or home without further notice to the representative or person.

(h) Upon the failure of a representative or person to enter into a storage agreement as provided by this subsection or upon termination of an agreement, unless the parties otherwise agree or the representative or person has sold or removed the manufactured dwelling or floating home, the landlord may sell or dispose of the property pursuant to this section without further notice to the representative or person.

(21) If a governmental agency determines that the condition of a manufactured dwelling, floating home or recreational vehicle abandoned under this section constitutes an extreme health or safety hazard under state or local law and the agency determines that the hazard endangers others in the facility and requires quick removal of the property, the landlord may sell or dispose of the property pursuant to this subsection. The landlord shall comply with all provisions of this section, except as follows:

(a) The date provided in subsection (6) of this section by which a tenant, lienholder, owner, personal representative or designated person must contact a landlord to arrange for the disposition of the property must be not less than 15 days after personal delivery or mailing of the notice required by subsection (3) of this section.

(b) The date provided in subsections (8) and (9) of this section by which a tenant, lienholder, owner, personal representative or designated person must remove the property must be not less than seven days after the tenant, lienholder, owner, personal representative or designated person contacts the landlord.

(c) The notice required by subsection (3) of this section must be as provided in subsection (5) of this section, except that:

(A) The dates and deadlines in the notice for contacting the landlord and removing the property must be consistent with this subsection;

(B) The notice must state that a governmental agency has determined that the property constitutes an extreme health or safety hazard and must be removed quickly; and

(C) The landlord shall attach a copy of the agency's determination to the notice.

(d) If the tenant, a lienholder, owner, personal representative or designated person does not remove the property within the time allowed, the landlord or a buyer at a sale by the landlord under subsection (11) of this section shall promptly remove the property from the facility.

(e) A landlord is not required to enter into a storage agreement with a lienholder, owner, personal representative or designated person pursuant to subsection (19) of this section.

(22) In the case of an abandoned recreational vehicle, manufactured dwelling or floating home that is owned by someone other than the tenant, the provisions of this section regarding the rights and responsibilities of a tenant to the abandoned vehicle, dwelling or home shall also apply to that owner, with regard only to the vehicle, dwelling or home, and not to any goods left inside or outside the vehicle, dwelling or home.

(23) In the case of an abandoned motor vehicle, the procedure authorized by ORS 98.830 and 98.835 for removal of abandoned motor vehicles from private property may be used by a landlord as an alternative to the procedures required in this section.

(24)(a) A landlord may sell or dispose of a tenant's abandoned personal property without complying with the provisions of this section if, after termination of the tenancy or no more than seven days prior to the termination of the tenancy, the following parties so agree in a writing entered into in good faith:

(A) The landlord;

(B) The tenant, or for an abandonment as the result of the death of a tenant who was the only tenant, the personal representative, designated person or other person entitled to possession of the personal proper-

ty, such as an heir or devisee, as described in subsection (20) of this section; and
(C) In the case of a manufactured dwelling, floating home or recreational vehicle, any owner and any lienholder.
(b) A landlord may not, as part of a rental agreement, require a tenant, a personal representative, a designated person or any lienholder or owner to waive any right provided by this section.
(25) Until personal property is conclusively presumed to be abandoned under subsection (9) of this section, a landlord does not have a lien pursuant to ORS 87.152 for storing the personal property.
Note: For transition provisions regarding secured transactions, see notes under 79.0628.

90.427 Termination of periodic tenancies; landlord remedies for tenant holdover. (1) The landlord or the tenant may terminate a week-to-week tenancy by a written notice given to the other at least 10 days before the termination date specified in the notice.
(2) The landlord or the tenant may terminate a month-to-month tenancy by giving to the other, at any time during the tenancy, not less than 30 days' notice in writing prior to the date designated in the notice for the termination of the tenancy.
(3) The tenancy shall terminate on the date designated and without regard to the expiration of the period for which, by the terms of the tenancy, rents are to be paid. Unless otherwise agreed, rent is uniformly apportionable from day to day.
(4) If the tenant remains in possession without the landlord's consent after expiration of the term of the rental agreement or its termination, the landlord may bring an action for possession. In addition, the landlord may recover from the tenant any actual damages resulting from the tenant holding over, including the value of any rent accruing from the expiration or termination of the rental agreement until the landlord knows or should know that the tenant has relinquished possession to the landlord. If the landlord consents to the tenant's continued occupancy, ORS 90.240 (6) applies.
(5) Subsections (1) and (2) of this section shall not apply to a month-to-month tenancy subject to ORS 90.429 or other tenancy created by a rental agreement subject to ORS 90.505 to 90.840.
90.429 Termination of tenancy for certain rented spaces not covered by ORS 90.505 to 90.840. If a tenancy consists of rented space for a manufactured dwelling or floating home that is owned by the tenant, but the tenancy is not subject to ORS 90.505 to 90.840 because the space is not in a facility, the landlord may terminate a month-to-month tenancy without a cause specified in ORS 90.400 only by delivering a written notice of termination to the tenant not less than 180 days before the termination date designated in that notice.
90.430 Claims for possession, rent, damages after termination of rental agreement. If the rental agreement is terminated, the landlord may have a claim for possession and for rent and a separate claim for actual damages for breach of the rental agreement.
90.435 Limitation on recovery of possession of premises. A landlord may not recover or take possession of the dwelling unit by action or otherwise, including willful diminution of services to the tenant by interrupting or causing the interruption of heat, running water, hot water, electricity or other essential service to the tenant, except in case of abandonment, relinquishment or as permitted in this chapter in the manner provided in ORS 105.105 to 105.168.

MISCELLANEOUS

90.450 Right of city to recover from owner for costs of relocating tenant due to condemnation; defense. (1) A city with a population that exceeds 300,000 shall have a right of action against the owner of any premises to recover the reasonable costs of relocation incurred by the city because the condition of the premises causes condemnation and relocation of the tenants at public expense. In order to recover the costs, the city must allege and prove that, due to action or inaction of the owner, the premises are or have been in multiple and material violation of applicable health or safety codes for a period of more than 30 days and that the violation endangers the health or safety of the tenants or the public, or both.
(2) It shall be an affirmative defense to recovery of relocation costs incurred for any tenant that the condition was caused by the action or negligence of that tenant.
(3) The official responsible for city code enforcement shall notify the owner in writing when the official finds the premises to be in a condition that may cause tenant relocation. The notice shall also inform the owner of the potential liability for relocation costs.
(4) A landlord may not terminate a rental agreement because of the receipt of the notice required by subsection (3) of this section except for the reasons set forth in ORS 90.385 (4). The owner is not liable for

tenant relocation costs if the termination is for the reasons set forth in ORS 90.385 (4)(b).
(5) The action provided in subsection (1) of this section is in addition to any other action that may be brought against an owner under any other provision of law.
90.453 Termination by tenant who is victim of domestic violence, sexual assault or stalking; verification statement. (1) As used in this section, "verification" means:
(a) A copy of a valid order of protection issued by a court pursuant to ORS 30.866, 107.095 (1)(c), 107.716, 107.718, 124.015. 124.020 or 163.738 or any other court order that restrains a person from contact with the tenant;
(b) A copy of a police report regarding an act of domestic violence, sexual assault or stalking against the tenant or a minor member of the tenant's household; or
(c) A statement by a law enforcement office that the tenant has reported to the officer that the tenant or a minor member of the tenant's household is a victim of domestic violence, sexual assault or stalking.
(2) If a tenant gives a landlord at least 14 days' written notice, with verification that the tenant has been the victim of domestic violence, sexual assault or stalking within the 90 days preceding the date of the notice, and the notice so requests, the landlord shall release the tenant from the rental agreement. The notice given by the tenant must specify the release date.
(3) A tenant who is released from a rental agreement pursuant to subsection (2) of this section:
(a) Is not liable for rent or damages the dwelling unit incurred after the release date; and
(b) Is not subject to any fee solely because of termination of the rental agreement.
(4) Notwithstanding the release from a rental agreement of a tenant who is a victim, any other tenant remains subject to the rental agreement.
(5) A verification statement by a law enforcement officer must be in substantially the following form:

LAW ENFORCEMENT OFFICER VERIFICATION

____

Name of law enforcement officer

____

Name of tenant

Part 1. Statement by Tenant

I, ____________________________ (Name of tenant), do hereby state as follows:
(A) I or a minor member of my household have been abused, sexually assaulted or stalked as defined by ORS 124.015, 135.230, 147.450 or 163.732.
(B) The most recent incident(s) that I rely on in support of this statement occurred on the following date(s): ____________
I make this statement in support of my request to be released from my rental agreement

____

(Signature of tenant)

Date: ____________

Part 2. Statement by Law Enforcement Officer

I, ____________________________ (Name of law enforcement officer), do hereby verify as follows:
(A) I am a law enforcement officer.
(B) My name, business address and business telephone are as follows:

____

____

____

I am employed by ____________________________
(Name and address of law enforcement agency)
(C) I verify that the person who signed the statement above has informed me that the person or a minor member of the person's household is a victim of domestic violence, sexual assault or stalking, based on incidents that occurred on the dates listed above.
(D) I reasonably the statement of the person above that the person or a minor member of the person's household is a victim of domestic violence, sexual assault or stalking. I understand that the person who made the statement may use this document as a basis for gaining a release from the rental agreement with the person's landlord.

____

(Signature of law enforcement officer making this statement)

Date: ____________

90.456 Other tenants remaining in dwelling unit following tenant termination or exclusion due to domestic violence, sexual assault or stalking. Notwithstanding the release of a victim from a rental agreement under ORS 90.453 or the exclusion of a perpetrator of domestic violence, sexual assault or stalking as provided in ORS 90.459, if there are any remaining tenants of the dwelling unit, the tenancy shall continue for those tenants. Any fee, security deposit or prepaid rent paid by the victim, perpetrator or other tenants shall be applied, accounted for or refunded by the landlord following termination of the tenancy and delivery of possession by the remaining tenants as provided in ORS 90.300 and 90.302.

90.459 Change of locks at request of tenant who is victim of domestic violence, sexual assault or stalking. (1) A tenant may give actual notice to the landlord that the tenant is a victim of domestic violence, sexual assault or stalking and may request that the locks to the dwelling unit be changed. A tenant is not required to provide verification of the domestic violence, sexual assault or stalking to initiate the changing of the locks.
(2) A landlord who receives a request under subsection (1) of this section shall promptly change the locks to the tenant's dwelling unit at the tenant's expense or shall give the tenant permission to change the locks. If a landlord fails to promptly act, the tenant may change the locks without the landlord's permission. If the tenant changes the locks, the tenant shall give a key to the landlord.
(3) If the perpetrator of the domestic violence, sexual assault or stalking is a tenant in the same dwelling unit as the victim:
(a) Before the landlord or tenant changes the locks under this section, the tenant must provide the landlord with a copy of any order issued by a court pursuant to ORS 107.716, 107.718, 124.015 or 124.020 that orders the perpetrator to move out of the dwelling unit.
(b) The landlord has no duty under the rental agreement or by law to allow the perpetrator access to the dwelling unit or provide keys to the perpetrator, during the term of the court order or after the expiration of the court order, or to provide the perpetrator access to the perpetrator's personal property within the dwelling unit. Notwithstanding ORS 90.425, 90.435 or 90.675, if a landlord complies completely and in good faith with this section, the landlord is not liable to a perpetrator excluded from the dwelling unit.
(c) The perpetrator is jointly liable with any other tenant of the dwelling unit for rent or damages to the dwelling unit incurred prior to the time the perpetrator was excluded from the dwelling unit.
(d) Except as provided in subsection (2) of this section, the landlord may not require the tenant to pay additional rent or an additional deposit or fee because of the exclusion of the perpetrator.

90.472 Termination by tenant called into active state service by Governor. (1) As used in this section, "state service member" means a member of the organized militia who is called into active service of the state by the Governor under ORS 399.065 (1) for 90 or more consecutive days.
(2) A ten ant may terminate a rental agreement upon written notice if the tenant provides the landlord with proof of official orders showing that the tenant is a state service member.
(3) A termination of a rental agreement under this section is effective the earlier of:
(a) Thirty days after the date the next rental payment is due; or
(b) On the last day of the month after the month in which written notice is given.
(4) Notwithstanding ORS 99.300 (5)(a), 90.302 (3)(d) and 90.430, a tenant who terminates a lease under subsection (2) of this section is not:
(a) Subject to a penalty, fee, charge or loss of deposit because of the termination; or
(b) Liable for any rent beyond the effective date of the termination as determined under subsection (3) of this section.

90.475 Termination by tenant due to service with Armed Forces. (1) A tenant may terminate a rental agreement upon written notice if the tenant provides the landlord with proof of official orders showing that the tenant is:
(a) Enlisting for active service in the Armed Forces of the United States;
(b) Serving as a member of a National Guard or other reserve component or an active service component of the Armed Forces of the United States and ordered to active service outside the area for a period that will exceed 90 days;
(c) Terminating active service in the Armed Forces of the United States; or
(d) A member of the Public Health Service of the United States Department of Health and Human Services detailed by proper authority for duty with the Army or Navy of the United States and:
(A) Ordered to active service outside the area for a period that will exceed 90 days; or
(B) Terminating the duty and moving outside the area within the period that the member is entitled by federal law to the storage or shipment of household goods.
(2) As used in subsection (1) of this section, "Armed Forces of the United States" means the Air Force, Army, Coast Guard, Marine Corps or Navy of the United States.
(3) A termination of a rental agreement under this section is effective on the earlier of:
(a) A date determined under the provisions of any applicable federal law; or

(b) The later of:
(A) 30 days after delivery of the notice;
(B) 30 days before the earliest reporting date on orders for active service;
(C) A date specified in the notice; or
(D) 90 days before the effective date of the orders if terminating duty described under subsection (1)(d)(B) of this section or terminating any active service described in this section.
(4) Notwithstanding ORS 90.300 (5)(a), 90.302 (3)(d) and 90.430, a tenant who terminates a lease under subsection (1) of this section is not:
(a) Subject to a penalty, fee, charge or loss of deposit because of the termination; or
(b) Liable for any rent beyond the effective date of the termination as determined under subsection (3) of this section.
Note: Section 3, chapter 276, Oregon Laws 1999, provides:
Sec. 3. Section 2 of this 1999 Act [90.475] applies to rental agreements entered into, extended or renewed on or after the effective date of this 1999 Act [June 18, 1999].

MANUFACTURED DWELLING AND FLOATING HOME SPACES (General Provisions)

90.505 "Rent a space for a manufactured dwelling or floating home" defined; application of statutes. (1) As used in ORS 90.505 to 90.840, "rent a space for a manufactured dwelling or floating home," or similar wording, means a transaction creating a rental agreement in which the owner of a manufactured dwelling or floating home secures the right to locate the dwelling or home on the real property of another in a facility for use as a residence in return for value, and in which the owner of the manufactured dwelling or floating home retains no interest in the real property at the end of the transaction.
(2) Unless otherwise provided, ORS 90.100 to 90.450 apply to rental agreements that are subject to ORS 90.505 to 90.840. However, to the extent of inconsistency, the applicable provisions of ORS 90.505 to 90.840 control over the provisions of ORS 90.100 to 90.450.

90.510 Statement of policy; rental agreement; rules and regulations; utility or service charge; remedies. (1) Every landlord who rents a space for a manufactured dwelling or floating home shall provide a written statement of policy to prospective and existing tenants. The purpose of the statement of policy is to provide disclosure of the landlord's policies to prospective tenants and to existing tenants who have not previously received a statement of policy. The statement of policy is not a part of the rental agreement. The statement of policy shall provide all of the following information in summary form:
(a) The location and approximate size of the space to be rented.
(b) The federal fair-housing age classification and present zoning that affect the use of the rented space.
(c) The facility policy regarding rent adjustment and a rent history for the space to be rented. The rent history must, at a minimum, show the rent amounts on January 1 of each of the five preceding calendar years or during the length of the landlord's ownership, leasing or subleasing of the facility, whichever period is shorter.
(d) All personal property, services and facilities to be provided by the landlord.
(e) All installation charges imposed by the landlord and installation fees imposed by government agencies.
(f) The facility policy regarding rental agreement termination including, but not limited to, closure of the facility.
(g) The facility policy regarding facility sale.
(h) The facility policy regarding informal dispute resolution.
(i) Utilities and services available, the person furnishing them and the person responsible for payment.
(j) If a tenants' association exists for the facility, a one-page summary about the tenants' association that shall be provided to the landlord by the tenants' association.
(k) Any facility policy regarding the removal of a manufactured dwelling, including a statement that removal requirements may impact the market value of a dwelling.
(2) The rental agreement and the facility rules and regulations shall be attached as an exhibit to the statement of policy. If the recipient of the statement of policy is a tenant, the rental agreement attached to the statement of policy shall be a copy of the agreement entered by the landlord and tenant.
(3)(a) Prospective tenants shall receive a copy of the statement of policy before signing a rental agreement;
(b) Existing tenants who have not previously received a copy of the statement of policy and who are on month-to-month rental agreements shall receive a copy of the statement of policy at the time a 90-day notice of a rent increase is issued; and

(c) All other existing tenants who have not previously received a copy of the statement of policy shall receive a copy of the statement of policy upon the expiration of their rental agreement and before signing a new agreement.
(4) Every landlord who rents a space for a manufactured dwelling or floating home shall provide a written rental agreement, except as provided by ORS 90.710 (2)(d), that shall be signed by the landlord and tenant and that cannot be unilaterally amended by one of the parties to the contract except by:
(a) Mutual agreement of the parties;
(b) Actions pursuant to ORS 90.530 or 90.600; or
(c) Those provisions required by changes in statute or ordinance.
(5) The agreement required by subsection (4) of this section shall specify:
(a) The location and approximate size of the rented space;
(b) The federal fair-housing age classification;
(c) The rent per month;
(d) All personal property, services and facilities to be provided by the landlord;
(e) All security deposits, fees and installation charges imposed by the landlord;
(f) Improvements that the tenant may or must make to the rental space, including plant materials and landscaping;
(g) Provisions for dealing with improvements to the rental space at the termination of the tenancy;
(h) Any conditions the landlord applies in approving a purchaser of a manufactured dwelling or floating home as a tenant in the event the tenant elects to sell the home. Those conditions shall be in conformance with state and federal law and may include, but are not limited to, conditions as to pets, number of occupants and screening or admission criteria;
(i) That the tenant may not sell the tenant's manufactured dwelling or floating home to a person who intends to leave the manufactured dwelling or floating home on the rental space until the landlord has accepted the person as a tenant;
(j) The term of the tenancy;
(k) The process by which the rental agreement or rules and regulations may be changed, which shall identify that the rules and regulations may be changed with 60 days' notice unless tenants of at least 51 percent of the eligible spaces file an objection within 30 days; and
(L) The process by which notices shall be given by either landlord or tenant.
(6) Every landlord who rents a space for a manufactured dwelling or floating home shall provide rules and regulations concerning the tenant's use and occupancy of the premises. A violation of the rules and regulations may be cause for termination of a rental agreement. However, this subsection does not create a presumption that all rules and regulations are identical for all tenants at all times. A rule or regulation shall be enforceable against the tenant only if:
(a) The rule or regulation:
(A) Promotes the convenience, safety or welfare of the tenants;
(B) Preserves the landlord's property from abusive use; or
(C) Makes a fair distribution of services and facilities held out for the general use of the tenants.
(b) The rule or regulation:
(A) Is reasonably related to the purpose for which it is adopted and is reasonably applied;
(B) Is sufficiently explicit in its prohibition, direction or limitation of the tenant's conduct to fairly inform the tenant of what the tenant shall or shall not do to comply; and
(C) Is not for the purpose of evading the obligations of the landlord.
(7)(a) A landlord who rents a space for a manufactured dwelling or floating home may adopt a rule or regulation regarding occupancy guidelines. If adopted, an occupancy guideline in a facility shall be based on reasonable factors and shall not be more restrictive than limiting occupancy to two people per bedroom.
(b) As used in this subsection:
(A) "Reasonable factors" may include but are not limited to:
(i) The size of the dwelling.
(ii) The size of the rented space.
(iii) Any discriminatory impact for reasons identified in ORS 659A.421.
(iv) Limitations placed on utility services governed by a permit for water or sewage disposal.
(B) "Bedroom" means a room that is intended to be used primarily for sleeping purposes and does not include bathrooms, toilet compartments, closets, halls, storage or utility space and similar areas.
(8)(a) If a written rental agreement so provides, a landlord may require a tenant to pay to the landlord a utility or service charge that has been billed by a utility or service provider to the landlord for utility or service provided directly to the tenant's dwelling unit

or to a common area available to the tenant as part of the tenancy. A utility or service charge that shall be assessed to a tenant for a common area must be described in the written rental agreement separately and distinctly from such a charge for the tenant's dwelling unit. A landlord may not increase the utility or service charge to the tenant by adding any costs of the landlord, such as a handling or administrative charge, other than those costs billed to the landlord by the provider for utilities or services as provided by this subsection.
(b) A utility or service charge is not rent or a fee. Nonpayment of a utility or service charge shall not constitute grounds for termination of a rental agreement for nonpayment of rent pursuant to ORS 90.400 (2), but shall constitute grounds for termination of a rental agreement for cause pursuant to ORS 90.630.
(c) As used in this section, "utility or service" has the meaning given that term in ORS 90.315 (1).
(9) Intentional and deliberate failure of the landlord to comply with subsections (1) to (3) of this section is cause for suit or action to remedy the violation or to recover actual damages. The prevailing party is entitled to reasonable attorney fees and court costs.
(10) A receipt signed by the potential tenant or tenants for documents required to be delivered by the landlord pursuant to subsections (1) to (3) of this section is a defense for the landlord in an action against the landlord for nondelivery of the documents.
(11) A suit or action arising under subsection (9) of this section must be commenced within one year after the discovery or identification of the alleged violation.
(12) Every landlord who publishes a directory of tenants and tenant services must include a one-page summary regarding any tenants' association. The tenants' association shall provide the summary to the landlord.
Note: See note under 90.302.

90.512 Definitions for ORS 90.514 and 90.518. As used in ORS 90.514 and 90.518:
(1) "Buyer" has the meaning given that term in ORS 72.1030.
(2) "Improvements" has the meaning given that term in ORS 646.400.
(3) "Provider" means a contractor licensed under ORS chapter 701 who adds improvements to a manufactured dwelling park.
(4) "Statement of estimated costs" means a written list of the charges, fees, services, goods and accessories that a provider knows or should know are associated with the making of an improvement contracted by the provider and the total estimated cost to the buyer for the improvement.

90.514 Disclosure to prospective tenant of improvements required under rental agreement. (1) Before a prospective tenant signs a rental agreement for space in a manufactured dwelling park, the landlord must provide the prospective tenant with a written statement that discloses the improvements that the park will require under the rental agreement. The written statement must be in the format developed by the Attorney General pursuant to ORS 90.516 and include at least the following:
(a) A notice that the tenant may select the provider of an improvement.
(b) Separately stated and identifiable information for each required improvement that specifies:
(A) The dimensions, materials and finish for improvements to be constructed;
(B) The installation charges imposed by the landlord and the installation fees imposed by government agencies;
(C) The system development charges to be paid by the tenant; and
(D) The site preparation requirements and restrictions, including, but not limited to, requirements and restrictions on the use of plants and landscaping.
(c) Identification of the improvements that belong to the tenant and the improvements that must remain with the manufactured dwelling park.
(2) Except as provided in ORS 41.740, a written statement provided under this section is considered to contain all of the terms relating to improvements that a prospective tenant must make under the rental agreement. There may be no evidence of the terms of the written statement other than the contents of the written statement.

90.516 Model statement for disclosure of improvements required under rental agreement; rules. The Attorney General, by rule, shall adopt a model written statement for use by manufactured dwelling park landlords pursuant to ORS 90.514.

90.518 Provider statement of estimated cost of improvements. (1) A provider hired to make improvements shall give the buyer of the provider's services a statement of estimated costs for the improvements contracted by the provider prior to the date that the manufactured dwelling is delivered to a manufactured dwelling park.

(2) If a provider fails to give a statement of estimated costs or knowingly fails to give a complete statement of estimated costs, a buyer who does not have actual notice of the total cost for an improvement and suffers an ascertainable loss due to the failure by the provider may bring an action to recover the greater of actual damages or $200.

(3) Except as provided in ORS 41.740, a statement of estimated costs given under this section is considered to contain all of the terms of the agreement between the buyer and the provider hired to make improvements. There may be no evidence of the terms of the statement of estimated costs other than the contents of the statement of estimated costs.

90.525 Unreasonable conditions of rental or occupancy prohibited. (1) No landlord shall impose conditions of rental or occupancy which unreasonably restrict the tenant or prospective tenant in choosing a fuel supplier, furnishings, goods, services or accessories.

(2) No landlord of a facility shall require the prospective tenant to purchase a manufactured dwelling or floating home from a particular dealer or one of a group of dealers.

(3) No landlord renting a space for a manufactured dwelling or floating home shall give preference to a prospective tenant who purchased a manufactured dwelling or floating home from a particular dealer.

(4) No manufactured dwelling or floating home dealer shall require, as a condition of sale, a purchaser to rent a space for a manufactured dwelling or floating home in a particular facility or one of a group of facilities.

90.528 Use of common areas or facilities. (1) A landlord who rents a space for a manufactured dwelling may require a deposit for the use of common areas or facilities by a tenant or tenants. The amount of any deposit charged for the use of common areas or facilities shall be reasonably based on the potential cleaning cost or other costs associated with the use of the area or facility. Conditions for return of a deposit shall be stated in writing and made available to the tenant or tenants placing the deposit.

(2) No tenant shall be required to acquire a bond or insurance policy as a precondition for the use of common areas or facilities.

(3) A landlord who rents a space for a manufactured dwelling shall not prohibit use of a common area or facility if the purpose of the prohibition is to prevent the use of the area or facility for tenant association meetings, tenant organizing meetings or other lawful tenant activities.

Note: 90.528 was enacted into law by the Legislative Assembly but was not added to or made a part of ORS chapter 90 or any series therein by legislative action. See Preface to Oregon Revised Statutes for further explanation.

90.530 Pets in facilities; rental agreements. (1) Notwithstanding a change in the rules and regulations of a manufactured dwelling or floating home facility that would prohibit pets, a tenant may keep a pet that is otherwise legally living with the tenant at the time the landlord provides notice of the proposed change to the rules and regulations of the facility. The tenant may replace a pet with a pet similar to the one living with the tenant at the time the landlord provided notice of the proposed change. New rules and regulations that regulate the activities of pets shall apply to all pets in the facility, including those pets that were living in the facility prior to the adoption of the new rules or regulations.

(2) A rental agreement between a landlord renting a space for a manufactured dwelling or floating home and a tenant renting the space must comply with the following:

(a) A landlord may not charge a one-time, monthly or other periodic amount based on the tenant's possession of a pet.

(b) A landlord may provide written rules regarding control, sanitation, number, type and size of pets. The landlord may require the tenant to sign a pet agreement and to provide proof of liability insurance. The landlord may require the tenant to make the landlord a co-insured for the purpose of receiving notice in the case of cancellation of the insurance.

(c) A landlord may charge a tenant an amount for a violation of a written pet agreement or rules relating to pets not to exceed $50 for each violation.

90.540 Permissible forms of tenancy; minimum fixed term. A rental agreement for a space for a manufactured dwelling or floating home must be a month-to-month or fixed term tenancy. A rental agreement for a fixed term tenancy must have a duration or term of at least two years.

90.545 Fixed term tenancy expiration; renewal or extension; new rental agreements; tenant refusal of new rental agreement; written storage agreement upon termination of tenancy. (1) Except if renewed or extended as provided by this section, a fixed term tenancy for space for a manufactured dwelling or floating home shall, upon reaching its ending date, automatically renew as a month-to-month tenancy

having the same terms and conditions, other than duration and rent increases pursuant to ORS 90.600, unless the tenancy is terminated pursuant to ORS 90.380 (5)(b), 90.400 (2), (3) or (9), 90.630 or 90.632.
(2) To renew or extend a fixed term tenancy for another term, of any duration that is consistent with ORS 90.540, the landlord shall submit the proposed new rental agreement to the tenant at least 60 days prior to the ending date of the term. The landlord shall include with the proposed agreement a written statement that summarizes any new or revised terms, conditions, rules or regulations.
(3) Notwithstanding ORS 90.610 (3), a landlord's proposed new rental agreement may include new or revised terms, conditions, rules or regulations, if the new or revised terms, conditions, rules or regulations:
(a)(A) Fairly implement a statute or ordinance adopted after the creation of the existing agreement; or
(B) Are the same as those offered to new or prospective tenants in the facility at the time the proposed agreement is submitted to the tenant and for the six-month period preceding the submission of the proposed agreement or, if there have been no new or prospective tenants during the six-month period, are the same as are customary for the rental market;
(b) Are consistent with the rights and remedies provided to tenants under this chapter, including the right to keep a pet pursuant to ORS 90.530;
(c) Do not relate to the age, size, style, construction material or year of construction of the manufactured dwelling or floating home contrary to ORS 90.632 (2); and
(d) Do not require an alteration of the manufactured dwelling or floating home or alteration or new construction of an accessory building or structure.
(4) A tenant shall accept or reject a landlord's proposed new rental agreement at least 30 days prior to the ending of the term by giving written notice to the landlord.
(5) If a landlord fails to submit a proposed new rental agreement as provided by subsection (2) of this section, the tenancy renews as a month-to- month tenancy as provided by subsection (1) of this section.
(6) If a tenant fails to accept or unreasonably rejects a landlord's proposed new rental agreement as provided by subsection (4) of this section, the fixed term tenancy terminates on the ending date without further notice and the landlord may take possession by complying with ORS 105.105 to 105.168.
(7) If a tenancy terminates under conditions described in subsection (6) of this section, and the tenant surrenders or delivers possession of the premises to the landlord prior to the filing of an action pursuant to ORS 105.110, the tenant has the right to enter into a written storage agreement with the landlord, with the tenant having the same rights and responsibilities as a lienholder under ORS 90.675 (19), except that the landlord may limit the term of the storage agreement to not exceed six months. Unless the parties agree otherwise, the storage agreement must commence upon the date of the termination of the tenancy. The rights under ORS 90.675 of any lienholder are delayed until the end of the tenant storage agreement.

(Landlord and Tenant Relations)

90.600 Increases in rent; notice; meeting with tenants; effect of failure to meet. (1) If a rental agreement is a month-to-month tenancy to which ORS 90.505 to 90.840 apply, the landlord may not increase the rent unless the landlord gives notice in writing to each affected tenant at least 90 days prior to the effective date of the rent increase specifying the amount of the increase, the amount of the new rent and the date on which the increase becomes effective.
(2) This section does not create a right to increase rent that does not otherwise exist.
(3) This section does not require a landlord to compromise, justify or reduce a rent increase that the landlord otherwise is entitled to impose.
(4) Neither ORS 90.510 (1), requiring a landlord to provide a statement of policy, nor ORS 90.510 (4), requiring a landlord to provide a written rental agreement, create a basis for tenant challenge of a rent increase, judicially or otherwise.
(5)(a) The tenants who reside in a facility may elect one committee of seven or fewer members in a facility-wide election to represent the tenants. One tenant of record for each rented space may vote in the election. Upon written request from the tenants' committee, the landlord or a representative of the landlord shall meet with the committee within 10 to 30 days of the request to discuss the tenants' nonrent concerns regarding the facility. Unless the parties agree otherwise, upon a request from the tenants' committee, a landlord or representative of the landlord shall meet with the tenants' committee at least once, but not more than twice, each calendar year. The meeting shall be held on the premises if the facility has suitable meeting space for that purpose, or at a location reasonably convenient to the tenants. After the meeting, the tenants' committee shall send

a written summary of the issues and concerns addressed at the meeting to the landlord. The landlord or the landlord's representative shall make a good faith response in writing to the committee's summary within 60 days.
(b) The tenants' committee is entitled to informal dispute resolution in accordance with ORS 446.547 if the landlord or landlord's representative fails to meet with the tenants' committee or fails to respond in good faith to the written summary as required by paragraph (a) of this subsection.
90.605 Persons authorized to receive notice and demands on landlord's behalf; written notice to change designated person. Any person authorized by the landlord of a facility to receive notices and demands on the landlord's behalf retains this authority until the authorized person is notified otherwise. Written notice of any change in the name or address of the person authorized to receive notices and demands shall be delivered to the residence of each person who rents a space for a manufactured dwelling or floating home or, if specified in writing by the tenant, to another specified address.
90.610 Informal dispute resolution; notice of proposed change in rule or regulation; objection to change by tenant. (1) As used in this section, "eligible space" means each space in the facility as long as:
(a) The space is rented to a tenant and the tenancy is subject to ORS 90.505 to 90.840; and
(b) The tenant who occupies the space has not:
(A) Previously agreed to a rental agreement that includes the proposed rule or regulation change; or
(B) Become subject to the proposed rule or regulation change as a result of a change in rules or regulations previously adopted in a manner consistent with this section.
(2) Notwithstanding ORS 90.245 (1), the parties to a rental agreement to which ORS 90.505 to 90.840 applies shall provide for a process establishing informal dispute resolution of disputes that may arise concerning the rental agreement for a manufactured dwelling or floating home space.
(3) The landlord may propose changes in rules or regulations, including changes that make a substantial modification of the landlord's bargain with a tenant, by giving written notice of the proposed rule or regulation change, and unless tenants of at least 51 percent of the eligible spaces in the facility object in writing within 30 days of the date the notice was served, the change shall become effective for all tenants of those spaces on a date not less than 60 days after the date that the notice was served by the landlord.
(4) One tenant of record per eligible space may object to the rule or regulation change through either:
(a) A signed and dated written communication to the landlord; or
(b) A petition format that is signed and dated by tenants of eligible spaces and that includes a copy of the proposed rule or regulation and a copy of the notice.
(5) If a tenant of an eligible space signs both a written communication to the landlord and a petition under subsection (4) of this section, or signs more than one written communication or petition, only the latest signature of the tenant may be counted.
(6) Notwithstanding subsection (4) of this section, a proxy may be used only if a tenant has a disability that prevents the tenant from objecting to the rule or regulation change in writing.
(7) The landlord's notice of a proposed change in rules or regulations required by subsection (3) of this section must be given or served as provided in ORS 90.155 and must include:
(a) Language of the existing rule or regulation and the language that would be added or deleted by the proposed rule or regulation change; and
(b) A statement substantially in the following form, with all blank spaces in the notice to be filled in by the landlord:

NOTICE OF PROPOSED RULE
OR REGULATION CHANGE

The landlord intends to change a rule or regulation in this facility.
The change will go into effect unless tenants of at least 51 percent of the eligible spaces object in writing within 30 days. Any objection must be signed and dated by a tenant of an eligible space.
The number of eligible spaces as of the date of this notice is: ______. Those eligible spaces are (space or street identification): ______________________
The last day for a tenant of an eligible space to deliver a written objection to the landlord is ______________
(landlord fill in date).
Unless tenants in at least 51 percent of the eligible spaces object, the proposed rule or regulation will go into effect on ______________.
The parties may attempt to resolve disagreements regarding the proposed rule or regulation change by using the facility's informal dispute resolution process.
(8) A good faith mistake by the landlord in complet-

ing those portions of the notice relating to the number of eligible spaces that have tenants entitled to vote or relating to space or street identification numbers does not invalidate the notice or the proposed rule or regulation change.

(9) After the effective date of the rule or regulation change, when a tenant continues to engage in an activity affected by the new rule or regulation to which the landlord objects, the landlord may give the tenant a notice of termination of the tenancy pursuant to ORS 90.630. The notice shall include a statement that the tenant may request a resolution through the facility's informal dispute resolution process by giving the landlord a written request within seven days from the date the notice was served. If the tenant requests an informal dispute resolution, the landlord may not file an action for possession pursuant to ORS 105.105 to 105.168 until 30 days after the date of the tenant's request for informal dispute resolution or the date the informal dispute resolution is complete, whichever occurs first.

(10) An agreement under this section may not require informal dispute resolution of disputes relating to:
(a) Facility closure;
(b) Facility sale; or
(c) Rent, including but not limited to amount, increase and nonpayment.

(11) ORS 90.510 (1) to (3), requiring a landlord to provide a statement of policy, do not create a basis for a tenant to demand informal dispute resolution of a rent increase.

90.620 Termination by tenant; notice to landlord. (1) The tenant who rents a space for a manufactured dwelling or floating home may terminate a rental agreement that is a month-to-month or fixed term tenancy without cause by giving to the landlord, at any time during the tenancy, not less than 30 days' notice in writing prior to the date designated in the notice for the termination of the tenancy.

(2) The tenant may terminate a rental agreement that is a month-to-month or fixed term tenancy for cause pursuant to ORS 90.315, 90.360 (1), 90.365 (2), 90.375 or 90.380.

(3) A tenant may not be required to give the landlord more than 30 days' written notice to terminate.

90.630 Termination by landlord; causes; notice; cure; nonpayment of rent. (1) Except as provided in subsection (4) of this section, the landlord may terminate a rental agreement that is a month-to-month or fixed term tenancy for space for a manufactured dwelling or floating home by giving to the tenant not less than 30 days' notice in writing before the date designated in the notice for termination if the tenant:
(a) Violates a law or ordinance related to the tenant's conduct as a tenant, including but not limited to a material noncompliance with ORS 90.740;
(b) Violates a rule or rental agreement provision related to the tenant's conduct as a tenant and imposed as a condition of occupancy, including but not limited to a material noncompliance with a rental agreement regarding a program of recovery in drug and alcohol free housing; or
(c) Fails to pay a:
(A) Late charge pursuant to ORS 90.260;
(B) Fee pursuant to ORS 90.302; or
(C) Utility or service charge pursuant to ORS 90.510 (8).

(2) A violation making a tenant subject to termination under subsection (1) of this section includes a tenant's failure to maintain the space as required by law, ordinance, rental agreement or rule, but does not include the physical condition of the dwelling or home. Termination of a rental agreement based upon the physical condition of a dwelling or home shall only be as provided in ORS 90.632.

(3) The notice required by subsection (1) of this section shall state facts sufficient to notify the tenant of the reasons for termination of the tenancy.

(4) The tenant may avoid termination of the tenancy by correcting the violation within the 30-day period specified in subsection (1) of this section. However, if substantially the same act or omission which constituted a prior violation of which notice was given recurs within six months after the date of the notice, the landlord may terminate the tenancy upon at least 20 days' written notice specifying the violation and the date of termination of the tenancy.

(5) The landlord of a facility may terminate a rental agreement that is a month-to-month or fixed term tenancy for a facility space if the facility or a portion of it that includes the space is to be closed and the land or leasehold converted to a different use, which is not required by the exercise of eminent domain or by order of state or local agencies, by:
(a) Not less than 365 days' notice in writing before the date designated in the notice for termination; or
(b) Not less than 180 days' notice in writing before the date designated in the notice for termination, if the landlord finds space acceptable to the tenant to which the tenant can move the manufactured dwelling or

floating home and the landlord pays the cost of moving and set-up expenses or $3,500, whichever is less.
(6) The landlord may:
(a) Provide greater financial incentive to encourage the tenant to accept an earlier termination date than that provided in subsection (5) of this section; or
(b) Contract with the tenant for a mutually acceptable arrangement to assist the tenant's move.
(7) The Housing and Community Services Department shall adopt rules to implement the provisions of subsection (5) of this section.
(8)(a) A landlord may not increase the rent for the purpose of offsetting the payments required under this section.
(b) There shall be no increase in the rent after a notice of termination is given pursuant to this section.
(9) This section does not limit a landlord's right to terminate a tenancy for nonpayment of rent pursuant to ORS 90.400 (2) or for other cause pursuant to ORS 90.380 (5)(b), 90.400 (3) or (9) or 90.632 by complying with ORS 105.105 to 105.168.
(10) A tenancy shall terminate on the date designated in the notice and without regard to the expiration of the period for which, by the terms of the rental agreement, rents are to be paid. Unless otherwise agreed, rent is uniformly apportionable from day to day.
(11) Nothing in subsection (5) of this section shall prevent a landlord from relocating a floating home to another comparable space in the same facility or another facility owned by the same owner in the same city if the landlord desires or is required to make repairs, to remodel or to modify the tenant's original space.
(12)(a) Notwithstanding any other provision of this section or ORS 90.400, the landlord may terminate the rental agreement for space for a manufactured dwelling or floating home because of repeated late payment of rent by giving the tenant not less than 30 days' notice in writing before the date designated in that notice for termination and may take possession in the manner provided in ORS 105.105 to 105.168 if:
(A) The tenant has not paid the monthly rent prior to the eighth day of the rental period as described in ORS 90.400 (2)(b)(A) or the fifth day of the rental period as described in ORS 90.400 (2)(b)(B) in at least three of the preceding 12 months and the landlord has given the tenant a notice for nonpayment of rent pursuant to ORS 90.400 (2)(b) during each of those three instances of nonpayment;
(B) The landlord warns the tenant of the risk of a 30-day notice for termination with no right to correct the cause, upon the occurrence of a third notice for nonpayment of rent within a 12-month period. The warning must be contained in at least two notices for nonpayment of rent that precede the third notice within a 12-month period or in separate written notices that are given concurrent with, or a reasonable time after, each of the two notices for nonpayment of rent; and
(C) The 30-day notice of termination states facts sufficient to notify the tenant of the cause for termination of the tenancy and is given to the tenant concurrent with or after the third or a subsequent notice for nonpayment of rent.
(b) Notwithstanding subsection (2) of this section, a tenant who receives a 30-day notice of termination pursuant to this subsection shall have no right to correct the cause for the notice.
(c) The landlord may give a copy of the notice required by paragraph (a) of this subsection to any lienholder of the manufactured dwelling or floating home by first class mail with certificate of mailing or by any other method allowed by ORS 90.150 (2) and (3). A landlord is not liable to a tenant for any damages incurred by the tenant as a result of the landlord giving a copy of the notice in good faith to a lienholder. A lienholder's rights and obligations regarding an abandoned manufactured dwelling or floating home shall be as provided under ORS 90.675.

90.632 Termination of tenancy due to physical condition of manufactured dwelling or floating home; correction of condition by tenant. (1) A landlord may terminate a month-to-month or fixed term rental agreement and require the tenant to remove a manufactured dwelling or floating home from a facility, due to the physical condition of the manufactured dwelling or floating home, only by complying with this section and ORS 105.105 to 105.168. A termination shall include removal of the dwelling or home.
(2) A landlord shall not require removal of a manufactured dwelling or floating home, or consider a dwelling or home to be in disrepair or deteriorated, because of the age, size, style or original construction material of the dwelling or home or because the dwelling or home was built prior to adoption of the National Manufactured Home Construction and Safety Standards Act of 1974 (42 U.S.C. 5403), in compliance with the standards of that Act in effect at that time or in compliance with the state building code as defined in ORS 455.010.
(3) Except as provided in subsection (5) of this section, if the tenant's dwelling or home is in disrepair

or is deteriorated, a landlord may terminate a rental agreement and require the removal of a dwelling or home by giving to the tenant not less than 30 days' written notice before the date designated in the notice for termination.

(4) The notice required by subsection (3) of this section shall:

(a) State facts sufficient to notify the tenant of the causes or reasons for termination of the tenancy and removal of the dwelling or home;

(b) State that the tenant can avoid termination and removal by correcting the cause for termination and removal within the notice period;

(c) Describe what is required to correct the cause for termination;

(d) Describe the tenant's right to give the landlord a written notice of correction, where to give the notice and the deadline for giving the notice in order to ensure a response by the landlord, all as provided by subsection (6) of this section; and

(e) Describe the tenant's right to have the termination and correction period extended as provided by subsection (7) of this section.

(5) The tenant may avoid termination of the tenancy by correcting the cause within the period specified. However, if substantially the same condition that constituted a prior cause for termination of which notice was given recurs within 12 months after the date of the notice, the landlord may terminate the tenancy and require the removal of the dwelling or home upon at least 30 days' written notice specifying the violation and the date of termination of the tenancy.

(6) During the termination notice or extension period, the tenant may give the landlord written notice that the tenant has corrected the cause for termination. Within a reasonable time after the tenant's notice of correction, the landlord shall respond to the tenant in writing, stating whether the landlord agrees that the cause has been corrected. If the tenant's notice of correction is given at least 14 days prior to the end of the termination notice or extension period, failure by the landlord to respond as required by this subsection shall be a defense to a termination based upon the landlord's notice for termination.

(7) Except when the disrepair or deterioration creates a risk of imminent and serious harm to other dwellings, homes or persons within the facility, the 30-day period provided for the tenant to correct the cause for termination and removal shall be extended by at least:

(a) An additional 60 days if:

(A) The necessary correction involves exterior painting, roof repair, concrete pouring or similar work and the weather prevents that work during a substantial portion of the 30-day period; or

(B) The nature or extent of the correction work is such that it cannot reasonably be completed within 30 days because of factors such as the amount of work necessary, the type and complexity of the work and the availability of necessary repair persons; or

(b) An additional six months if the disrepair or deterioration has existed for more than the preceding 12 months with the landlord's knowledge or acceptance as described in ORS 90.415 (1).

(8) In order to have the period for correction extended as provided in subsection (7) of this section, a tenant must give the landlord written notice describing the necessity for an extension in order to complete the correction work. The notice must be given a reasonable amount of time prior to the end of the notice for termination period.

(9) A tenancy shall terminate on the date designated in the notice and without regard to the expiration of the period for which, by the terms of the rental agreement, rents are to be paid. Unless otherwise agreed, rent is uniformly apportionable from day to day.

(10) This section does not limit a landlord's right to terminate a tenancy for nonpayment of rent pursuant to ORS 90.400 (2) or for other cause pursuant to ORS 90.380 (5)(b), 90.400 (3) or (9) or 90.630 by complying with ORS 105.105 to 105.168.

(11) A landlord may give a copy of the notice for termination required by this section to any lienholder of the dwelling or home, by first class mail with certificate of mailing or by any other method allowed by ORS 90.150 (2) and (3). A landlord is not liable to a tenant for any damages incurred by the tenant as a result of the landlord giving a copy of the notice in good faith to a lienholder.

(12) When a tenant has been given a notice for termination pursuant to this section and has subsequently abandoned the dwelling or home as described in ORS 90.675 (2), any lienholder shall have the same rights as provided by ORS 90.675, including the right to correct the cause of the notice, within the 90-day period provided by ORS 90.675 (19) notwithstanding the expiration of the notice period provided by this section for the tenant to correct the cause.

90.635 Closure of facility; notice to tenant of tax credit; rules. (1) If a facility is closed or a portion of a facility is closed, resulting in the termination of the

rental agreement between the landlord of the facility and a tenant renting space for a manufactured dwelling, whether because of the exercise of eminent domain, by order of the state or local agencies, or as provided under ORS 90.630 (5), the landlord shall provide notice to the tenant of the tax credit provided under ORS 316.153. The notice shall state the eligibility requirements for the credit, information on how to apply for the credit and any other information required by the Office of the Manufactured Dwelling Park Community Relations by rule.
(2) The landlord shall send the notice described under subsection (1) of this section to a tenant affected by a facility closure on or before:
(a) The date notice of rental termination must be given to the tenant under ORS 90.630 (5), if applicable; or
(b) In the event of facility closure by exercise of eminent domain or by order of a state or local agency, within 15 days of the date the landlord received notice of the closure.
(3) The landlord shall forward to the office a list of the names and addresses of tenants to whom notice under this section has been sent.
(4) The office may adopt rules to implement this section, including rules specifying the form and content of the notice described under this section.

(Ownership Change)

90.675 Disposition of manufactured dwelling or floating home left in facility; notice; sale; limitation on landlord liability; tax cancellation; storage agreements; hazardous property. (1) As used in this section:
(a) "Current market value" means the amount in cash, as determined by the county assessor, that could reasonably be expected to be paid for personal property by an informed buyer to an informed seller, each acting without compulsion in an arms-length transaction occurring on the assessment date for the tax year or on the date of a subsequent reappraisal by the county assessor.
(b) "Dispose of the personal property" means that, if reasonably appropriate, the landlord may throw away the property or may give it without consideration to a nonprofit organization or to a person unrelated to the landlord. The landlord may not retain the property for personal use or benefit.
(c) "Lienholder" means any lienholder of abandoned personal property, if the lien is of record or the lienholder is actually known to the landlord.
(d) "Of record" means:
(A) For a manufactured dwelling, that a security interest has been properly recorded with the Department of Transportation pursuant to ORS 802.200 (1)(a)(A) and 803.097 for a dwelling registered and titled by the department pursuant to ORS 820.500.
(B) For a floating home, that a security interest has been properly recorded with the State Marine Board pursuant to ORS 830.740 to 830.755 for a home registered and titled with the board pursuant to ORS 830.715.
(e) "Personal property" means only a manufactured dwelling or floating home located in a facility and subject to ORS 90.505 to 90.840. "Personal property" does not include goods left inside a manufactured dwelling or floating home or left upon a rented space and subject to disposition under ORS 90.425.
(2) A landlord may not store, sell or dispose of abandoned personal property except as provided by this section. This section governs the rights and obligations of landlords, tenants and any lienholders in any personal property abandoned or left upon the premises by the tenant or any lienholder in the following circumstances:
(a) The tenancy has ended by termination or expiration of a rental agreement or by relinquishment or abandonment of the premises and the landlord reasonably believes under all the circumstances that the tenant has left the personal property upon the premises with no intention of asserting any further claim to the premises or to the personal property;
(b) The tenant has been absent from the premises continuously for seven days after termination of a tenancy by a court order that has not been executed; or
(c) The landlord receives possession of the premises from the sheriff pursuant to ORS 105.161.
(3) Prior to selling or disposing of the tenant's personal property under this section, the landlord must give a written notice to the tenant that shall be:
(a) Personally delivered to the tenant; or
(b) Sent by first class mail addressed and mailed to the tenant at:
(A) The premises;
(B) Any post-office box held by the tenant and actually known to the landlord; and
(C) The most recent forwarding address if provided by the tenant or actually known to the landlord.
(4)(a) A landlord shall also give a copy of the notice described in subsection (3) of this section to:
(A) Any lienholder of the personal property;
(B) The tax collector of the county where the personal property is located; and

(C) The assessor of the county where the personal property is located.
(b) The landlord shall give the notice copy required by this subsection by personal delivery or first class mail, except that for any lienholder, mail service shall be both by first class mail and by certified mail with return receipt requested.
(c) A notice to lienholders under paragraph (a)(A) of this subsection must be sent to each lienholder at each address:
(A) Actually known to the landlord;
(B) Of record; and
(C) Provided to the landlord by the lienholder in a written notice that identifies the personal property subject to the lien and that was sent to the landlord by certified mail with return receipt requested within the preceding five years. The notice must identify the personal property by describing the physical address of the property.
(5) The notice required under subsection (3) of this section shall state that:
(a) The personal property left upon the premises is considered abandoned;
(b) The tenant or any lienholder must contact the landlord by a specified date, as provided in subsection (6) of this section, to arrange for the removal of the abandoned personal property;
(c) The personal property is stored on the rented space;
(d) The tenant or any lienholder, except as provided by subsection (18) of this section, may arrange for removal of the personal property by contacting the landlord at a described telephone number or address on or before the specified date;
(e) The landlord shall make the personal property available for removal by the tenant or any lienholder, except as provided by subsection (18) of this section, by appointment at reasonable times;
(f) If the personal property is considered to be abandoned pursuant to subsection (2)(a) or (b) of this section, the landlord may require payment of storage charges, as provided by subsection (7)(b) of this section, prior to releasing the personal property to the tenant or any lienholder;
(g) If the personal property is considered to be abandoned pursuant to subsection (2)(c) of this section, the landlord may not require payment of storage charges prior to releasing the personal property;
(h) If the tenant or any lienholder fails to contact the landlord by the specified date or fails to remove the personal property within 30 days after that contact, the landlord may sell or dispose of the personal property. If the landlord reasonably believes the county assessor will determine that the current market value of the personal property is $8,000 or less, and the landlord intends to dispose of the property if it is not claimed, the notice shall state that belief and intent; and
(i) If applicable, there is a lienholder that has a right to claim the personal property, except as provided by subsection (18) of this section.
(6) For purposes of subsection (5) of this section, the specified date by which a tenant or lienholder must contact a landlord to arrange for the disposition of abandoned personal property shall be not less than 45 days after personal delivery or mailing of the notice.
(7) After notifying the tenant as required by subsection (3) of this section, the landlord:
(a) Shall store the abandoned personal property of the tenant on the rented space and shall exercise reasonable care for the personal property; and
(b) Is entitled to reasonable or actual storage charges and costs incidental to storage or disposal. The storage charge shall be no greater than the monthly space rent last payable by the tenant.
(8) If a tenant or lienholder, upon the receipt of the notice provided by subsection (3) or (4) of this section or otherwise, responds by actual notice to the landlord on or before the specified date in the landlord's notice that the tenant or lienholder intends to remove the personal property from the premises, the landlord must make that personal property available for removal by the tenant or lienholder by appointment at reasonable times during the 30 days following the date of the response, subject to subsection (18) of this section. If the personal property is considered to be abandoned pursuant to subsection (2)(a) or (b) of this section, but not pursuant to subsection (2)(c) of this section, the landlord may require payment of storage charges, as provided in subsection (7)(b) of this section, prior to allowing the tenant or lienholder to remove the personal property. Acceptance by a landlord of such payment does not operate to create or reinstate a tenancy or create a waiver pursuant to ORS 90.415.
(9) Except as provided in subsections (18) to (20) of this section, if the tenant or lienholder does not respond within the time provided by the landlord's notice, or the tenant or lienholder does not remove the personal property within 30 days after responding to the landlord or by any date agreed to with the

landlord, whichever is later, the personal property is conclusively presumed to be abandoned. The tenant and any lienholder that have been given notice pursuant to subsection (3) or (4) of this section shall, except with regard to the distribution of sale proceeds pursuant to subsection (13) of this section, have no further right, title or interest to the personal property and may not claim or sell the property.

(10) If the personal property is presumed to be abandoned under subsection (9) of this section, the landlord then may:

(a) Sell the personal property at a public or private sale, provided that prior to the sale:

(A) The landlord may seek to transfer the certificate of title and registration to the personal property by complying with the requirements of the appropriate state agency; and

(B) The landlord shall:

(i) Place a notice in a newspaper of general circulation in the county in which the personal property is located. The notice shall state:

(I) That the personal property is abandoned;

(II) The tenant's name;

(III) The address and any space number where the personal property is located, and if actually known to the landlord, the plate, registration or other identification number as noted on the title;

(IV) Whether the sale is by private bidding or public auction;

(V) Whether the landlord is accepting sealed bids and, if so, the last date on which bids will be accepted; and

(VI) The name and telephone number of the person to contact to inspect the personal property;

(ii) At a reasonable time prior to the sale, give a copy of the notice required by sub-subparagraph (i) of this subparagraph to the tenant and to any lienholder, by personal delivery or first class mail, except that for any lienholder, mail service shall be by first class mail with certificate of mailing;

(iii) Obtain an affidavit of publication from the newspaper to show that the notice required under sub-subparagraph (i) of this subparagraph ran in the newspaper at least one day in each of two consecutive weeks prior to the date scheduled for the sale or the last date bids will be accepted; and

(iv) Obtain written proof from the county that all property taxes on the personal property have been paid or, if not paid, that the county has authorized the sale, with the sale proceeds to be distributed pursuant to subsection (13) of this section; or

(b) Destroy or otherwise dispose of the personal property if the landlord determines from the county assessor that the current market value of the property is $8,000 or less.

(11)(a) A public or private sale authorized by this section shall be conducted consistent with the terms listed in subsection (10)(a)(B)(i) of this section. Every aspect of the sale including the method, manner, time, place and terms must be commercially reasonable.

(b) If there is no buyer at a sale described under paragraph (a) of this subsection, the personal property is considered to be worth $8,000 or less, regardless of current market value, and the landlord shall destroy or otherwise dispose of the personal property.

(12) Notwithstanding ORS 446.155 (1) and (2), unless a landlord intentionally misrepresents the condition of personal property, the landlord is not liable for the condition of the personal property to:

(a) A buyer of the personal property at a sale pursuant to subsection (10)(a) of this section, with or without consideration; or

(b) A person or nonprofit organization to whom the landlord gives the personal property pursuant to subsection (1)(b), (10)(b) or (11)(b) of this section.

(13)(a) The landlord may deduct from the proceeds of the sale:

(A) The reasonable or actual cost of notice, storage and sale; and

(B) Unpaid rent.

(b) After deducting the amounts listed in paragraph (a) of this subsection, the landlord shall remit the remaining proceeds, if any, to the county tax collector to the extent of any unpaid property taxes owed on the dwelling or home.

(c) After deducting the amounts listed in paragraphs (a) and (b) of this subsection, if applicable, the landlord shall remit the remaining proceeds, if any, to any lienholder to the extent of any unpaid balance owed on the lien on the personal property.

(d) After deducting the amounts listed in paragraphs (a), (b) and (c) of this subsection, if applicable, the landlord shall remit to the tenant the remaining proceeds, if any, together with an itemized accounting.

(e) If the tenant cannot after due diligence be found, the remaining proceeds shall be deposited with the county treasurer of the county in which the sale occurred, and if not claimed within three years shall revert to the general fund of the county available for general purposes.

(14) The county tax collector shall cancel all unpaid property taxes as provided under ORS 311.790 only under circumstances described in paragraph (a), (b), (c) or (d) of this subsection:
(a) The landlord disposes of the personal property after a determination described in subsection (10)(b) of this section.
(b) There is no buyer of the personal property at a sale described under subsection (11) of this section.
(c)(A) There is a buyer of the personal property at a sale described under subsection (11) of this section;
(B) The current market value of the personal property is $8,000 or less; and
(C) The proceeds of the sale are insufficient to satisfy the unpaid property taxes owed on the personal property after distribution of the proceeds pursuant to subsection (13) of this section.
(d)(A) The landlord buys the personal property at a sale described under subsection (11) of this section;
(B) The current market value of the personal property is more than $8,000;
(C) The proceeds of the sale are insufficient to satisfy the unpaid property taxes owed on the personal property after distribution of the proceeds pursuant to subsection (13) of this section; and
(D) The landlord disposes of the personal property.
(15) The landlord is not responsible for any loss to the tenant or lienholder resulting from storage of personal property in compliance with this section unless the loss was caused by the landlord's deliberate or negligent act. In the event of a deliberate and malicious violation, the landlord is liable for twice the actual damages sustained by the tenant or lienholder.
(16) Complete compliance in good faith with this section shall constitute a complete defense in any action brought by a tenant or lienholder against a landlord for loss or damage to such personal property disposed of pursuant to this section.
(17) If a landlord does not comply with this section:
(a) The tenant is relieved of any liability for damage to the premises caused by conduct that was not deliberate, intentional or grossly negligent and for unpaid rent and may recover from the landlord up to twice the actual damages sustained by the tenant;
(b) A lienholder aggrieved by the noncompliance may recover from the landlord the actual damages sustained by the lienholder. ORS 90.255 does not authorize an award of attorney fees to the prevailing party in any action arising under this paragraph; and
(c) A county tax collector aggrieved by the noncompliance may recover from the landlord the actual damages sustained by the tax collector, if the noncompliance is part of an effort by the landlord to defraud the tax collector. ORS 90.255 does not authorize an award of attorney fees to the prevailing party in any action arising under this paragraph.
(18) The provisions of this section regarding the rights and responsibilities of a tenant to the abandoned personal property shall also apply to any lienholder, except that the lienholder may not sell or remove the dwelling or home unless:
(a) The lienholder has foreclosed its lien on the manufactured dwelling or floating home;
(b) The tenant or a personal representative or designated person described in subsection (20) of this section has waived all rights under this section pursuant to subsection (22) of this section; or
(c) The notice and response periods provided by subsections (6) and (8) of this section have expired.
(19)(a) Except as provided by subsection (20)(d) and (e) of this section, if a lienholder makes a timely response to a notice of abandoned personal property pursuant to subsections (6) and (8) of this section and so requests, a landlord shall enter into a written storage agreement with the lienholder providing that the personal property may not be sold or disposed of by the landlord for up to 12 months. A storage agreement entitles the lienholder to store the personal property on the previously rented space during the term of the agreement, but does not entitle anyone to occupy the personal property.
(b) The lienholder's right to a storage agreement arises upon the failure of the tenant or, in the case of a deceased tenant, the personal representative, designated person, heir or devisee to remove or sell the dwelling or home within the allotted time.
(c) To exercise the right to a storage agreement under this subsection, in addition to contacting the landlord with a timely response as described in paragraph (a) of this subsection, the lienholder must enter into the proposed storage agreement within 60 days after the landlord gives a copy of the agreement to the lienholder. The landlord shall give a copy of the proposed storage agreement to the lienholder in the same manner as provided by subsection (4)(b) of this section. The landlord may include a copy of the proposed storage agreement with the notice of abandoned property required by subsection (4) of this section. A lienholder enters into a storage agree-

ment by signing a copy of the agreement provided by the landlord and personally delivering or mailing the signed copy to the landlord within the 60-day period.

(d) The storage agreement may require, in addition to other provisions agreed to by the landlord and the lienholder, that:

(A) The lienholder make timely periodic payment of all storage charges, as described in subsection (7)(b) of this section, accruing from the commencement of the 45-day period described in subsection (6) of this section. A storage charge may include a utility or service charge, as described in ORS 90.510 (8), if limited to charges for electricity, water, sewer service and natural gas and if incidental to the storage of personal property. A storage charge may not be due more frequently than monthly;

(B) The lienholder pay a late charge or fee for failure to pay a storage charge by the date required in the agreement, if the amount of the late charge is no greater than for late charges imposed on facility tenants;

(C) The lienholder maintain the personal property and the space on which the personal property is stored in a manner consistent with the rights and obligations described in the rental agreement that the landlord currently provides to tenants as required by ORS 90.510 (4); and

(D) The lienholder repair any defects in the physical condition of the personal property that existed prior to the lienholder entering into the storage agreement, if the defects and necessary repairs are reasonably described in the storage agreement and, for homes that were first placed on the space within the previous 24 months, the repairs are reasonably consistent with facility standards in effect at the time of placement. The lienholder shall have 90 days after entering into the storage agreement to make the repairs. Failure to make the repairs within the allotted time constitutes a violation of the storage agreement and the landlord may terminate the agreement by giving at least 14 days' written notice to the lienholder stating facts sufficient to notify the lienholder of the reason for termination. Unless the lienholder corrects the violation within the notice period, the agreement terminates as provided and the landlord may sell or dispose of the property without further notice to the lienholder.

(e) Notwithstanding subsection (7)(b) of this section, a landlord may increase the storage charge if the increase is part of a facility-wide rent increase for all facility tenants, the increase is no greater than the increase for other tenants and the landlord gives the lienholder written notice consistent with the requirements of ORS 90.600 (1).

(f) During the term of an agreement described under this subsection, the lienholder shall have the right to remove or sell the property, subject to the provisions of its lien. Selling the property includes a sale to a purchaser who wishes to leave the property on the rented space and become a tenant, subject to the provisions of ORS 90.680. The landlord may condition approval for occupancy of any purchaser of the property upon payment of all unpaid storage charges and maintenance costs.

(g)(A) Except as provided in paragraph (d)(D) of this subsection, if the lienholder violates the storage agreement, the landlord may terminate the agreement by giving at least 90 days' written notice to the lienholder stating facts sufficient to notify the lienholder of the reason for the termination. Unless the lienholder corrects the violation within the notice period, the agreement terminates as provided and the landlord may sell or dispose of the property without further notice to the lienholder.

(B) After a landlord gives a termination notice pursuant to subparagraph (A) of this paragraph for failure of the lienholder to pay a storage charge and the lienholder corrects the violation, if the lienholder again violates the storage agreement by failing to pay a subsequent storage charge, the landlord may terminate the agreement by giving at least 30 days' written notice to the lienholder stating facts sufficient to notify the lienholder of the reason for termination. Unless the lienholder corrects the violation within the notice period, the agreement terminates as provided and the landlord may sell or dispose of the property without further notice to the lienholder.

(C) A lienholder may terminate a storage agreement at any time upon at least 14 days' written notice to the landlord and may remove the property from the facility if the lienholder has paid all storage charges and other charges as provided in the agreement.

(h) Upon the failure of a lienholder to enter into a storage agreement as provided by this subsection or upon termination of an agreement, unless the parties otherwise agree or the lienholder has sold or removed the property, the landlord may sell or dispose of the property pursuant to this section without further notice to the lienholder.

(20) If the personal property is considered abandoned as a result of the death of a tenant who was the only tenant, this section applies, except as follows:

(a) The provisions of this section regarding the rights and responsibilities of a tenant to the abandoned personal property shall apply to any personal representative named in a will or appointed by a court to act for the deceased tenant or any person designated in writing by the tenant to be contacted by the landlord in the event of the tenant's death.
(b) The notice required by subsection (3) of this section shall be:
(A) Sent by first class mail to the deceased tenant at the premises; and
(B) Personally delivered or sent by first class mail to any personal representative or designated person if actually known to the landlord.
(c) The notice described in subsection (5) of this section shall refer to any personal representative or designated person, instead of the deceased tenant, and shall incorporate the provisions of this subsection.
(d) If a personal representative, designated person or other person entitled to possession of the property, such as an heir or devisee, responds by actual notice to a landlord within the 45-day period provided by subsection (6) of this section and so requests, the landlord shall enter into a written storage agreement with the representative or person providing that the personal property may not be sold or disposed of by the landlord for up to 90 days or until conclusion of any probate proceedings, whichever is later. A storage agreement entitles the representative or person to store the personal property on the previously rented space during the term of the agreement, but does not entitle anyone to occupy the personal property. If such an agreement is entered, the landlord may not enter a similar agreement with a lienholder pursuant to subsection (19) of this section until the agreement with the personal representative or designated person ends.
(e) If a personal representative or other person requests that a landlord enter into a storage agreement, subsection (19)(c) to (e) and (g)(C) of this section applies, with the representative or person having the rights and responsibilities of a lienholder with regard to the storage agreement.
(f) During the term of an agreement described under paragraph (d) of this subsection, the representative or person shall have the right to remove or sell the property, including a sale to a purchaser or a transfer to an heir or devisee where the purchaser, heir or devisee wishes to leave the property on the rented space and become a tenant, subject to the provisions of ORS 90.680. The landlord also may condition approval for occupancy of any purchaser, heir or devisee of the property upon payment of all unpaid storage charges and maintenance costs.
(g) If the representative or person violates the storage agreement, the landlord may terminate the agreement by giving at least 30 days' written notice to the representative or person stating facts sufficient to notify the representative or person of the reason for the termination. Unless the representative or person corrects the violation within the notice period, the agreement terminates as provided and the landlord may sell or dispose of the property without further notice to the representative or person.
(h) Upon the failure of a representative or person to enter into a storage agreement as provided by this subsection or upon termination of an agreement, unless the parties otherwise agree or the representative or person has sold or removed the property, the landlord may sell or dispose of the property pursuant to this section without further notice to the representative or person.
(21) If a governmental agency determines that the condition of personal property abandoned under this section constitutes an extreme health or safety hazard under state or local law and the agency determines that the hazard endangers others in the facility and requires quick removal of the property, the landlord may sell or dispose of the property pursuant to this subsection. The landlord shall comply with all provisions of this section, except as follows:
(a) The date provided in subsection (6) of this section by which a tenant, lienholder, personal representative or designated person must contact a landlord to arrange for the disposition of the property shall be not less than 15 days after personal delivery or mailing of the notice required by subsection (3) of this section.
(b) The date provided in subsections (8) and (9) of this section by which a tenant, lienholder, personal representative or designated person must remove the property shall be not less than seven days after the tenant, lienholder, personal representative or designated person contacts the landlord.
(c) The notice required by subsection (3) of this section shall be as provided in subsection (5) of this section, except that:
(A) The dates and deadlines in the notice for contacting the landlord and removing the property shall be consistent with this subsection;
(B) The notice shall state that a governmental agency has determined that the property constitutes an ex-

treme health or safety hazard and must be removed quickly; and
(C) The landlord shall attach a copy of the agency's determination to the notice.
(d) If the tenant, a lienholder or a personal representative or designated person does not remove the property within the time allowed, the landlord or a buyer at a sale by the landlord under subsection (11) of this section shall promptly remove the property from the facility.
(e) A landlord is not required to enter into a storage agreement with a lienholder, personal representative or designated person pursuant to subsection (19) of this section.
(22)(a) A landlord may sell or dispose of a tenant's abandoned personal property without complying with the provisions of this section if, after termination of the tenancy or no more than seven days prior to the termination of the tenancy, the following parties so agree in a writing entered into in good faith:
(A) The landlord;
(B) The tenant, or for an abandonment as the result of the death of a tenant who was the only tenant, the personal representative, designated person or other person entitled to possession of the personal property, such as an heir or devisee, as described in subsection (20) of this section; and
(C) Any lienholder.
(b) A landlord may not, as part of a rental agreement, as a condition to approving a sale of property on rented space under ORS 90.680 or in any other manner, require a tenant, a personal representative, a designated person or any lienholder to waive any right provided by this section.
(23) Until personal property is conclusively presumed to be abandoned under subsection (9) of this section, a landlord does not have a lien pursuant to ORS 87.152 for storing the personal property.

Note: The 2003 Legislative Session enacted amendments to ORS 90.675 with an operative date of May 1, 2005. The foregoing is the text of the statute that is in effect until then. The text of the statute that will become effective on May 1, 2005 is included below.

90.675 Disposition of manufactured dwelling or floating home left in facility; notice; sale; limitation on landlord liability; tax cancellation; storage agreements; hazardous property. (1) As used in this section:
(a) "Current market value" means the amount in cash, as determined by the county assessor, that could reasonably be expected to be paid for personal property by an informed buyer to an informed seller, each acting without compulsion in an arms-length transaction occurring on the assessment date for the tax year or on the date of a subsequent reappraisal by the county assessor.
(b) "Dispose of the personal property" means that, if reasonably appropriate, the landlord may throw away the property or may give it without consideration to a nonprofit organization or to a person unrelated to the landlord. The landlord may not retain the property for personal use or benefit.
(c) "Lienholder" means any lienholder of abandoned personal property, if the lien is of record or the lienholder is actually known to the landlord.
(d) "Of record" means:
(A) For a manufactured dwelling, that a security interest has been properly recorded with the Department of Transportation pursuant to ORS 802.200 (1)(a)(A) and 803.097 for a dwelling registered and titled by the department pursuant to ORS 820.500.
(B) For a floating home, that a security interest has been properly recorded with the State Marine Board pursuant to ORS 830.740 to 830.755 for a home registered and titled with the board pursuant to ORS 830.715.
(e) "Personal property" means only a manufactured dwelling or floating home located in a facility and subject to ORS 90.505 to 90.840. "Personal property" does not include goods left inside a manufactured dwelling or floating home or left upon a rented space and subject to disposition under ORS 90.425.
(2) A landlord may not store, sell or dispose of abandoned personal property except as provided by this section. This section governs the rights and obligations of landlords, tenants and any lienholders in any personal property abandoned or left upon the premises by the tenant or any lienholder in the following circumstances:
(a) The tenancy has ended by termination or expiration of a rental agreement or by relinquishment or abandonment of the premises and the landlord reasonably believes under all the circumstances that the tenant has left the personal property upon the premises with no intention of asserting any further claim to the premises or to the personal property;
(b) The tenant has been absent from the premises continuously for seven days after termination of a tenancy by a court order that has not been executed; or

(c) The landlord receives possession of the premises from the sheriff pursuant to ORS 105.161.
(3) Prior to selling or disposing of the tenant's personal property under this section, the landlord must give a written notice to the tenant that must be:
(a) Personally delivered to the tenant; or
(b) Sent by first class mail addressed and mailed to the tenant at:
(A) The premises;
(B) Any post-office box held by the tenant and actually known to the landlord; and
(C) The most recent forwarding address if provided by the tenant or actually known to the landlord.
(4)(a) A landlord shall also give a copy of the notice described in subsection (3) of this section to:
(A) Any lienholder of the personal property;
(B) The tax collector of the county where the personal property is located; and
(C) The assessor of the county where the personal property is located.
(b) The landlord shall give the notice copy required by this subsection by personal delivery or first class mail, except that for any lienholder, mail service shall be both by first class mail and by certified mail with return receipt requested.
(c) A notice to lienholders under paragraph (a)(A) of this subsection must be sent to each lienholder at each address:
(A) Actually known to the landlord;
(B) Of record; and
(C) Provided to the landlord by the lienholder in a written notice that identifies the personal property subject to the lien and that was sent to the landlord by certified mail with return receipt requested within the preceding five years. The notice must identify the personal property by describing the physical address of the property.
(5) The notice required under subsection (3) of this section must state that:
(a) The personal property left upon the premises is considered abandoned;
(b) The tenant or any lienholder must contact the landlord by a specified date, as provided in subsection (6) of this section, to arrange for the removal of the abandoned personal property;
(c) The personal property is stored on the rented space;
(d) The tenant or any lienholder, except as provided by subsection (18) of this section, may arrange for removal of the personal property by contacting the landlord at a described telephone number or address on or before the specified date;
(e) The landlord shall make the personal property available for removal by the tenant or any lienholder, except as provided by subsection (18) of this section, by appointment at reasonable times;
(f) If the personal property is considered to be abandoned pursuant to subsection (2)(a) or (b) of this section, the landlord may require payment of storage charges, as provided by subsection (7)(b) of this section, prior to releasing the personal property to the tenant or any lienholder;
(g) If the personal property is considered to be abandoned pursuant to subsection (2)(c) of this section, the landlord may not require payment of storage charges prior to releasing the personal property;
(h) If the tenant or any lienholder fails to contact the landlord by the specified date or fails to remove the personal property within 30 days after that contact, the landlord may sell or dispose of the personal property. If the landlord reasonably believes the county assessor will determine that the current market value of the personal property is $8,000 or less, and the landlord intends to dispose of the property if it is not claimed, the notice shall state that belief and intent; and
(i) If applicable, there is a lienholder that has a right to claim the personal property, except as provided by subsection (18) of this section.
(6) For purposes of subsection (5) of this section, the specified date by which a tenant or lienholder must contact a landlord to arrange for the disposition of abandoned personal property shall be not less than 45 days after personal delivery or mailing of the notice.
(7) After notifying the tenant as required by subsection (3) of this section, the landlord:
(a) Shall store the abandoned personal property of the tenant on the rented space and shall exercise reasonable care for the personal property; and
(b) Is entitled to reasonable or actual storage charges and costs incidental to storage or disposal. The storage charge may be no greater than the monthly space rent last payable by the tenant.
(8) If a tenant or lienholder, upon the receipt of the notice provided by subsection (3) or (4) of this section or otherwise, responds by actual notice to the landlord on or before the specified date in the landlord's notice that the tenant or lienholder intends to remove the personal property from the premises, the landlord must make that personal property available for

removal by the tenant or lienholder by appointment at reasonable times during the 30 days following the date of the response, subject to subsection (18) of this section. If the personal property is considered to be abandoned pursuant to subsection (2)(a) or (b) of this section, but not pursuant to subsection (2)(c) of this section, the landlord may require payment of storage charges, as provided in subsection (7)(b) of this section, prior to allowing the tenant or lienholder to remove the personal property. Acceptance by a landlord of such payment does not operate to create or reinstate a tenancy or create a waiver pursuant to ORS 90.415.

(9) Except as provided in subsections (18) to (20) of this section, if the tenant or lienholder does not respond within the time provided by the landlord's notice, or the tenant or lienholder does not remove the personal property within 30 days after responding to the landlord or by any date agreed to with the landlord, whichever is later, the personal property is conclusively presumed to be abandoned. The tenant and any lienholder that have been given notice pursuant to subsection (3) or (4) of this section shall, except with regard to the distribution of sale proceeds pursuant to subsection (13) of this section, have no further right, title or interest to the personal property and may not claim or sell the property.

(10) If the personal property is presumed to be abandoned under subsection (9) of this section, the landlord then may:

(a) Sell the personal property at a public or private sale, provided that prior to the sale:

(A) The landlord may seek to transfer ownership of record of the personal property by complying with the requirements of the appropriate state agency; and

(B) The landlord shall:

(i) Place a notice in a newspaper of general circulation in the county in which the personal property is located. The notice shall state:

(I) That the personal property is abandoned;

(II) The tenant's name;

(III) The address and any space number where the personal property is located, and any plate, registration or other identification number for a floating home noted on the title, if actually known to the landlord;

(IV) Whether the sale is by private bidding or public auction;

(V) Whether the landlord is accepting sealed bids and, if so, the last date on which bids will be accepted; and

(VI) The name and telephone number of the person to contact to inspect the personal property;

(ii) At a reasonable time prior to the sale, give a copy of the notice required by sub-subparagraph (i) of this subparagraph to the tenant and to any lienholder, by personal delivery or first class mail, except that for any lienholder, mail service shall be by first class mail with certificate of mailing;

(iii) Obtain an affidavit of publication from the newspaper to show that the notice required under sub-subparagraph (i) of this subparagraph ran in the newspaper at least one day in each of two consecutive weeks prior to the date scheduled for the sale or the last date bids will be accepted; and

(iv) Obtain written proof from the county that all property taxes on the personal property have been paid or, if not paid, that the county has authorized the sale, with the sale proceeds to be distributed pursuant to subsection (13) of this section; or

(b) Destroy or otherwise dispose of the personal property if the landlord determines from the county assessor that the current market value of the property is $8,000 or less.

(11)(a) A public or private sale authorized by this section shall be conducted consistent with the terms listed in subsection (10)(a)(B)(i) of this section. Every aspect of the sale including the method, manner, time, place and terms must be commercially reasonable.

(b) If there is no buyer at a sale described under paragraph (a) of this subsection, the personal property is considered to be worth $8,000 or less, regardless of current market value, and the landlord shall destroy or otherwise dispose of the personal property.

(12) Notwithstanding ORS 446.155 (1) and (2), unless a landlord intentionally misrepresents the condition of personal property, the landlord is not liable for the condition of the personal property to:

(a) A buyer of the personal property at a sale pursuant to subsection (10)(a) of this section, with or without consideration; or

(b) A person or nonprofit organization to whom the landlord gives the personal property pursuant to subsection (1)(b), (10)(b) or (11)(b) of this section.

(13)(a) The landlord may deduct from the proceeds of the sale:

(A) The reasonable or actual cost of notice, storage and sale; and

(B) Unpaid rent.

(b) After deducting the amounts listed in paragraph (a) of this subsection, the landlord shall remit the re-

maining proceeds, if any, to the county tax collector to the extent of any unpaid property taxes owed on the dwelling or home.
(c) After deducting the amounts listed in paragraphs (a) and (b) of this subsection, if applicable, the landlord shall remit the remaining proceeds, if any, to any lienholder to the extent of any unpaid balance owed on the lien on the personal property.
(d) After deducting the amounts listed in paragraphs (a), (b) and (c) of this subsection, if applicable, the landlord shall remit to the tenant the remaining proceeds, if any, together with an itemized accounting.
(e) If the tenant cannot after due diligence be found, the remaining proceeds shall be deposited with the county treasurer of the county in which the sale occurred. If not claimed within three years the deposited proceeds revert to the general fund of the county available for general purposes.
(14) The county tax collector shall cancel all unpaid property taxes as provided under ORS 311.790 only under one of the following circumstances:
(a) The landlord disposes of the personal property after a determination described in subsection (10)(b) of this section.
(b) There is no buyer of the personal property at a sale described under subsection (11) of this section.
(c)(A) There is a buyer of the personal property at a sale described under subsection (11) of this section;
(B) The current market value of the personal property is $8,000 or less; and
(C) The proceeds of the sale are insufficient to satisfy the unpaid property taxes owed on the personal property after distribution of the proceeds pursuant to subsection (13) of this section.
(d)(A) The landlord buys the personal property at a sale described under subsection (11) of this section;
(B) The current market value of the personal property is more than $8,000;
(C) The proceeds of the sale are insufficient to satisfy the unpaid property taxes owed on the personal property after distribution of the proceeds pursuant to subsection (13) of this section; and
(D) The landlord disposes of the personal property.
(15) The landlord is not responsible for any loss to the tenant or lienholder resulting from storage of personal property in compliance with this section unless the loss was caused by the landlord's deliberate or negligent act. In the event of a deliberate and malicious violation, the landlord is liable for twice the actual damages sustained by the tenant or lienholder.
(16) Complete compliance in good faith with this section shall constitute a complete defense in any action brought by a tenant or lienholder against a landlord for loss or damage to such personal property disposed of pursuant to this section.
(17) If a landlord does not comply with this section:
(a) The tenant is relieved of any liability for damage to the premises caused by conduct that was not deliberate, intentional or grossly negligent and for unpaid rent and may recover from the landlord up to twice the actual damages sustained by the tenant;
(b) A lienholder aggrieved by the noncompliance may recover from the landlord the actual damages sustained by the lienholder. ORS 90.255 does not authorize an award of attorney fees to the prevailing party in any action arising under this paragraph; and
(c) A county tax collector aggrieved by the noncompliance may recover from the landlord the actual damages sustained by the tax collector, if the noncompliance is part of an effort by the landlord to defraud the tax collector. ORS 90.255 does not authorize an award of attorney fees to the prevailing party in any action arising under this paragraph.
(18) The provisions of this section regarding the rights and responsibilities of a tenant to the abandoned personal property shall also apply to any lienholder, except that the lienholder may not sell or remove the dwelling or home unless:
(a) The lienholder has foreclosed its lien on the manufactured dwelling or floating home;
(b) The tenant or a personal representative or designated person described in subsection (20) of this section has waived all rights under this section pursuant to subsection (22) of this section; or
(c) The notice and response periods provided by subsections (6) and (8) of this section have expired.
(19)(a) Except as provided by subsection (20)(d) and (e) of this section, if a lienholder makes a timely response to a notice of abandoned personal property pursuant to subsections (6) and (8) of this section and so requests, a landlord shall enter into a written storage agreement with the lienholder providing that the personal property may not be sold or disposed of by the landlord for up to 12 months. A storage agreement entitles the lienholder to store the personal property on the previously rented space during the term of the agreement, but does not entitle anyone to occupy the personal property.
(b) The lienholder's right to a storage agreement arises upon the failure of the tenant or, in the case of

a deceased tenant, the personal representative, designated person, heir or devisee to remove or sell the dwelling or home within the allotted time.

(c) To exercise the right to a storage agreement under this subsection, in addition to contacting the landlord with a timely response as described in paragraph (a) of this subsection, the lienholder must enter into the proposed storage agreement within 60 days after the landlord gives a copy of the agreement to the lienholder. The landlord shall give a copy of the proposed storage agreement to the lienholder in the same manner as provided by subsection (4)(b) of this section. The landlord may include a copy of the proposed storage agreement with the notice of abandoned property required by subsection (4) of this section. A lienholder enters into a storage agreement by signing a copy of the agreement provided by the landlord and personally delivering or mailing the signed copy to the landlord within the 60-day period.

(d) The storage agreement may require, in addition to other provisions agreed to by the landlord and the lienholder, that:

(A) The lienholder make timely periodic payment of all storage charges, as described in subsection (7)(b) of this section, accruing from the commencement of the 45-day period described in subsection (6) of this section. A storage charge may include a utility or service charge, as described in ORS 90.510 (8), if limited to charges for electricity, water, sewer service and natural gas and if incidental to the storage of personal property. A storage charge may not be due more frequently than monthly;

(B) The lienholder pay a late charge or fee for failure to pay a storage charge by the date required in the agreement, if the amount of the late charge is no greater than for late charges imposed on facility tenants;

(C) The lienholder maintain the personal property and the space on which the personal property is stored in a manner consistent with the rights and obligations described in the rental agreement that the landlord currently provides to tenants as required by ORS 90.510 (4); and

(D) The lienholder repair any defects in the physical condition of the personal property that existed prior to the lienholder entering into the storage agreement, if the defects and necessary repairs are reasonably described in the storage agreement and, for homes that were first placed on the space within the previous 24 months, the repairs are reasonably consistent with facility standards in effect at the time of placement. The lienholder shall have 90 days after entering into the storage agreement to make the repairs. Failure to make the repairs within the allotted time constitutes a violation of the storage agreement and the landlord may terminate the agreement by giving at least 14 days' written notice to the lienholder stating facts sufficient to notify the lienholder of the reason for termination. Unless the lienholder corrects the violation within the notice period, the agreement terminates as provided and the landlord may sell or dispose of the property without further notice to the lienholder.

(e) Notwithstanding subsection (7)(b) of this section, a landlord may increase the storage charge if the increase is part of a facility-wide rent increase for all facility tenants, the increase is no greater than the increase for other tenants and the landlord gives the lienholder written notice consistent with the requirements of ORS 90.600 (1).

(f) During the term of an agreement described under this subsection, the lienholder shall have the right to remove or sell the property, subject to the provisions of its lien. Selling the property includes a sale to a purchaser who wishes to leave the property on the rented space and become a tenant, subject to the provisions of ORS 90.680. The landlord may condition approval for occupancy of any purchaser of the property upon payment of all unpaid storage charges and maintenance costs.

(g)(A) Except as provided in paragraph (d)(D) of this subsection, if the lienholder violates the storage agreement, the landlord may terminate the agreement by giving at least 90 days' written notice to the lienholder stating facts sufficient to notify the lienholder of the reason for the termination. Unless the lienholder corrects the violation within the notice period, the agreement terminates as provided and the landlord may sell or dispose of the property without further notice to the lienholder.

(B) After a landlord gives a termination notice pursuant to subparagraph (A) of this paragraph for failure of the lienholder to pay a storage charge and the lienholder corrects the violation, if the lienholder again violates the storage agreement by failing to pay a subsequent storage charge, the landlord may terminate the agreement by giving at least 30 days' written notice to the lienholder stating facts sufficient to notify the lienholder of the reason for termination. Unless the lienholder corrects the violation within the notice period, the agreement terminates as provided and the landlord may sell or dispose of the property without further notice to the lienholder.

(C) A lienholder may terminate a storage agreement at any time upon at least 14 days' written notice to the landlord and may remove the property from the facility if the lienholder has paid all storage charges and other charges as provided in the agreement.

(h) Upon the failure of a lienholder to enter into a storage agreement as provided by this subsection or upon termination of an agreement, unless the parties otherwise agree or the lienholder has sold or removed the property, the landlord may sell or dispose of the property pursuant to this section without further notice to the lienholder.

(20) If the personal property is considered abandoned as a result of the death of a tenant who was the only tenant, this section applies, except as follows:

(a) The provisions of this section regarding the rights and responsibilities of a tenant to the abandoned personal property shall apply to any personal representative named in a will or appointed by a court to act for the deceased tenant or any person designated in writing by the tenant to be contacted by the landlord in the event of the tenant's death.

(b) The notice required by subsection (3) of this section must be:

(A) Sent by first class mail to the deceased tenant at the premises; and

(B) Personally delivered or sent by first class mail to any personal representative or designated person if actually known to the landlord.

(c) The notice described in subsection (5) of this section must refer to any personal representative or designated person, instead of the deceased tenant, and must incorporate the provisions of this subsection.

(d) If a personal representative, designated person or other person entitled to possession of the property, such as an heir or devisee, responds by actual notice to a landlord within the 45-day period provided by subsection (6) of this section and so requests, the landlord shall enter into a written storage agreement with the representative or person providing that the personal property may not be sold or disposed of by the landlord for up to 90 days or until conclusion of any probate proceedings, whichever is later. A storage agreement entitles the representative or person to store the personal property on the previously rented space during the term of the agreement, but does not entitle anyone to occupy the personal property. If such an agreement is entered, the landlord may not enter a similar agreement with a lienholder pursuant to subsection (19) of this section until the agreement with the personal representative or designated person ends.

(e) If a personal representative or other person requests that a landlord enter into a storage agreement, subsection (19)(c) to (e) and (g)(C) of this section applies, with the representative or person having the rights and responsibilities of a lienholder with regard to the storage agreement.

(f) During the term of an agreement described under paragraph (d) of this subsection, the representative or person shall have the right to remove or sell the property, including a sale to a purchaser or a transfer to an heir or devisee where the purchaser, heir or devisee wishes to leave the property on the rented space and become a tenant, subject to the provisions of ORS 90.680. The landlord also may condition approval for occupancy of any purchaser, heir or devisee of the property upon payment of all unpaid storage charges and maintenance costs.

(g) If the representative or person violates the storage agreement, the landlord may terminate the agreement by giving at least 30 days' written notice to the representative or person stating facts sufficient to notify the representative or person of the reason for the termination. Unless the representative or person corrects the violation within the notice period, the agreement terminates as provided and the landlord may sell or dispose of the property without further notice to the representative or person.

(h) Upon the failure of a representative or person to enter into a storage agreement as provided by this subsection or upon termination of an agreement, unless the parties otherwise agree or the representative or person has sold or removed the property, the landlord may sell or dispose of the property pursuant to this section without further notice to the representative or person.

(21) If a governmental agency determines that the condition of personal property abandoned under this section constitutes an extreme health or safety hazard under state or local law and the agency determines that the hazard endangers others in the facility and requires quick removal of the property, the landlord may sell or dispose of the property pursuant to this subsection. The landlord shall comply with all provisions of this section, except as follows:

(a) The date provided in subsection (6) of this section by which a tenant, lienholder, personal representative or designated person must contact a landlord to arrange for the disposition of the property must be not

less than 15 days after personal delivery or mailing of the notice required by subsection (3) of this section.
(b) The date provided in subsections (8) and (9) of this section by which a tenant, lienholder, personal representative or designated person must remove the property must be not less than seven days after the tenant, lienholder, personal representative or designated person contacts the landlord.
(c) The notice required by subsection (3) of this section must be as provided in subsection (5) of this section, except that:
(A) The dates and deadlines in the notice for contacting the landlord and removing the property must be consistent with this subsection;
(B) The notice must state that a governmental agency has determined that the property constitutes an extreme health or safety hazard and must be removed quickly; and
(C) The landlord shall attach a copy of the agency's determination to the notice.
(d) If the tenant, a lienholder or a personal representative or designated person does not remove the property within the time allowed, the landlord or a buyer at a sale by the landlord under subsection (11) of this section shall promptly remove the property from the facility.
(e) A landlord is not required to enter into a storage agreement with a lienholder, personal representative or designated person pursuant to subsection (19) of this section.
(22)(a) A landlord may sell or dispose of a tenant's abandoned personal property without complying with the provisions of this section if, after termination of the tenancy or no more than seven days prior to the termination of the tenancy, the following parties so agree in a writing entered into in good faith:
(A) The landlord;
(B) The tenant, or for an abandonment as the result of the death of a tenant who was the only tenant, the personal representative, designated person or other person entitled to possession of the personal property, such as an heir or devisee, as described in subsection (20) of this section; and
(C) Any lienholder.
(b) A landlord may not, as part of a rental agreement, as a condition to approving a sale of property on rented space under ORS 90.680 or in any other manner, require a tenant, a personal representative, a designated person or any lienholder to waive any right provided by this section.
(23) Until personal property is conclusively presumed to be abandoned under subsection (9) of this section, a landlord does not have a lien pursuant to ORS 87.152 for storing the personal property.

90.680 Sale of dwelling or home on rented space; duties and rights of seller, prospective purchaser and landlord. (1) A landlord shall not deny any manufactured dwelling or floating home space tenant the right to sell a manufactured dwelling or floating home on a rented space or require the tenant to remove the dwelling or home from the space solely on the basis of the sale.
(2) The landlord may not exact a commission or fee for the sale of a manufactured dwelling or floating home on a rented space unless the landlord has acted as agent for the seller pursuant to written contract.
(3) The landlord may not deny the tenant the right to place a "for sale" sign on or in a manufactured dwelling or floating home owned by the tenant. The size, placement and character of such signs shall be subject to reasonable rules of the landlord.
(4) If the prospective purchaser of a manufactured dwelling or floating home desires to leave the dwelling or home on the rented space and become a tenant, the landlord may require:
(a) Except when a termination or abandonment occurs, that a tenant give not more than 10 days' notice in writing prior to the sale of the dwelling or home on a rented space;
(b) That prior to the sale, the prospective purchaser submit to the landlord a complete and accurate written application for occupancy of the dwelling or home as a tenant after the sale is finalized and that a prospective purchaser may not occupy the dwelling or home until after the prospective purchaser is accepted by the landlord as a tenant;
(c) That a tenant give notice to any lienholder, prospective purchaser or person licensed to sell dwellings or homes of the requirements of paragraphs (b) and (d) of this subsection, the location of all properly functioning smoke alarms and any other rules and regulations of the facility such as those described in ORS 90.510 (5)(b), (f), (h) and (i); and
(d) If the sale is not by a lienholder, that the prospective purchaser pay in full all rents, fees, deposits or charges owed by the tenant as authorized under ORS 90.140 and the rental agreement, prior to the landlord's acceptance of the prospective purchaser as a tenant.

(5) If a landlord requires a prospective purchaser to submit an application for occupancy as a tenant under subsection (4) of this section, at the time that the landlord gives the prospective purchaser an application the landlord shall also give the prospective purchaser copies of the statement of policy, the rental agreement and the facility rules and regulations, including any conditions imposed on a subsequent sale, all as provided by ORS 90.510. The terms of the statement, rental agreement and rules and regulations need not be the same as those in the selling tenant's statement, rental agreement and rules and regulations.
(6) The following apply if a landlord receives an application for tenancy from a prospective purchaser under subsection (4) of this section:
(a) The landlord shall accept or reject the prospective purchaser's application within seven days following the day the landlord receives a complete and accurate written application. An application is not complete until the prospective purchaser pays any required applicant screening charge and provides the landlord with all information and documentation, including any financial data and references, required by the landlord pursuant to ORS 90.510 (5)(h). The landlord and the prospective purchaser may agree to a longer time period for the landlord to evaluate the prospective purchaser's application or to allow the prospective purchaser to address any failure to meet the landlord's screening or admission criteria. If a tenant has not previously given the landlord the 10 days' notice required under subsection (4)(a) of this section, the period provided for the landlord to accept or reject a complete and accurate written application is extended to 10 days.
(b) The landlord may not unreasonably reject a prospective purchaser as a tenant. Reasonable cause for rejection includes, but is not limited to, failure of the prospective purchaser to meet the landlord's conditions for approval as provided in ORS 90.510 (5)(h) or failure of the purchaser's references to respond to the landlord's timely request for verification within the time allowed for acceptance or rejection under paragraph (a) of this subsection. Except as provided in paragraph (c) of this subsection, the landlord shall furnish to the seller and purchaser a written statement of the reasons for the rejection.
(c) If a rejection under paragraph (b) of this subsection is based upon a consumer report, as defined in 15 U.S.C. 1681a for purposes of the federal Fair Credit Reporting Act, the landlord shall not disclose the contents of the report to anyone other than the purchaser. The landlord shall disclose to the seller in writing that the rejection is based upon information contained within a consumer report and that the landlord cannot disclose the information within the report.
(7) The following apply if a landlord does not require a prospective purchaser to submit an application for occupancy as a tenant under subsection (4) of this section or if the landlord does not accept or reject the prospective purchaser as a tenant within the time required under subsection (6) of this section:
(a) The landlord waives any right to bring an action against the tenant under the rental agreement for breach of the landlord's right to establish conditions upon and approve a prospective purchaser of the tenant's dwelling or home;
(b) The prospective purchaser, upon completion of the sale, may occupy the dwelling or home as a tenant under the same conditions and terms as the tenant who sold the dwelling or home; and
(c) If the prospective purchaser becomes a new tenant, the landlord may only impose conditions or terms on the tenancy that are inconsistent with the terms and conditions of the seller's rental agreement if the new tenant agrees in writing.
(8) A landlord may not, because of the age, size, style or original construction material of the dwelling or home or because the dwelling or home was built prior to adoption of the National Manufactured Home Construction and Safety Standards Act of 1974 (42 U.S.C. 5403), in compliance with the standards of that Act in effect at that time or in compliance with the state building code as defined in ORS 455.010:
(a) Reject an application for tenancy from a prospective purchaser of an existing dwelling or home on a rented space within a facility; or
(b) Require a prospective purchaser of an existing dwelling or home on a rented space within a facility to remove the dwelling or home from the rented space.
(9) A tenant who has received a notice pursuant to ORS 90.632 has the right to sell the tenant's dwelling or home in compliance with this section during the notice period. The tenant shall provide a prospective purchaser with a copy of any outstanding notice given pursuant to ORS 90.632 prior to a sale. The landlord may also give any prospective purchaser a copy of any such notice. The landlord may require as

a condition of tenancy that a prospective purchaser who desires to leave the dwelling or home on the rented space and become a tenant must comply with the notice within the notice period consistent with ORS 90.632. If the tenancy has been terminated pursuant to ORS 90.632, or the notice period provided in ORS 90.632 has expired without a correction of cause or extension of time to correct, a prospective purchaser does not have a right to leave the dwelling or home on the rented space and become a tenant.

(10) Except as provided by subsection (9) of this section, after a tenancy has ended and during the period provided by ORS 90.675 (6) and (8), a former tenant retains the right to sell the tenant's dwelling or home to a purchaser who wishes to leave the dwelling or home on the rented space and become a tenant as provided by this section, if the former tenant makes timely periodic payment of all storage charges as provided by ORS 90.675 (7)(b), maintains the dwelling or home and the rented space on which it is stored and enters the premises only with the written permission of the landlord. Payment of the storage charges or maintenance of the dwelling or home and the space does not create or reinstate a tenancy or create a waiver pursuant to ORS 90.415. A former tenant has no right to enter the premises without the written permission of the landlord, including entry to maintain the dwelling or home or the space or to facilitate a sale.

(Actions)

90.710 Causes of action; limit on cause of action of tenant; attorney fees. (1) Any person aggrieved by a violation of ORS 90.525, 90.630, 90.680 or 90.765 shall have a cause of action against the violator thereof for any damages sustained as a result of the violation or $200, whichever is greater.

(2)(a) Except as provided in paragraphs (b) and (c) of this subsection, a tenant shall have a cause of action against the landlord for a violation of ORS 90.510 (4) for any damages sustained as a result of such violation, or $100, whichever is greater.

(b) However, the tenant shall have no cause of action if, within 10 days after the tenant requests a written agreement from the landlord, the landlord offers to enter into a written agreement which does not substantially alter the terms of the oral agreement made when the tenant rented the space and which complies with this chapter.

(c) If, within 10 days after being served with a complaint alleging a violation of ORS 90.510, the landlord offers to enter into a written rental agreement with each of the other tenants of the landlord which does not substantially alter the terms of the oral agreement made when each tenant rented the space and which complies with this chapter, then the landlord shall not be subject to any further liability to such other tenants for previous violations of ORS 90.510.

(d) Notwithstanding ORS 41.580 (1), if a landlord and a tenant mutually agree on the terms of an oral agreement for renting residential property, but the tenant refuses to sign a written memorandum of that agreement after it has been reduced to writing by the landlord and offered to the tenant for the tenant's signature, the oral agreement shall be enforceable notwithstanding the tenant's refusal to sign.

(e) A purchaser shall have a cause of action against a seller for damages sustained or $100, whichever is greater, who sells the tenant's manufactured dwelling or floating home to the purchaser before the landlord has accepted the purchaser as a tenant if:

(A) The landlord rejects the purchaser as a tenant; and

(B) The seller knew the purchaser intended to leave the manufactured dwelling or floating home on the space.

(3) The court may award reasonable attorney fees to the prevailing party in an action under this section.

90.720 Action to enjoin violation of ORS 90.750 or 90.755. In addition to the tenant's cause of action under ORS 90.710, any tenant prevented from exercising the rights in ORS 90.750 or 90.755 may bring an action in the appropriate court having jurisdiction in the county in which the alleged infringement occurred, and upon favorable adjudication, the court shall enjoin the enforcement of any provision contained in any bylaw, rental agreement, regulation or rule, pertaining to a facility, which operates to deprive the tenant of these rights.

(Landlord Rights and Obligations)

90.725 Landlord access to rented space. (1) A landlord or a landlord's agent may enter onto a rented space, not including the tenant's manufactured dwelling or floating home or an accessory building or structure, in order to inspect the space, make necessary or agreed repairs, decorations, alterations or improvements, supply necessary or agreed services, perform agreed yard maintenance, equipment servicing or grounds keeping or exhibit the space to prospective or actual purchasers of the facility, mortgagees, tenants, workers or contractors. The right of access of the landlord or landlord's agent is limited as follows:

(a) A landlord or landlord's agent may enter upon the rented space without consent of the tenant and without notice to the tenant for the purpose of serving notices required or permitted under this chapter, the rental agreement or any provision of applicable law.
(b) In case of an emergency, a landlord or landlord's agent may enter the rented space without consent of the tenant, without notice to the tenant and at any time. "Emergency" includes but is not limited to a repair problem that, unless remedied immediately, is likely to cause serious damage to the premises. If a landlord or landlord's agent makes an emergency entry in the tenant's absence, the landlord shall give the tenant actual notice within 24 hours after the entry, and the notice shall include the fact of the entry, the date and time of the entry, the nature of the emergency and the names of the persons who entered.
(c) If the tenant requests repairs or maintenance in writing, the landlord or landlord's agent, without further notice, may enter upon demand, in the tenant's absence or without consent of the tenant, for the purpose of making the requested repairs until the repairs are completed. The tenant's written request may specify allowable times. Otherwise, the entry must be at a reasonable time. The authorization to enter provided by the tenant's written request expires after seven days, unless the repairs are in progress and the landlord or landlord's agent is making a reasonable effort to complete the repairs in a timely manner. If the person entering to do the repairs is not the landlord, upon request of the tenant, the person must show the tenant written evidence from the landlord authorizing that person to act for the landlord in making the repairs.
(d)(A) If a written agreement requires the landlord to perform yard maintenance, equipment servicing or grounds keeping for the space:
(i) A landlord and tenant may agree that the landlord or landlord's agent may enter for that purpose upon the space, without notice to the tenant, at reasonable times and with reasonable frequency. The terms of the right of entry must be described in the rental agreement or in a separate written agreement.
(ii) A tenant may deny consent for a landlord or landlord's agent to enter upon the space pursuant to this paragraph if the entry is at an unreasonable time or with unreasonable frequency. The tenant must assert the denial by giving actual notice of the denial to the landlord or landlord's agent prior to, or at the time of, the attempted entry.
(B) As used in this paragraph:
(i) "Yard maintenance, equipment servicing or grounds keeping" includes, but is not limited to, servicing individual septic tank systems or water pumps, weeding, mowing grass and pruning trees and shrubs.
(ii) "Unreasonable time" refers to a time of day, day of the week or particular time that conflicts with the tenant's reasonable and specific plans to use the space.
(e) In all other cases, unless there is an agreement between the landlord and the tenant to the contrary regarding a specific entry, the landlord shall give the tenant at least 24 hours' actual notice of the intent of the landlord to enter and the landlord or landlord's agent may enter only at reasonable times. The landlord or landlord's agent may not enter if the tenant, after receiving the landlord's notice, denies consent to enter. The tenant must assert this denial of consent by giving actual notice of the denial to the landlord or the landlord's agent prior to, or at the time of, the attempt by the landlord or landlord's agent to enter.
(2) A landlord shall not abuse the right of access or use it to harass the tenant. A tenant shall not unreasonably withhold consent from the landlord to enter.
(3) A landlord has no other right of access except:
(a) Pursuant to court order;
(b) As permitted by ORS 90.410 (2); or
(c) When the tenant has abandoned or relinquished the premises.
(4) If a landlord is required by a governmental agency to enter a rented space, but the landlord fails to gain entry after a good faith effort in compliance with this section, the landlord shall not be found in violation of any state statute or local ordinance due to the failure.
(5) If the tenant refuses to allow lawful access, the landlord may obtain injunctive relief to compel access or may terminate the rental agreement pursuant to ORS 90.630 (1) and take possession in the manner provided in ORS 105.105 to 105.168. In addition, the landlord may recover actual damages.
(6) If the landlord makes an unlawful entry or a lawful entry in an unreasonable manner or makes repeated demands for entry otherwise lawful but that have the effect of unreasonably harassing the tenant, the tenant may obtain injunctive relief to prevent the reoccurrence of the conduct or may terminate the rental agreement pursuant to ORS 90.620 (1). In addition, the tenant may recover actual damages not less than an amount equal to one month's rent.

90.730 Landlord to maintain rented space and common areas in habitable condition. (1) A landlord who rents a space for a manufactured dwelling or floating home shall at all times during the tenancy maintain the rented space and the facility common areas in a habitable condition. The landlord does not have a duty to maintain a dwelling or home. A landlord's habitability duty under this section includes only the matters described in subsections (2) and (3) of this section.

(2) For purposes of this section, a rented space is considered unhabitable if it substantially lacks:

(a) A sewage disposal system and a connection to the space approved under applicable law at the time of installation and maintained in good working order to the extent that the sewage disposal system can be controlled by the landlord;

(b) If required by applicable law, a drainage system reasonably capable of disposing of storm water, ground water and subsurface water, approved under applicable law at the time of installation and maintained in good working order;

(c) A water supply and a connection to the space approved under applicable law at the time of installation and maintained so as to provide safe drinking water and to be in good working order to the extent that the water supply system can be controlled by the landlord;

(d) An electrical supply and a connection to the space approved under applicable law at the time of installation and maintained in good working order to the extent that the electrical supply system can be controlled by the landlord;

(e) At the time of commencement of the rental agreement, buildings, grounds and appurtenances that are kept in every part safe for normal and reasonably foreseeable uses, clean, sanitary and free from all accumulations of debris, filth, rubbish, garbage, rodents and vermin;

(f) Except as otherwise provided by local ordinance or by written agreement between the landlord and the tenant, an adequate number of appropriate receptacles for garbage and rubbish in clean condition and good repair at the time of commencement of the rental agreement, and for which the landlord shall provide and maintain appropriate serviceable receptacles thereafter and arrange for their removal; and

(g) Completion of any landlord-provided space improvements, including but not limited to installation of carports, garages, driveways and sidewalks, approved under applicable law at the time of installation.

(3)(a) For purposes of this section, "facility common areas" means all areas under control of the landlord and held out for the general use of tenants.

(b) A facility common area is considered unhabitable if it substantially lacks:

(A) Buildings, grounds and appurtenances that are kept in every part safe for normal and reasonably foreseeable uses, clean, sanitary and free from all accumulations of debris, filth, rubbish, garbage, rodents and vermin;

(B) Safety from the hazards of fire; and

(C) Trees, shrubbery and grass maintained in a safe manner.

(4) The landlord and tenant may agree in writing that the tenant is to perform specified repairs, maintenance tasks and minor remodeling only if:

(a) The agreement of the parties is entered into in good faith and not for the purpose of evading the obligations of the landlord;

(b) The agreement does not diminish the obligations of the landlord to other tenants on the premises; and

(c) The terms and conditions of the agreement are clearly and fairly disclosed and adequate consideration for the agreement is specifically stated.

(Tenant Rights and Obligations)

90.740 Tenant obligations. A tenant shall:

(1) Install the tenant's manufactured dwelling or floating home and any accessory building or structure on a rented space in compliance with applicable laws and the rental agreement.

(2) Except as provided by the rental agreement, dispose from the dwelling or home and the rented space all ashes, garbage, rubbish and other waste in a clean, safe and legal manner. With regard to needles, syringes and other infectious waste, as defined in ORS 459.386, the tenant may not dispose of these items by placing them in garbage receptacles or in any other place or manner except as authorized by state and local governmental agencies.

(3) Behave, and require persons on the premises with the consent of the tenant to behave, in compliance with the rental agreement and with any laws or ordinances that relate to the tenant's behavior as a tenant.

(4) Except as provided by the rental agreement:

(a) Use the rented space and the facility common areas in a reasonable manner considering the purposes for which they were designed and intended;

(b) Keep the rented space in every part free from all accumulations of debris, filth, rubbish, garbage, rodents and vermin as the condition of the rented space

permits and to the extent that the tenant is responsible for causing the problem. The tenant shall cooperate to a reasonable extent in assisting the landlord in any reasonable effort to remedy the problem;
(c) Keep the dwelling or home, and the rented space, safe from the hazards of fire;
(d) Install and maintain in the dwelling or home a smoke alarm approved under applicable law;
(e) Install and maintain storm water drains on the roof of the dwelling or home and connect the drains to the drainage system, if any;
(f) Use electrical, water, storm water drainage and sewage disposal systems in a reasonable manner and maintain the connections to those systems;
(g) Refrain from deliberately or negligently destroying, defacing, damaging, impairing or removing any part of the facility, other than the tenant's own dwelling or home, or knowingly permitting any person to do so;
(h) Maintain, water and mow or prune any trees, shrubbery or grass on the rented space; and
(i) Behave, and require persons on the premises with the consent of the tenant to behave, in a manner that does not disturb the peaceful enjoyment of the premises by neighbors.

90.750 Right to assemble or canvass in facility; limitations. No provision contained in any bylaw, rental agreement, regulation or rule pertaining to a facility shall:
(1) Infringe upon the right of persons who rent spaces in a facility to peaceably assemble in an open public meeting for any lawful purpose, at reasonable times and in a reasonable manner, in the common areas or recreational areas of the facility. Reasonable times shall include daily the hours between 8 a.m. and 10 p.m.
(2) Infringe upon the right of persons who rent spaces in a facility to communicate or assemble among themselves, at reasonable times and in a reasonable manner, for the purpose of discussing any matter, including but not limited to any matter relating to the facility or manufactured dwelling or floating home living. The discussions may be held in the common areas or recreational areas of the facility, including halls or centers, or any resident's dwelling unit or floating home. The landlord of a facility, however, may enforce reasonable rules and regulations including but not limited to place, scheduling, occupancy densities and utilities.
(3) Prohibit any person who rents a space for a manufactured dwelling or floating home from canvassing other persons in the same facility for purposes described in this section. As used in this subsection, "canvassing" includes door-to-door contact, an oral or written request, the distribution, the circulation, the posting or the publication of a notice or newsletter or a general announcement or any other matter relevant to the membership of a tenants' association.
(4) This section is not intended to require a landlord to permit any person to solicit money, except that a tenants' association member, whether or not a tenant of the facility, may personally collect delinquent dues owed by an existing member of a tenants' association.
(5) This section is not intended to require a landlord to permit any person to disregard a tenant's request not to be canvassed.

90.755 Right to speak on political issues; limitations; placement of political signs. (1) No provision in any bylaw, rental agreement, regulation or rule shall infringe upon the right of a person who rents a space for a manufactured dwelling or floating home to invite public officers, candidates for public office or officers or representatives of a tenant organization to appear and speak upon matters of public interest in the common areas or recreational areas of the facility at reasonable times and in a reasonable manner in an open public meeting. The landlord of a facility, however, may enforce reasonable rules and regulations relating to the time, place and scheduling of the speakers that will protect the interests of the majority of the homeowners.
(2) The landlord shall allow the tenant to place political signs on or in a manufactured dwelling or floating home owned by the tenant. The size, placement and character of such signs shall be subject to the reasonable rules of the landlord.

90.760 Notice to tenants' association when park becomes subject to listing agreement. (1) A tenants' association or a facility purchase association may give written notice to the landlord of a facility in which some or all of the members of the associations reside as tenants requesting that the associations be notified, by first class mail to no more than three specified persons and addresses for each association, in the event the facility becomes subject to a listing agreement for the sale of all or part of the facility.
(2) If an association requests notice pursuant to subsection (1) of this section, the landlord shall give written notice to the persons and addresses designated in the request as soon as all or any portion of the facility becomes subject to a listing agreement entered into by or on behalf of the owner.

90.765 Prohibitions on retaliatory conduct by landlord. (1) In addition to the prohibitions of ORS 90.385, a landlord who rents a space for a manufactured dwelling or floating home may not retaliate by increasing rent or decreasing services, by serving a notice to terminate the tenancy or by bringing or threatening to bring an action for possession after:
(a) The tenant has expressed an intention to complain to agencies listed in ORS 90.385;
(b) The tenant has made any complaint to the landlord which is in good faith;
(c) The tenant has filed or expressed intent to file a complaint under ORS 659A.820; or
(d) The tenant has performed or expressed intent to perform any other act for the purpose of asserting, protecting or invoking the protection of any right secured to tenants under any federal, state or local law.
(2) If the landlord acts in violation of subsection (1) of this section the tenant is entitled to the remedies provided in ORS 90.710 (1) and has a defense in any retaliatory action against the tenant for possession.
90.771 Confidentiality of information regarding disputes. (1) In order to foster the role of the Office of the Manufactured Dwelling Park Community Relations in mediating and resolving disputes between landlords and tenants of manufactured dwelling and floating home facilities, the Housing and Community Services Department shall establish procedures to maintain the confidentiality of information received by the office pertaining to individual landlords and tenants of facilities and to landlord-tenant disputes. The procedures must comply with the provisions of this section.
(2) Except as provided in subsection (3) of this section, the department shall treat as confidential and not disclose:
(a) The identity of a landlord, tenant or complainant involved in a dispute or of a person who provides information to the department in response to a department investigation of a dispute;
(b) Information provided to the department by a landlord, tenant, complainant or other person relating to a dispute; or
(c) Information discovered by the department in investigating a dispute.
(3) The department may disclose:
(a) Information described in subsection (2) of this section to a state agency; and
(b) Information described in subsection (2) of this section if the landlord, tenant, complainant or other person who provided the information being disclosed, or the legal representative thereof, consents orally or in writing to the disclosure and specifies to whom the disclosure may be made. Only the landlord, tenant, complainant or other person who provided the information to the department may authorize or deny the disclosure of the information.
(4) This section does not prohibit the department from compiling and disclosing examples and statistics that demonstrate information such as the type of dispute, frequency of occurrence and geographical area where the dispute occurred if the identity of the landlord, tenant, complainant and other persons are protected.
90.775 Rules; adoption. The Housing and Community Services Department may adopt rules necessary to carry out the provisions of ORS 90.771.

(Facility Purchase by Tenants)

90.800 Policy. (1) The State of Oregon encourages affordable housing options for all Oregonians. One housing alternative chosen by many Oregonians is facility living. The Legislative Assembly finds that many facility residents would like to join together to purchase the facility in which they live in order to have greater control over the costs and environment of their housing. The Legislative Assembly also finds that current market conditions place residents at a disadvantage with other potential investors in the purchase of facilities.
(2) It is the policy of the State of Oregon to encourage facility residents to participate in the housing marketplace by insuring that technical assistance, financing opportunities, notice of sale of facilities and the option to purchase facilities are made available to residents who choose to participate in the purchase of a facility.
(3) The purpose of ORS 90.100, 90.630, 90.760, 90.800 to 90.840, 308.905, 446.003, 456.579 and 456.581 is to strengthen the private housing market in Oregon by encouraging all Oregonians to have the ability to participate in the purchase of housing of their choice.
90.810 Association notification of possible sale of facility. (1) A facility owner shall notify, as described in ORS 90.760, the tenants' association and a facility purchase association within 10 days of receipt of:
(a) Any written offer received by the owner or agent of the owner to purchase the facility which the owner intends to consider; or
(b) Any listing agreement entered into, by the owner or agent of the owner, to effect the sale of the facility.

(2) The notice required by subsection (1) of this section shall be mailed to any association and facility purchase association.

90.815 Incorporation of facility purchase association. A facility purchase association shall comply with the provisions of ORS chapters 60, 62 and 65 before making the offer provided for under ORS 90.820.

90.820 Facility purchase by association or nonprofit corporation; procedures. (1) Within 14 days of delivery by or on behalf of the facility owner of the notice required by ORS 90.760 (2) or 90.810, a tenants' association or facility purchase association may notify the owner of the facility in which the tenants reside by certified mail or personal service at the address disclosed to the tenants under ORS 90.305 (1)(a) that the association, or a tenants' association supported nonprofit organization, is interested in purchasing the facility.

(2) Upon delivery of the notice required by subsection (1) of this section, the owner shall negotiate in good faith with the association or organization and provide the association or organization an opportunity to purchase the facility as the owner would any bona fide third party potential purchaser.

(3) A facility purchase association or tenants' association actively involved in negotiations with a facility owner may waive or reduce the time periods for notice described in this section. A facility purchase association or tenants' association may authorize a tenants' association supported nonprofit organization to waive notice on behalf of the association.

(4) This section, ORS 90.760 (2) and 90.810 do not apply to:

(a) Any sale or transfer to a person who would be included within the table of descent and distribution if the facility owner were to die intestate.

(b) Any transfer by gift, devise or operation of law.

(c) Any transfer by a corporation to an affiliate. As used in this paragraph, "affiliate" means any shareholder of the transferring corporation, any corporation or entity owned or controlled, directly or indirectly, by the transferring corporation or any other corporation or entity owned or controlled, directly or indirectly, by any shareholder of the transferring corporation.

(d) Any transfer by a partnership to any of its partners.

(e) Any conveyance of an interest in a facility incidental to the financing of the facility.

(f) Any conveyance resulting from the foreclosure of a mortgage, deed of trust or other instrument encumbering a facility or any deed given in lieu of a foreclosure.

(g) Any sale or transfer between or among joint tenants or tenants in common owning a facility.

(h) Any exchange of a facility for other real property, whether or not the exchange also involves the payment of cash or other boot.

(i) The purchase of a facility by a governmental entity under that entity's powers of eminent domain.

90.830 Facility owner affidavit of compliance with procedures. (1) A facility owner may at any time record, in the County Clerk Lien Record of the county where a facility is situated, an affidavit in which the facility owner certifies that:

(a) With reference to an offer by the owner for the sale of the facility, the owner has complied with the provisions of ORS 90.820;

(b) With reference to an offer received by the owner for the purchase of the facility, or with reference to a counteroffer that the owner intends to make, or has made, for the sale of the facility, the owner has complied with the provisions of ORS 90.820;

(c) Notwithstanding compliance with the provisions of ORS 90.820, no contract for the sale of the facility has been executed between the owner and a facility purchase association, tenants' association or tenants' association supported nonprofit organization;

(d) The provisions of ORS 90.820 are inapplicable to a particular sale or transfer of the facility by the owner, and compliance with those subsections is not required; or

(e) A particular sale or transfer of the facility is exempted from the provisions of this section and ORS 90.820.

(2) Any party acquiring an interest in a facility, and any and all title insurance companies and attorneys preparing, furnishing or examining any evidence of title, have the absolute right to rely on the truth and accuracy of all statements appearing in the affidavit and are under no obligation to inquire further as to any matter or fact relating to the facility owner's compliance with the provisions of ORS 90.820.

(3) It is the purpose and intention of this section to preserve the marketability of title to facilities, and, accordingly, the provisions of this section shall be liberally construed in order that all persons may rely on the record title to facilities.

90.840 Park purchase funds, loans. (1) The Director of the Housing and Community Services Department may lend funds available to the Housing and Community Services Department to provide

funds necessary to carry out the provisions of ORS 456.581 (2). Such funds advanced shall be repaid to the Housing and Community Services Department as determined by the director.
(2) Notwithstanding any budget limitation, the director may spend funds available from the Mobile Home Parks Purchase Account to employ personnel to carry out the provisions of ORS 456.581 (1).

(Dealer Sales of Manufactured Dwellings)

90.860 Definitions for ORS 90.865 to 90.875. As used in ORS 90.865 to 90.875:
(1) "Buyer" has the meaning given that term in ORS 72.1030;
(2) "Facility" has the meaning given that term in ORS 90.100;
(3) "Landlord" has the meaning given that term in ORS 90.100;
(4) "Manufactured dwelling" has the meaning given that term in ORS 90.100;
(5) "Manufactured dwelling park" has the meaning given that term in ORS 446.003;
(6) "Purchase money security interest" has the meaning given that term in ORS 79.1070;
(7) "Secured party" has the meaning given that term in ORS 79.1050; and
(8) "Seller" has the meaning given that term in ORS 72.1030.
Note: 90.860 to 90.875 were enacted into law by the Legislative Assembly but were not added to or made a part of ORS chapter 90 or any series therein by legislative action. See Preface to Oregon Revised Statutes for further explanation.
Note: 79.1050 and 79.1070 were repealed by section 187, chapter 445, Oregon Laws 2001. The text of 90.860 was not amended by enactment of the Legislative Assembly to reflect the repeal. Editorial adjustment of 90.860 for the repeal of 79.1050 and 79.1070 has not been made.

90.865 Dealer notice of rent payments and financing. A seller of a manufactured dwelling acting as a vehicle dealer under ORS chapter 822 must provide notice under ORS 90.870 if the manufactured dwelling is to be placed in a facility and the seller:
(1) Pays a portion of the rent for the dwelling; or
(2) Provides financing or assists the buyer in arranging financing that results in a party taking a purchase money security interest in the dwelling and the seller knows that a portion of the proceeds from the financing is to be used to pay a portion of the rent for the dwelling.
Note: See first note under 90.860.

The 2003 Legislative Session enacted amendments to 90.865 with an operative date of May 1, 2005. The text of the statute operative on that date is provided below.

90.865 Dealer notice of rent payments and financing. A seller of a manufactured dwelling who is subject to ORS 446.666 to 446.756 must provide notice under ORS 90.870 if the manufactured dwelling is to be placed in a facility and the seller:
(1) Pays a portion of the rent for the dwelling; or
(2) Provides financing or assists the buyer in arranging financing that results in a party taking a purchase money security interest in the dwelling and the seller knows that a portion of the proceeds from the financing is to be used to pay a portion of the rent for the dwelling.
Note: See first note under 90.860.

90.870 Manner of giving notice; persons entitled to notice. (1) A seller subject to ORS 90.865 must give notice by certified mail to the parties listed in subsection (2) of this section prior to the date the manufactured dwelling is delivered to the facility. The notice must be in writing and include:
(a) A statement that a portion of the rent is being paid by the seller or out of the proceeds from financing; and
(b) The amount and duration of rent that is being paid by the seller or out of the proceeds from financing.
(2) A seller subject to ORS 90.865 must give notice under subsection (1) of this section to:
(a) The buyer;
(b) The landlord; and
(c) The secured party, if any, taking a purchase money security interest in the manufactured dwelling.
Note: See first note under 90.860.

90.875 Remedy for failure to give notice. If a seller fails to provide notice under ORS 90.870, a buyer, landlord or secured party without actual notice that suffers an ascertainable loss as a result of the failure may bring an individual action to recover actual damages or $200, whichever is greater.

Chapter 91 – Tenancy
2003 Edition
Creation and Termination
of Tenancies

91.010 When tenancy is deemed to exist. A tenancy is deemed to exist under this chapter and ORS 105.115 and 105.120 when one has let real estate as a landlord to another.

91.020 Tenancies classified. Tenancies are as follows: Tenancy at sufferance, tenancy at will, tenancy for years, tenancy from year to year, tenancy from month to month, tenancy by entirety and tenancy for life. The times and conditions of the holdings shall determine the nature and character of the tenancy.

91.030 Tenancy by entirety or for life. A tenancy by entirety and a tenancy for life shall be such as now fixed and defined by the laws of the State of Oregon.

91.040 Tenancy at sufferance. One who comes into possession of the real estate of another lawfully, but who holds over by wrong after the termination of the term, is considered as a tenant at sufferance. No notice is required to terminate a tenancy at sufferance.

91.050 Tenancy at will. One who enters into the possession of real estate with the consent of the owners, under circumstances not showing an intention to create a freehold interest, is considered a tenant at will. When the rent reserved in the lease at will is payable at periods of less than three months, a notice to terminate the tenancy is sufficient if it is equal to the interval between the times of payment of rent. The notice to terminate a tenancy at will is sufficient if given for the prescribed period prior to the expiration of the period for which, by the terms of the lease and holding, rents are to be paid.

91.060 Tenancy from year to year. One who enters into the possession of real estate with the consent of the owner, and no certain time is mentioned, but an annual rent is reserved, is considered a tenant from year to year. A notice to terminate a tenancy from year to year is sufficient if it is given 60 days prior to the expiration of the period for which, by the terms of the lease and holding, rents are to be paid.

91.070 Tenancy from month to month. One who holds the lands or tenements of another, under the demise of the other, and no certain time has been mentioned, but a monthly rental has been reserved, is considered a tenant from month to month. Except as otherwise provided by statute or agreement, such tenancy may only be terminated by either the landlord or tenant giving the other, at any time during the tenancy, not less than 30 days' notice in writing prior to the date designated in the notice for the termination of the tenancy. The tenancy shall terminate on the date designated and without regard to the expiration of the period for which, by the terms of the tenancy and holding, rents are to be paid.

91.080 Termination when expiration of tenancy fixed by terms of lease. A tenant entering into the possession of real estate may, by the terms of the lease, fix the date of expiration of the tenancy, and when so fixed, no notice is required to render the holding of the tenant wrongful and by force after the expiration of the term as fixed by the lease.

91.090 Termination of tenancy by failure to pay rent; reinstatement. The failure of a tenant to pay the rent reserved by the terms of the lease for the period of 10 days, unless a different period is stipulated in the lease, after it becomes due and payable, operates to terminate the tenancy. No notice to quit or pay the rent is required to render the holding of such tenant thereafter wrongful; however, if the landlord, after such default in payment of rent, accepts payment thereof, the lease is reinstated for the full period fixed by its terms, subject to termination by subsequent defaults in payment of rent.

91.100 Waiver of notice. Any person entering into the possession of real estate under written lease, as the tenant of another, may, by the terms of the lease of the person, waive the giving of any notice prescribed by ORS 91.050 to 91.070.

91.110 Notices to be in writing; how served. All notices required by ORS 91.050 to 91.070 and by ORS 105.120, must be in writing and must be served upon the tenant by being delivered to the tenant in person or by being posted in a conspicuous place on the leased premises in case of the absence of the tenant, or by being left at the residence or place of abode.

91.115 Tenant not to deny landlord's title. A tenant is not permitted to deny the title of the tenant's landlord at the time of the commencement of the relation.

Eviction of Nontenants

91.120 Eviction of employee; notice required. An employee described in ORS 90.110 (7) may only be evicted pursuant to ORS 105.105 to 105.168 after at least 24 hours' written notice of the termination of employment or a notice period set forth in a written employment contract, whichever is longer. This section does not create the relationship of landlord and tenant between a landlord and such employee.

91.130 Eviction of purchaser or seller of property; notice required. A dwelling unit purchaser or seller described in ORS 90.110 (2) may only be evicted pursuant to ORS 105.105 to 105.168 after at least 24 hours' written notice of the termination of the occupancy or a notice period set forth in a written agreement of sale, whichever is longer. This section does not create the relationship of landlord and tenant between the seller and purchaser.

RENT

91.210 Rents payable in advance unless otherwise agreed; demand unnecessary. Unless otherwise expressly provided by the lease or terms of holding, all rents reserved under the lease or terms of holding are due and payable in advance. The tenant shall pay or tender payment thereof on or prior to the first day of the rent paying period provided in the lease or by the terms of the holding, and no demand therefor is necessary to render a tenant in default.

91.220 Tenant in possession liable for rent; remedies for recovery. (1) Every person in possession of land out of which any rent is due, whether it was originally demised in fee, or for any other estate of freehold, or for any term of years, is liable for the amount or proportion of rent due from the land in possession of the person, although it is only a part of what was originally demised.

(2) Such rent may be recovered in an action at law, and the deed of demise, or other instrument in writing, if there is any, showing the provisions of the lease, may be used in evidence by either party to prove the amount due from the defendant.

(3) This section shall not deprive landlords of any other legal remedy for the recovery of their rents, whether secured to them by their leases or provided by law.

91.225 Local rent control prohibited; exclusions; exceptions. (1) The Legislative Assembly finds that there is a social and economic need to insure an adequate supply of affordable housing for Oregonians. The Legislative Assembly also finds that the imposition of general restrictions on housing rents will disrupt an orderly housing market, increase deferred maintenance of existing housing stock, lead to abandonment of existing rental units and create a property tax shift from rental-owned to owner-occupied housing. Therefore, the Legislative Assembly declares that the imposition of rent control on housing in the State of Oregon is a matter of statewide concern.

(2) Except as provided in subsections (3) to (5) of this section, a city or county shall not enact any ordinance or resolution which controls the rent that may be charged for the rental of any dwelling unit.

(3) This section does not impair the right of any state agency, city, county or urban renewal agency as defined by ORS 457.035 to reserve to itself the right to approve rent increases, establish base rents or establish limitations on rents on any residential property for which it has entered into a contract under which certain benefits are applied to the property for the expressed purpose of providing reduced rents for low income tenants. Such benefits include, but are not limited to, property tax exemptions, long-term financing, rent subsidies, code enforcement procedures and zoning density bonuses.

(4) Cities and counties are not prohibited from including in condominium conversion ordinances a requirement that, during the notification period specified in ORS 100.305, the owner or developer may not raise the rents of any affected tenant except in a proportional amount equal to the percentage increase in the All Items Portland Consumer Price Index since the date of the last rent increase for the dwelling unit then occupied by the affected tenant.

(5) Cities, counties and state agencies may impose temporary rent controls when a natural or man-made disaster that materially eliminates a significant portion of the rental housing supply occurs, but must remove the controls when the rental housing supply is restored to substantially normal levels.

(6) As used in this section, "dwelling unit" and "rent" have the meaning given those terms in ORS 90.100.

(7) This section is applicable throughout this state and in all cities and counties therein. The electors or the governing body of a city or county shall not enact, and the governing body shall not enforce, any ordinance, resolution or other regulation that is inconsistent with this section.

EMBLEMENTS

91.230 Farm tenant's right to emblements. When the leasing or occupation is for the purpose of farming or agriculture, the tenant or person in possession shall, after the termination of the lease or occupancy, have free access to the premises to cultivate and harvest or gather any crop or produce of the soil planted or sown by the tenant or person in possession before the service of notice to quit.

MATTERS RELATING TO GAMBLING LEASES

91.240 Gambling leases prohibited; status of rental contracts; termination; recovery of possession. (1) No person shall let or rent any house, room, shop

or other building, or any boat, booth, garden or other place, knowing or having reason to believe it will be used for gambling purposes.
(2) All contracts for the rent of a room, building or place in violation of subsection (1) of this section are void between the parties.
(3) Any person letting or renting any room, building, or place mentioned in subsection (1) of this section which is at any time used by the lessee or occupant thereof, or any other person with the knowledge or consent of the lessee or occupant, for gambling purposes, upon discovery thereof, may avoid and terminate such lease or contract of occupancy, and recover immediate possession of such building or other place by an action at law for that purpose to be brought before any justice of the peace of the county in which the use is permitted.

91.245 Penalty for letting or renting a place for gambling purposes. Violation of ORS 91.240 (1) results in a forfeiture of twice the amount of the rent of such building or other place for six months to be recovered by action at law instituted by the district attorney in the name of the state.

UTILITY CLAIMS

91.255 Transfer of claim; prohibition; limitations.
(1) As used in this section, "municipal utility" means any city, county or district that provides or delivers electricity, natural gas, domestic water, sewer service or garbage or refuse service. A "municipal utility" does not include a people's utility district.
(2) A utility company shall not transfer a claim against a tenant to the owner of the real property without the written consent of the owner.
(3) A municipal utility shall not transfer a claim against a tenant to the owner of the real property unless the municipal utility provided notice of the delinquent status to the tenant and mailed a copy of the notice of delinquency by first class mail to the last address of the owner or owner's agent that is on file with the utility, within 30 days from the time the payment is due on the account.
(4) A municipal utility shall not deny or shut off its service to any subsequent tenant based on any lien for an unpaid claim for services furnished to a previous tenant who has vacated the premises unless the utility notified the owner or the owner's agent of any delinquency by mailing a copy of the notice of delinquency by first class mail to the last address of the owner or owner's agent that is on file with the utility, at the time the notice was sent to the previous tenant.
(5) A municipal utility may not provide service to a tenant if the tenant has a previous unpaid bill with the municipal utility unless that municipal utility and tenant agree to a plan for repayment of unpaid utility bills.
(6) A municipal utility shall have the same policy regarding the disconnection of services for nonpayment of an outstanding amount for a single family residence occupied by a tenant and for a single family residence occupied by the owner.
(7) A municipal utility shall provide information to the owner or owner's agent regarding the status of a tenant's account upon request, within a reasonable amount of time. If a request is made verbally, the municipal utility shall provide the information verbally. If a municipal utility discloses information under this subsection, the municipal utility shall not be held responsible for the disclosure of information to a person who is not an owner or owner's agent.
(8) Subsections (5) and (6) of this section apply only if a municipal utility intends to file a lien for unpaid utility services or intends to deny service to a subsequent tenant based on a claim for unpaid services to a previous tenant.
(9) Subsection (7) of this section applies only if a municipal utility intends to file a lien for unpaid utility services or intends to deny service to a subsequent tenant based on a claim for unpaid services to a previous tenant.
(10) Nothing in this section creates, expands or abridges any authority of a municipal utility to transfer a claim, based upon any contract, ordinance or lien.
(11) Nothing in this section shall abridge any procedural due process protections such as notice and hearing that a tenant or subsequent tenant is entitled to under a contract, utility policy, rule, statute or the state and federal Constitutions, prior to the denial or shutoff of service.

Note: 91.255 was enacted into law by the Legislative Assembly but was not added to or made a part of ORS chapter 91 or any series therein by legislative action. See Preface to Oregon Revised Statutes for further explanation.

Chapter 105 – Property Rights
2003 Edition

Actions for Recovery of Real Property

105.005 Right of action; recovery; damages. (1) Any person who has a legal estate in real property and a present right to the possession of the property, may recover possession of the property, with damages for withholding possession, by an action at law. The action shall be commenced against the person in the actual possession of the property at the time, or if the property is not in the actual possession of anyone, then against the person acting as the owner of the property.

(2) In an action brought under subsection (1) of this section or in a separate action for damages only, a person who, throughout the vesting period, used or occupied land of another with the honest and objectively reasonable belief that the person was the actual legal owner of the land shall not be liable for:

(a) Double or treble damages under ORS 105.810 (1) to (3) or 105.815; or

(b) The value of the use or occupation of the land by the person throughout the vesting period.

105.010 Contents of complaint. The plaintiff in the complaint shall set forth:

(1) The nature of the estate of the plaintiff in the property, whether it be in fee, for life, or for a term of years; including, when necessary, for whose life and the duration of the term.

(2) That the plaintiff is entitled to the possession thereof.

(3) That the defendant wrongfully withholds the property from the plaintiff to the damage of the plaintiff for such sum as is therein claimed.

(4) A description of the property with such certainty as to enable the possession thereof to be delivered if there is recovery.

105.015 Answer. The defendant shall not be allowed to give in evidence any estate, license or right of possession in the property in the defendant or another, unless the same is pleaded in the answer. If pleaded, the nature and duration of the estate, license or right of possession shall be set forth with the certainty and particularity required in a complaint. If the defendant does not defend for the whole of the property, the defendant shall specify for what particular part the defendant does defend.

105.020 Substitution of landlord for tenant. A defendant who is in actual possession may, for answer, plead that the defendant is in possession only as tenant of another; naming the landlord and the place of residence of the landlord. Thereupon the landlord, if the landlord applies therefor, shall be made defendant in place of the tenant and the action shall proceed in all respects as if originally commenced against the landlord. If the landlord does not apply to be made defendant within the day the tenant is allowed to answer, the landlord shall not be allowed to, but shall be made defendant if the plaintiff requires it. If the landlord is made defendant on motion of the plaintiff the landlord shall be required to appear and answer within 10 days from notice of the pendency of the action and the order making the landlord defendant, or such further notice as the court or judge thereof may prescribe.

105.025 Verdict. The jury by their verdict shall find as follows:

(1) If the verdict is for the plaintiff, that the plaintiff is entitled to the possession of all or a part of the property described in the complaint, or that the plaintiff owns an undivided share or interest in all or a part of the property; including the nature and duration of the estate of the plaintiff in such property.

(2) If the verdict is for the defendant, that the plaintiff is not entitled to the possession of the property described in the complaint, or the part that the defendant defends, and the estate, license or right to possession in such property established on the trial by the defendant, if any, as the same is required to be pleaded.

105.030 Damages for withholding; setoff for improvements. The plaintiff shall only be entitled to recover damages for withholding the property for the term of six years next preceding the commencement of the action, and for any period that may elapse from the commencement to the time of giving a verdict, excluding the value of the use of permanent improvements made by the defendant. When permanent improvements have been made upon the property by the defendant, or those under whom the defendant claims, while holding under color of title in good faith and adverse to the claim of the plaintiff, the value of the improvements at the time of trial shall be allowed as a setoff against such damages.

105.035 Judgment when plaintiff's right to possession expires. If the right of the plaintiff to the possession of the property expires after the commencement of the action and before the trial, the verdict shall be given according to the fact and judgment shall be given only for the damages.

105.040 Order to make survey. (1) The court or judge thereof may, on motion, and after notice to the adverse party, or cause shown, grant an order allowing the party applying therefor to enter upon the property in controversy and make survey and admeasurement thereof for the purposes of the action.
(2) The order shall describe the property. A copy of the order shall be served upon the defendant, and thereupon the party may enter upon the property, and make the survey and admeasurement. If any unnecessary injury is done to the premises, the applying party is liable therefor.
105.045 Action not prejudiced by alienation by person in possession. An action for the recovery of the possession of real property against a person in possession is not prejudiced by any alienation made by such person, either before or after the commencement of the action. If the alienation is made after the commencement of the action, and the defendant does not satisfy the judgment recovered for damages for withholding the possession, the damages may be recovered by action against the purchaser.
105.050 Cotenant shall prove ouster. In an action by a tenant in common of real property against a cotenant, the plaintiff shall show, in addition to the evidence of right of possession, that the defendant either denied the plaintiff's right or did some act amounting to a denial.
105.055 Conclusiveness of judgment. (1) Except as provided in subsection (2) of this section, the judgment in an action to recover the possession of real property is conclusive as to the estate in the property and the right to the possession thereof, so far as the same is thereby determined, upon the party against whom the judgment is given, and against all persons claiming from, through or under such party, after the commencement of the action.
(2) When service of the summons is made by publication and judgment is given for want of an answer, at any time within two years from the entry thereof the defendant or the successor in interest of the defendant as to the whole or any part of the property, shall, upon application to the court or judge thereof, be entitled to an order vacating the judgment and granting the defendant a new trial upon the payment of the costs of the action.
(3) In an action against a tenant the judgment is conclusive against a landlord, who has been made defendant in place of the tenant, to the same extent as if the action had been originally commenced against the landlord.
105.060 Effect of new trial on plaintiff's possession. If the plaintiff has taken possession of the property before the judgment is set aside and a new trial granted as provided in ORS 105.055 (2), the possession is not thereby affected in any way. If judgment is given for the defendant in the new trial, the defendant is entitled to restitution by execution in the same manner as if the defendant were plaintiff.
105.070 Rights of donee under Donation Law. In an action at law for the recovery of the possession of real property, if either party claims the property as a donee of the United States under the Act of Congress approved September 27, 1850, commonly called the Donation Law, or the Acts amendatory thereto, such party from the date of settlement of the party on the property, as provided in said Acts, is deemed to have a legal estate in fee in the property. The estate shall continue upon the condition that the party performs the conditions required by such Acts, and is unconditional and indefeasible after the performance of such condition. If both plaintiff and defendant claim title to the same real property by virtue of settlement under such Acts, the settlement and the performance of the subsequent conditions shall be conclusively presumed in favor of the party having, or claiming under, the elder patent certificate or patent, unless it appears upon the face of such certificate or patent that it is absolutely void.
105.075 Notice to quit; action to recover possession not affected by forcible entry or wrongful detainer. In any action to recover the possession of real property, as provided for in ORS 105.005, notice to quit, when necessary, may be given as prescribed in ORS 91.050 to 91.110 and 105.120. Nothing in ORS 105.105 to 105.168 prevents such action from being maintained for the recovery of the possession of real property although the entry of the defendant is forcible or the holding is unlawful and with force as defined in ORS 105.105.
105.080 Reimbursement of tenants in common obtaining possession; lien. In all cases where property in this state is or has been claimed or owned by residents of this state in common with others, and such residents have obtained or shall obtain the possession of the property at their own cost, expense or labor, they are entitled to reimbursement from the remaining claimant in common of the property, according to their proportionate interest therein. Residents so obtaining possession of such property have a lien upon it until the remaining claimant has paid or tendered such proportionate share of the reasonable costs, expenses or labor aforesaid.

FORCIBLE ENTRY AND WRONGFUL DETAINER

105.105 Entry to be lawful and peaceable only. No person shall enter upon any land, tenement or other real property unless the right of entry is given by law. When the right of entry is given by law the entry shall be made in a peaceable manner and without force.

105.110 Action for forcible entry or wrongful detainer. When a forcible entry is made upon any premises, or when an entry is made in a peaceable manner and possession is held by force, the person entitled to the premises may maintain in the county where the property is situated an action to recover the possession of the premises in the circuit court or before any justice of the peace of the county.

105.111 Stay of eviction for state service member. (1) As used in this section, "state service member" means a member the organized militia who is called into active service of the state by the Governor under ORS 399.065 (1) for 30 or more consecutive days.

(2) In an action pursuant to ORS 105.110, the court may stay the eviction of the defendant for up to 90 days if:

(a) The defendant is a state service member;

(b) The agree-upon rent does not exceed $1,200 per month; and

(c) The premises are occupied chiefly for dwelling purposes by the spouse, children or other dependents of the defendant.

(3) If the defendant requests a stay of the eviction for up to 90 days and the defendant can prove that the ability of the defendant to pay the agreed-upon rent is materially affected by being called into active service, the court may grant the stay of the eviction.

105.112 Action by tenant to recover personal property; forms. (1) A tenant or former tenant may bring an action to recover personal property taken or retained by a landlord in violation of ORS chapter 90.

(2) An action under this section shall be governed by the provisions of ORS 105.105 to 105.168 except that:

(a) The complaint shall be in substantially the following form and shall be available from the court clerk:

IN THE ________ COURT FOR

THE COUNTY OF ________

(Tenant),)
)
)
vs.) No. ________
)
(Landlord),)
)
Defendant(s).)

COMPLAINT FOR RETURN

OF PERSONAL PROPERTY

I

Defendant(s) (is) (are) in possession of the following personal property belonging to the plaintiff(s):

____

____

____

[ ] See attached list.

II

Defendant(s) took the personal property alleged in paragraph I from premises rented by plaintiff(s) from defendant(s) at:

________________ (street and number)

________________ (city)

________________ (county)

III

Plaintiff(s) (is) (are) entitled to possession of the personal property because:

____ Defendant(s) took the personal property wrongfully because plaintiff(s) had not abandoned the property, and because either there was no court order awarding defendant(s) possession of the premises or the plaintiff(s) (was) (were) not continuously absent from the premises for seven days after such an order when defendant(s) removed the personal property.

____ Defendant(s) lawfully took possession of the personal property after enforcement of a court order for possession of the premises pursuant to ORS 105.165, but refused to return the personal property to plaintiff(s) without payment although plaintiff(s) demanded return of the property within the time provided by ORS 90.425 or 90.675.

____ Defendant(s) lawfully took possession of the personal property pursuant to ORS 105.161, but refused to return the personal property to plaintiff(s) although plaintiff(s) offered payment of all sums due for storage and any costs of removal of the personal property and demanded return of the property within the time provided by ORS 90.425 or 90.675.

____ Other: ________________________

____

Wherefore, plaintiff(s) pray(s) for possession of the personal property and costs and disbursements incurred herein.

________ ________________________

Date Signature of Plaintiff(s)

____

____

(b) The complaint shall be signed by the plaintiff or an

attorney representing the plaintiff as provided by ORCP 17 or verified by an agent or employee of the plaintiff or an agent or employee of an agent of the plaintiff.
(c) The answer shall be in substantially the following form and shall be available from the court clerk:

IN THE ________ COURT FOR
THE COUNTY OF ________

(Tenant),)
Plaintiff(s),)
)
vs.) No. ________
)
(Landlord),)
)
Defendant(s).)

ANSWER

I (we) deny that the plaintiff(s) is (are) entitled to possession of the personal property subject of the complaint because:

___ The defendant(s) did not take and do not have possession of any of the property listed in the complaint.

___ The defendant(s) took possession of the personal property as provided in ORS 90.425 or 90.675 after giving written notice that it was considered abandoned, and the plaintiff(s) did not make a timely demand for return of the property.

___ The defendant(s) took possession of the personal property as provided in ORS 90.425 or 90.675 after giving written notice that it was considered abandoned, but not after a sheriff's enforcement of an eviction judgment against the plaintiff(s) as provided in ORS 105.165, and the plaintiff(s) refused to pay charges lawfully due for storage.

___ Other: ________________________________
____

I (we) ask that the plaintiff(s) take nothing by the complaint and that I (we) be awarded my (our) costs and disbursements.

________ ________________________
Date Signature of Plaintiff(s)

(d) The issue at trial shall be limited to whether the plaintiff is entitled to possession of the personal property listed in the complaint.
(e) No claim for damages shall be asserted by either party in the action for possession of the personal property under this section, but each party may pursue any claim for damages in a separate action.
(f) A party may join an action for possession of personal property with an action for damages or a claim for other relief, but the proceeding is not governed by the provisions of ORS 105.105 to 105.168.
(g) If the court determines that the plaintiff is entitled to possession of the personal property that is the subject of the complaint, the court shall enter an order directing the sheriff to seize the personal property to which the court finds the plaintiff entitled, and to deliver that property to the plaintiff. The court may provide that the defendant have a period of time to deliver the property to the plaintiff voluntarily before execution. The costs of execution may be recovered in the manner provided in ORS 18.910.
(h) Subject to the provisions of ORCP 68, a prevailing party who has been represented by counsel may recover attorney fees as provided by ORS 90.255.

105.113 Form of summons. Notwithstanding ORCP 7 C, for premises to which ORS chapter 90 or ORS 91.120 applies, the summons must be in substantially the following form and be available from the court clerk:

IN THE CIRCUIT COURT
FOR THE COUNTY OF ________
No. ________
SUMMONS
RESIDENTIAL EVICTION

PLAINTIFF (Landlord or agent):
____
____
vs.
DEFENDANT (Tenants/Occupants):
____
____
To: ________________________ (Street address and city of property occupied by defendant)
________________ (Mailing address if different)

NOTICE TO TENANTS:
READ THESE PAPERS CAREFULLY
YOUR LANDLORD WANTS TO EVICT YOU

________, ________ AT ________ AM/PM, you must come to the County Court House located at ________________________. You do not have to pay any fees to the court for this first hearing.

• If you do not appear in court and your landlord does, your landlord will win automatically and can have the Sheriff physically remove you.
• If you do show up in court and your landlord does not, this eviction action will be dropped.
• If both of you show up:
• The judge may ask you to try to reach an agreement with your landlord, but this is voluntary. Trained me-

diators may be available free of charge to help resolve disputes.

• The court will schedule a trial if you and your landlord do not reach an agreement or if you do not agree to move out.

If You Want a Trial, You Must:

• Show up in court at the time scheduled above;

• On the same day, file an Answer with the Court giving a legal reason why you should not be evicted (the Court can give you a form);

• Give a copy of the Answer to your landlord (or your landlord's agent or attorney); and

• Pay a filing fee of ________ (the judge may allow payment to be deferred in certain circumstances).

If You Have Questions, You Should See an Attorney Immediately. If you need help finding an attorney, you can call the Oregon State Bar's Lawyer Referral Service at 503-684-3763 or toll-free in Oregon at 800-452-7636.

____

Signature of Plaintiff (landlord or agent)

Plaintiff's address:

____

____

Plaintiff's telephone number: ____________

I certify that this is a true copy of the original summons:

____

Signature of Plaintiff (landlord or agent)

105.115 Causes of unlawful holding by force. (1) Except as provided by subsections (2) and (3) of this section, the following are causes of unlawful holding by force within the meaning of ORS 105.110, 105.123 and 105.126:

(a) When the tenant or person in possession of any premises fails or refuses to pay rent within 10 days after it is due under the lease or agreement under which the tenant or person in possession holds, or to deliver possession of the premises after being in default on payment of rent for 10 days.

(b) When the lease by its terms has expired and has not been renewed, or when the tenant or person in possession is holding from month to month, or year to year, and remains in possession after notice to quit as provided in ORS 105.120, or is holding contrary to any condition or covenant of the lease or is holding possession without any written lease or agreement.

(2) In the case of a dwelling unit to which ORS chapter 90 applies:

(a) The following are causes of unlawful holding by force within the meaning of ORS 105.110 and 105.123:

(A) When the tenant or person in possession of any premises fails or refuses to pay rent within 72 hours or 144 hours, as the case may be, of the notice required by ORS 90.400 (2).

(B) When a rental agreement by its terms has expired and has not been renewed, or when the tenant or person in possession remains in possession after a valid notice terminating the tenancy pursuant to ORS chapter 90, or is holding contrary to any valid condition or covenant of the rental agreement or ORS chapter 90.

(b) A landlord may not file an action for the return of possession of a dwelling unit based on a cause of unlawful holding by force as described in paragraph (a) of this subsection until after the expiration of a rental agreement for a fixed term tenancy or after the expiration of the time period provided in a notice terminating the tenancy.

(3) In an action under subsection (2) of this section, ORS chapter 90 shall be applied to determine the rights of the parties, including:

(a) Whether and in what amount rent is due;

(b) Whether a tenancy or rental agreement has been validly terminated; and

(c) Whether the tenant is entitled to remedies for retaliatory conduct by the landlord as provided by ORS 90.385 and 90.765.

105.120 Notice necessary to maintain action in certain cases; waiver of notice; effect of advance payments of rent. (1) Except as provided in subsection (2) of this section, an action for the recovery of the possession of the premises may be maintained in cases provided in ORS 105.115 (1)(b), when the notice to terminate the tenancy or to quit has been served upon the tenant or person in possession in the manner prescribed by ORS 91.110 and for the period prescribed by ORS 91.060 to 91.080 before the commencement of the action, unless the leasing or occupation is for the purpose of farming or agriculture, in which case the notice must be served for a period of 90 days before the commencement of the action. Any person entering into the possession of real estate under written lease as the tenant of another may, by the terms of the lease, waive the giving of any notice required by this subsection.

(2) An action for the recovery of the possession of a dwelling unit to which ORS chapter 90 applies may be maintained in situations described in ORS 105.115 (2) when the notice to terminate the tenancy or to quit has been served by the tenant upon the landlord or by the landlord upon the tenant or person in possession in the manner prescribed by ORS 90.155.

(3) Except when a tenancy involves a dwelling unit subject to ORS chapter 90, the service of a notice to quit upon a tenant or person in possession does not authorize an action to be maintained against the tenant or person in possession for the possession of premises before the expiration of any period for which the tenant or person has paid the rent of the premises in advance.

(4) An action to recover possession of a dwelling unit subject to ORS chapter 90 may not be brought or filed against a tenant or person in possession based upon a notice under ORS 90.427 to terminate the tenancy until after the expiration of any period for which the tenant or person has paid the rent of the dwelling unit in advance, unless:

(a) The only other money paid by the tenant was collected as a last month's rent deposit as provided under ORS 90.300; or

(b) The only unused rent was paid by the tenant for a rental period extending beyond the termination date specified in a valid outstanding notice to terminate the tenancy and the landlord refunded the unused rent within six days after receipt by delivering the unused rent to the tenant in person or by first class mailing.

105.123 Complaint. (1) In an action pursuant to ORS 105.110, it is sufficient to state in the complaint:

(a) A description of the premises with convenient certainty;

(b) That the defendant is in possession of the premises;

(c) That, in the case of a dwelling unit to which ORS chapter 90 does not apply, the defendant entered upon the premises with force or unlawfully holds the premises with force; and

(d) That the plaintiff is entitled to the possession of the premises.

(2) The plaintiff may include, at the plaintiff's option, the defendant's Social Security number in the complaint for the purpose of accuracy in tenant screening information. This subsection does not require a tenant to have a Social Security number in order to enter into a rental agreement.

105.124 Form of complaint if ORS chapter 90 applies. For a complaint described in ORS 105.123, if ORS chapter 90 applies to the dwelling unit:

(1) The complaint must be in substantially the following form and be available from the clerk of the court:

In the Circuit Court
for the County of ________
No. ________

Residential Eviction Complaint

Plaintiff (Landlord or agent):
____
____
Address: ________________
City: ________________
State: ____________ Zip: ____________
Telephone: ____________

vs.

Defendant (Tenants/Occupants):
____
____
Mailing Address: ________________
City: ________________
State: ____________ Zip: ____________
Telephone: ____________
Defendant's Social Security number ____________
(Optional information for purposes of identification.)

1.

Tenants are in possession of the dwelling unit, premises or rental property described above or located at:
____

2.

Landlord is entitled to possession of the property because of:

____ 24-hour notice for personal injury, substantial damage, extremely outrageous act or unlawful occupant. ORS 90.400 (3).

____ 24-hour or 48-hour notice for violation of a drug or alcohol program. ORS 90.400 (9).

____ 72-hour or 144-hour notice for nonpayment of rent. ORS 90.400 (2).

____ 7-day notice with stated cause in a week-to-week tenancy. ORS 90.400 (1)(a) and (e)(A).

____ 10-day notice for a pet violation, a repeat violation in a month-to-month tenancy or without stated cause in a week-to-week tenancy. ORS 90.405, 90.400 (1)(d) or 90.427 (1).

____ 20-day notice for a repeat violation. ORS 90.630 (4).

____ 30-day or 180-day notice without stated cause in a month-to-month tenancy. ORS 90.427 (2) or 90.429.

____ 30-day notice with stated cause. ORS 90.400 (1), 90.630 or 90.632.

____ Other notice ________________

____ No notice (explain) ________________

A Copy of the Notice Relied Upon, If Any, Is Attached

3.

If the landlord uses an attorney, the case goes to trial and the landlord wins in court, the landlord can col-

lect attorney fees from the defendant pursuant to ORS 90.255 and 105.137 (3).
Landlord requests judgment for possession of the premises, court costs, disbursements and attorney fees.
I certify that the allegations and factual assertions in this complaint are true to the best of my knowledge.

____

Signature of landlord or agent.
(2) The complaint must be signed by the plaintiff or an attorney representing the plaintiff as provided by ORCP 17, or verified by an agent or employee of the plaintiff or an agent or employee of an agent of the plaintiff.
(3) A copy of the notice relied upon, if any, must be attached to the complaint.
Note: Section 56, chapter 596, Oregon Laws 2001, provides:
Sec. 56. Notwithstanding sections 5, 6, 15 and 16 of this 2001 Act, prior to January 1, 2004, a clerk of the court may:
(1) Make available either the forms set forth in sections 5 and 6 of this 2001 Act [105.124 and 105.126] or the form set forth in ORS 105.125 (1999 Edition) for plaintiff use in bringing an eviction complaint.
(2) Use either the forms set forth in sections 15 and 16 of this 2001 Act [105.152 and 105.153] or the form set forth in ORS 105.154 (2) (1999 Edition) for issuing a notice of restitution.
105.126 Form of complaint if ORS chapter 90 does not apply. For a complaint described in ORS 105.123, if ORS chapter 90 does not apply to the premises:
(1) The complaint must be in substantially the following form and be available from the clerk of the court:

IN THE CIRCUIT COURT
FOR THE COUNTY OF ________
No. ________
EVICTION COMPLAINT
(Tenancy not covered by ORS chapter 90)
No. ________

(Landlord),
Plaintiff(s)
vs.
(Tenant),
Defendant(s)

1.

Defendant is in possession of the following premises:

____

______________________________ (city)

2.

Defendant entered upon the premises with force or is unlawfully holding the premises with force.

3.

Plaintiff is entitled to possession of the premises, because:
____ 30-day notice (month-to-month tenancy)
____ 30-day notice (cause)
____ Other notice (explain) ____________
____ No notice (explain) ____________
A COPY OF ANY NOTICE RELIED UPON IS ATTACHED
Wherefore, plaintiff prays for possession of the premises, costs and disbursements and attorney fees, if applicable.

____

Plaintiff
(2) A copy of the notice relied upon, if any, must be attached to the complaint.
105.130 How action conducted; fees; surcharge. (1) Except as provided in this section and ORS 105.135, 105.137 and 105.140 to 105.161, an action pursuant to ORS 105.110 shall be conducted in all respects as other actions in courts of this state.
(2) Upon filing a complaint in the case of a dwelling unit to which ORS chapter 90 applies, the clerk shall:
(a) Collect a filing fee of $12;
(b) Collect any other fee authorized by law or ordinance; and
(c) With the assistance of the plaintiff or an agent of the plaintiff, complete the applicable summons and provide to the plaintiff or an agent of the plaintiff sufficient copies of the summons and complaint for service.
(3) After a complaint is filed under subsection (2) of this section, if the defendant demands a trial, the plaintiff shall pay an additional filing fee of $26 and the defendant shall pay a filing fee of $26.
(4) An action pursuant to ORS 105.110 shall be brought in the name of a person entitled to possession as plaintiff. The plaintiff may appear in person or through an attorney. In an action to which ORS chapter 90 applies, the plaintiff may also appear through a nonattorney who is an agent or employee of the plaintiff or an agent or employee of an agent of the plaintiff.
(5) Notwithstanding ORS 9.160, 9.320 and ORS chapter 180, a state agency may appear in an action brought pursuant to ORS 105.110 through an officer or employee of the agency if:
(a) The Attorney General consents to the representation of the agency by an officer or employee in the particular action or in the class of actions that includes the particular action; and

(b) The agency, by rule, authorizes an officer or employee to appear on its behalf in the particular type of action being conducted.
(6) In addition to the fees charged under subsection (2) of this section, the clerk shall collect a surcharge from the plaintiff at the time a complaint is filed that is subject to the filing fees established by subsection (2) of this section and from a defendant at the time a defendant demands a trial in the action. The surcharge shall be deposited by the State Court Administrator into the State Treasury to the credit of the Housing and Community Services Department Low Income Rental Housing Fund established by ORS 458.350. The amount of the surcharge shall be $10.
(7) Fees and surcharges provided for in this section may not be refunded.
(8)(a) In addition to the fees provided for in subsection (2) of this section, for the period commencing September 1, 2003, and ending June 30, 2005, upon filing a complaint in the case of a dwelling unit to which ORS chapter 90 applies, the clerk shall collect a surcharge of $4.
(b) In addition to the fees provided for in subsection (3) of this section, for the period commencing September 1, 2003, and ending June 30, 2005, if the defendant demands a trial after a complaint is filed under subsection (2) of this section, the plaintiff shall pay a surcharge of $8 and the defendant shall pay a surcharge of $8.

Note: The 2003 Legislative Session enacted amendments to 105.130 with an operative date of July 1, 2005. The following is the text of 105.130 which becomes effective then.

105.130 How action conducted; fees; surcharge.
(1) Except as provided in this section and ORS 105.135, 105.137 and 105.140 to 105.161, an action pursuant to ORS 105.110 shall be conducted in all respects as other actions in courts of this state.
(2) Upon filing a complaint in the case of a dwelling unit to which ORS chapter 90 applies, the clerk shall:
(a) Collect a filing fee of $13;
(b) Collect any other fee authorized by law or ordinance; and
(c) With the assistance of the plaintiff or an agent of the plaintiff, complete the applicable summons and provide to the plaintiff or an agent of the plaintiff sufficient copies of the summons and complaint for service.
(3) After a complaint is filed under subsection (2) of this section, if the defendant demands a trial, the plaintiff shall pay an additional filing fee of $29 and the defendant shall pay a filing fee of $29.
(4) An action pursuant to ORS 105.110 shall be brought in the name of a person entitled to possession as plaintiff. The plaintiff may appear in person or through an attorney. In an action to which ORS chapter 90 applies, the plaintiff may also appear through a nonattorney who is an agent or employee of the plaintiff or an agent or employee of an agent of the plaintiff.
(5) Notwithstanding ORS 9.160, 9.320 and ORS chapter 180, a state agency may appear in an action brought pursuant to ORS 105.110 through an officer or employee of the agency if:
(a) The Attorney General consents to the representation of the agency by an officer or employee in the particular action or in the class of actions that includes the particular action; and
(b) The agency, by rule, authorizes an officer or employee to appear on its behalf in the particular type of action being conducted.
(6) In addition to the fees charged under subsection (2) of this section, the clerk shall collect a surcharge from the plaintiff at the time a complaint is filed that is subject to the filing fees established by subsection (2) of this section and from a defendant at the time a defendant demands a trial in the action. The surcharge shall be deposited by the State Court Administrator into the State Treasury to the credit of the Housing and Community Services Department Low Income Rental Housing Fund established by ORS 458.350. The amount of the surcharge shall be $10.
(7) Fees and surcharges provided for in this section may not be refunded.

105.132 Assertion of counterclaim. No person named as a defendant in an action brought under ORS 105.105 to 105.168 may assert a counterclaim unless the right to do so is otherwise provided by statute.
105.135 Service and return of summons; posting; contents. (1) Except as provided in this section, the summons shall be served and returned as in other actions.
(2) At the time the clerk collects the filing fee under ORS 105.130, the clerk shall enter the first appearance date on the summons. That date shall be seven days after the judicial day next following payment of filing fees unless no judge is available for first appearance

at that time, in which case the clerk may extend the first appearance date for up to seven additional days. At the request of the plaintiff, the clerk may enter a date more than seven days after the judicial day next following payment of filing fees if a judge will be available.

(3) Notwithstanding ORCP 10, by the end of the judicial day next following the payment of filing fees:

(a) The clerk shall mail a true copy of the summons and complaint by first class mail to the defendant at the premises.

(b) The process server shall serve the defendant with a true copy of the summons and complaint at the premises by personal delivery to the defendant or, if the defendant is not available for service, by attaching a true copy of the summons and complaint in a secure manner to the main entrance to that portion of the premises of which the defendant has possession.

(4) The process server shall indicate the manner in which service was accomplished by promptly filing with the clerk a certificate of service as provided by ORCP 7 F(2)(a).

(5) In the case of premises to which ORS chapter 90 applies, the summons shall inform the defendant of the procedures, rights and responsibilities of the parties as specified in ORS 105.137.

105.137 Effect of failure of party to appear; appearance by attorney; scheduling of trial; unrepresented defendant. In the case of a dwelling unit to which ORS chapter 90 applies:

(1) If the plaintiff appears and the defendant fails to appear at the first appearance, a default judgment shall be entered against the defendant in favor of the plaintiff for possession of the premises and costs and disbursements.

(2) If the defendant appears and the plaintiff fails to appear at the first appearance, an order shall be entered dismissing the complaint and awarding costs and disbursements against the plaintiff in favor of the defendant.

(3) An attorney at law shall be entitled to appear on behalf of any party, but no attorney fees may be awarded if the defendant does not contest the action.

(4) The plaintiff or an agent of the plaintiff may obtain a continuance of the action for as long as the plaintiff or the agent of the plaintiff deems necessary to obtain the services of an attorney at law.

(5) If both parties appear in court on the date contained in the summons, the court shall set the matter for trial as soon as practicable, unless the court is advised by the parties that the matter has been settled. The trial shall be scheduled no later than 15 days from the date of such appearance. If the matter is not tried within the 15-day period, and the delay in trial is not attributable to the landlord, the court shall order the defendant to pay rent that is accruing into court, provided the court finds after hearing that entry of such an order is just and equitable.

(6)(a) The court shall permit an unrepresented defendant to proceed to trial by directing the defendant to file an answer in writing on a form which shall be available from the court clerk, and to serve a copy upon the plaintiff on the same day as first appearance.

(b) The answer shall be in substantially the following form:

IN THE ________ COURT FOR
THE COUNTY OF ________

(Landlord),)
)
Plaintiff(s),)
)
vs.) No. ________
)
(Tenant),)
)
Defendant(s).)

ANSWER

I (we) deny that the plaintiff(s) is (are) entitled to possession because:

___ The landlord did not make repairs.

List any repair problems: ____________________

____

___ The landlord is attempting to evict me (us) because of my (our) complaints (or the eviction is otherwise retaliatory).

___ The eviction notice is wrong.

___ List any other defenses: ____________________

____

____

I (we) may be entitled as the prevailing party to recover attorney fees from plaintiff(s) if I (we) obtain legal services to defend this action pursuant to ORS 90.255.

I (we) ask that the plaintiff(s) not be awarded possession of the premises and that I (we) be awarded my (our) costs and disbursements and attorney fees, if applicable, or a prevailing party fee.

________ ____________________
Date Signature of defendant(s)

(7) If an unrepresented defendant files an answer as provided in subsection (6) of this section, the answer

shall not limit the defenses available to the defendant at trial under ORS chapter 90. If such a defendant seeks to assert at trial a defense not fairly raised by the answer, the plaintiff shall be entitled to a reasonable continuance for the purposes of preparing to meet the defense.

105.138 Compelling arbitration; procedure. (1) Notwithstanding ORS 105.137 (5), if a party to an action to which ORS 90.505 to 90.840 apply moves for an order compelling arbitration and abating the proceedings, the court shall summarily determine whether the controversy between the parties is subject to an arbitration agreement enforceable under ORS 90.610 (2) and, if so, shall issue an order compelling the parties to submit to arbitration in accordance with the agreement and abating the action for not more than 30 days, unless the parties agree to an order of abatement for a longer period acceptable to the court.

(2) If the court issues an order compelling arbitration under subsection (1) of this section, the court may not order the payment of rent into court pending the arbitration unless the court finds such an order is necessary to protect the rights of the parties.

105.139 Burden of proof in certain cases. If a landlord brings an action for possession under ORS 90.400 (3)(f) and the person in possession contends that the tenant has not vacated the premises, the burden of proof is on the defendant as to that issue.

105.140 Continuance. No continuance shall be granted to a defendant for a longer period than two days unless:

(1) The defendant gives an undertaking to the adverse party with good and sufficient security, to be approved by the court, conditioned for the payment of the rent that may accrue if judgment is rendered against the defendant; or

(2) In an action for the recovery of the possession of a dwelling unit to which ORS chapter 90 applies, the court orders a defendant to pay rent into court as it becomes due from the commencement of the action until entry of a general judgment in the action. If a defendant fails to pay rent into court as ordered under this subsection, the action shall be tried forthwith.

105.145 Judgment on trial by court; duties of parties to stipulated agreement. (1) If an action is tried by the court without a jury, and after hearing the evidence the court concludes that the complaint is not true, the court shall enter judgment against the plaintiff for costs and disbursements. If the court finds the complaint true or if judgment is rendered by default, it shall render a general judgment against the defendant and in favor of the plaintiff, for restitution of the premises and the costs and disbursements of the action. If the court finds the complaint true in part, it shall render judgment for the restitution of such part only, and the costs and disbursements shall be taxed as the court deems just and equitable.

(2) If, as a result of a court-sponsored or other mediation or otherwise, the plaintiff and defendant agree, in the manner provided by ORCP 67 F for judgment by stipulation, that the defendant shall perform in a certain manner or that the plaintiff shall be paid moneys agreed to be owing by the defendant and that as a result of that performance or payment the defendant shall retain possession of the premises, including retention of possession contingent upon that performance or payment of moneys by the defendant by a certain date, the court shall enter an order or judgment to that effect. In addition, if the plaintiff and defendant agree that the plaintiff shall perform in a certain manner or pay moneys to the defendant by a certain date, the court shall enter an order or judgment to that effect.

(3) If, as provided by subsection (2) of this section, the parties enter an order or judgment by stipulation that requires the defendant to perform in a certain manner or make a payment by a certain date and the defendant later demonstrates compliance with the stipulation, the court shall enter a judgment of dismissal in favor of the defendant.

105.146 Failure of defendant to perform as ordered; judgment of restitution. (1) In an action to recover possession of the premises, if the court has entered an order by stipulation that provides for the defendant to retain possession of the premises contingent upon the defendant's performance or payment of moneys by a certain date as provided under ORS 105.145 (2), and the defendant fails to comply with the order, the plaintiff may obtain and enforce a judgment of restitution of the premises pursuant to this section and ORS 105.148 and 105.149.

(2) A plaintiff may obtain and enforce a judgment of restitution based upon an order entered as provided under ORS 105.145 (2), provided the order includes only:

(a) Future performance or conduct as described in the order for a period of not more than six months following entry of the order;

(b) Payment of past due rent and other past due amounts pursuant to a schedule provided in the or-

der for a period of not more than six months following entry of the order;
(c) Payment of rent due for future rental periods that follow entry of the order pursuant to a schedule provided in the order for not more than the first three monthly rental periods following entry of the order; and
(d) Payment of any costs, disbursements or attorney fees pursuant to a schedule provided in the order.
(3) The order shall contain a statement providing that 12 months following the entry of the order, the court shall automatically dismiss the order without further notice to either the plaintiff or the defendant.
(4) If the defendant fails to comply with the order, the plaintiff may file with the clerk of the court an affidavit of noncompliance describing how the defendant has failed to comply. The plaintiff shall attach a copy of the order to the affidavit. The affidavit or the order must include the terms of the underlying settlement agreement or stipulation or have a copy of the agreement attached.
(5) Upon receipt of a plaintiff's affidavit:
(a) The court shall enter a judgment of restitution; and
(b) The clerk shall issue a notice of restitution as provided by ORS 105.151 and attach to the notice a copy of the plaintiff's affidavit of noncompliance and any attachments for service.
(6) The court shall establish a procedure that allows the defendant to request a hearing on the plaintiff's affidavit of noncompliance and delay expiration of the notice of restitution period or execution upon a judgment of restitution pending the hearing.
(7) The court shall enter a judgment dismissing the plaintiff's action in favor of the defendant without assessment of costs, disbursements, prevailing party fee or attorney fees against either party except as provided in the order and without further notice to either party:
(a) Upon receipt of a writing signed by the plaintiff showing compliance with or satisfaction of the order; or
(b) Twelve months following entry of the order, unless the plaintiff has filed an affidavit of noncompliance and the court has found in favor of the plaintiff on the affidavit.
Note: 105.146 to 105.149 were added to and made a part of 105.105 to 105.168 by legislative action but were not added to any smaller series therein. See Preface to Oregon Revised Statutes for further explanation.

105.148 Contesting plaintiff's affidavit of noncompliance; delaying execution upon judgment of restitution. (1) To contest a plaintiff's affidavit of noncompliance under ORS 105.146 and delay expiration of the notice of restitution period or execution upon the judgment of restitution, a defendant shall file a request for hearing with the clerk of the court. The request must be filed prior to issuance by the clerk of a writ of execution of judgment of restitution and must include a statement by the defendant describing how the defendant complied with the order or describing why the defendant should not be required to comply.
(2) The clerk shall make available a document providing for a request for hearing by a defendant. The document must be in substantially the following form:

IN THE CIRCUIT COURT
FOR THE COUNTY OF ________
Defendant's Request for Hearing to
Contest an Affidavit of Noncompliance
Case No. ________

Landlord or agent (Plaintiff):
____
vs.
Tenant/Occupant (Defendant):
____
Address of Property:
____
____

1. My landlord has filed a statement with the court saying that I have not complied with a court-approved agreement and that as a result my landlord is entitled to possession of the property.
2. I deny that the landlord is entitled to possession of the property because (The reason must be one of the following. You must check one or more of these responses and explain in section 3.):
____ a. The landlord is wrong. As explained below, I did comply with the agreement.
____ b. Before I could comply with the agreement, the landlord was supposed to do what is described below, which the landlord did not do.
____ c. The landlord and I changed the agreement and I complied with the agreement as changed. The change we agreed to is explained below.
____ d. The landlord prevented me from keeping the agreement. The way that the landlord did that is explained below.
____ e. The agreement was not made in good faith as required by ORS 90.130. The lack of good faith is explained below.
____ f. The portion of the agreement described below was unconscionable as described in ORS 90.135.
____ g. The landlord is required by law or contract to have good cause to force me to move out and my

alleged conduct or performance does not meet the standard of good cause, as explained below.

____ h. The landlord is claiming that I did not pay rent for a period of time following the date of the agreement. I did not pay that rent because I have claims for money against the landlord to offset the rent. Those claims arise from the landlord's violation of the Residential Landlord and Tenant Act or the rental agreement since the date of the court order and are explained below.

3. Here is my explanation for the reason or reasons checked above:

____

____

4. I understand that if I lose in court, I may be responsible for the landlord's costs, disbursements, any attorney fees and a prevailing party fee.

I swear the above statements are true.

(Signature of tenant)

____

Subscribed and sworn to before me this ______ day of ____________________, 2 ______.

Trial court administrator / clerk / notary

____

Note: See note under 105.146.

105.149 Hearing on compliance with order. (1) Upon receipt of a timely filed request for hearing described in ORS 105.148, the clerk of the court shall:

(a) Schedule a hearing on the defendant's request as soon as practicable;

(b) Notify both parties of the hearing date; and

(c) Mail or send by facsimile a copy of the defendant's request to the plaintiff.

(2)(a) At the hearing, except as provided in paragraph (b) of this subsection, the court may consider only the following issues:

(A) Whether the defendant complied with the order.

(B) Whether the plaintiff complied with any requirement of the order that is a predicate to compliance by the defendant.

(C) Whether the parties agreed to modify the order and complied with the modified order.

(D) Whether one party unfairly prevented compliance by the other party.

(b) If ORS chapter 90 applies to a dwelling unit, in addition to the issues described in paragraph (a) of this subsection, the court may consider the following issues:

(A) Whether the stipulated agreement was entered into in good faith as required by ORS 90.130 or is unconscionable as described in ORS 90.135.

(B) Whether, for a defendant whose noncompliance concerns performance or conduct, the noncompliance constitutes good cause for purposes of an applicable law or contract that requires the plaintiff to have good cause for terminating the tenancy.

(C) Whether, for a defendant whose noncompliance concerns a failure to pay rent due for future rental periods pursuant to ORS 105.146 (2)(c), the defendant has claims against the plaintiff for moneys that offset the rent. The defendant's claims must be pursuant to ORS chapter 90 or the rental agreement and must have arisen after the entry of the order.

(c) The defendant may not raise defenses or claims involving issues other than issues described in paragraphs (a) and (b) of this subsection.

(3) If the court finds in favor of the plaintiff after the hearing, the clerk may issue a writ of execution of judgment of restitution. If the defendant did not appear at the hearing, the clerk may issue the writ immediately. If the defendant did appear, the clerk may issue the writ no earlier than 24 hours after the court's ruling. Further notice to the defendant is not required.

(4) If the court finds in favor of the defendant after the hearing, the court shall set aside the judgment. The court may reinstate the order, terminate the order and enter a judgment dismissing the plaintiff's action in favor of the defendant, enter a new order or schedule a trial on the plaintiff's action as soon as practicable.

Note: See note under 105.146.

105.151 Enforcement of judgment of restitution; notice of restitution. (1) If the court renders judgment for restitution of the premises to the plaintiff, the plaintiff may only enforce that judgment in the following manner:

(a) Issuance by the clerk of the court and service upon the defendant of a notice of restitution that shall give the defendant four days to move out of the premises, including removal of all personal property; and

(b) After the expiration of the four-day period provided in the notice of restitution, issuance by the clerk of the court and service by the sheriff upon the defendant of a writ of execution of judgment of restitution, directing the sheriff to enforce the judgment by removing the defendant and by returning possession of the premises to the plaintiff, along with an eviction trespass notice from the sheriff.

(2) Following entry of judgment for restitution of the premises in favor of a plaintiff, or any date for possession as specified in the judgment, whichever

is later, the plaintiff may request that the clerk of the court in which the judgment is entered issue a notice of restitution. The notice of restitution shall order the defendant to move out of the premises, including removing all personal property, in no less than four days. The plaintiff may direct the clerk to extend the notice period beyond four days. Following payment of any required fees, the clerk shall issue the notice.

(3) This section does not prevent a landlord in a tenancy to which ORS chapter 90 does not apply from exercising a right of entry provided by law and described in ORS 105.105 in order to recover possession of the premises, provided that the right of entry is stated in the rental agreement between the parties.

105.152 Form of notice of restitution for judgment entered under ORS 105.146. If the court entered a judgment pursuant to ORS 105.146, a notice of restitution issued by the clerk of the court pursuant to ORS 105.151 must be in substantially the following form:

IN THE CIRCUIT COURT
FOR THE COUNTY OF ________
Notice of Restitution because of not complying with a court-approved agreement
Case No. ________

To: ______________________________
(Tenant/Defendant)

____
(Address of rental property)

You and your landlord made a court-approved agreement allowing you to stay in the property. Your landlord claims that you have not kept that agreement. (A copy of the landlord's claim is attached.) Unless you can prove to the court why you should not have to move out, you must move by the MOVE OUT DATE listed below. If you do not, the landlord can have the Sheriff physically remove you.

If you believe that you have kept the agreement or that you have a legal reason for not keeping the agreement, you are entitled to a court hearing. Legal reasons are listed in ORS 105.148 and 105.149. They include the landlord interfering with your effort to keep the agreement and your complying with a modification of the agreement made by you and your landlord.

To request a hearing, you must go to the court and complete a form explaining why you believe that you have kept (or should not be required to keep) the agreement. You have to do this before ________ AM/PM on ________.

The Sheriff will not physically remove you from the property before the hearing.

If the judge rules against you at the hearing, the landlord can have the Sheriff physically remove you 24 hours later.

DEADLINE TO MOVE OUT
MOVE OUT DATE: ________

If you do not request a hearing, you must move out of the property no later than 11:59 PM on the Move Out Date.

If you and everyone else living there do not move out by that time, the Sheriff will physically remove you. You must also move all of your belongings by that time. Anything you leave behind will be stored or disposed of as allowed by law.

____
Deputy Court Administrator

Note: See note under 105.124.

105.153 Form of notice of restitution for judgment not entered under ORS 105.146. If a court entered a judgment other than pursuant to ORS 105.146, a notice of restitution issued by the clerk of the court pursuant to ORS 105.151 must be in substantially the following form:

IN THE CIRCUIT COURT FOR
THE COUNTY OF ________
NOTICE OF RESTITUTION
Case No. ________

To: ______________________________
(Defendant/Tenant)

____

____
(Address of property)

DEADLINE TO MOVE OUT
MOVE OUT DATE: ________

The Court has ordered you to move out of the property. You must move out no later than 11:59 PM on the Move Out Date.

If you and everyone else living there do not move out by that time, the Sheriff will physically remove you. You must also move all of your belongings by that time. Anything you leave behind will be stored or disposed of as allowed by law.

____
Deputy Court Administrator

105.156 Form of writ of execution for judgment of restitution. The writ of execution of judgment of restitution referred to in ORS 105.151 must be in substantially the following form:

State of Oregon,) WRIT OF
) ss. EXECUTION OF
) JUDGMENT OF
) RESTITUTION
County of ________)

To the Sheriff:

This was an eviction action for possession of the following premises:

____

______________________ (city)

______________________ (county)

Judgment was rendered on ________ (date) that the plaintiff have restitution of the premises on or after ________ (date), and also that the plaintiff recover costs and disbursements in the sum of $ ________.

In the name of the State of Oregon, you are ordered to enforce and serve this writ on the defendant, in the manner provided in ORS 105.161 (1), after the four-day period provided in the notice of restitution.

If the defendant has not moved out of the premises by the end of the four-day period or any delay requested by the plaintiff, whichever is later, and if the plaintiff has paid all fees for enforcement of this execution, you shall immediately make legal service of this writ and an eviction trespass notice on the defendant. You shall remove the defendant and any other person subject to the judgment, if present, from the premises and return possession of the premises to the plaintiff.

The plaintiff shall be responsible for removing, storing and disposing of any personal property left by the defendant on the premises following the removal of the defendant and the return of possession of the premises, as provided by ORS 105.165.

DATED this ______ day of ________, ______.

____
Deputy Court Administrator

____
Plaintiff

____
Address

____
City/State/Zip

105.157 Form of eviction trespass notice. The eviction trespass notice referred to in ORS 105.151 must be in substantially the following form:

EVICTION TRESPASS NOTICE

Occupants of these premises located at:

____

____

____

have been evicted by an order of the court in ________ vs. ________, Case Number ________.

Trespassing or entering into or upon these premises without written consent of the landlord will result in arrest and prosecution.

Any personal property present on these premises at the time this notice was served, (date) ________, is in the possession of the landlord and may be redeemed by contacting the landlord at:

____

____

____

DATED ________________

________________ SHERIFF

105.158 Service of notice of restitution. (1) For purposes of this section, "process server" means any competent person 18 years of age or older who:

(a) Is a resident of the State of Oregon;

(b) Is not the plaintiff, a relative of the plaintiff or an agent of the plaintiff for purposes of management of the premises;

(c) Is a person regularly employed in the business of serving process; and

(d) Charges a fee no greater than that set by ORS 21.410 (1)(a) for service of the notice of restitution.

(2) The sheriff or a process server shall serve the notice of restitution under ORS 105.152 or 105.153 in the manner provided by this subsection. Notwithstanding ORCP 10, by the end of the next judicial day following the payment of fees:

(a) The sheriff or process server shall mail a copy of the notice of restitution by first class mail to the defendant at the premises; and

(b) The sheriff or process server shall serve the notice of restitution at the premises by personal delivery to the defendant or, if the defendant is not available for service, by attaching a copy of the notice in a secure manner to the main entrance to that portion of the premises of which the defendant has possession.

(3) If service of the notice of restitution is made by a process server, by the end of the next judicial day following service the process server shall file with the clerk of the court a certificate of service in the same manner as provided by ORCP 7 F(2)(a).

105.159 Computation of time before plaintiff may request writ of execution. (1) Notwithstanding ORCP 10, the four-day period specified in ORS 105.151 (2) shall:

(a) Commence at 12:01 AM on the day following mailing and service of the notice of restitution pursuant to ORS 105.158, including a Saturday or a Sunday or other legal holiday; and

(b) End on the fourth calendar day following the mailing and service except that if the fourth day is a

Saturday or a Sunday or other legal holiday, the period shall end at 12 midnight of the day preceding the next judicial day.
(2) Except as provided in subsection (3) of this section, at any time after the expiration of the period provided in the notice of restitution, the plaintiff may request that the clerk of the court issue a writ of execution of judgment of restitution directing the sheriff to enforce the judgment of restitution by returning possession of the premises to the plaintiff. Following payment of any required fees, the clerk shall issue the writ in substantially the form provided by ORS 105.156.
(3) Unless the judgment otherwise provides, the clerk may not issue a notice of restitution or a writ of execution of judgment of restitution more than 60 days after the judgment is entered or after any date for possession as specified in the judgment, whichever is later.

105.161 Service and enforcement of writ of execution and eviction trespass notice. (1) Following issuance of the writ of execution of judgment of restitution and payment of any fees required by the sheriff, the sheriff shall immediately enforce and serve the writ upon the defendant, along with the eviction trespass notice, as follows:
(a) The sheriff shall mail a copy of the writ and the eviction trespass notice by first class mail to the defendant at the premises;
(b) The sheriff shall serve the writ and the eviction trespass notice at the premises by personal delivery to the defendant or, if the defendant is not available for service, by attaching the writ and notice in a secure manner to the main entrance to that portion of the premises of which the defendant has possession;
(c) Immediately following the service of the writ and the eviction trespass notice, the sheriff shall return possession of the premises to the plaintiff by removing the defendant or any other person subject to the judgment; and
(d) Following the sheriff's removal of the defendant and return of possession of the premises to the plaintiff, the plaintiff shall be responsible for removing, storing and disposal of any personal property left by the defendant on the premises, as provided by ORS 105.165.
(2) Following issuance of the writ, at the plaintiff's request, the sheriff shall delay enforcement and service of the writ.
(3) Any writ not enforced and served within 30 days following issuance shall expire and become unenforceable.
(4) A judgment may not be enforced if the parties have entered a new rental agreement or if the plaintiff has accepted rent for a period of occupancy beginning after the judgment was entered.

105.165 Alternative method of removing, storing and disposing of tenant's personal property; requirements; landlord liability. (1) In the case of a dwelling unit to which ORS chapter 90 applies, the landlord may elect to remove, store and dispose of all or part of the personal property left by the tenant upon the premises following restitution of the premises pursuant to ORS 105.161, provided that:
(a) The sheriff or process server shall first serve the notice of restitution and the sheriff shall thereafter deliver possession of the premises to the landlord, as provided in ORS 105.161; and
(b) The landlord shall store and dispose of the personal property of the tenant pursuant to ORS 90.425 or 90.675, except that if the tenant claims that property within the time provided in ORS 90.425 or 90.675, the landlord must make that property available for removal by the tenant by appointment at reasonable times and without the payment of any costs, charges or other sums, and the notice to the tenant shall so state.
(2) Any cost incurred by the landlord for execution pursuant to ORS 105.151 or 105.158 to 105.161 or for removal, storage or sale of the tenant's property under this section and not recovered pursuant to ORS 90.425 (12) or 90.675 (12) shall be added to the judgment.
(3) If the landlord fails to permit the tenant to recover possession of the tenant's personal property under subsection (1)(b) of this section, the tenant may recover, in addition to any other amount provided by law, twice the actual damages or twice the monthly rent, whichever is greater.
(4) If the tenant's personal property includes a manufactured dwelling or floating home, the landlord shall use the alternative method provided by this section for the dwelling or home. The landlord may use the alternative method provided by this section for all or part of the tenant's other personal property. If a landlord elects to use this alternative method for part of the tenant's other property, the remaining portion, not including any manufactured dwelling or floating home, shall be removed by the sheriff pursuant to ORS 105.161.

105.168 Minor as party in proceedings pertaining to residential dwellings. Notwithstanding ORCP 27 or any other provision of law, a minor, as defined in ORS 109.697 and who is a tenant as defined under ORS

90.100, may appear as a party without appointment of a guardian or guardian ad litem in an action for forcible entry or wrongful detainer, under ORS 105.105 to 105.168 regarding possession of a residential dwelling unit to which ORS chapter 90 applies, or in an action based upon a contract for a residential dwelling unit or for utility services provided to that unit.

*****

MODIFICATION OF LEASE TERMS

105.190 Covenant of good faith and fair dealing; rights and obligations of parties. Whenever a covenant of good faith and fair dealing is implied in the lease of real property, a party's rights or duties under such covenant may be modified only by express provision in the lease agreement.

The remainder of ORS Chapter 105 is not included here as it pertains to easement owner obligations, suits for partition, housing receivership, seller's property disclosure, unlawful gambling and controlled substances, and suits to quiet title, all of which do not pertain generally to property management. The full text is available on the internet or in any public library.

Index